MENLO SCHOOL · MENLO COLLEGE
founded 1915

Gift of

College Student Council

Library Fund

Established Fall of 1972

The Art of Ancient Mesopotamia

Anton Moortgat

The Art of
Ancient Mesopotamia

The Classical Art of the Near East

Phaidon · London & New York

All rights reserved by Phaidon Press Ltd.,
5 Cromwell Place, London SW 7
First published 1969

Phaidon Publishers Inc., New York
Distributors in the United States: Frederick A. Praeger Inc.
111 Fourth Avenue, New York, N. Y. 10003
Library of Congress Catalog Card Number: 69-12789

Translated by JUDITH FILSON

SBN 7148 1371 0

Printed and bound by Boss-Druck, Kleve
Made in Germany

Contents

To my wife for many years of collaboration

Anton Moortgat

Foreword

It was not easy for me to arrange my ideas in the form in which they now appear in the text of the present volume. These are the ideas I have expressed since 1941 while lecturing in Berlin, initially at the Friedrich-Wilhelm University and latterly, since 1948, at the Free University. This text is the basis of the book, as its function is to convey to the reader an understanding of the organic unity of ancient Mesopotamian architecture and art, as it developed over the course of many centuries.

It might appear as though the plates and figures in the text are subordinate to this main task, but in reality their purpose is equally fundamental as they, better than any written description, can provide a vivid picture of the individual works of art. If even a few of the plates enable the reader to appreciate directly something of the essential nature of the Sumerian, Akkadian or Assyrian art-form, that in itself will have justified the very great trouble – not perhaps immediately apparent – which we have taken to assemble photographs suitable for reproduction as plates, from numerous museums and collec-

tions. It is particularly in this respect that I have to thank my many friends, colleagues and students for their help: Mr. Karl Gutbrod, head of the publishing firm M. DuMont Schauberg in Cologne; Mr. Siegfried Hagen, of the same firm; my wife, Dr. Ursula Moortgat-Correns; Dr. Peter Calmeyer; and especially Mr. Johannes Boese, assistant in my Department.

The German manuscript of this book went to the publishers at the beginning of 1966. It was not possible to take into consideration anything published after that date.

The chronological system which underlies this essay in art history is the so-called 'Short Chronology', which can also be found in tabular form in my history of the Near East in Antiquity (Alexander Scharff and Anton Moortgat, *Ägypten und Vorderasien im Altertum,* Munich 1950). The reader is referred to the Notes at the end of the book where he will find listed most important works on the subject written before 1966.

A.M.

Introduction

The culture of Ancient Mesopotamia, which began in the third millennium B.C. under the Sumerians and Akkadians and culminated in the second and first millennia B.C. under the Babylonians and Assyrians, was produced by a succession of races of the most varied origin and language. Yet it displays an integrated spiritual organism, of which the overriding unity, combined at the same time with internal diversity, lends itself for comparison with that of the Christian West after the period of late Antiquity.

The unity of this Mesopotamian culture is based not so much on the geo-political necessities of the 'Land of the Two Rivers' and its geographical nature, but rather on a comprehensive religious outlook on the world, which – in spite of its long historical development and all its local variations – was nevertheless homogeneous, with its essential character held in common.

Just as the Western world during the Middle Ages had Christianity as its foundation, so the ancient Near Eastern world received its basic character from the Sumero-Akkadian religion, in its social, political and economic aspects as well as in its spiritual and ethical ones. Individual man and his society, which was transformed from a theocratic, socialist temple-city into a great state with a god-king at its head, and then developed into the Assyrian and Chaldaean world empires, accepted the law of their existence from metaphysical powers, with whom they maintained contact in this and the next world, indirectly or directly, through priests and princes. Western culture, however, obtains the unity of its structure from the fundamental principles laid down in antiquity. In Mesopotamia, the models on which the foundations of classical art were based had been created by the Sumerians and Akkadians in the first half of the third millennium B.C.

Anyone wishing to grasp the essence and unity of Mesopotamian architecture and art can only attempt to understand the conceptions of god generally accepted then, and the ideas of kingship directly bound up with them, by studying the buildings and works of art which have been rediscovered. The uniformity of tradition linking these works of art arises from the organic unity of these conceptions of god and king, their complexity from the outward variations between them, as well as from the different levels of technical skill and from the feeling for style prevailing at any one time among the ever-changing races participating: Sumerians, Akkadians, Canaanites, Assyrians, Kassites, Hurrians or Mitannians. Following on the course of political events, after the Sumerians and Akkadians, the Canaanites in Babylon and the Assyrians in the area between the rivers Tigris and Zab became the wielders of central power in Mesopotamia, and correspondingly their gods, Marduk and Ashur, became the spiritual heads of the whole civilization of the Land of the Two Rivers. Thus too the art of the Babylonians and the Assyrians necessarily became the heir of Sumerian and Akkadian art. It formed with the latter the central classical stem of ancient Near Eastern art, in comparison with which all the other arts, such as that of the Elamites, Hittites or Phoenicians, were of only peripheral importance.

This classical Mesopotamian art from 3000 to 550 B.C. is a collective form of expression. It mirrors the Sumero-Akkadian and Babylonian-Assyrian concept of god and king, and because of this the history of the art of this centre of the ancient Near Eastern culture was much more narrowly circumscribed and easier to grasp than the history of art of many later Western areas, where art has become largely the means of expressing individual feelings, personal ideals of beauty or a philosophy of life.

Yet anyone who understands how incomplete is our knowledge today of the basic Sumerian concepts concerning the world and life, and who perceives how fragmentary our stock of their works of art still remains, and how uncertain we are still of the historical sequence, will not underestimate the difficulties facing the writing of a truthful history of the art of Ancient Mesopotamia.

I Sumero-Akkadian Art

A THE PROTOHISTORICAL PERIOD
(The Uruk VI–IV and Jamdat Nasr Periods)

1 Architecture

About 3000 B.C., in Uruk (modern Warka), the sacred place of Inanna, the Sumerian 'Lady of Heaven', there arose a complex of buildings which even today would be numbered amongst the most splendid and impressive architectural works, were they in a better state of preservation. In the so-called archaic levels of Eanna, the 'House of Heaven', we have been able to identify both the beginnings of the cuneiform script and the origins of the cylinder seal, at that time reserved for the use of the temple administration and bearing the first considerable friezes composed of figures. Here the crumbled ruins of the oldest of the large cult buildings of mankind, the first evidence of a truly monumental architecture, lay buried until their rediscovery at the beginning of the century.

During the same period, in a second sacred area of the city of Uruk, situated to the north-west of the Eanna sanctuary, in the older precinct of Anu (in the plan of the city UVB 7, Plate 1, square K XVII), another temple must have been given its final shape on a site it had already occupied for many centuries. Like the temple of Enki, the Sumerian water-god in Eridu, the most ancient Sumerian centre of civiliz-ation in the neighbourhood of the Persian Gulf, it must

have already been started in prehistoric times, in the Uruk or 'Ubaid periods, and being of far smaller di-mensions than the buildings in Eanna, and owing to continued decay and to equally continuous rebuild-ing on the same site, after being levelled or filled in, it must gradually have become a 'High Temple', i.e. a temple on a disproportionately high platform. In this way it became the prototype of the Ziggurat, which later was to be such a significant feature of Sumero-Babylonian architecture.

Here, right at the beginning of Sumerian architec-ture, we encounter one of its most characteristic features which, with the sun-dried mud brick, the basic element of Sumerian architecture, is in keeping with the inner nature of Near Eastern man and his attitude to life, for whom nothing is final but for whom, on the contrary, everything seems to rotate in a constant cycle of development and disintegration. It was not only the high temple itself which was shaped out of this cycle. In the same way the whole 'tell', the mound of ruins itself, had grown out of the crumbling and rebuilding over a thousand years of a village, a sanctuary or a city, and contributed to the outward structure of the whole settlement and even to an extent determined the appearance of the ancient Near Eastern landscape.

We know the ground-plan of important parts of the Eanna sanctuary during the first phases of the Protohistorical Period (Uruk V and IV), and also in part the elevation, in two phases which followed quickly one upon the other but which, however, present important modifications in building technique and style[1] (Fig. 1). The first phase includes Levels V and IV c-b, the second phase Level IVa.

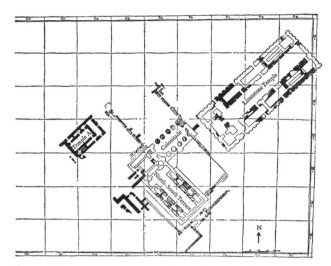

Fig. 1   Eanna sanctuary at Uruk (Warka), Level V-IVb
(After: ZANF 15, 1950, Pl. 1)

a   T   *uk V Period*

 largest building of the first phase is the so-called *Limestone Temple*. It was possible to reconstruct its ground an with certainty primarily because of the exact symmetry prevailing in this kind of architecture. The building was constructed on an elongated, rectangular plan, 70 m. × 30 m., with its corners facing the cardinal points of the compass. The stumps of those walls – which were evidently not just foundations but free-standing outside walls, since their outer surface is decorated regularly with niches – are built of limestone blocks. This is a remarkarble exception to the general development of architecture in the Land of the Two Rivers. It can only be explained in the light of the special importance of the building and it was already abandoned by the second phase of building in the sanctuary. The problem as to whether only the lower part or the full height of the Limestone Temple's walls was built of stone cannot be resolved. It appears to have been the sole attempt on the part of the Sumerian architect to escape from the necessity of building with perishable material, but the attempt soon failed, indeed was bound to fail, not so much because the stone was not available – it was no easier in that countryside to

obtain roof timbers – than because it did not have any relationship with the essential character of this kind of architecture.

The nucleus of the layout is a T-shaped court, 62 m. long and about 11.5 m. wide. This width, which can only be spanned by the very largest tree trunks, nevertheless cannot be used as evidence that the cruciform room was an open courtyard, as remains of fallen joists were found in it (UVB 21, p. 16 f.), albeit from a later rebuilding (Uruk IV). We are dealing here with a covered and not an open courtyard.[2] On each of the two sides of the long room there were four rooms exactly corresponding, of which one room on each side had steps leading to the flat roof. Except for the rooms with steps, they were all accessible from the outside as well as from the hall, through doors placed opposite each other. On the southern short side of the building is the room which was clearly the most important in the whole building, flanked on each side by a smaller annexe room. It is reached from the long room through a broad doorway, embellished with niches, which lies on the longitudinal axis of the whole building.

Apart from its impressive dimensions and the niche decoration of its walls, which was an unmistakable feature of cult building in the Near East for thousands of years, right back to earliest prehistory, there is nothing in the other furnishings (cult niches, altar, podium) to indicate any special cult significance or ritual use of the building.

The Limestone Temple is indeed the largest building in this first phase of the Eanna sanctuary, but it is not the only one. Indeed, it is very closely linked with another, extensive complex of which we have discovered only part. Thus to the south-west there is an L-shaped terrace made of clay *Patzen* – that is, of unburnt mud bricks of exceptionally large size. The terrace consists of two parts, set at right angles to each other, which enclose a court lying at a lower level. The south-western part of the terrace, known as the 'North-South Terrace', had a building on it, the so-called 'Temple A', of which the plan is exactly like that of the Limestone Temple, but it is built of mud and is considerably smaller than the other. On the north-west terrace, on the other hand, there is part of a building of a quite exceptional character, a colonnade about 30 m. wide composed of two rows of huge pillar-shaped supports, which have a diameter of over 2 m. Only at the point where the colonnade meets the wall do they become half-columns. The Limestone Temple, Temple A and the 'Colonnade' lie round a rectangular court which was about 2 m. lower, with its entrance on the south-east. Its perimeter walls were at first built of *Patzen* – the exceptionally large unburnt mud bricks – and later of the sun-dried mud bricks known as *Riemchen*, that is, small bricks of the dimensions 6 × 6 × 16 cm.

In contrast to the attempt made in the Limestone Temple to improve on the perishable nature of the sun-dried brick by using building stone, here in the Colonnade and in the court next to it another method was tried. Building with mud and reed, or mud and wood, as had been the custom in the Land of the Two Rivers for many centuries, indeed for a millennium, had produced its own laws and evolved its own styles.[3] The matting with which they had tried to protect the mud walls is here, perhaps for the first time to any great extent, transformed into a wall-casing, consisting of thousands of nail-shaped *clay cones,* which were set closely together in a clay bed. The cones have flat heads – or heads decorated by incisions – and are coloured black, white or red. The way in which they are arranged forms a mosaic pattern which so clearly has the appearance of a textile that we may perhaps assume that their origin, in all probability, lay in the earlier reed mats with which the walls were hung. This type of wall-casing of baked clay cones was used not only for the long walls of the court, which are broken up into a series of half-columns, but also for the *north-west wall,* which forms a sort of *platform,* and for the round pillars of the Colonnade itself (Pls. 1, 2). This method of making mud walls durable by means of a mosaic covering is typical of the whole Protohistorical Period. It had the advantage over stone building that the assemblage of small pieces of coloured material, in the way the clay cones were used here, was somehow in keeping with the Sumerian character. It is a treatment which prevailed not only in architecture but also to a great extent in other branches of art, to the end of Sumerian history. For it would seem that to a Sumerian the complete thing was not primary but grew for him out of the composition and arrangement of its component parts.

It is possible that the mosaic facing of clay cones, which superseded the original mat covering, itself represents a second transformation, from a *stone cone mosaic* (Pl. 2; Fig. 2). Such a facing on mud walls with coloured stone can be seen in a building dating from Level IV at Uruk (Warka), on a building lying between the two main sanctuaries of Anu and Inanna. There, while the walls of the court are mixed with clay cones, the walls of the building itself, which stands in the court, have been reinforced with a mosaic from white alabaster cones as well as with red and black limestone cones.[4] The whole edifice looks like a switch from the purely stone building of the Limestone Temple to a mud building strengthened by a stone facing.

All this leads us to the supposition that in the same way the pillar-like supports in the Colonnade with their cone mosaic facing are only a substitute for earlier stone pillars, as pillars and columns are structural building elements which are alien to the real character of mud brick building. The pillar is thus excluded from the development of Sumerian architecture. The pillar, and very soon the arch also, were known to Sumerian builders as a structural method

Fig. 2 Reconstruction of the Stone Cone Temple at Uruk (After: UVB 15, Pl. 41)

for overcoming the forces of gravity, but neither ever became a decisive influence in the architecture of the classical period of the ancient Near East. Sumerian architecture, as we have seen it here, does not attempt to express in artistic form the tectonic of building – that is, the interplay of the stresses of load and support, the overcoming of the forces of gravity through the structural elements of a building. Rather does Sumerian architecture express itself from the beginning, as we have seen, in the disposition of the ground-plan and the decoration of the wall surfaces. The actual framework of its buildings was clad in a skin, or rather a garment. And in this it resembles ancient Near Eastern sculpture.

b The Uruk IVa Period

Characteristics which appeared in Sumerian architecture during the first phase of the Protohistorical Period (Uruk V–IV c–d) as alien to its real nature – such as building in stone or the emphasis laid on tectonic forces by the use of pillars – disappeared completely in the second Protohistorical phase of the Eanna sanctuary, which is the equivalent of Level IVa. From the architectural point of view this phase represents the peak in the development of this fundamental period of culture. The sanctuary had experienced a complete transformation. It is true that we again find two examples of two buildings of unequal size placed at right angles to each other, but their siting had been altered[5] (Fig. 3). In the place where the Limestone Temple had been, there was now only a large store and administrative building. The Main Temple D, clearly the successor to the Limestone Temple, now occupied the whole area which was previously covered by the terraces, Colonnade and Temple A, as well as that of the large cone-mosaic court. North-west of the Main Temple D lay Temple C, a building of the same type as the Limestone Temple, and standing in a clear relation to the Main Temple D. It is actually the best preserved example of this type of temple. It is not necessary here to describe its ground-plan in detail. It only differs from that of the Limestone Temple inasmuch as the block at its end (the 'Kopfbau') is

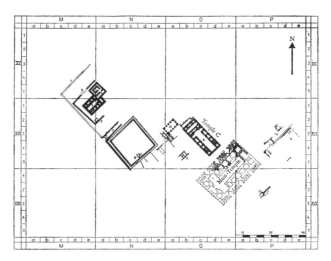

Fig. 3   Eanna sanctuary at Uruk, Level IVa
(After: UVB 21, Pl. 31)

only connected with the complex round the central court to a very small extent, whereas it stretches mainly towards the north-west. It is also remarkable that none of the outside walls of the whole building show any trace of the architectural feature of niches, whereas the entire expanse of the inner rooms of the block round the main room, the 'Kopfbau', is decorated with very small niches. Perhaps this shows that only this north-west part of the main room complex in Temple C was intended for religious use and that the central courtyard complex was meant to be used for administration.

The embellishment with niches of the outside walls of Temple D as well as of its inside walls represents an increase which should not be considered just as pure ornament, but rather as a positive contribution to the room design. Whereas the shorter sides of the huge building – it must have occupied an area of about 55 × 80 m. – were decorated with the customary wall arrangement of niches in three steps, in the long walls the niches amount to independent rooms, owing to their exceptional depth, and also to their cruciform shape. Each set of three niches, about 1.5 m. deep, is followed by a cruciform niche of about 6 m. deep and over 5 m. wide. In whatever way the elevation of the walls was carried out in detail – if one can restore even part of this extraordinary building in one's imagination from the fragment of the ground-plan which survives – inevitably one is struck by the marked lightening of the brick mass, of which as it were only a fragile shell still survives, the product of a gay and abstract imagination. Here again the aesthetic form of the architecture does not arise out of an emphasis laid on the constructive elements of the building and their sublimation by embellishment. Indeed, it is altogether quite impossible to explain the 'niche' architecture as a development of mud-brick building. Again, at Temple D at Uruk, the most developed cult building of the Sumerian Protohistorical Period, the artistic style of the elevation does not reflect its inner tectonic forces, but is an ornamental covering. Yet that is not to say that the embellishment of walls with niches may not in part owe its origin to an older, different method of building. Such an origin must certainly lie very far back in prehistory, and probably also outside Mesopotamia, since the oldest known buildings in the country, even in neolithic times, were made of mud. Whilst the ornamental covering with cone mosaic may have been suggested by an architecture of reed and mud, the wall arrangement of niches may represent a transference to mud building of an age-old technique of building with wooden posts, an idea which has recently become increasingly more probable.[6]

c The Jamdat Nasr Period

The impressive buildings in the sanctuary of Innin, which date from the first phase of the Protohistorical Period, represent a completely new development, heralding the birth of a great civilization. By contrast, the High Temple in the Anu precinct at Uruk (UVB 7, Pl. 1, K XVII) – right through to its final, highly developed form, which belongs to the second phase of the Protohistorical Period – is the culmination of a tradition of many centuries. This was apparent from the numerous layers of rebuilding laid bare by the excavations[7] (Fig. 4). The cycle of collapse and rebuilding had made it too into a high temple, that is to say this had brought about its raised site. The origins of this temple undoubtedly lay far back in prehistory, though it was possibly not so old as a similar building which has recently been excavated.

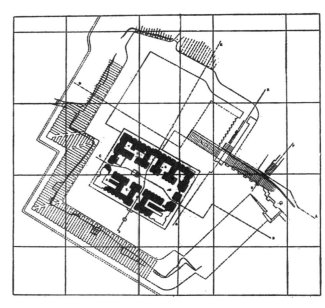

Fig. 4　The 'White Temple' on the Anu Ziggurat at Uruk (After: H. J. Lenzen, *Die Entwicklung der Zikkurat*, 1941, Pl. 2 b)

This is the temple at Eridu[8] (Fig. 5), the city of the water-god Enki, which was probably the principal temple of the Sumerian world before its leadership was transferred to the main sanctuary of Innin at Eanna in Uruk. As far back as the middle chalcolithic age, from a very small, primitive beginning – a chapel

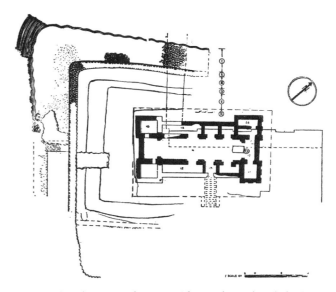

Fig. 5　Temples VII and VI at Eridu (modern Abu-Shahrain) (After: Sumer 3, No. 2, Fig. 2)

covering a bare 2 × 3 metres – there had developed in Eridu a temple with an elongated rectangular central space, flanked on both sides by a row of smaller rooms; one of these rooms was the staircase landing. The entrance to the temple is on one of the long sides. At one of the shorter ends of the main hall there is a stage-like podium, and at the opposite end a hearth or altar. Through constant rebuilding the temple rose so far above the level of its surroundings that below it a simple terrace – or possibly one with two tiers – had grown up and this could only be reached by a stairway.

The so-called 'White Temple' on the Anu terrace or 'ziggurat' at Uruk so resembles these prehistoric buildings at Eridu in all details that it would be reasonable to assume that it too had had a long series of similar predecessors, even if this had not been proved by the excavations. However, this White Temple has been preserved beneath the casing of another, later temple, and – together with a few fragments of stone vessels in architectural form from the Protohistorical Period – it provides the best medium for the reconstruction of the elevation of this type of building.[9] Probably there is a genetic connection between the ground-plan of the High Temple and that of the Limestone Temple, Temple C and Temple D in Eanna. The resemblance is especially marked in the buildings situated at the head of the complex (the 'Kopfbau'), in the general grouping of the rooms and in the way in which the niches are arranged on the walls. The White Temple is thus the best evidence of the development which went on continuously from the first to the second half of the Protohistorical Period, the so-called Jamdat Nasr Period.[10] In recent times we have discovered two further examples of this type of temple, which are also of importance because of the way in which they are embellished. These are the temple at *Tell 'Uqair*[11] with its wall paintings (Fig. 6) and the 'Temple of the Thousand Eyes' at *Tell Brak*[12] (Fig. 7) in Northern Mesopotamia, of which the cult podium is decorated in true Sumerian style with gold and brightly coloured stones. The tradition of architecture which can be studied here in the White Temple and in its related buildings corresponds to the unbroken development of writing and that of a section of the sculpture (see

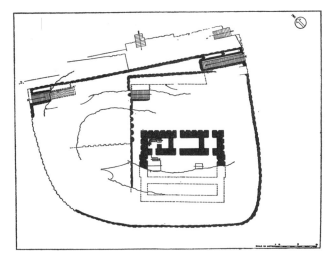

Fig. 6 'Painted Temple' at Tell 'Uqair
(After: JNES 2, Pl. V)

Sections 2 and 3 below). In the Eanna Sanctuary at Uruk, on the other hand, at the point of transition from the period of Uruk IV to the Jamdat Nasr period, there was a change which cannot only have had external causes. It is true that building was still carried out using *Riemchen* bricks and that the walls were still decorated with cone mosaics, but in other respects the whole design of the sanctuary at this period (Uruk III) gives the impression af a completely new beginning[13] (Fig. 8). The centre of the whole

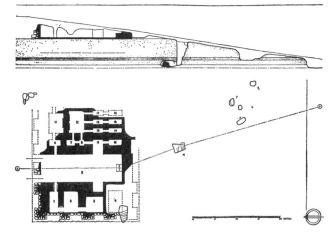

Fig. 7 'Temple of the Thousand Eyes' at Tell Brak
(After: Iraq 9, 1947, Pl. LVII)

layout was now really a raised terrace, on which a temple must have been built, possibly in the style of the contemporary White Temple. The terrace underwent several transformations at short intervals (Uruk III a–c), not only affecting its height but also its dimensions. It seems as if now the goddess Innin was accorded for the first time a High Temple, such as the other gods, Anu and Enki, had already possessed before. Round this high temple there also arose numerous dwelling houses and administrative offices, as well as the places for sacrifices *(Opferstätten)* – all of which were constantly rebuilt. By this time the buildings were arranged in several groups, each group round a court, and all inside a girdle of buildings.

There is a remarkable contrast between the inner and the outer development of the Eanna sanctuary. The building of the High Temple seems to suggest that only now was Innin accorded equal status to Anu, as a city divinity of Uruk, and perhaps was only now deemed 'Lady of Heaven', after having originally been a goddess of life, closely bound up with the chthonic sphere. Rooms containing places for sacrifice show how extensively her power and reputation had spread. In contrast to this, however, there was a clear step backwards as regards the style of the building and as far as the clarity, precision and boldness of conception in the layout were concerned, as well as in the technique of the brickwork. In the ground-plan some of the rooms are completely unlit and in others the thick walls of *Patzen* bricks take up more space than the room they surround. One feels that the great architectural boldness of the Uruk IV period has given way to a petty clumsiness. No longer is there any harmony or symmetry controlling the style of Eanna architecture. Thus it stands in contrast to the High Temple of Anu, the final form of which – the White Temple – fully maintains the high artistic level achieved during the period Uruk VI–Uruk IV.

2 Sculpture in the round

Judging from the sculpture known to us at the present time, sculpture in the round in Mesopotamia before 3000 B.C. did not progress beyond the undoubtedly expressive but idol-like terra-cottas dating from the late 'Ubaid period, such as those found in Ur and Eridu. At that time male and female figures were kneaded from clay into shapes completely divorced from nature. Individual parts of the body are over-emphasized, others are carelessly modelled and reduced in size. Painting is used to help produce an effect of plasticity and it underlines the daemonic character of these objects, which are mere craft products.[14] No direct path links this ceramic style of prehistoric objects moulded in the round with the first real sculpture in the round from the historical period of Mesopotamia. However, what had hitherto been hidden in obscurity – the beginning of a plastic art in stone, rising above the purely craftsman level to the rank of true art – is gradually taking shape for us, though as yet not clearly defined. For many decades now we have known of a series of badly preserved figures in gypsum which came from Uruk. These had been discovered in excavations there in the years 1912/13, in the debris under the paving of the Parthian Temple[15] (Pls. 3–5). Hitherto they have not received much attention as they were in such a

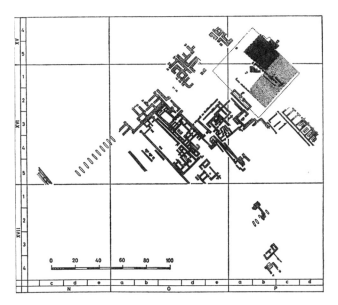

Fig. 8   Eanna Sanctuary at Uruk, Level III a–c
(After: UVB 20, Pl. 30)

fragmentary condition. They were also incorrectly held to be Parthian because of the place where they were found, and they were thus excluded from the history of Sumerian plastic art. Added to this, these figures were identified by Jordan, the excavator who found them, as images of squatting men, while in fact they represent conquered enemies with their arms pinioned behind their backs, as is shown clearly in Plate 3. It is also probable that their knees were fastened to their necks, like those of the conquered enemy in the great seal impressions[16] from the period Uruk IV. The stone figures in Plates 3 and 4 can only be explained in this way. Thus they seem to have a direct relation in detail to a find from the Uruk IV period, and this allows one to presume that the art of stone sculpture in the round of human figures may have been started in this creative epoch. There is still further evidence to help us date the gypsum figures from the Parthian Temple in the Uruk IV period. With them, under the rubble of the temple, were found not only mosaic cones,[17] which belong to Sumerian Protohistory, but also one object[18] (Pl. 5), which despite its utterly fragmentary condition, can be identified as a man with a curious beard, like a disk-shaped ruff, standing clear of the entire chin and both cheeks. This kind of beard also recalls other figures sculptured in the round in stone, which very recent research has shown belong to the Protohistorical Period in Sumer. For this same 'detachable' beard can be seen on a stone statuette, 25 cm. high, made of grey limestone and now in Zürich (Pls. 8–10), which was connected by Alfred Boissier with two similar statuettes in the Louvre[19] as early as 1912 (Pls. 6, 7). These statuettes from Zürich and Paris, which because of their beards are connected with the little gypsum figures of bound prisoners from Warka, represent a completely naked man, who seems to be wearing a padded band round his forehead and has both arms lying across his breast in such a way that it looks as though the elbows were tied together, while his legs and feet are shown separated only by a vertical central groove. In the Ancient East only a prisoner was portrayed naked. The hair and beard of this figure, however, seem to suggest that he was a prince. The wide, padded diadem was worn by princes of the Uruk IV and Jamdat Nasr periods. The plank-like modelling of the legs

and feet of the Zürich and Paris figures, with the same width from top to bottom, and divided only by a groove, links the Zürich and Paris figures with one of a naked woman excavated at Warka. It was found in the rubble from the Jamdat Nasr period[20] (Pl. 11). The front view of this statuette shows, in practically unrelated juxtaposition, a very soft and naturally modelled female bosom next to a lower trunk rather like that of a wooden idol. The feet have become a pedestal, the legs are completely embedded in the block of stone, and only a scratched line indicates the pubic area and the division between the legs. The style of the arms is in complete contrast to that of the breast, and they hang down limp on each side of the body as if they were sleeves made of material. Representation and abstract formula are presented side by side, unconnected, in a way we shall find again and again in the Protohistorical Period of Sumer.

The small statuette of a woman, from Level IV of the Sin Temple in Khafaje[21] (Pl. 12), which dates from the Jamdat Nasr period and which for a long time was the sole evidence for the existence of Protohistorical sculpture in the round in Sumer, is a coarse piece of craftsmanship. The modelling of the upper part of the naked body, with its heavy breasts, and of the fleshy face with its hooked nose, gives no hint of a spiritualizing abstraction. This creature seems completely tied down to the animal world. If we have here the portrait of a female slave, we get quite a different impression from the statuette of a man, of which we unfortunately only possess the upper half. It was found in a vessel of a late period at Warka[22] (Pl. 13). The statue was about a third life-size, and though only part of it has survived – from the crown of the head to just below the waist – it shows nevertheless that the Sumerian sculptor in the Protohistorical Period (Uruk IV–Jamdat Nasr period) could create a complete human portrait in the round out of stone. Indeed, it is created in a way which corresponds to the spirit of that age, in which the material and the transcendental merged into each other. That the statuette is a product of the Protohistorical Period can be shown beyond doubt by a number of unmistakable factual details. The half-length skirt with its characteristic padded girdle below the naked upper body is how the princes are dressed in the hunting stele from Warka (Uruk) (cf. p. 14; Pl. 14),[23] and on the seal impressions from Warka (see below). Like the stone figure they can be recognised by their distinctive head-dress, a calotte, tied to the forehead and neck by a padded band, with the appearance of a cap. We have already met the 'detachable' beard, such as the one on this statuette, in the gypsum figures from Warka, Zürich and Paris (p. 8, Pls. 3–10). The unusual horizontal grooving on the beard should also be mentioned, as yet another peculiarity of the statuette characteristic of the Protohistorical Period. It can be seen again on the male figure in the net garment on the so-called 'Preusser' seal, one of the most significant examples of protohistorical glyptic from Warka (p. 13; Pl. B 1). This highly stylized, wig-type beard which seems to be a contrast in style to the almost tangible muscularity of the back and of the upper arm, revealed by the play of light and shade, actually lifts the man's face right out of this world. Thus during the Sumerian Protohistorical Period the statue as a work of art has been created – the portrait in the round of a man or of a god in human shape.

3 Relief and other two-dimensional art

In the Land of the Two Rivers before about 3000 B.C. there had been only two vehicles for two-dimensional art: painted pottery and the stamp seal. Ever since the early chalcolithic age painted ware had answered the urge for abstract decoration. In glyptic, however, for the first time a narrative art, based on observation of the outside world, had come into existence (Moortgat, *Entstehung*, Pl. 18a). Even during a completely prehistoric age,[24] in the late chalcolithic era, the Ubaid II period, a point had been reached when the round or rectangular flat area on the stamp was no longer regarded merely as part of a tool which one decorated, but as a surface prepared for a design, and the artist contrived to compose an appropriate picture. In this way the abstract principle of mirror-like symmetry already stands beside the free, irregular division of the picture.

a The Uruk VI–IV Period

During the first phase of the Protohistorical Period (Uruk VI–IV) it is evidently once more in the field of glyptic that one finds a continued development. A new shape of seal was created, for a purpose which is no longer easily explained: the *cylinder seal,* a stone roller of which the surface of the cylinder offers a considerably larger surface for a design than did the stamp seal. The picture area is a strip which returns back into itself, and when it is rolled onto clay it produces a continuous frieze. Whether this shape of seal was happened on by chance or whether it was consciously invented, right from the beginning it reflected the Sumerian character to an extraordinary extent and remained for ever true to the culture imprinted by the Sumerian spirit, in a way that is only equalled by the cuneiform script. The cycle, which is born from itself and finds its fulfilment again in itself, is something which we shall encounter again and again in innumerable small and large pictorial compositions in the ancient Near East. It can be regarded as a structural principle basic to Sumerian art, and it may owe its origin to an attitude to life which was deeply rooted.

We have only a few examples[25] of original cylinder seals dating from the Uruk VI–IV period: but we have numerous fragments of clay jug stoppers which bear impressions of cylinder seals.

The *pictorial repertoire* presented by this material is very varied. It includes certain themes[26] which retained their importance and set the pattern in Near Eastern art (Pls. A 2; L 1–4): the cult procession, and scenes of sacrifice, battle and hunting. On the other hand, however, we also find motifs which are characteristic only of the Protohistorical Period, and were not continued at all, or not for long, in later periods: for example, wild animals in open country, or animals and mixed composite creatures in heraldic form. The subject-matter illustrates with great clarity the central importance to the Sumerians of the worship of their gods and of their ruler as war leader and high priest. Yet wild and domesticated animals also occupy an important place as motifs, as symbols of the powers promoting or threatening man's life. Sometimes, too, they are combined into composite creatures, such as, for example, the lion-headed eagle or the snake-dragon (Pl. A 1). The herd in echelon formation with the symbol of Innin appears only exceptionally and points to the next period, the Jamdat Nasr period.

It is impossible[27] to discover a difference in form between the seal impressions from the two phases of the Uruk VI–IV period, as one can with the architecture of this period, even though the animal pictures in the heraldic compositions were largely discovered in the later sub-divisions of Level IV.

Naturalism and *symbolic abstraction* not only participate in the themes but also, from the beginning, dictate the pattern of Sumerian art, in the single figure as well as in the composition of pictures. These two fundamental forms of all pictorial art do to some extent struggle for the soul of the Near Eastern artist throughout all the centuries, yet the conflict is never resolved once and for all time, as it was, for instance, in Egyptian art or again in Byzantine art. Rather they condition the character of the different periods of art by their continually changing relationship to each other: sometimes they confront each other face to face in a single work, at other times symbolism threatens to displace naturalism, or representational art triumphs over any form of abstraction. Here, in the beginning the fundamental methods of art do not have quite equal force. It is true that there is a series of seal impressions which particularly favour the mirror-like, non-realistic arrangement of animals and mixed creatures (Pls. A 3; M 1–2) – dating right back to the period of the Limestone Temple[28] and occurring with increasing frequency until the next period, the Jamdat Nasr period.[29] In spite of this, the main impression we get from the plastic art of this creative period is one of a naturalistic, vigorous spirituality, for which a world of the profane, distinct from the religious, the supernatural, actually did not yet exist. Even in those cases where the stone-cutter has composed artifical heraldic groups with his animal figures, with symbolic significance, the single animal-like figures still remain noticeably true to nature. The stone-cutter is visibly striving for shapes which are rounded, solid and close to life; even indeed when he is depicting fabulous beings, the elements of which they are com-

bined are extraordinarily carefully observed.[30] It must have been the very same stone-cutters who depicted groups of animals sometimes in a free natural attitude and arrangement, and sometimes in a heraldic, abstract composition: the ibex on the seal impression UVB 2, Fig. 32 cannot be told apart from that on the impression UVB 5, Pl. 26a. How high a degree of freedom and harmony in the reproduction of animal forms was achieved by the stone-cutters of this great period is shown on a fragment of a large jug stopper decorated with an impression consisting of two registers.[31] An actual cylinder seal in the British Museum[32] has a very similar subject, but in this case the strong marks left by the use of the drill enable one to appreciate the delicate workmanship of the former piece.

A few examples of scenes in which prince, priests, warriors and prisoners appear, provide evidence that in the visual art of the period the human figure could also be handled with complete success.[33] Here, all of a sudden, the artist has successfully shown his knowledge of human physiognomy: the composition of the picture, that is the spatial arrangement of the individual figures within the framework of the picture, is here free of all abstract design, in contrast to the pictures of the heraldic type.

Whether the art of stone-cutting was the only branch of two-dimensional art during the Uruk VI–IV period or whether there were other media cannot yet be decided. The fact is, however, that all the two-dimensional art which has survived from this period is the work of the stone-cutter, and it had as its focal point Uruk, the metropolis of the great Sumerian civilization.

b   The Jamdat Nasr Period

The second phase of the Protohistorical Period in Sumer, the so-called Jamdat Nasr period,[34] is named after a small excavation site in the vicinity of Kish and Babylon. Strictly speaking, it corresponds to the building period Uruk IIIb,[35] if one goes by the stage in the development of writing on the clay tablets of Jamdat Nasr. A wider interpretation of the Jamdat Nasr period includes the Levels Uruk III-II.

On the one hand this period contributes to art a normal development from the seed sown in the preceding epoch, through all types of expansion and enrichment of the different kinds of art and styles, but on the other hand, as in the architecture of the period, it produces completely alien phenomena, which at first suggest a retrograde movement or a decline, but which became of decisive importance for the future of Sumerian art. In this instance the course of art is more difficult even than usual to understand by purely formal observation. Rather we have to grasp its pattern from the content of its designs and the attitude to life underlying them, however difficult this may be and however incomplete our understanding still remains.

i The Uruk IV tradition

Those works of art from the Jamdat Nasr period which developed further the subject-matter and style of the Uruk IV period form the peak of the artistic achievement in the Protohistorical Period and enable us to fill the great architecture of the time with a tangible life. Uruk continues as the centre of Sumerian culture, which had, however, meanwhile extended its influence over the whole of the Near East, even as far as the Nile valley.[36]

At the same time new branches of art appear to have been developed: reliefs (high and low) were suddenly employed to decorate cult vessels, of which the outside surfaces, like that of the cylinder seal, provided the Sumerian sculptor with the opportunity to devise a pictorial frieze returning round into itself. At the same time the first *stele* decorated with relief appeared, to serve as a pattern for the future. *Sculpture in the round*, mainly of animal subjects but sometimes of humans as well, was probably started with the amulet in stone, which was so popular in the Jamdat Nasr period, or with the amulet-like stamp seal. Yet another subject for plastic art in the round was the *vessel in the shape of a whole animal*. Different limbs of the body were assembled from various materials, stone or metal, and this resulted in some of the most important works of art in all branches of Sumerian art. Wall painting and painting on pottery started originally as imitation and as a substitute for

other, more costly techniques. Reliefs vary from decidedly flat reliefs to exaggeratedly high reliefs – even to the extent of parts being modelled in the round, projecting from the surface of the relief – every degree being exemplified on numberless stone vessels or fragments of them: bowls, libation jars, high cylinder-shaped provision vessels. The supporting stands and feet of relatively quite small bowls are elaborated into sculptured groups. Some of the vessels are decorated with an exaggeratedly high relief which projects grotesquely, overpowering the whole object. As in the architecture, these reveal to us an aspect of the Sumerian character in whose make-up the tectonic plays no part. Plastic decoration is not used here, as it is by the Greeks, to emphasize the structure of a vessel, but rather as an ornamental veil, and its meaning[37] is undoubtedly related to the cult ceremony in which these valuable vessels were used (Pls. 15, 16).

The sculptured groups and high relief on the cult vessels employ for their subjects the domestic animal (ox and sheep) and the beast of prey (lion and eagle), either singly, in rows or in combat. Sometimes a naked hero is added as protector of the domestic animals against the animals of prey. Their style is the same as that we saw in the glyptic of the Uruk IV period, only the rounding of the body forms is frequently increased to an inflated disproportion, and they are often carved in a careless and coarse way; the hands and the paws of the lion are an example of this. Yet this is not to deny the liveliness of imagination and composition of these early works of art. Because there is so much inner, scintillating vitality we can overlook the often stiff and abstract arrangement of the figures in groups of a heraldic symmetry.

Quite a different impression is conveyed by the two most important alabaster vessels which have survived, the outside surfaces of which are decorated with extensive friezes. One is an object shaped like a trough[38] (Pls. 17, 18) and the other is a tall alabaster vase, shaped like a chalice[39] (Pl. 19), both from Uruk (Warka). In spite of the particular importance attaching to the subject-matter portrayed on these, the bas-reliefs on the two vessels seem to be subordinated in their arrangement to the construction of the vessel itself, indeed, they even stress its special shape.

Whereas on the tall alabaster vase, which is almost cylindrical in shape, the three rows of friezes, one above the other, together with the narrow raised bands which separate them, accentuate the base, border and central area of the vase and the series of pictures follow the circular design, in the case of the trough the narrow borders of the design frame the wide and short sides of the vessel. The picture's composition, of completely mirror-like symmetry within the surrounding framework, indicates the desire for the abstract symbolism of a religious conception, which must be related to the worship of the goddess Innana of Uruk. The symbolic standard, made of a bundle tied with rings, plays an important role in the picture. It is the standard which, as we know, became the prototype for the later cuneiform ideogram for Innana. The sacred herd of maned sheep (ram, ewe and lamb) is arranged in symmetrical duplication round a reed hut crowned on the right and left by the sign of the goddess. On the short sides of the trough two ringed bundles are combined with two lambs and two rosettes of eight petals. Abstract formalism, however, has been confined to the composition of the picture, exactly as in the heraldic scenes of glyptic from the preceding epoch, while the animal figures themselves are shown completely realistically. In the history of art, this trough with its reliefs represents the most perfect example of something we have already seen, in principle, in the heraldic scenes on the cylinder seals of the Uruk IV period: naturalistic individual portraits within an abstract composition.

In an even more splendid way, the relief on the large chalice-shaped alabaster vase[40] (Pl. 19; Fig. 9) achieves the aim of the other trend in art, a trend already noted in the freely-constructed, narrative scenes in the stone-cutting of the Uruk IV period (cf. p. 8), in the battle scenes and the cultic processions (Pls. L 1–3). The three friezes, placed one above the other, are doubtless all part of the same theme, which is a comprehensive picture of a cult procession with a long parade of figures offering sacrifices and of sacrificial animals. The leader of this parade is a man whose appearance has had to be reconstructed from surviving traces and from other fragmentary scenes. He is dressed in a garment made

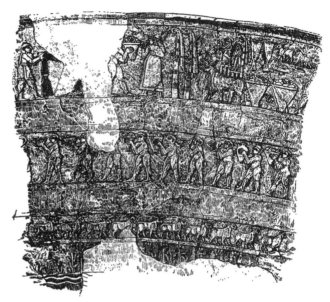

Fig. 9 Alabaster vase from Uruk
(After: Heinrich, *Kleinfunde*, Pl. 38)

of transparent netting and is accompanied by two assistants, one carrying a basket of fruit and the other a large cloth girdle (Pl. 20). In the middle frieze numerous naked servants walk in procession carrying baskets, ewers and libation jars, containing fruit and drinks. Below this passes a procession of the sacrificial sheep, and below these a scene symbolizing the source of all life, a row of ears of barley and palm shoots, as if above a stretch of water. The whole procession is being received by a woman in a cloak, with a heavy mane of hair and a pointed head-dress with horns (Pl. 21). She is standing in front of two standards of ringed bundles, at the entrance to a temple or storehouse, in which there are already various vessels containing gifts. Amongst these there are vessels in the shape of whole animals, a lion and a goat, as well as a stepped pedestal with ringed bundles and sheep on either side. On the pedestal two human figures are standing praying and sacrificing. No-one now queries the real meaning of this composite scene. The goddess Innin herself, or her substitute, a high priestess, is receiving her bridegroom on New Year's Day to celebrate the Sacred Marriage.[41] This bridegroom, who is known from later written sources, is the half-mythical King of Uruk, Dumuzi, or, as he is called by the Semites,

Tammuz, and simultaneously he is a shepherd[42]. In this figure we are dealing with one of the essential and fundamental elements of Sumerian culture, which began in Uruk, the city of Innin. Life, *eternal* life, personified in the goddess, and the procreative yet simultaneously transitory life, symbolized by the King Dumuzi, this is the dual principle which presided over the cosmos, the world of the gods as well as the community of men, which Dumuzi unites – individual human beings as well as animal and plant and, finally, mountain and water.

It is difficult to decide whether this frieze was intended to represent a mythical event, that is to say an incident from the life of the goddess Innin and her lover – this would seem possible if the head-dress of the main female figure really is horned and thus would be the first divine crown – or whether it was meant to represent a cult ceremony, such as took place every New Year in imitation of the myth. However, we may perhaps come nearest to the truth if we simply avoid this sharp distinction between Myth and Reality. The protohistorical world of Sumer, as it came to maturity in Uruk, is indeed in every direction – sociological/political as well as religious/artistic – a union of the sacred world of the gods and the profane world of humans, of the real and the metaphysical, of nature and the abstract: in some ways it was a golden age, in which the life of the gods and the life of humans still intermingled. Man, not yet as an individual separated from his community, has through his princes the closest possible relationship with the gods, and has in a way taken part in eternal life.[43] He is not yet so conscious of his existence as an individual and does not yet sense, as he will later, the terror of death. He still lives like the animals and plants, the eternal life of nature and her mysterious powers. This attitude to life had allowed the higher organization of the Sumerian temple-city to emerge from the prehistoric peasant communities and village cultures, a happy constellation – perhaps unique. The same attitude is apparent in the best works of art of the period, and the alabaster vase doubtless counts as one of them. Following a natural order – from the life-giving properties of the beneficial plants and the domesticated animals, to the men reaping the harvest, with the

king leading them as their mediator with the goddess – the sculptor has, without showing a rigid constraint, turned the powerful figures of his men and animals into an organic composite picture, in which the hierarchy within the cosmos is indicated only by the relative size of the figures. His world is separated into three divisions: at the bottom water, plants and animals, mankind in the middle and the king with the goddess at the summit.

The abstract principle of picture composition used in this work consists merely of a simple arrangement of rows and of rythmic repetition. And the frieze, as imaginary space, is lifted from the vessel's surface by broad bands, framing it above and below. If the central figure of a woman with the horned head-gear does indeed represent the goddess herself, then she is shown for the first time in purely human form, in front of her two standards of ringed bundles, these being her abstract symbols. In this way representation of the deity in human form would also have been initiated in this period of Protohistory, an event of great importance to Near Eastern art. Moreover this kind of anthropomorphism follows naturally from the particular attitude to life shown during this period, which has already been described.

The stone-cutter of the Jamdat Nasr period, the maker of the *cylinder seal*, went through the same stages of development both as regards subject-matter as well as style, which we have already seen in the development of the relief. For him too the royal shepherd and the hunter Dumuzi, the sacred herds and pens, are once again the main subjects of his art (Pls. A 4; A 6). It is useful to compare two cylinder seals with the same theme but different compositions; the seals are in London[44] and Berlin[45] (Pls. A 5; B 1). On both there is a picture showing the ruler in a net garment feeding the sacred sheep of Innin, identified by the presence of the ringed bundle standard. The seal in the British Museum presents a mythical and, at the same time, a ritual scene. The ruler is approaching two sheep, holding towards them in both hands a branch on which there is a rosette with eight petals. Two more sheep, again shown between the ringed bundles of the goddess, are approaching the king. The other seal has the same pictorial elements: the king,

once more in the net garment,[46] branches with rosettes, maned sheep and the ringed bundle of Innin,
but now they are arranged in a different, closely knit,
symmetrical composition, no longer suggesting a cult
ritual or the mythical episode which inspired it. This
time man and tree are formally merged in such a way
that we can recognize in them the incarnate spirit of
vegetation, Dumuzi, seen here bestowing life on the
sacred herd. Here once again art has achieved a movement towards the symbolic, though with complete
naturalism of the individual figures, solely by the use
of an abstract composition.

Beside the reliefs on vessels the Near East is also
indebted to its Protohistorical Period for the *stele*
decorated with relief, that is an upright, magical
stone block, used initially for reports in pictorial
form, later also for written reports of the king's
deeds. A basalt fragment[47] of one such stele was found
at Warka, measuring 80 cm. high and about 60 cm.
broad (Pl. 14). Only its front side has been slightly
smoothed to make a surface for a relief. The reliefs
on this face are not distributed freely, but form an
irregular pattern. Although the picture area has
been levelled, it was not framed or marked off from its
surroundings. There are two distinct episodes shown
on it: in them the king, who can be recognized by his
diadem, wig and beard, is shown fighting a lion, in
one picture with a spear and in the other with a bow
and arrow. The episodes are carved one above the
other, not separated by a band or even by a base
line. How far removed we are here from the abstract
or consecutive narrative works of art which have
been described above! The magical block of stone
itself, on which the scene is carved, has not yet been
cut into any shape. The concept of a picture surface
as an abstract form for expressing the idea of time
and space, in which the events depicted take place,
has not yet been grasped. The figures float in time and
space on the surface of the block of stone. Pictorial
composition in this work is at a far more primitive
level than it was with the vessels or with the cylinder
seals.

We may say, in short, that the reliefs of the Jamdat
Nasr period, which carried forward the traditions of
the Uruk IV period in quite new categories of art,
continued to portray individual figures of man and

beast in the same naturalistic manner, but found
various solutions to the problem of using the 'picture
surface' as an abstract equivalent of space and time,
as well as for the arrangement of the figures inside it.
These solutions correspond to various stages of development, and existed side by side during the same
period.

In some of the stone-ware decorated with reliefs, it
was already noticeable that the sculptor in the Jamdat
Nasr period felt an urge to move from relief towards
sculpture in the round. The relief was raised to such
an extent that it became almost completely detached
from the surface of the picture. This also seems to
have been the case with certain wall reliefs[48] of the
late Uruk III period, amongst which some of the
most outstanding examples of plastic animal art ever
found have been rediscovered. Animals are shown
lying with their bodies stretched out along the wall,
but with their heads projecting at a right angle.
Whereas the surface of their bodies is shown by incised lines, suggesting the hide, the heads of the rams
in particular are shown in strong plastic modelling
with the individual features in high relief. The lack
of symmetry of the horns increases even more the
illusion of real life, which makes one suspect the
existence of a deeply rooted understanding of the
essential nature of these sacred animals by the sculptors of the period.

Another ram's head,[49] probably from an animal in
a recumbent position, used as part of a vessel, gives
an even stronger impression of daemonic mystery
(Pls. 22, 23). It was particularly in these splendid
likenesses of domestic animals, which with water and
useful plants constituted the main support of their
existence, that the Sumerians of the Protohistorical
Period found an especially happy way to express
their attitude to life. These animals and plants are,
therefore, not purely material elements of nature but
just as much the symbols of a transcendental principle.

This is probably also the reason why the animal
motif and form was used for an extraordinarily large
number of amulets – pendants in the shape of domestic animals, and also in the shape of their enemies the
animals of prey, or of animals possessing a frequent
and rapid rate of reproduction such as frogs and fish,

and lastly of composite creatures, which combined the might of two animals[50] (Pl. B 2). These amulets, carved in the round, have a connection with the stamp seal as well as with the cylinder seal, a sign that the seal, which was at first probably only a sign or device for the individual, was soon attributed magic properties as a means of protection. The amulet animal figures were halved longitudinally down their centre, and generally had crude signs on their flat half, made with an engraving tool or drill.[51] On the cylinder seals the amulet animals were on the knob at the upper end of the metal rod which passed through the boring of the cylinder or were fashioned directly out of the stone.[52]

Some of these little figures are of particular importance because they represent the earliest examples of toreutic, *metal plastic art*. We have not yet discovered any specimen of metal plastic art on a larger scale from the Protohistorical Period, but it is almost certain that such works must have existed, since large-scale castings would in theory have been no more difficult to produce than the small amulets of copper and silver.[53] They too must have been a solid casting, as this was the method used for casting amulets.

Nothing is more characteristic of Sumerian art than their fondness for making up figures out of a variety of pieces using different materials, and by so doing obtaining at the same time a colour contrast. For this work they used coloured stones, especially black and white, though lapis lazuli was also a great favourite. No less popular was the combination of stone with metal, copper (bronze) as well as silver and gold. This partiality of the Sumerians led them to make their reliefs with inlaid friezes and incrustations, and in the field of sculpture in the round it produced a technique which was to attain its final peak in Greece, thousand of years later, in plastic art in chryselephantine. Several circumstances favoured this combining of different materials. The mosaic-like decoration of an ornament or a figure certainly corresponds to a particular way of thinking, an analytical rather than a synthetical outlook. However, another equally strong motive behind the composite work may have been their love of bright colours and gay iridescence. The southerner experiences the shape of things in sharply outlined and contrasting coloured

surfaces. The inlaid objects, the incrustations, are really coloured drawings. Moreover, the application of metal parts to a stone statuette, particularly in the case of extremities such as ears, horns, tail and legs, was in no small way caused by the difficulty, indeed the impossibility, of carving such fragile parts out of stone. Thus the Protohistorical Period had already recognized and profited from the way in which the material determines the style in art. It is certainly no coincidence that nearly all the amulets of four-legged animals made of stone are shown lying down, that is to say with their legs close to the main part of the body, and only the the little bronze lion from the 'Sammelfund' found at Warka is standing upright on his legs[54] (Fig. 10). It was the material he was using which compelled the sculptor of the ram's head (Pls. 22, 23)[55] not to project the long horns out from the head but to leave them as part of the block, whereas pegged horns of cattle, made of bronze,[56] have been found which must have stuck out freely from the animals' heads, the heads probably being made of some other material.

The most beautiful example of an animal statuette with inlay is a stone figure,[57] about 8 cm. long, which has a white body with its head turned at a right angle and is made of limestone (Pl. 25). Large irregular pieces of some other coloured stone had been inset in its shoulder blades and hind-quarters, probably in order to suggest the spotted colouring of the animal.

Fig. 10 Bronze lion amulet from Uruk. Redrawn (After: Heinrich, *Kleinfunde*, Pl. 13 a)

On the animal's loins, back and neck, as well as between its eyes, we can still trace the cavities for five-petalled flowers, which were probably inlaid with coloured stones. None of the extremities has survived – ears, horns, tail or legs – except for the silver hind legs which, like the rest of the body, are modelled in a remarkably life-like way. The aim of the sculpture – what the sculptor was striving to achieve – was to free it from the limitations of its material, stone, and this could only be realized with the help of metal. That the organic unity of the object as a whole suffered as a result did not hinder the Sumerians, who preferred coordination to subordination.

To this category of polychrome, composite – if one may use the term in this way – sculpture belongs the *mask or face of a woman* in marble. The mask, like the little bull just described, was discovered at Warka in a layer from the Jamdat Nasr period and clearly represents the peak of all the surviving art of the Protohistorical Period[58] (Pl. 26).

The mask is almost life-size and is possibly the earliest work of art sculptured in the round of really high quality. It is not a fragment in the usual sense of the word, that is to say it is not a piece broken off a complete statue, but is a portion of the composite portrait of a woman which had its many parts made up of different materials. For that reason the back of the head is missing, and the rear side has been cut flat and has drill holes where it was fastened to other parts. For that reason too the hair is only outlined and on the crown there is a deep groove ready to receive a gold wig. The eyebrows, joined above the nose, were probably originally inlaid with lapis lazuli, and the eyeballs, made from some other material, were sunk in the deep eye sockets provided for them, surrounded by delicately shaped lids.

The head is carved out of fine-grained marble, thus suggesting a translucent skin, and if in imagination we add the missing parts of the head, we become aware of a discord affecting the whole thing, which we have encountered already in those reliefs in which completely naturalistic individual figures were inserted in a schematic, heraldic-type pattern. Here a similar contrast in style divides the conventional, standardized upper part of the head from the mouth, austere and almost portrait-like, and the delicately

indicated lines between the nose and corners of the mouth. These present an expression which must have been based on an individual personality. Or is it just this tension between realism and symbolism, which we have met already in many other works of art from the Protohistorical Period, which gives them exceptional merit and meaning?

ii   New developments

Just as in architecture, new trends emerged in works of art during the Jamdat Nasr period which cannot be classified merely as developments of those from the first phase of the Protohistorical Period. No more than in the architecture, can they be explained simply by the label 'bad quality' or 'decadent', even though many of them can be counted as works of lesser quality.

In Tell Brak, in Northern Mesopotamia, far from the centre of Sumer in the Protohistorical Period, a temple existed in the Jamdat Nasr period, which resembled that at the so-called Anu Ziggurat at Warka (Uruk) and the even older temples in Eridu. When it was excavated the stone mask of a woman[59] was discovered which differs in its essentials from the female head from Warka (Pl. 27). When comparing the two one must discount the differences in the national characteristics of the subjects and the provincial quality of the head from Tell Brak. All the naturalism which the head from Uruk shows has been deliberately avoided in the Tell Brak head, in favour of an intentional abstraction, a rejection of natural forms as inessential in favour of a transformation – almost deformation – of nature in obedience to inner laws of form. Here for the first time in the Protohistorical Period the human form itself, a female face, is alienated from nature in order that its spiritual essence can be expressed. With this work a new principle is introduced into the art of the Jamdat Nasr period, which does indeed mark the end of its golden age, yet belongs to the future.

A second stone head[60] from Tell Brak goes even further in this direction. In this parts of the face, especially the forehead and eyes, are completely out of proportion, undoubtedly because the head represents a god (Pl. 28). In the formation of the eyes this shows the greatest resemblance to a small fragment of a gypsum stucco relief[61] painted black, white and red from the archaic Temple of Ishtar in Ashur (Fig. 11). Of this only a fragment just 15 cm. high has been preserved, but perhaps it enables us to understand a similar, though larger cult relief of the goddess Ishtar (= Innin). The body, facing forwards, stands out in high relief from the surface. The goddess is shown naked except for heavy jewellery on her neck, breasts and hips. Her eyebrows are exaggeratedly large, and her eyes are oval, with the outside corners drawn right down so that they practically cover her cheekbones, exactly as in the stone mask from Tell Brak. The goddess on the stucco relief is standing narrowly compressed within a rectangular ornamental framework. The entire interior pattern, as well as the decoration of the frame, is carried out in red and black paint over the light background of the gypsum. This small work of art thus represents a combination of relief and painting. The relief as such is completely in the tradition of the art from the Protohistorical Period, but the painting – like the stone mask from Tell Brak – underlines the feeling for transcendental abstraction in a new way.

Painting became of greater importance in the Jamdat Nasr period because, like the composite sculpture using many different materials, it met the desire for

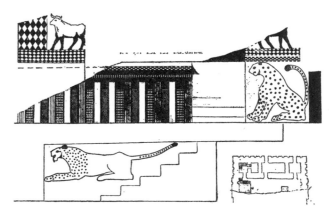

Fig. 12   Painting on the cult platform of the temple at Tell 'Uqair
(After: JNES 2, 1943, Pl. X)

brightness. But painting did not achieve the rank of a separate art form, developing a style from its own nature. It was not only used in the service of some other art, architecture, sculpture or pottery, either as wall-painting, decoration on pottery or reliefs. It was also clearly employed as a substitute for other, undoubtedly more expensive techniques. In the Temple of 'Uqair[62] the front of the cult platform has a painted decoration (Fig. 12) which is clearly an imitation of a clay cone mosaic, such as the ones we have seen on the temple podium in the cone mosaic court at Warka (cf. Pls. 1, 2); on the other hand this kind of podium front may also be finished in expensive stones and metal, as it was in the Temple of Tell Brak.[63] Thus the polychrome painting on pottery, which is typical of the Jamdat Nasr period, was also apparently only an imitation of the stone ewers inlaid with lapis lazuli, shell and mother of pearl, such as the original one from Warka[64] (Pl. 24). The decoration of a vase from Khafaje[65] (Fig. 13) seems to be a substitute for an inlay of triangular, square and lozenge-shaped little plaques of different colours, of which large numbers were uncovered in the level of the same period at Warka.[66] Perhaps the small stucco relief from the Temple of Ishtar in Ashur with all its colours is also only a copy of a large cult relief made up of coloured stones and metal. In this way the stone masks from Tell Brak and the face of the woman from Warka might also have originated in similar cult reliefs.

Fig. 11   Fragment of gypsum stucco relief of Ishtar from Ashur
(After: WVDOG 39, Pl. 28 c)

Fig. 13   Painted vase from Khafaje
(After: OIP 63, Colour Plate 6)

The highly developed civilization created by the
umerians in their Protohistorical Period about 3,000
c. and the art and architecture which emerged as
e expression of this culture spread rapidly from its
centre, the sanctuary of Innin at Uruk, not only
throughout the land of the Sumerians but also over
all the neighbouring territories of the Near East, over
Iran as well as North Mesopotamia and Northern
Syria, indeed doubtless into Egypt too. This vast area
may well have contributed in technical matters to
the development of Sumerian art. Certainly materials must have been imported from abroad, from
the wooden joists for building to metals and stones,
shells and lapis lazuli, and perhaps also some technical
knowledge for their application. It is, however, in-
spiring to observe how the sudden flowering in all
branches of art resulted naturally from a central attitude to life, from a concept of the life force which
has created everything, which sustains everything,
ever renewing itself in the species and in the community, even after death, and which stands in direct relationship to the divinity and comes from the myth
of the royal shepherd, who is chosen as the lover and

husband of Innin, the Lady of Heaven. The basic
concept underlying the iconographic repertoire of the
Protohistorical Period in Uruk circled round this
figure of Tammuz who, as we have recently learned,
must die, descend to the underworld for half a year
to save the goddess from the demons of death in the
underworld, and then rise again from the dead for
the next half year. The Protohistorical Period not only
personified in him the profound idea that all higher
life can only be maintained with the help of and at
the cost of life itself, but also affirmed this idea joy-
fully because it made possible a more highly organized state and social community in the temple-city.
And from this all-embracing conception of the Protohistorical Period of the Sumerian world there arose
the first great monumental temple architecture, as
well as all the art which existed essentially to serve
it: reliefs on the stone ewers and on the first stele, the
cylinder seal which was created for the administration of the temple, the painted cult relief, all kinds
of wall and pottery painting, polychrome and composite sculpture. The life of the human community,
founded on the life of the domestic animal and the
beneficial plants, but at the same time bound up with
the eternal life of the divinity – this was the idea
which gave birth to an art in whose forms naturalism
and transcendental abstraction combined harmoni-
ously. The real greatness of such an achievement can
only be assessed when one considers that it was perfected here for the first time and pointed the way for
all future periods.

B   THE FIRST TRANSITION PERIOD AND THE MESILIM PERIOD
(Disintegration and reconstruction)

Even during the Jamdat Nasr period, when the
Eanna sanctuary was completely re-arranged, many
features appeared in its architecture which do not fit
into the picture of interior and exterior harmony
which we have learnt to expect as characteristic of
the Protohistorical Period. We may possibly be able

to explain these features as being due to the transformation of the goddess Innin from a mother-goddess figure into a supreme 'Lady of Heaven' (see p. 7). These features are not only contrary to the symmetry of the ground-plan and elevation, but also to the laws of building, and they seem to lead to a formlessness and chaos. They have their counterpart in the decoration of a complete group of cylinder seals and stamp seals of the Jamdat Nasr period (see pp. 30–1, under *glyptic),* which led many scholars to regard this period as one wholly decadent. Yet this cannot be the case, because the great style of the Protohistorical Period and the so-called 'decadent' style are combined in one and the same object as, for example, in the stamp seal in the shape of a recumbent gazelle[67] (Pl. B 2). In fact we have to recognize that even in the Jamdat Nasr period itself there were the first beginnings of a new trend which, after an interim period of disintegration of all standards, was then to lead on to a reconstruction of the Sumerian world in a different guise, to the art of the period we call the Mesilim Period.

1 Architecture

There was a fundamental change in architecture, extending from the individual brick to the technique of making foundations, from the individual layout to the overall ground-plan of the whole complex – a change which enables us to imagine how great an upheaval there must have been between the Jamdat Nasr and the Mesilim Periods.

The purely outward aspect of the change showed itself straight away in the *building technique.* The *Patzen* and *Riemchen* bricks and the cone mosaics, all typical of the Protohistorical Period, slowly vanished and their place was taken by a building method using the so-called *plano-convex* brick (Fig. 14), that is – a brick basically unsuitable for construction, with its upper side curved, which cannot be used in ordinary bonders and courses but has to be laid sideways and in a herringbone pattern, one above the other.[68] A similar tendency to soften and round off the rec-

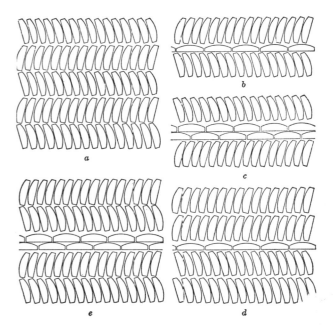

Fig. 14 Plano-convex bricks (Diagram)
(After: Christian, *Altertumskunde,* Pl. 148, 2)

tangular appearance, a tendency demonstrated by the use of the plano-convex brick, can also be seen in many of the ground-plans of individual rooms, as well as in the perimeter walls of sanctuaries, and in the brick-structure in the so-called Temple Oval at Khafaje and in the High Temple at Al 'Ubaid (see pp. 20–1).

The technique for *building foundations* was completely new. Whereas in the Protohistorical Period the temples were built on a levelled stretch of ground, now there is a change, and the walls of the building were buried deep in the earth in excavated trenches. In this way there was an actual merging between the rising building and the earth carrying it. The idea that a building, especially a temple, is fixed immovably in the earth, found its expression in strange foundation figures, actually large pegs or nails, of which the upper part is shaped as a human (Pl. 29). Later they were also engraved with foundation inscriptions and carried square stone tablets on their heads.[69] They were placed at each of the four corners of the building and were also sometimes arranged round it in an oval in the ground, and may have provided a magical defence against the demoniacal powers which might otherwise have risen out of the depths to harm the building.

In addition to their wish to lay the foundations of the sacred building inside the earth and not on top of it, another idea unknown in earlier times emerges: that it was desirable to separate the temple from its unclean, profane surroundings. The Temple Oval at Khafaje, which has been mentioned already, was only begun at the height of the Mesilim Period, and no longer had trenches for the walls of the temple: instead, its entire complex was built in an eight metre deep excavation, which had previously been filled with pure white sand.

Moreover it was in the Mesilim Period that for the first time the custom arose whereby the sacred building was cut off from its immediate surroundings by placing a second wall round the foundation walls. This looked like a thick, protective wall and was known as the *kisu*[70] (Fig. 15). This custom continued down to the late Babylonian period.

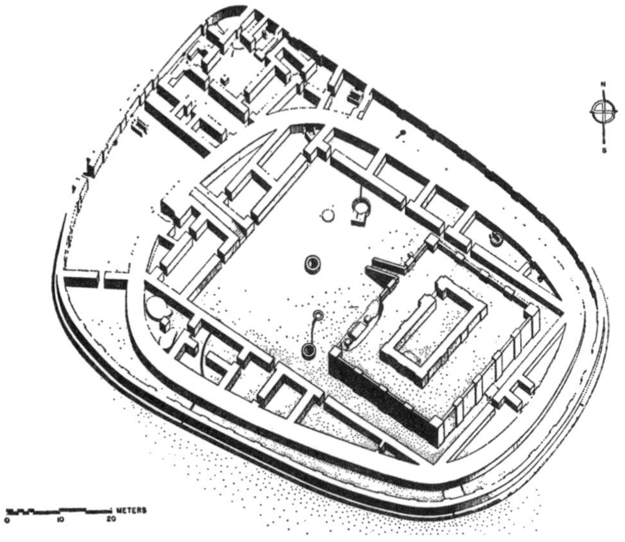

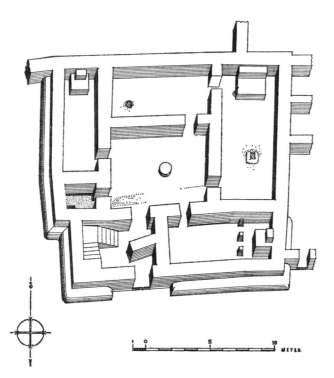

Fig. 15 'Square Temple' (Abu Temple) with its *kisu* wall, at Tell Asmar
(After: OIP 58, p. 176, Fig. 133)

Fig. 16 'Temple Oval' at Khafaje
(After: OIP 53, Pl. V)

All these technical building details suggest a change in the state of mind of the Sumerians, and particularly a growing dualism in their attitude to life, an attitude which divided the divine area from the profane, in contrast to their earlier, harmonious blending, achieved in the previous period. This interpretation of the new architectural features is supported by the surrounding of the sacred area of the gods by a wall which cuts it off from the world around it and protects it from other parts of the temple-city[71] (Figs. 16, 17, 18).

It is during the Mesilim Period that we first encounter in Kish a vast, monumental building, which is not a temple, nor part of a sanctuary but a *palace*, that is, the residence and administrative centre of a city ruler[72] (Fig. 19). According to the level at which it was found, this belongs to the Mesilim Period and was built in two parts: a southern part had been added to the older, northern complex. The northern part is surrounded by a double wall. The monumental entrance was formed by a doorway flanked by towers and with a flight of steps leading to it. The heart of the palace seems to be a square courtyard, on the north, west and south sides of which lie rectangular rooms, while on the east side there are smaller domestic offices. The southern building added

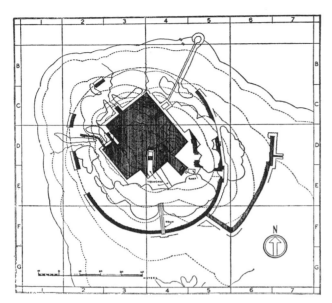

Fig. 17   High Temple with enclosure wall at Al 'Ubaid
(After: Iraq 5, p. 10, Fig. 2)

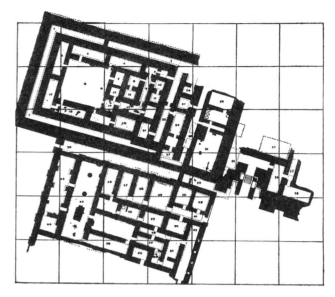

Fig. 19   Palace at Kish
(After: Christian, *Altertumskunde*, Pl. 151, 2)

later consisted of two large rooms to the west, very long and rectangular in shape. On the long axis of the larger of these, a row of bases may well have carried wooden pillars for the support of the roof. The whole ground-plan of this building, the oldest secular building in Sumer, displays a character utterly unlike anything known until then. It faces com-

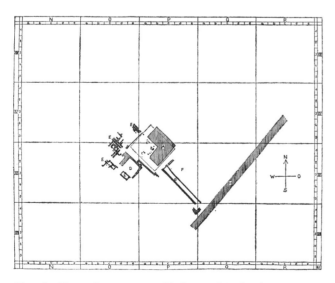

Fig. 18   Eanna Sancturary at Uruk, Level Arch. I b
(After: H. J. Lenzen, *Die Entwicklung der Zikkurat*, Pl. 5)

pletely in on itself, and shows signs of having been strongly fortified. Its plan is rectangular and exact. It has nothing in common with the chaotic loss of form which had already begun in the Jamdat Nasr period and which prevailed through the period of transition down to the Mesilim Period. On the contrary, it represents a good example of the new, ordered architectural idiom of the fully developed Mesilim Period.[73]

The same attitude to life which was apparent in the strongly fortified palace and in the walled sanctuaries also showed itself in the *city walls,* which were probably begun about this period. The oldest form of the city wall of Uruk[74] (Fig. 20) consisted of a double rampart about 9.5 km. in circumference: the inner wall had a core 4 to 5 m. thick of plano-convex bricks. The excavations revealed numerous semi-circular towers and two gates with rectangular towers. We know this city wall belonged to the Mesilim Period, because of the way in which it was built. In the most famous epic poem of the ancient Near Eastern world, the wall is the work of the hero Gilgamesh, the half-mythical king who ruled over Uruk after Tammuz. However Gilgamesh, originally the Lord of Kullab, unlike Tammuz the shepherd is not bound to Inanna (Ishtar), the principal goddess

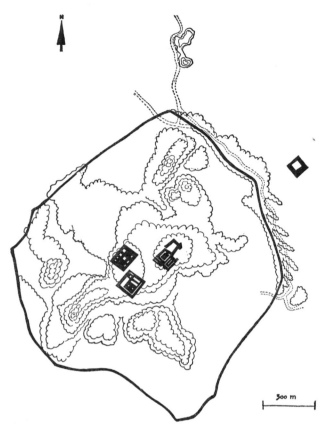

500 m

Fig. 20   City wall at Uruk. Redrawn
(After: UVB 7, Pl. 1)

of the city of Uruk, which he fortified, but stands in
opposition to her. He no longer seeks life through an
alliance with her but, after endless trials, is forced
to recognize that eternal life is withheld from man
by the gods. Man is no longer the beloved of the
gods, but their servant. Only great deeds can outlive
the death of a hero. Life itself, however, the gods
retain in their own hands as the goal – never
attained – of mortal longing. This attitude to life,
expressed with the utmost clarity in the Gilgamesh
epic, represents a clear break with that of the Innin-
Tammuz cult, and must be the same attitude which
caused the golden age of the Protohistorical Period
to disintegrate and was also the basis of the dualism
of the Mesilim Period. Just as it brought about the
enclosing of sanctuaries, palaces and cities, so too it
caused the remodelling of the *temple ground-plan.*

It may be that the shape of the temple cella, ʋ
arose at the end of the Jamdat Nasr period and
developed further in the transition period dow   .
the Mesilim Period, owes its layout to the type of
cella found in the Protohistorical Period, with its
extended, rectangular central room flanked on both
sides by smaller rooms. The most distinct example
of this we have seen in the White Temple at Uruk
(Warka). However, it cannot be denied that the
individual temple, as well as the sacred area, finally
achieved an entirely new appearance at the end of
this period of transformation of the entire architecture of the Mesilim Period. This transformation must
have corresponded to a new conception, possibly also
to a new function within the cult. Unfortunately
archaeological exploration of the centre of Sumerian
culture during this period has not yet recovered any
appreciable remains of sacred cellae. We have to
turn for information to the somewhat peripheral
region round the Diyala, where it is possible that
alien influences from the east or north may also have
played some part. In Khafaje, Tell Asmar (Eshnunna)
and Tell Agrab the foundations of sanctuaries have
been excavated, in many layers one above the other,
and these have revealed the transformation from the
Jamdat Nasr period through the transition period
leading to the Mesilim Period. The five oldest Levels,
I–V, of the so-called Sin Temple at Khafaje all date
back to the Jamdat Nasr period. The original layout
of the temple[75] (Fig. 21) shows a long, rectangular
room as its cella. It has a platform for cult purposes
on its north-western short side. To the north-east the
cella is flanked by a kind of sacristy and two small
entrance rooms. They are situated as far away as
possible from the Holy of Holies, and compelled
anyone coming in to make a turn of ninety degrees if
he wished to look at the divinity. On the south-west
side of the cella there was a single, very narrow room
which probably once had a staircase in it. The resemblance to the White Temple cannot be doubted:
equally, however, the differences cannot be ignored:
the side on which there is the room for the staircase
seems to be curtailed, and particularly on the north-
east side, in front of the entrance to the temple, the
architect has attempted to create a court by means of
irregular enclosure walls. There seems to be a round

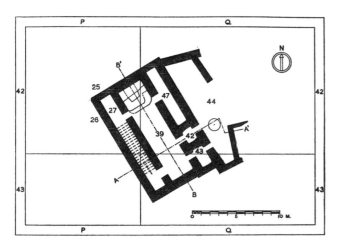

Fig. 21   Sin Temple at Khafaje, Level I
(After: OIP 58, Pl. 2 A)

place of sacrifice, an *Opferstätte*, in the court. Thus the Sin Temple, lying in the middle of a city settlement, is no longer a free-standing monument, facing the outside world in every direction. On the contrary it is trying to shut itself off from the outside world, to turn in on itself. And this is the characteristic feature which dominated the further development of cult building in Sumer. The temple itself became a sort of courtyard-house, as exemplified already in the Sin Temple at Khafaje in its fifth building level: that is to say, it became a dwelling-place for the god and, like the human dwelling-place, was primarily an enclosed space within which covered rooms were built. Whereas the planning of the Sin Temple at Level V[76] (Fig. 22) still shows signs of indecision, by the Level following this[77] (Fig. 23), belonging to the transition period prior to the Mesilim Period, for the first time the temple had regained an ordered and balanced design. All the rooms were grouped round a courtyard, which was reached by a flight of steps, and through a large entrance hall. There were several small rooms for the priests on the south side of this court. The main cella has kept its rectangular shape, and has its entrance door right at the end of one of its long sides, as far away as possible from the platform on the northern short side. The entrance rooms have been transformed into a large antecella. The sacristy rooms lie to the north of the cellae. The Holy of Holies is the most difficult part to reach, even when the temple court has been entered. The whole building is a sacred, secluded place, in which the god has his dwelling and where he receives the worship and the sacrifices due to him from those consecrated by him, the priesthood. The temples no longer form a great community with the people, a temple-city, as they did in the Protohistorical Period, but now they are more like monasteries, cutting themselves off from the profane world and the palace of the ruler.

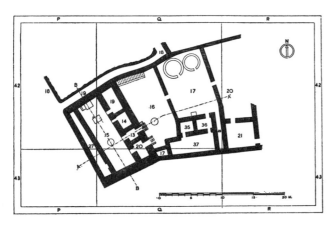

Fig. 22   Sin Temple at Khafaje, Level V
(After: OIP 58, Pl. 5 A)

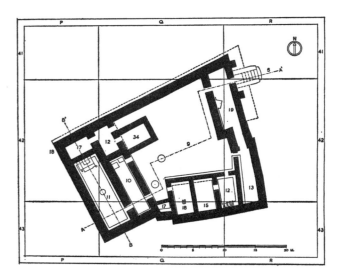

Fig. 23   Sin Temple at Khafaje, Level VI
(After: OIP 58, Pl. 6)

On the various ground-plans of the temples of
the god Abu at Eshnunna (Tell Asmar) – of which
many levels, one on top of the other, were excavated – a development can be observed which is very
like that at the Sin Temple at Khafaje. The very
oldest shrine[78] (Fig. 24), a little shrine which goes
back as far as the end of the Jamdat Nasr period, is
completely amorphous, and owes its shape probably
to chance, conditioned by the restricted space available between the surrounding houses. It is possible to
identify a cella with irregular long walls, which
change their direction, a podium against one of the
short walls, and at the other end a circuitous entrance
through a small antechamber. In the following
stratum[79] (Fig. 25), during the transitional period
prior to the Mesilim Period, the shrine was completely replanned: the altar was transferred from
the west to the east side, the rooms were given
straight-sided walls, and the essential parts of the
whole ground-plan now resembled an ordinary Near
Eastern courtyard-house, like the Sin Temple at
Khafaje. The enclosed sacred area is of an irregular
design. The cella now assumes a rectangular shape
and occupies the largest space inside the court. It has
its podium on the eastern, short wall and its entrance in the southern, long wall. To its west there is
a forecourt with a round table for sacrifices and
there is a small gate-house at the northern end of
the forecourt.

Not until the height of the Mesilim Period[80] does
the so-called Abu shrine become a truly represen-
tative example of a temple planned as a courtyard-
house, facing inward on itself (Fig. 26). In this case
the enclosed area has an almost square shape. There
is now a rectangular cella on both the western and
eastern sides of the square inner court, a priests'
room to the south, and to the north a third cella and
an entrance hall. The separation of the temple from
its profane surroundings is emphasized further by
means of a *kisu* (see p. 20).

There are temples of the same courtyard-house
type in several other parts of the Sumerian sphere of
influence (Ashur, Mari) dating from the transitional
period and the Mesilim Period. But they show only
local divergencies and do not have any new features
of importance.

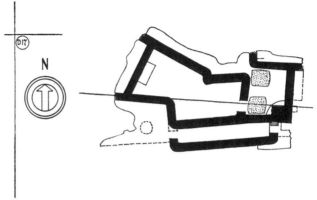

Fig. 24   Abu Temple at Tell Asmar (Earliest Shrine)
(After: OIP 58, Pl. 19 A)

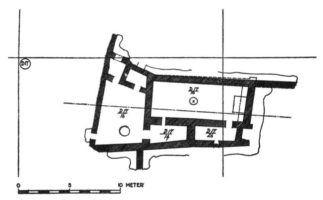

Fig. 25   Abu Temple at Tell Asmar (Archaic Shrine I)
(After: OIP 58, Pl. 19 B)

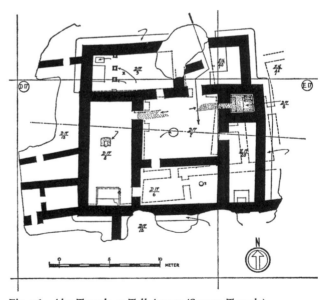

Fig. 26   Abu Temple at Tell Asmar (Square Temple)
(After: OIP 58, Pl. 22)

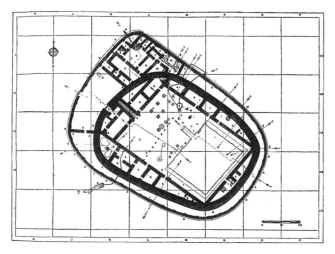

Fig. 27 'Temple Oval' at Khafaje
(After: OIP 53, Pl. IV)

We know today of two *shrines* dating from the Mesilim Period which – though differing greatly in external appearance – yet arise, each in its own fashion, from the same dualistic way of thought prevailing in this period, and they express this dualism in monumental form. These are the so-called Temple Oval at Khafaje[81] (Fig. 27) and the Shara

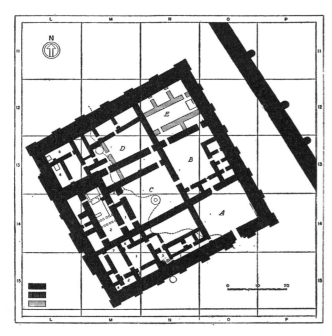

Fig. 28 Shara Temple at Tell Agrab
(After: OIP 58, Fig. 203)

Temple at Tell Agrab[82] (Fig. 28). In them not only has the sacred cella been given its new shape, but the form of the whole temple complex, with the priests' house and the administrative rooms, is conceived as a unity, and projected in accordance with a precise plan. At Khafaje there is a high temple on a terrace raised 6 m. within a rectangular court. The whole complex was at first surrounded by an oval encircling wall, and later by a second oval wall. Between these two perimeter walls arose a priests' house which in its ground-plan is related to an element of the great Shara Shrine at Tell Agrab. But whereas for the Temple Oval at Khafaje the rounded form of encircling wall was still used, dating from the transitional period prior to the Mesilim Period, at the Shara Temple an almost square perimeter wall with tower buttresses was substituted. This perimeter wall, several metres thick, surrounded the various main components of the vast sanctuary in a well-planned design. Several rectangular complexes of rooms grouped around a courtyard were juxtaposed. In the western area, which is the only part that has survived, looking from south to north we can recognize the priests' house, the main shrine with its main cella 19 m. long on a bent axis between the antechamber and side rooms, and in addition a second shrine with two cellae with bent axes, leading off an inner court, similar to the so-called Square Temple of Abu at Eshnunna (Tell Asmar) (see p. 20).

With the Shara Temple of Tell Agrab, which was finally completed in the Mesilim Period, we reach the end of the difficult internal and external reshaping of Sumerian architecture, which took place after the breakdown of its first period of great artistic achievement.

2 Art

The dualism in the Sumerian attitude to life that we noticed penetrating their architecture after the Jamdat Nasr period, also resulted in a considerable revolution in art. As in architecture, in art too a complete reconstruction of style was only achieved at

the height of the Mesilim Period and after the collapse of all the old laws of style, a collapse which led
at times to a state of chaos. This reconstruction applied to style, to all kinds of works of art, their
subject-matter and their form.

At the time of the first great period of Sumerian
civilization the cylinder seal and stone cult vessels
were the main media for artistic design, but now
other media attained increased importance: one such
group consisted of stone maces, decorated with reliefs,
which served as votive objects. One had on it the
name of a King Mesilim of Kish, and the whole
period has derived its name from this, the first 'historical' object. Another group consisted of peculiar
stone plaques, square in shape and decorated with
reliefs, with a hole pierced in the centre, presumably
votive reliefs. In addition, there were many figures
in the round, in stone and bronze, which were for the
most part votive statuettes.

*a The transition from the Jamdat Nasr Period to
the Mesilim Period*

As yet it is difficult to find stratigraphical evidence
for this transition. No sculpture has yet been found
in the building levels of the Early Dynastic Period I
in the Diyala region. It is easier to use palaeography
when trying to trace the development of art during
this obscure period, even though the greatest caution
must be exercised in so doing.

An amulet from Khafaje[83] (Pl. 37) in the shape of
a lion-headed eagle (of which Sumerian Protohistory
had produced numerous examples) and made of slate,
worked quite flat, no longer presents a somewhat
bloated, full shape. Its style has changed into a
wooden aridity, which is more typical of the following
Mesilim Period, and the stratum at Khafaje, Sin
Temple VIII, where it was found also suggests this.
The outside surface of the object has been completely
covered by an inscription which is not at variance
with its dating in this transition period, although it
has not yet been possible to decipher the whole text.
Of greater interest in the history of sculpture is the
'Personnage aux plumes' from Telloh, now in the
Louvre[84] (Pl. 30), which has been known to us for a

long time. This scene, incised rather than modelled,
shows a male figure in a net skirt with a naked upper
body and a heavy mane of hair lying on the nape of
the neck. Two leaves decorated with a herring-bone
pattern rise from the crown of his head. There are
faint suggestions of a beard. The man is standing
with his left hand raised in greeting, in front of two
symbolic maces taller than the man himself. The god
Ningirsu is mentioned in the inscription. The maces,
as well as the leaves in his hair, most probably represent the symbol of this god. Thureau-Dangin considers the inscription on the 'Personnage aux plumes'
to be one of the oldest from Telloh. The plaque must
belong to the transitional period between the Protohistorical Period and the historical era. The head-
dress, which probably has no connection with feathers,
may be the very ancient form of the crown of the
Sumerian gods, in which a vegetation element was
predominant, before the bull's horn became part
of it.

With the help of its inscription another work of
art can be attributed to the transition from the Jamdat Nasr to the Mesilim Period. This is a small *stele*[85]
(Pls. 31–34) covered on all sides by reliefs, which
reached New York through the art trade either from
Larsa or Umma. Divided into several individual
scenes, it shows the meeting between a male and a
female principal character, both accompanied by a
train of followers. An altar, or a temple door, is
placed between the man and woman. The women,
including the principal woman, who is carrying a
vessel, are depicted just like the principal female
figure on the great alabaster vase from Warka,[86] and
they thus show the strength of the strong tradition
of the Jamdat Nasr period. The male principal figure,
on the other hand, is clearly different from the men
in the net garments, both in his dress and bearing.
His dress has a thick padded girdle and a simple,
wide tufted hem. His beard is long and pointed. The
upper part of his body no longer seems to be quite
naked. His hands are clasped across his breast with
his elbows sticking out abruptly from his body. The
attendants are wearing a dress slit vertically in front,
with one half hitched high to allow free movement.
This type of male attire is quite usual in the Mesilim
Period.

However, we find the most marked break with the first period of great achievement in Sumerian art not in the few reliefs surviving from the transitional period prior to the Mesilim Period, but in the *glyptic* of this time.

In addition to the group of large cylinder seals with exceptionally realistic and lively figures of great plasticity, the Jamdat Nasr period had always produced another group of small cylinder seals and stamp seals, with ornamental designs very carelessly drilled[87] (Pls. C 1–3). The bow drill was used a great deal when making them, and it is not unlikely they were influenced by Iranian art. At this time, at the end of the Jamdat Nasr civilization, in glyptic the divorce from naturalism and materialism was taken even further. Where plants and animals do still appear as components of a design, they are not only reduced to mere lines and dots, but are included with other, purely ornamental elements in an abstract pattern which completely fills the available space and has no purpose beyond abstract symbolism[88] (Pls. C 4–6).

In the layer of rubbish under the Royal Cemetery at Ur (Seal Impression Stratum = SIS 4–5) impressions from many different periods[89] were found, as this must have been a rubbish heap. Most of them are certainly older than the Mesilim Period, and more recent than the Jamdat Nasr period, and this has been confirmed by the ductus of the script on the clay tablets found with them.[90] Here one sometimes has an impression of a complete disintegration of all that had been achieved by earlier art. Ornamental devices and figures are interlocked and intertwined and cover the entire surface of the picture without any apparent significance as objects, while the surface of the picture itself is no longer used as a symbol of space but is purely a background for an ornamental pattern.

Cuneiform signs are also used as decoration, or, more precisely, signs resembling cuneiform characters, for they are not yet readable.[91] Here a degree of decline has been reached from which there was only one possible step left, a turning back, if all art in the real meaning of the word was not to come to an end.

b Mesilim Period

In the Mesilim Period itself, which was a new period of great achievement in the history of Sumerian art, the sculptor and the carver again had the vitality and the means to transform the unnatural and the abstract into a new positive method of art. Their art was no longer used to express a balanced combination of the physical and the metaphysical world, but solely for a transcendental concept of god and king. Their task was to show only one form of existence, remote from the profane world, in pictures which indeed resembled nature but which were transfigured with the aid of intellectual abstract laws of form. In this way Sumerian art avoided being limited to mere decoration, like the art of the Old Germanic or Islamic world, and it resulted in their retaining a world based on real figures and shapes from nature, with its rich variety, yet they were also able to endow this world with a spiritual meaning.

Our store of works of art from the Mesilim Period has been enriched in quantity as well as in variety owing to the excavations of the last decades. These not only form a group homogeneous in subject and style, which is clearly distinct from all the art of the preceding age as well as from that of the following periods, but they can also in general be identified by palaeography and by stratigraphy, except when by chance they have got into the wrong environment. It was especially in the strata excavated in the Diyala sites, to which we also owe our knowledge of the architecture of the Mesilim Period from its birth to its maturity, that numerous reliefs and statues in the round belonging to this period were discovered. But also in Kish, the city of Mesilim, in Telloh and Shurrupak (Fara), in Nippur, Ur and Mari a number of important works have come to light, and these are proof that the new style extended over the whole area of Sumerian civilization. At the same time it should perhaps not be overlooked that the northern part of this civilization, where the Semitic element had always been more prominent than further south, has so far produced the most numerous examples of this style.

This historical assumption has been confirmed in the last two years in a surprising manner through new discoveries in excavations in the North Syrian, North Mesopotamian mound, Tell Chuera, lying about half-way between the Khabur and the Balikh, not far south of Tell Abiad (Harran).[92] These discoveries show that at a distance of about 600 km. north-west of the centre of Sumerian civilization, not only the same type of ceramics and the same toggle pins came to light, but also the same type of statuettes of praying figures made in alabaster, in a very good style, and dating from the Mesilim Period. Thus the northern district of Mesopotamia seems to have become more important than the south during the middle of the third millennium B.C. It is more than likely that the pre-Akkadian Semites played a part in this. Furthermore the oldest historical inscription found in the Sumerian area, on a *votive mace* decorated in relief, originated from a King Mesilim from the northern city of Kish, the predecessor of later Babylon. The date of this votive offering, found in Telloh, can be attributed to the period between the Jamdat Nasr period and that of Ur I on the basis of the ductus of the writing, and this provides a fixed date which is of importance to the history of art. The vertical sides of this massive mace-head[93] (Pls. 35, 36), 19 cm. in height, are decorated all round with a continuous frieze of a series of lions. Each lion is springing on the back of the one in front, but with his head facing outwards. The relief covers almost the whole exterior surface of the mace-head. The bodies of the animals have been carved out flatly, the manes have been kept inside the body's outline, and are stylized by an arrangement of short, parallel incised lines, in the form of segments of a circle. The animals' faces look like masks, with their eyes and tongues originally filled with inlay and with a sharply angled skull-line, on which the ears have been placed like handles. These creatures give one the impression that they were composed intellectually, if one compares them with the full-blooded lions of the preceding period (cf. Pls. 15, 16). This is true to an even greater degree of the composite creature carved on the top surface of the mace-head, a lion-headed eagle, presented with its front view facing us. Even as early as from the Uruk IV period there are examples of this demon, but it is only now in the Mesilim Period that, for the first time, it is given its character of a superior power,

threatening the life of man, by means of the heraldic-like arrangement of its outspread wings and claws, its mask-like lion's head, and the deliberate stylization of its feathers. The relief itself remains flat like a drawing.

The feeling for abstraction in the Mesilim Period must understandably have given rise to their preference for a flat relief, and even more to the move towards a linear style, towards *drawing*. We think it may also be possible to assign to the period of King Mesilim of Kish a particularly beautiful example of pure contour drawing. This is on the bronze lance head[94] (Fig. 29) from Telloh, dedicated by a king of Kish – the inscription is incomplete – which on account of its size must have been a divine standard. The lion, in keeping with the space available for decoration, is in an upright position, standing erect on its hind legs, its outline engraved with a light and certain touch, with very few interior lines. It is almost the classic example of the true Mesilim Period style. Divorce from reality can scarcely be taken further in a work of art; here the abstract use of a motif based on nature has reached its peak, and has thereby become a symbol for an idea. What a

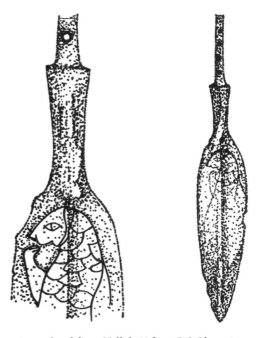

Fig. 29   Lance head from Telloh (After: DC Pl. 5, 1)

difference lies between this shadowy creature and the compact, muscular lion from the Jamdat Nasr period!

The style of the Mesilim Period is less pronounced, though still unmistakable in its general direction, in a similar work of art which can be assigned to this period with the aid of stratigraphy and palaeography. This is a mace-head from the Shara Temple at Tell Agrab[95] on which four lions' heads are carved completely in the round (Pl. 38). Here again however the animals' heads are marked with an angled line round the skull, just like that on the Mesilim mace, and their manes are stylized to the same degree.

In the earliest Sumerian royal palace known to us, the palace under Cemetery A at Kish (see pp. 20–1), a large number of fragments of *inlay-work*[96] were found in the courtyard, immediately behind the entrance. These are parts from various wall friezes (Pls. 39–41). They include figures of walking sheep, squatting men, probably milking, women playing musical instruments, and warriors with prisoners. The motif as well as the technique of the inlay is clearly connected with older Sumerian art. Even in the Jamdat Nasr period there were already wall decorations at Uruk in the form of rows of sheep. These were in high relief, almost carved in the round, and some of them were, perhaps, amongst the most lively animal portraits of that period (see p. 14). Again, from the transitional period we know of burnt clay figures of animals for inlaying: this time they are flat and their surface is decorated with impressed circles, a feature probably recalling the technique of cone mosaics from the first Protohistorical Period.[97] Here then, in the Mesilim Period, inlay carries on the tradition. Figures made of bright yellow limestone were inlaid in the dark grey slate – the figures being completely flat, their outlines clear-cut, the interior lines sketched in delicately – inlaid in such a way that they were on the same plane as the dark background surrounding them. A few individual figures, predominantly human, are typical of the Mesilim Period; for instance, the men and women in short crinoline skirts with padded girdles and tufted hems, and the women musicians. Their thin wooden legs with peculiar feet, of which the arch is exaggeratedly high, are characteristic. So are the warriors[98] with long, thin limbs, large

noses and long pointed beards (Pl. 41), whose costume was rather like the ones we have already met on the Stele from Larsa (see p. 26). The tall head-gear is conical and gets wider at the top. Their long dress is held together by a padded girdle, and its lower part is slit, with half of it hitched up over the knee. This type of man is completely new.

For the first time, as far as we know, in the Mesilim Period square or rectangular *stone plaques* were made with a hole pierced in the centre (Pl. 42). They provide a main source for the history of relief during this phase of the period. But their practical purpose is still not clear (holders for standards? wall-decoration? foundation reliefs?).[99] The best of these provide us with our earliest glimpse of the mature style of relief from this important epoch. Their subject-matter is of prime significance to our understanding of the whole of Sumerian art and indeed of a large part of all the art of the ancient Near East which came after it.[100]

In the Inanna Temple at Nippur, at Levels VII B and VIII, the most recent American excavations have unearthed several fragments of votive plaques coming from that area and dating from the Imdugud-Sukurru and Mesilim Periods. Donald P. Hansen has published full details about them and has investigated them thoroughly in JNES XXII pp. 145 ff. ('New votive plaques from Nippur'). Whereas their subject-matter is fully in accord with the votive plaques known to us already, which are based on the 'Symposium', Hansen rightly points out the difference in style of the Nippur tablets, which is also in accordance with their origin as established by stratigraphy. They probably extend from the first Transitional period to the Ur I period (ED I to ED IIIa). What sounds strange about them, coming from the great city of Nippur, is the lack of uniformity and cohesion in their style, as well as in the quality of most of their workmanship. Their clumsy, almost rustic character shows that Nippur must indeed have been a religious rather than an aesthetic centre in Sumer. If a coherent style did exist in the Mesilim period, it certainly did not originate in Nippur.

The central motif of all the votive reliefs is the so-called 'Symposium' scene. This shows a central, female figure seated on a throne, opposite a seated man whose rank is clearly lower than hers. Both are always shown with a drinking beaker in one hand, and in the other they are generally holding a branch. A large mixing bowl is often shown placed between them. Servants wait on them. In addition to the servants musicians and dancers are often present. Gifts of all kinds, drinks, vessels and boxes, as well as sacrificial animals, are being presented. The procession of men bearing gifts, which sometimes includes a chariot drawn by four animals, at times stretches into a third register. One of the main characters at the feast has presumably just got out of the chariot. The chariot is, however, sometimes replaced by a boat, the second mode of conveyance for man and god in Sumer, a land rich in canals. Individual motifs are sometimes drawn sketchily, sometimes in detail. But it is most important to observe that in this cycle the scenes centred on the Symposium are closely bound up with a second group of pictures, concerning the hero protecting domestic animals from beasts of prey. In this group, standing at his side is a composite creature[101] (Pls. 45, 46) combining the inseparable companions, man and ox, just as in earlier reliefs their two enemies, the lion and eagle, were combined as the lion-headed eagle. The inner relationship linking these two sets of pictures in a unified cycle is not only illustrated in the cylinder seal scenes composed of two registers,[102] but also on a votive relief from the Shara Temple at Tell Agrab[103] (Pl. 49): the two upper registers of this contain a complete 'Symposium' scene, and in the third register at the bottom a man is shown on the left hurling a spear to save an ox, which has already collapsed before the onslaught of a lion. Both groups of subjects, the cult meeting of a woman and man with the procession of gifts, and the protection of domestic animals by a hero from lion and eagle, have their origin in the art of the Jamdat Nasr period (see pp. 13–14). And yet since then a marked change in the art-form has occurred: for the first time we find relief no longer used as decoration of an exterior surface of a seal, vessel, mace or weapon, when through being used in that way it was forced either to form part of the object on which it was carved, or to distort the surface of the object itself. Furthermore the figures no longer represent just a decorative element on the pictorial

surface as they did in the transitional period. Now the sculptor creates a *pictorial scene independent* of the object's function, when he not only smoothes down the surface but frames it carefully, dividing it into registers (Pl. 42) (examples of this are easy to recognize in the votive plaques from Khafaje, Ur and Tell Agrab,[104] on which similar arrangements of scenes are used). The pictorial surface as such is an abstract concept characteristic of the Mesilim Period. Art at that time did not function in the spatial reality of this world but in an ideal vacuum, which it created itself and which it separated carefully from reality with the help of a frame. The idea of abstract space also imposes its own laws on the figures appearing within it. The figures – in their movement, bearing, size and relationship to each other – have to submit themselves to the latent powers which control the pictorial scene, the horizontal and vertical co-ordinates, the slanting diagonals. Here then, perhaps for the first time, use is made of the principle of isocephaly (the horizontal alignment of heads and eyes): for example, the heads of the sitting and standing figures of the symposium,[105] and also those of men and animals are shown at an even height. All the features which had already emerged in the Proto-historical Period as abstract laws governing the arrangement of the figures in relation to each other within the picture were again employed by the artists of the Mesilim Period: the arrangement of rows, the mirror-like confrontation, symmetry, the upright posture of four-footed animals standing on their hind legs in heraldic groups. Some arrangements went further, as when the individual figures of the four-footed animals are shown in echelon crossways[106] (Pl. 46) and so merge into a plaited, criss-cross frieze, or when the groups of figures to the left and right of the picture's axis are no longer arranged on a fixed equilibrium but a fluid one[107] (Pl. 42). Now, however, in the Mesilim Period all the figures and groups of figures arranged in this way are subordinated to the inexorable power of their pictorial surface, the abstract space in which they exist.

Two-dimensional art in the Mesilim Period was really only taken to its logical conclusion by the stone-carvers. It is true that the subject-matter of the *glyptic* of this period produced no innovations. The men who carved the cylinder seals were themselves still dominated by the cycle of the 'symposium' and of the hero protecting the domestic animals against beasts of prey – the tree of life with two animals also belongs to this sequence. Yet the actual drinking scene is not shown so often, probably because in it style could not be used to make the seal picture into a heraldic symbol of the powers promoting and threatening life, entirely remote from nature (Pl. D 1).

The shape of the cylinder seal provides a pictorial surface on the actual seal itself of a uniformly broad, continuous frieze returning into itself, and on the impression provides an unending band. In this frieze all the individual components have to be arranged according to the restricted space available, and not according to the laws of nature. The four-footed animal fits in better if it is standing on its hind or fore legs,[108] the human figure is more easily adapted to the frieze if it is in the 'knee-running' position.[109] This interweaving of figures, human and animal, the so-called *'Figurenband'*, the 'figured band', is an invention of the glyptic in the Mesilim Period: the individual figures overlap each other and together form an abstract pattern remote from nature. Even so the urge to reject reality was not yet satisfied. Pictorial abstraction led on to contractions in the picture, such as had never before been seen in Near Eastern art and which did not appear again. Like the composite creatures, which were made up out of various natural elements, in order to symbolize a supernatural power, now at this period the components of, say, a three-figure motif were compressed into an abstract abbreviation: the hero, who is overpowering two lions, is transformed into a heraldic pattern consisting of the upper part of a human body and, below, of the hindquarters of two lions, or alternatively their forequarters. The hero in the middle is gripping his own two lion-tails on the right and left. Instead of the human hero sometimes it is the upper part of the bull-man which is combined with the parts of the two lions[110] (Pl. D 3).

The composition of the *individual figures* of men and animals also conformed with the trend towards abstraction. Though in general the clothes and hair of the humans, and the shape of the lions and cattle, are the same in the glyptic as those used in the art of relief,[111] yet it cannot be denied that the seal-cutter of the Mesilim Period often goes much further in stylizing the figures of men and animals than does the contemporary sculptor. In the glyptic, not only are the bodies exaggeratedly rigid and elongated,[112] but the actual extremities, the lower parts of arms and legs on men, the front and back feet on animals, are often tapered to a mere line.[113] Again, a further step towards abstract treatment is often taken with the faces of heroes and animals drawn front view, particularly in the contracted motifs referred to above, in which abstract treatment is carried to its limit. As an example of this, if we look at an impression from Fara[114] we can see a nose and ring of locks of hair made so geometric in form that they have been reduced to spherical ornaments: the lions' heads, seen from above, have been rendered as trellis-like rectangles. It is only if one thinks back to the way in which the same subject – the hero overpowering animals – was handled in high relief on decorated stone vessels in the Jamdat Nasr period, when individual shapes were carved with the utmost exuberance, with an almost puffed-up closeness to nature – it is only then that one appreciates how wide a gulf separates the two periods in their fundamental approach to all art, and therefore in their whole being. Symbolism and abstract presentation cannot be taken further (Pl. D 2).

Characteristic of the Mesilim Period are the numerous examples of *sculptured figures in the round* of men and women worshipping, which must have been placed in the cellae of the temples as votive figures. We do not know of any earlier examples of this kind of art, unless we include in this category the 11 cm. high figure of a standing servant-woman,[115] with her upper body naked, which was discovered in Level IV of the Sin Temple at Khafaje (Pl. 12). This, however, had nothing of the beseeching, imploring, passionate self-devotion to the gods which we can see in all the statuettes from the Mesilim Period, in so far as they are relatively successful in quality. The figures in the round from the Mesilim Period are without exception statuettes, and at the most are only a third of life-size. Man in the first Proto-historical Period of Sumer was to some extent linked in bodily union with the Divine through the king and his sacred marriage: the statuettes of worshippers from the Mesilim Period, on the other hand, are the best example of the feeling that a wide gulf divided man and his world from the divine world, a gulf which could only be bridged through prayer and sacrifice.

The same purpose which motivated relief and glyptic clearly also influenced three-dimensional art in the round during the Mesilim Period. Here again there was an attempt to idealize the human shape by replacing the natural, living forms whenever possible by a solid geometric, contrived composition. This form of abstraction was used in particular for the statuettes made of stone, because, when working with stone as a material, it was very difficult to adopt the usual method to achieve abstract expression – by means of exaggeratedly long and thin figures. The block of stone as a medium is not in keeping with the character of the Mesilim Period, and there are some signs that for this reason just at that time a second method of producing figures in the round, *sculpture in bronze*, had attained particular importance, and indeed had begun to exert an influence on style as a whole, reacting on sculpture in stone.

It is true that there are many fewer works of art in bronze still surviving than there are stone statuettes. But this should not mislead us as they are much more perishable, and their material is far more in demand than stone. We know that *large statues* in the round in bronze existed in the Mesilim Period because of the chance survival of a fragment from the Shara Temple at Tell Agrab, the front part of a human foot,[116] beautifully cast, and almost life-size (Pl. 50). The slender toes, completely separate from each other, with carefully outlined nails, must have been part of a large statue. The large, open space between the individual toes is evidence of the attempt to free as far as possible the individual limbs from the mass of the sculpture. We may imagine what such a bronze statue from the Mesilim Period would have looked like when whole, with the help of the bronze statuettes found at Khafaje and Tell Agrab, even though these latter were only parts of cult stands. The two best examples[117] show a naked, belted man with the typically long hair and beard of the Mesilim Period, slender and fine limbed, standing in a walking posture, the upper part of his body leaning forwards slightly, his head turned a little upward, the upper and lower parts of his arms quite clear of his body, and with both hands clasped and stretched forward (Pl. 52). The whole statue suggests admirably the fervour of a worshipper and expresses a submissive devotion to god which is in complete accordance with the essential character of the Mesilim Period.

Besides this there exists another example which shows how the toreutic art of this period was able to achieve freedom from the mass of the material. The Near Eastern Department of the Berlin State Museum has possessed for a long time a bull's head made of bronze[118] (Pl. 53), about half life-size. Completely in keeping with the spirit of this period, it combines the stylization of natural forms as an ornament with the desire to free all the extremities as far as possible from the material. Mouth and nostrils have the form of a double volute. The two sides of the upper part of the head are shaped rather like a tube, out of which the splendidly curved horns rise up. One has to recall the rams' heads from the Jamdat Nasr period, when the stone-cutters made the horns lying alongside the head,[119] if one is to appreciate the way in which this bull's head seems almost to float detached, with no trace of heavy massiveness. Only bronze casting could achieve this, because it was in tune with the essential character of the period, a period which scorned all base matter. The difficulties inherent in the tasks which the metal workers of the Mesilim Period set themselves is shown by the small bronze portrait of a team of four horses with a charioteer,[120] which comes from the Shara Temple at Tell Agrab (Pl. 51). Although it is an astonishing technical achievement, yet it is too small (7.2 cm. high) and its surface is in too bad condition for it to possess any artistic merit now.

An alabaster statuette from the Nintu Temple (discovered in Level VI)[121] looks like an imitation of one of the bronze statuettes mentioned above from the Temple Oval I at Khafaje:[122] it is true that in the brittle stone the proportions have necessarily been somewhat compressed and that the sculptor has not dared to separate the legs from each other or the hands from the breast, but otherwise the somewhat buckled posture and general appearance is the same (Pl. 54). The sculptors went astonishingly far at times with kneeling figures, especially that of a naked serving man wearing a girdle, from Tell Agrab[123] (Pls. 55, 56). He is carrying a large mixing vessel on his head, which he is supporting with both hands raised. Both legs are carved completely independently of each other, the left knee raised high and the right knee on the ground. The whole statuette is in the spirit of a work cast in bronze transferred to limestone, and in a way is a subject in conflict with the material in which it is made.

The great majority of *stone statuettes* from the Mesilim Period still surviving were discovered in temples. They represent the entire temple hierarchy, which in these esoteric sanctuaries maintained communion with the gods, and range from ministering priests to the high priest himself and the princes. Portraits of this kind have been found in many cities of the Sumerian region, but nowhere in such quantities as in the temples in the Diyala area, at Eshnunna (Tell Asmar), Khafaje and Tell Agrab.[124] Most of the statuettes are of men. Without exception they are wearing long rectangular beards and wigs with a wide, central parting. This wig hangs down each side of the face onto the chest, where it often merges into the beard. Some of the men of lower rank are sometimes shown as bald-headed. The upper part of the body is always naked. The men always wear a half-length skirt, held up by a thick padded girdle and decorated with a tufted hem at the bottom. Both hands are clasped together in front of the chest and occasionally they hold a beaker. Eyeballs and pupils are inlaid in special material or are carved in the form of discs on the eyeball. The feet and the shanks are either with or without supports according to whether they need them for stability, and are carved free from the stone. Elbows are pointed and jut out. Beard and wig are stylized, with horizontal wavy or zig-zag lines. Hands are generally too small, sometimes quite stunted. The back is very often divided into two halves by a sharply incised vertical line. This generalized picture includes many variations amongst the numerous statuettes and fragments of statuettes. They also vary considerably in quality.

In the most carelessly-made works, rejection of naturalism leads towards stereometric compositions[125] in which we can detect few traces of the feeling prevalent in this period for the transcendental (Pl. 57). The feet in particular are so clumsy that they appear almost grotesque. Against that, in the better examples[126] the main impression created is of the contrast between the cone-shaped skirt and the completely geometrized upper body, so that once again one senses the influence of toreutic, in the exaggerated detachment of the upper arms from the body (Pl. 58). The shoulders are carved very wide, at the expense of the chest. The profile seems quite unreal, with the huge projecting nose, and protruding lips, which carry on the rhythm of the waves of the wig and beard. The lower legs are completely chiselled out of the gypsum, with great skill, and are protected from breaking by a support left standing at the back.

The statuettes of an officiating priest[127] with his head shaved bare is particularly expressive because of the way in which he is shown gazing upward as though seeking his god, in a manner which is very much in keeping with the character of this epoch. This statuette belongs to a large hoard of statues which had been buried at a place identified positively through stratigraphy as Level I of the 'Square Temple' at Eshnunna. Therefore this work was undoubtedly made at the height of the Mesilim Period,[128] a period to which the later stages of building levels at the Square Temple no longer belonged.[129]

A statuette[130] from the Sin Temple (Level IX) at Khafaje (Pl. 60) introduces another variation in style. By leaving a broad slab of stone standing behind the lower legs and by not detaching the elbows from the body, it was possible to keep the legs and lower arms very slender, in keeping with a style truly in tune with the spirit of the Mesilim Period. The effect is the more striking because the skirt is decorated especially sumptuously. The lower tufts are very long and have been given a pronounced plastic appearance, while in addition the upper part of the skirt up to the girdle is covered with four rows of short tufts. This would seem to represent a change in the style of skirt which thereafter was to acquire even greater significance. The small relief at the back of the foot support is important; it shows us part of a motif from the

Figurenband (cf. p. 31) – a hero with a bison rearing up high on its hind legs, its head facing backwards. The hero is shown in a style which could only belong to the Mesilim Period, with his face and hair completely schematized, and this supports the attribution of the whole statuette to this period. Unfortunately the head of the statuette is missing. One may perhaps imagine it most easily by examining a fragment[131] which was found in the Temple Oval II at Khafaje. Although this is badly preserved one can still recognize the same type with fine limbs and the same kind of pleasing facial features, which most likely belong to the end of the period.

Amongst the statuettes of the Mesilim Period two are of exceptional interest. These two are by far the largest of the hoard referred to above, excavated at the Square Temple at Eshnunna; they are of a man and a woman[132] and they may perhaps be related in their conception (Pls. 61, 62). They are both holding a small beaker in their tiny hands, which are quite out of proportion to the size of their bodies. It may be that this couple represent the principle characters of the cult marriage which we so often see illustrated on votive tablets. These two statuettes do not only have the stunted size of their hands in common; both are also the only figures from the hoard to have abnormally large eyes and, in these eyes, equally abnormally large pupils of black inlay. Both statuettes are shown raising their heads on high and gazing at the divinity. In this way they have both been endowed with a lofty, supernatural character. Because of this, the excavator H. Frankfort[133] considered that the male statuette represented the god Abu, the owner of the temple, and this belief was reinforced by the presence of a relief carved on the front of the base below the feet of the statuette: two goats, each lying in front of a bush, facing away from each other, with a bird of prey hovering over them. This is one of the classical subjects of the Protohistorical Period, from the group of scenes of the Innin/Tammuz myth (Fig. 30). But as the character represented by the statuette had none of the external attributes by which one could generally recognize the god, such as the horned cap, we consider it more likely that this is a portrait of a prince or high priest who had to represent the god at the cult marriage festival.

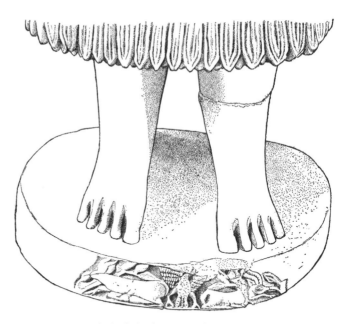

Fig. 30 Base relief of the large worshipper statuette from the hoard in the 'Square Temple', Tell Asmar. Redrawn (After: OIP 44, Pl. 6 A)

Nor does the female companion piece fit into the framework made up by the other numerous statuettes of women which are known to belong to this period, from the Square Temple at Eshnunna and more especially from the Nintu Temple VI, the Sin Temple VIII/IX and the Temple Oval at Khafaje. None has the exaggeratedly large eyes with the gigantic pupils, none is lifting up her head so high, none has so small a hair arrangement, and none such tiny hands, even though some resemble her in having their hands separated and they are sometimes shown holding a branch. But above all no other statuette has, like this one, a very small human figure (only its lower part has survived) standing on the same base next to the principle figure: this must presumably have been intended to indicate the motherly aspect of the woman represented. The sculptor has achieved a transcendental, elevated effect in this female figure more by superficial details, such as the over-large eyes and the smallness of the hands, than by anything like a variation in style, such as geometrizing or breaking-up the stone mass. Statuettes surviving unbroken are in a small minority in comparison with the large number of female heads found.[134, 135]

It does not seem as if the sculptor even attempted to achieve such an intensive impression of spiritualization in any of the other female statuettes and heads. Also, on the whole, the quality of the work is poorer than it was in the statues of the men. It is true that the shape of their bodies is invariably concealed by the heavy cloak, leaving only the right arm and part of the shoulder free, yet the plump faces under the luxuriant wreath of plaited hair seem gentle and sensual. Only the inlaid eyes seem unearthly.[136] It is only when the women's cloak is decorated with a pattern of short, incised scales[137] (Pl. 63) that the figures achieve any outward charm, such as was also typical of the male statuettes of this group. They must surely belong to the end of the Mesilim Period and are beginning to free themselves from the rigid restraint of this epoch.[138]

Recently, with the assistance of certain works of art from Mari, it has been possible to establish that such an escape from abstract patterns of composition did in fact take place already during the Mesilim Period itself in some of the sculpture in the round, in favour of a more determined swing towards living forms taken from nature. On two pieces of sculpture from the Ishtar Temple[139] (Pls. 64, 66) at Mari, a fragment of a statuette with an inscription of Idi-Narum and, above all, on a seated statue of Ebih-il, there are votive inscriptions which are the earliest known inscriptions in the Semitic language. The second of these, the seated figure of Ebih-il can, with the aid of palaeography, be attributed with certainty to the Mesilim Period[140] (Pl. 65). This has been confirmed archaeologically by means of a cylinder seal, which Parrot has recently published[141] (Pl. 67). It originated in the area of the Ishtar Temple and carries the legend Shar-il, of which the syllable 'il' (here meaning God) is written with the same sign, still half pictographic (the lower half of a dancer with one leg raised high), which is reproduced in the same form in the votive inscription on the statue of Ebih-il. This cylinder seal is an undoubted example of glyptic from the Mesilim Period.

The seated figure of Ebih-il, now attributed with certainty in this way to the Mesilim Period, shows us that during this period – as in the Jamdat Nasr period – there is still the same antinomy of representational and abstract art. No part of the statue of Ebih-il is just a stereometric framework, any more than in the bronze sculpture of this period which has just been described. The only features recalling the stone worshippers of the Mesilim Period are the schematic positioning of the hands clasped together in front of the chest and the too rapid tapering of the lower arms from the jutting-out elbows. Otherwise everything is completely unlike figures such as those from the hoard in the Square Temple at Eshnunna (see above): the soft modelling of the naked upper part of the body, the free, natural appearance of the fleece of the skirt, the beard carefully stylized with vertical curls and drilled holes and the head of completely normal size, with eyes inlaid in colour but natural in appearance. Unfortunately the feet are missing but the ankles, beautifully made, and the legs carved free of the chair reflect once more the influence of plastic work in bronze.

This influence is even more marked if we examine the seated figure of a singer, Ur-Nanshe[142] (Pls. 68, 69). Here the style cannot be distinguished from that of the statue of Ebih-il. It was found in the temple of Nini-Zaza at Mari, together with a fragment of another statuette of Ur-Nanshe portrayed as a woman playing a harp.[143] Both works have been identified through their inscriptions as votive gifts for the King Iblul-il. The statue of the harpist in particular shows a conflict with the technique of stonecutting, as her instrument is held completely free in space. The better preserved statue of Ur-Nanshe, a woman worshipping with her hands clasped together and squatting with crossed legs on a cushion, also displays great detachment in its whole design and a freedom of style rather like that in the statues from the Diyala area. The closest resemblance to the statue of Ebih-il expresses itself in the modelling of the naked (?) upper part of the body, in the slightly full, soft face with its delicate, aquiline nose, in the mouth, slightly smiling and with small lips, and in the completely corresponding stylization of the hair and the same inlay in the eyes.

How important this school of sculpture at Mari had become is only apparent if one compares their work with similar groups of sculpture from the Diyala region. From there too we have seated figures of men and figures sitting with their legs crossed. The best example of this kind came from Eshnunna[144] and was found in the vicinity of the Square Temple I. It is not well preserved, yet it could clearly never have been compared with the figure of Ur-Nanshe from Mari for freedom of all the limbs from the stone mass nor its particular charm.

More comparable are fragments found in the top stratum of the so-called Main Level at the Shara Temple (Tell Agrab), which show a similar delicacy of execution and visible striving towards a really lifelike portrait. This is particularly true of two similar male heads,[145] a female statuette[146] and a female head.[147]

Involuntarily one asks oneself whether perhaps this does not suggest a Semitic strain, which has already appeared in the inscriptions, and which had perhaps existed in the entire art of the Mesilim Period, especially in that type of sculpture in the round which resembled bronze work in its freedom, and especially at Mari on the Middle Euphrates. And does not the discord within the art of the Sumerian region, noticed so often already, derive at least partly from the symbiosis of the Semite and the Sumerian?

The sculpture found in the Diyala area and in the pre-Sargonic temples at Mari is of immense importance because it enables us to appreciate the existence of a unified style prevailing in the southern part of the Land of the Two Rivers during the second half of the third millennium. The statuettes excavated in the year 1963 at Tell Chuera in Northern Syria (see the back of the jacket of this book), though small in number, are nevertheless of greater importance historically, at least for anyone for whom history does not consist only of the written word. In all material respects they undoubtedly belong to the alabaster sculpture of the Mesilim Period from the Diyala and the Middle Euphrates region, yet they emphasize those basic traits which were still, on the whole, entirely new to the Sumer of the third millennium: features such as individual human personality, as, for example, it is revealed – though only very modestly – in the smallest statuette from Tell Chuera[148] (Pls. 70, 71), or the feeling for grace and elegance in dress and movement, which marks a second figure, clearly a prince of that area[149] (Pls. 72, 73).

The ridged hairstyle of a third statuette is a move in the same direction[150] (Pls. 74, 75). We cannot yet put a name to these figures, yet their whole being convinces us that they are not Sumerians but are probably related to and predecessors of the Semites, whom we shall shortly encounter at Mari. They were, after all, settled in the Syrian desert and nearer to Harran than to the centre of Sumerian civilization around Uruk and Ur. Apart from the artistic merit of their art, they represent the founders of the settlement at Tell Chuera in the third millennium B.C., with their clearly mixed culture made up of elements from Anatolia, Iraq, and North and West Syria – the first Semitic leaders of a great movement which under Sargon of Akkad led to the epoch-making foundation of the first Akkadian Empire. This movement, as we now recognize, was to run its course through many centuries, as did the movement of the later 'Canaanites'.

C THE SECOND TRANSITION PERIOD ('IMDUGUD–SUKURRU PERIOD') AND THE FIRST DYNASTY OF UR

There must have been a second transitional period, after the Mesilim Period, which had produced some of the most unusual works of art ever made in the ancient Near East, and before the next phase, which through its numerous texts is the first period to be seen in the full light of history (this is the period dominated by the Kings of the First Dynasty of Ur and the *ensis* of Lagash). The best evidence for this transitional period is to be seen in the clay tablets and the seal impressions from Shuruppak (Fara). The writing ductus on these tablets and in the legends on these seal impressions is older than that of the period of the First Dynasty of Ur and the *ensis* of Lagash. Yet this second transitional period is not a cultural turning-point, as was the first transitional period – that between the Jamdat Nasr and the Mesilim Periods. It is merely a stage on the way of a slow but continuous transformation. We can follow the development of the stone-cutters' art from the Mesilim Period up to the beginning of the Akkadian Period, embracing several phases which cannot always be identified consistently in other branches of art, such as architecture and pictorial art. But from the many figures in the round, from the reliefs and small objects from the temples in the Diyala region, of which many levels and sub-levels were examined, as well as from the numerous finds from Telloh, Ur, Al 'Ubaid and Mari, we are learning more and more to recognize the existence of a general development based on its own internal laws, and this can be confirmed by palaeography and stratigraphy. Judging from our knowledge of today, this development led away from the ideals of the Mesilim Period, without itself producing fundamentally new ideas or new formulas of its own.

1 Architecture

At all the temples which we know from the Mesilim Period, building continued during the second transitional period and the Ur I Period. These temples were transformed and renewed, but nowhere do we find fundamentally new plans or new shapes. The plano-convex brick was still used where it had been used before, until just before the end of the Ur I Period. Neither in Uruk nor in Ur itself, which now emerges as the centre of political and intellectual life, neither in the Diyala region nor in Ashur do we find architectural achievements which suggest a new attitude to life. It is only at Mari, on the Middle Euphrates, in a few sanctuaries – as, for example, the Nini-Zaza Temple[151] – that influences seem to operate which emanated from the west, from the Canaanite region. However, this remained a merely peripheral phenomenon.

The various kinds of buildings, the arrangements of the ground-plans and the building shapes themselves remained, by and large, the same as in the Mesilim Period. Only the rejection of rounded forms – for instance the conversion of the temple terrace

at Khafaje from an oval to a rectangle[152] or the abandonment of the plano-convex brick – indicate a withdrawal of certain features which had appeared after the Jamdat Nasr period.

2 Art

a Sculpture in the round

Practically no other works of art have survived in such large quantities as have the figures of the *worshipper,* a form known from the Mesilim Period, when it was placed as a substitute for the worshipper himself in the temple of a divinity he wished to honour. From the inscriptions on some of them we know that it was hoped in this way to obtain a prolongation of life with the help of the divinity. It is possible for us to examine a long series of these figures, both standing and seated, male and female, and to confirm the impression that just before the beginning of the Ur I Period there was a coarsening and superficiality in the work generally, even though some of the figures do still show signs of good workmanship. The style of the Mesilim Period had been unusually relaxed, and had shown the extremities of the body disengaged from the block of the figure, as is usual in bronze casting. This style was at first the main influence during the second transitional period – of which the duration is difficult to assess – and indeed it seems that for a short time there was a striving to show transient movement and a more realistic treatment of individual features. We can see an example of this in a head from the Temple Oval II.[153] There is also a statuette of the priest Urkisalla,[154] from the Sin Temple IX at Khafaje, of which the head is unfortunately badly damaged (Fig. 31). The body's upper part still clearly reflects the Mesilim tradition. A large free space has been left between the upper arms and the chest. Yet the naked upper body has been modelled delicately, as it was in the statue of Ebih-il from Mari, and the long skirt with its short fringed hem, if seen in profile, follows the movement of the left leg which is slightly ad-

Fig. 31 Statuette of Urkisalla from the Sin Temple IX at Khafaje.
Redrawn
(After: OIP 44, Pls. 48–50)

vanced in front, so that the whole statue is given an S-shaped swing. Only to be compared is a poorly preserved figure from Ashur (Fig. 32).[155]

Another statuette, unfortunately headless, from the archaic Ishtar Temple at Ashur[156] belongs entirely to the Mesilim Period in the geometrization of the naked upper part of the body and the complete disengagement of the arms. Like the bronze statues of the Mesilim Period it still has its feet arranged in a walking position, and this makes the long skirt form an S-curve. But this skirt shows for the first time the heavy tufted decoration in many horizontal rows one over the other, which then was to become typical during the entire period which followed, up to the Akkadian Period.

The closest parallel to the figure from Ashur just described is provided by an especially beautiful work from the Nintu Temple VI at Khafaje[157] (Pl. 76). It can no longer be attributed to the Mesilim Period, because of the elaborate tufted skirt and the baldness of the head, and it must accordingly belong to the second transitional period. However, it is still quite free from the block-like massiveness which was to come later. Unfortunately the feet are missing from the so-called '*Konsistorialrat*'[158] (consistorial councillor) from Ashur (Pl. 77), otherwise he would pre-

sumably look not unlike the two preceding statues. His small hands and the disengaged arms are still quite in the style of the Mesilim Period, though the full face and the well nourished, thick-set figure no longer suggest a withdrawal from the world. The bulk of the heavy tufted skirt is beginning to dominate the whole appearance[159] (Pls. 78–80). But the change to a block shape was not confined to the lower part of the body. The upper part as well, with its arms lying close beside it, was once again reduced to a single unit, so that the shape of the breast, elbows and hands quite lost the stereometric stylization of the Mesilim Period. The fragment of the statuette of Idi-Narum, the grain steward, found in the Ishtar Temple at Mari[160] (Pl. 64), shows this change in the appearance of the upper body when this style is fully developed, and it would perhaps be better not to assign such an early date to this statuette as to that of Ebih-il (see above). If indeed, as stated by Thur-eau-Dangin, the writing ductus suggests a period earlier than the first *ensi* of Lagash, Ur-Nanshe, we shall have to assign it to the second transitional period. In any case it must be later than that of Ebih-il on account of its style.

Two fragments of male figures[161] (Pls. 81, 82) with exceptionally long hair and long, stylized beards with holes dividing the strands – resembling in this the beard of Ebih-il – have been compared[162] with the peg-figure of King Lugalkisalsi[163] (Pl. 83). The stone has been left in the spaces between their arms and chest, under their armpits, while the shapes of the body have been moulded delicately. They may therefore perhaps be dated after Ebih-il, during the second transitional period.

With the votive figure of King Lamgi-Ma'ri from Mari[164] (Pl. 84) we pass into the period of the *ensis* of Lagash, of whom Ur-Nanshe was the first. This statuette conforms to the new style, except in the walking position of the feet, which still reflects the Mesilim Period. The tufted material, from which the skirt is made, on this occasion also covers the left shoulder and the left arm. Only the right arm stands out from the mass of the stone block. In addition to the clothes of the Ur I Period, the head-dress of the kings now appears for the first time, as in the splendid example of the golden wig[165] (Pl. 86) from the

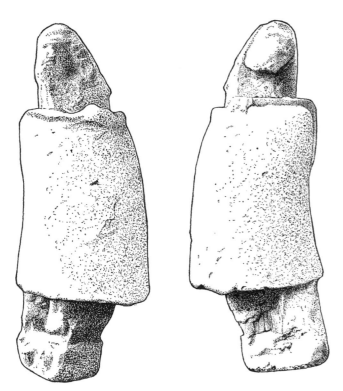

Fig. 32   Headless statuette from Ashur. Redrawn
(After: WVDOG 39, Pl. 34 c–e, Pl. 37 e)

tomb of the younger Mes-kalam-dug in the Royal
Cemetery at Ur: waved and parted hair with a
circlet of plaits fastened by a diadem, and a chignon
tied high up.

One of the statuettes from this period, which still
to a certain extent conforms to the laws of proportion, is the figure from Adab (Bismaya) bearing an
inscription of a king Lugaldalu.[166] Thureau-Dangin
considers the inscription to be earlier than Ur-
Nanshe. The treatment of the naked back would
accord with that theory, and like the still sharply
jutting elbows, it recalls the Mesilim Period. On the
other hand the very heavy and long skirt, together
with the feet placed side by side and chiselled out
only a little, indicate the Ur I Period.[167] The end of
this development is illustrated by two statuettes of
ensis of Lagash. The first of these is a very damaged
one of a son (Me'anesi) of Eannatum I in grey limestone[168] (Pl. 85), which reached the Baghdad Museum
through art dealers, but the other illustrates this

development even more clearly. It is the diorite statuette of Entemena, found at Ur[169] (Pls. 87, 88). This
stone is difficult to work, which no doubt accounts
for the coarseness of form in this statue, which is
imprisoned in its material. The feet are not even in
the axis of the body but are merely shown in front
view and in high relief. In this statue the two main
methods employed during the Mesilim Period in
order to rise above the limitations of the material –
the geometrization of natural forms and the disengagement of individual parts from the mass of the
stone – are again abandoned completely. With this
work then we have arrived at the beginning of a
new epoch, for, as we shall see, Entemena seems to
stand at almost the same stage of development as
A-anne-padda of Ur, the second king of his dynasty.[170]

In addition to the male statuettes there were many
statuettes of women, standing and seated, during the
whole time from the Mesilim Period through the
second transitional period and up to the end of the
Ur I Period. Even more numerous are the female
heads with a variety of hair-styles and head-dresses,
such as turbans and the *polos*-like hats, the significance of which we cannot always understand[171]
(Pls. 89–92).

In general the female statuettes, like the male
figures, gradually become more like a block. The
figure of a stout woman[172] (Pl. 93) from Level VI
of the Nintu Temple at Khafaje, shown by means of
stratigraphy to be from between the Mesilim Period
and that of Ur I, should be compared with the statuette of Urkisalla (see above). Her arms are still
typical of the Mesilim Period. On the other hand her
breasts, the modelling of which shows through the
dress, are evidence of the new feeling for a natural
rendering of the body. The lower part of the body
has already become massive. But the woman is not
yet wearing the tufted dress of the new period, as
worn already by a seated figure from the Ishtarat
Temple at Mari[173] (Pl. 95). On the seated figure the
heavy material is even pulled up over the high *polos*,
which is placed above the hair-style with side pieces,
so that only her face and upper body would show,
as though in a niche (the upper part of the body is
missing). In spite of the thick-set appearance of the

Fig. 33   Female statuette from the Ishtar Temple at Ashur. Redrawn (After: WVDOG 39, Pl. 35 a–d)

whole statue, the feet – carved independently as in the statue of Ebih-il – show how close this work still is to the Mesilim Period.

There is a female standing figure[174] (Fig. 33) in the same sort of style, one of the votive figures from the archaic Ishtar Temple at Ashur. Her whole body is just a column covered with heavy tufts, and only the feet remain free. Only the stunted hands and the right arm, shown clear of the body, remain from the Mesilim Period. The heavy hair-style has the appearance of a turban. This, and indeed the whole figure, may perhaps belong to the transition to the Ur I Period.[175]

A final reminder of the Mesilim Period is provided by the symmetrical pose of the tiny hands of the standing figure in the British Museum[176] (Pl. 94), but with this statuette we most probably have reached the end of the second transitional period. It is only her smooth cloak with its tufted hem which makes her seem still relatively slim.

And so the cloaked female figures followed the same path as had the male statuettes during the time of the First Dynasty of Ur, becoming imprisoned in the block (Pl. 96). At this stage several figures are shown with their right arm held close to the body,

with their hands clasped across their breast and with even the right shoulder covered[177] (Pls. 97, 98).

Finally the same coarseness and squatness which we noticed in the figures of Eannatum I and Entemena of Lagash can also be seen in two female standing figures from Lagash, which reached the Louvre and the British Museum respectively via the art dealers[178] (Pls. 99, 100, 101, 102). Their smooth hair is held by a head-band and hangs far down their backs. Their feet are still only shown as if in a niche. The whole weight of the medium imprisons these figures.

Still belonging to the transition from the Mesilim Period to the Ur I Period, a seated figure of a scribe Dudu[179] (Pl. 103) came into the possession of the Baghdad Museum a few years ago, and probably originated in Lagash. A delicately moulded naked upper body, a head shaved bald and a face with a slight smile rise above a crinoline-type tufted skirt. The feet are projecting in front of the seated man. If the donor is called A-imdugud, and this name is attested in the period of the Fara clay plaques,[180] this would fit in well the statue's style. All the more likely since a fragment of the seated figure from the Nintu Temple VII at Khafaje, which through stratigraphy can be assigned to the second transitional period, shows a marked resemblance to the Dudu statue.[181] A parallel to the figure from Mari, mentioned above, of a seated woman with a *polos* is provided by a second female figure, younger and shaped more like a block, with her feet drawn in close to her chair[182] (Pl. 104). Another statuette, of a seated couple,[183] again has none of the limbs cut free of the stone mass.

No motif was better adapted to the striving towards a presentation of the subject enclosed within its material than that of the worshipper squatting with his legs tucked under him (Pl. 105). The motif has been met with before,[184] in the Mesilim Period (see above), but the arms were always left clear of the body, in line with the preference at that time for stereometric forms. This is no longer the case with the figure known as Kurlil[185] from Al 'Ubaid (Pl. 106). Only the small hands and the sharply protruding elbows still recall the Mesilim Period. The squatting figure in the Ny Carlsberg Glyptotek[186]

(Pl. 107) has his elbows somewhat lowered, and it is noticeable that the individual features of the face, the hands and the lower legs have been rendered in a more realistic manner. In spite of this, the statuette as a whole has a more massive appearance than that of Kurlil.[187]

The climax of this tendency to imprison the subject in the medium, the aim of the artists at the end of the Ur I Period, was the figure of an official from Umma named Lupad[188] (Pl. 108). This shows a seated or squatting man, and it had to be reassembled from many fragments. Like the statuette of Entemena from Ur, this also was made from the hard stone diorite. If one judges this by the well rendered features of the face, by no means lacking in expression, one may conclude that the crude, heavy body with the lower arms and neckless head scarcely emerging from it, was the result of the spirit of the period rather than of a lack of technical skill.

b   Relief and two-dimensional art

The golden age of the Protohistorical Period united god and nature in one: when this was no longer possible, the Mesilim Period evolved the spiritualization of nature by means of art. This, however, gave rise to a tension which could not be carried through indefinitely, and so was bound at some stage to cause a reaction: thus, in the two-dimensional art of the Ur I Period, the transcendental which had permeated the Mesilim Period gave way to realism. It is the age in which gods become men.

It is possible to observe clearly in *glyptic*[189] (Pl. D 4) how the artists make use of the old motifs, in particular the figured band – but the drinking scene as well – without any new intellectual impulse, while they are slowly transforming the schematic aridity of the individual figures back into creatures of flesh and blood. When possible they infuse a plastic roundness into all the drawing, suppress the symbolic contractions (see p. 31) and, step by step, relax the control exercised by abstraction over the spatial design. The second transitional period is represented in glyptic by the impressions from Fara, which form a group round the one with the legend of Imdugud-Sukurru[190] (Pl. M 3) and which originated before the first *ensi* of Lagash, Ur-Nanshe. Humans and animals have been given plastic substance again, the lions' manes stand out indented above the outline of their bodies, the bisons have been given human faces. A cylinder seal in the Bibliothèque Nationale[191] shows us the figured band in an arrangement which corresponds approximately to the period of Ur-Nanshe, since here it is combined with a symposium scene in which human figures are dressed in tufted garments similar to those on the reliefs[192] (Pls. 109–112) of this prince (cf. Pl. E 2).

The shapes of the animals are even more exuberant on a seal from the period of Mes-kalam-dug, from a tomb in the Royal Cemetery at Ur[193] (Pl. E 1), and finally we have the impressions from the time of the very last of the *ensis*[194] of Lagash and of King Mes-anne-padda[195] of Ur, which are all practically identical in style. Towards the end of this development in the Ur I Period they even dare to relax the restraint imposed by the interweaving of the figures, and to arrange men and animals in groups of two, three and five, placed loosely next to each other[196] (Pl. E 3). The muscularity of the limbs both of men and beasts is shown with great plasticity, and this actually underlines a discrepancy between the intellectual character of the figured band, intended to symbolize the cycle of life and death, and the individual figures, full of life, who seem to belong entirely to this world. It is important to remember that they portrayed god in an entirely human shape, as for example on a cylinder seal[197] from this period, on which he can only be distinguished from his worshippers by his horned head-dress, and indeed his figure is remarkably true to nature (Pl. E 4). The anthropomorphism, so noticeable in the ancient Near East at all periods, the portrayal of the divinity in purely human form, is finally achieved in this seal. There will only be a transitory and occasional deviation from this.

Even the *engraving* on ivory and metal, a craft to which the style is least adapted, became subject to the general desire for compact forms, and thereby incidentally produced some of the most artistic works from this period. On a little shell plaque[198] from Ur, two divinities are shown – one leading the other by the hand – and their bodies, in their vast, bell-shaped garments, are no less in circumference than those of the princes of this period.[199] One of the finest examples of decorative art in Sumer, still in its best period, is the engraved silver vase[200] of Entemena from Telloh (Pl. 113). Two pictorial friezes encircle the shoulder and widest part of the vessel: the upper one of these shows cattle lying down, the lower several lion-headed eagles, their heads turned back, hovering above lions and goats. These friezes are among the very best in vase decoration. The designer has even found a way to reproduce the motif of the lion-headed eagle hovering over two animals in order to make a continuous frieze, a cycle – so in keeping with the Sumerian character – which returns into itself. The nearest equivalent of this motif can be seen on the somewhat similar bronze relief from the Temple of A-anne-padda at Al 'Ubaid.[201] The style differs from that of the Mesilim Period only in the individual figures, in the detailed drawing of the lines inside the feathers, and in the luxuriant manes of the lions, which are just like those on the Meskalam-dug seal (see above).

The main medium for relief in the Mesilim Period, the *votive plaque,* with a hole pierced in the centre, still appears in the Ur I Period, but with few exceptions[202] it has a different theme. Even the plaques referred to already (see Note 199), which were decorated with incised drawings and which came from Nippur and Telloh, showed gods on thrones being presented with libations and offerings. The mystic union between chthonic god and man no longer seems to be the main subject, but is replaced by the heavenly gods of the pantheon, who retain eternal life for themselves and whose favour man can only obtain through constant prayer and sacrifice. A badly preserved work from Telloh[203] is decorated with a libation scene, in front of an enthroned goddess of mountain and vegetation (Pl. 114). The same subject, though this time easier to recognize, is shown on a fragment of a relief-vase of Entemena[204] (Pl. 115). The best example of this kind of work is the small votive plaque found in the house of the divine bride *(Gigparku)* at Ur, in the sanctuary of the moon-god Nanna[205] (Pl. 116). Its top frieze shows a libation scene, with three priestesses in front of the enthroned

god – the bulkiness of his figure is noticeable. The subject of the lower frieze is probably a libation in front of the temple on the occasion of the induction of the *Nin-Dingir,* the divine bride. In the procession she is the only one turning her face to us and has exactly the same *en face* appearance as the enthroned goddesses of the period. Here again the decoration seems crude and rustic. The same is the case with a plaque of the High Priest Dudu from the period of Entemena[206] (Pl. 117) and it is in complete conformity with the coarse and massive style of the contemporary statuettes (see above). Moreover no attempt is made now to create a narrative scene: here only individual symbols are shown.

The votive plaques of Ur-Nanshe[207] (Pl. 109–112), the earliest *ensi* of Lagash, which were found at Telloh, scarcely deserve to be considered in a history of art because of the poor quality of their execution. Yet it is interesting to note that Ur-Nanshe introduced a theme otherwise scarcely used. In the so-called family reliefs, where the prince was shown with his wife, children and courtiers, all with their names added in the legends, he appears more than once as the builder of the temple, carrying the builders' basket on his head. And the motif of the basket bearer was to be of some significance in later art.

Far more important, however, was the appearance of a new category of relief – new at least in its perfected form: the *historical stele.* Since de Sarzec's excavations at the beginning of this century we have possessed what is still today the most important relief from this period, the 'Stele of the Vultures'. This is a memorial to Eannatum, the greatest of the *Ensis* of Lagash, and is of historical as well as of artistic interest[208] (Pls. 118–121). The stele, a limestone slab 1.88 m. high, 1.3 m. wide and 11 cm. thick, is rounded at the top, and is an admonitory stone commemorating a victory. It was erected by Eannatum on the border between Lagash and Umma, after his god Ningirsu had won back a disputed area (GU. EDIN) in battle with the city god of Umma. All four sides are covered with relief. Only part of the stele could be reconstructed from the many fragments. A detailed inscription fills the spaces between the pictures. From both the literary and the artistic point of view it is the first major composition of this nature, even though at an earlier stage there were some votive plaques created by artists who could illustrate a detailed theme, dividing it into individual parts and at the same time combining it into an unity. The main theme shows the god Ningirsu as conqueror: he is shown on the front side of the stele dressed as a king of the Protohistorical Period, with naked upper body, long skirt with a vertical border in front and a padded girdle. He also has a large chignon and a very long beard. In his left hand he is holding the enemy like fish caught in a net. The net has a fastener shaped like the symbol of death, the lion-headed eagle above two lions. The god is beating out the brains of the enemy with a mace. This figure of Ningirsu recalls the principal male figure of the Uruk IV and Jamdat Nasr periods, the fighting prince, or the man in the net garment, not only in his dress but also in the style which aims at complete corporeality. A smaller divinity who can be identified as a god because of his horned cap, together with a standard bearer, seem to have stood behind the figure of the fighting god. In the lower register there was probably the chariot from which Ningirsu had descended, and behind this the god's charioteer.

The reverse of the stele and its narrow side were decorated with various scenes from Eannatum's campaigns. In the top frieze we see him marching at the head of his phalanx of armed spearmen over the bodies of the fallen enemy (Pl. 119). Under the arched top of the stele the bodies are shown being devoured by vultures (Pl. 120). In the frieze below he is in his chariot, returning from the battle as a conqueror followed by his men, while in the register below this he is attending a libation ceremony and sacrificing animals beside a communal grave (Pl. 121). In the frieze right at the bottom, which is unfortunately in a bad state of preservation, there must have been another campaign sequence.

The dualism of the late Sumerian age is revealed clearly in this monument: whereas on the front side of the stele the conquest of Umma is still represented as a divine act, an act actually undertaken by a god who is completely tangible and presented in human form, yet in a symbolic manner, on the reverse side the artist is attempting to show human beings and their mortal world, completely in the spirit of the Ur I Period. To do this he not only employs the compact bodily shape of the individual figure, as for instance in the naked priest pouring wine at the burial scene,[209] which is just like the statuettes of the period: but the crowd scene itself appears for the first time as the subject of the picture, apparently because it corresponds to the spirit of this period. War is a collision of blocks of human beings, and in this picture it is not the movement which is recorded but rather as though everything were congealed, weighed down by pressure.

As opposed to the abstraction which pervades the Mesilim Period, in the Ur I Period the desire to make the transcendental natural, to bring the supernatural into comprehensible reality, also influenced the works of art composed of many coloured materials. It is possibly not a coincidence that we find the best examples of this art at precisely those places where the early Sumerian tradition of the Innin-Tammuz myth was maintained with the greatest vigour. One of these places is the temple of a goddess whose essential being must have resembled that of Inanna of Uruk, namely Ninhursag, the inhabitant of the sanctuary at Al 'Ubaid near Ur,[210] and the other is in the cemetery at Ur,[211] in the treasures of the pit graves which, by their nature, were linked to reflections on life and death.

In some way which we do not quite understand, the *picture friezes* found at the foot of the ziggurat at Al 'Ubaid (= El Obeid) must have been connected with the temple on top of it. Parts of several friezes[212] (Pls. 122–124) have been found, with birds and cattle cut out of shell or limestone, together with a pen from the sides of which two cows are coming: on its right, cows are being milked by squatting men, while on its left others are busy straining the milk and making it into butter. The lightly coloured figures have been set on dark slabs of slate, fastened with bitumen on to wood, and framed at the top and bottom by a rail of copper plate. Its connection with the numerous scenes of pens in the Protohistorical Period is obvious (see p. 13 above). But whereas then, in spite of all its realism, the scene was essentially related to the divinity, here in the milking scene it has been slightly changed into a *genre* type of picture.

The great goddess of life has become just a country-woman.

According to the inscription found there, the temple at Al 'Ubaid – the source of these friezes – originated in the reign of A-anne-padda, the second king of the First Dynasty of Ur, and they may therefore be assigned to the end of the Ur I Period.

The majority of the rich *treasures from the pit tombs* in the Royal Cemetery at Ur are, of course, only the work of craftsmen, and even the examples of inlay chosen for illustration in this book are not objects of great artistic value but merely decorations on implements and furnishings. Nevertheless they are of outstanding importance: like the pit tombs themselves, with the custom of burying the royal retinue – up to thirty people shared the death of their prince as an inevitable part of their own existence – these treasures bore witness to the continuance of the same conceptions about life and death which had been evolved during the Protohistorical Period of Sumerian civilization. Here in the actual tomb, figures in the round and flat objects made of coloured materials, still continued with the motif of the picture cycle from the Protohistorical Period: the tree of life and the man in the net garment, no longer in the conceptualized form of the Mesilim Period, but with an exuberant naturalism reinforced still more by the bright colours. Here not only the great gods of the heavenly pantheon but animals also are shown as humans. Animals which since the Protohistorical Period had symbolized chthonic and magic powers are now given human characteristics: indeed, by a reversal of all values, they are shown celebrating the most sacred ceremony of the cultic myth, the great festival of the Sacred Marriage, in a fantasy of feasting, music and dancing[213] (Fig. 34). Death itself, in the shape of a lion, celebrates the festival of life, symbolized in the row above by the hero with his arms round two bulls. These brightly coloured inlays, on the front end of a harp, represent an artistic peak, both in the freedom and, at the same time, the co-ordination of the composition, and in the observation of nature, even though the individual figures themselves are stylized.

Two he-goats, reaching far up into a bush,[214] provide the perfect example of polychrome art in the

Fig. 34   Front of harp with the 'Animal Orchestra' from Ur (After: UE 2, Pl. 105)

round. They are parts of a piece of furniture from the so-called Great Death Pit. The core of each is carved from wood, and its head and legs have been covered with beaten gold-leaf, the belly with silver-leaf. Horns, beard and mane are carved from lapis lazuli, the fleece from shell. The individual tufts of the fleece are stylized just like the tufts on the garments on stone statuettes of this period. The plant, its branches ending in rosettes, is also made out of wood covered in gold-leaf. The whole object stands on a base with a mosaic inlay of brightly coloured tesserae. The ancient symbol of life, the tree placed between nibbling animals, has never been illustrated in a more lively manner. The golden bull's head[215] on the front of a harp from the Great Death Pit should be compared with the bull's head from the Mesilim Period (Pl. 53). Here, in the head on the harp, we are looking at the head of an individual animal, radiating life, but the other was an intellectual and exaggerated abstraction. These two heads symbolize the two attitudes possible to a Sumerian when faced with the supernatural, the one leading him to transform reality into an abstract, the other to transform the transcendental into nature – once his unity of heaven and earth had been sundered at the end of the Protohistorical Period.

D THE AKKADIAN PERIOD

In the development of Sumerian art before this period we have only occasionally noticed phenomena which can certainly be traced to a non-Sumerian source. One thinks mainly of the statuettes of Ebih-il, Idi Narum and Lamgi-Ma'ri from Mari, which according to their inscriptions must undoubtedly be Semitic in origin. Yet they are so influenced by Sumerian culture that no one would dare label them Semitic art or explain their individual artistic character as due solely to the Semitic population of Mari.

The alabaster statuettes of the Mesilim Period found at Tell Chuera (see p. 36 and Pls. 70–75), the sensational site excavated during the last few years, in the extreme north of the Land of the Two Rivers, have a much more Semitic appearance, partly in their bearing and partly in their physiognomy. Where the art of the Akkadian Period is concerned, there is now no more room for doubt. Sumer was cut off from all sources of immigration, and its penetration by the Semites – infiltrating ceaselessly from the steppes – had now reached a stage when a general change in the religious and state systems and also in the social and cultural structure was effected.[216]

As far as we can tell from the meagre supply of surviving works of art, which we owe more to luck than to any systematic research, art provided this period with its most splendid outlet, a period imbued with a heroic spirit and a turbulent energy. At no other time do we miss a supply of monuments more sorely than we do here.

1 Architecture

We know only very little about the *buildings* of the Akkadian period, even though at many sites it has been possible to establish that the buildings of earlier periods were added to during the Akkadian Period. The brick used is now a large rectangular or square slab up to 52 × 52 cm. in size. The plano-convex

brick had been a typical element in building during the transitional period between the Jamdat Nasr and the Mesilim Periods, a period which was distinguished by few signs of firm discipline or precise, formal work, and this brick was no longer used during the Akkadian Period. It would have constituted a complete contradiction of the Akkadian feeling for style. The foundations of walls were placed in trenches. But this kind of detail tells one little of the essential spirit of the period. Another change seems more vital, a change which can be detected in the ground-plan of the age-old Abu Temple at Eshnunna (Tell Asmar). There the cella of the so-called Single Shrine Temple is divided into two halves by a partition wall[217] – and this is important when one considers that a cella divided into two halves, dating from the Mesilim Period, can also be seen at another site, at Tell Chuera in North Mesopotamia. Here, during the Mesilim Period, there had already been two instances of a temple plan showing a rectangular cella *in antis* and, at the same time, showing the cella divided into two equal parts, one behind the other.[218]

Had the principal cities of the Akkadian Empire – Sippar, the city of the sun-god Shamash, and Akkad, the city of the Heavenly Ishtar – been discovered and excavated, perhaps the same basic change could have been observed in the architecture of this period as that noticeable in the fragments of large and small works of art which have survived. However, a few ground-plans of buildings in peripheral areas enable us to appreciate that, with the mutation of the Sumerian king into an Akkadian god-king, the *palace* became of greater importance than it had been in Sumerian times, when the temple had dominated everything. The so-called Akkadian Palace at Eshnunna[219] (Fig. 35) is not a typical building and by no means a work of art, but rather an enlarged dwelling-house, and therefore it probably did not express directly the Akkadian concept of kingship. The position is different as regards the palaces at Tell Brak and Ashur, of which unfortunately only a few remains of the ground-plans still exist. Naram-Sin, the last but one of the great Akkadian rulers, erected a mighty building,[220] 100 m. square (Fig. 36), at the place in Tell Brak where the 'Temple of the Thou-

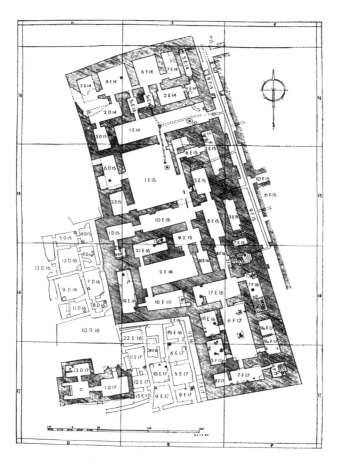

Fig. 35   'Akkadian Palace' at Tell Asmar
(After: OIC 17, Fig. 20)

shown by its resemblance to the original plan of the so-called 'Old Palace' at Ashur[221] (Fig. 37) which, I consider, may in all probability belong to the Akkadian Period, because an Akkadian clay tablet was found in the foundation trenches after they had become filled in.[222] The ground-plan is unmistakably the same as that at Tell Brak, with the same, almost square perimeter wall fencing in a complex of rectangular courts, onto which the different areas of the palace opened. Both groups of buildings could only have been erected from a plan which had been carefully considered before the building started. If one compares these two Akkadian buildings with the palace at Eshnunna, one might judge the latter to be essentially Sumerian, for its whole character is additive. Its ultimately achieved unity is secondary, and not the outcome of a primary, formal concept. And this difference is a key to the difference between Sumerian and Akkadian as a whole. The Akkadian Empire of the 'Four Regions of the World' also cor-

sand Eyes' had stood in the Protohistorical Period. The construction of a palace, at once a royal fortress and a caravanserai, on the sacred site of a temple was in itself an enormity which could probably only have been permitted to a god-king such as Naram-Sin. As well as a mighty gate-house, lying on the axis of the main court complex, three other smaller courtyard systems were enclosed by the almost square perimeter wall, 10 m. thick. The covered rooms would only have taken up very little space in comparison with the courtyards. Nothing has survived from the elevation or the inner layout of the rooms, only the harmonious and clear-cut design of the ground-plan itself enables us to gain a little insight into the particular nature of the Akkadian spirit. The fact that this imposing building is not just a work of purely military and economic significance is

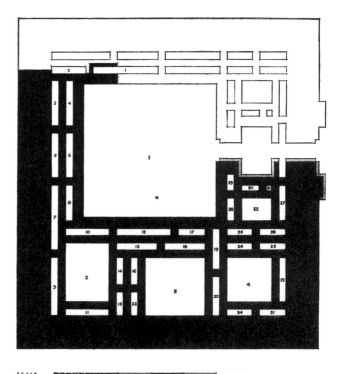

Fig. 36   'Palace' of Naram-Sin of Akkad at Tell Brak
(After: Iraq 9, Pl. LX)

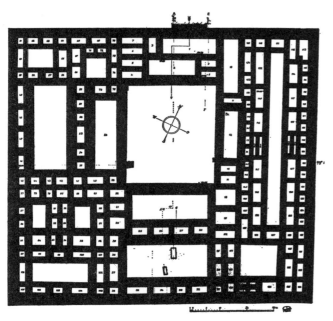

Fig. 37 'Old Palace' at Ashur (oldest layout)
(After: WVDOG 66, Pl. 3)

responded to a preconceived notion to which reality had to accommodate itself.

This palace at Ashur seems never to have been completed. However, the fact that the Akkadian rulers were active in Ashur is shown by the finding there of a spear-head with an inscription of Manish-tusu,[223] as well as of numerous fragments of basalt statues, of very great interest in the history of art (see below).

2 Art

Although it is true that the Akkadian Period only lasted for a century and a half, three to four generations of a powerful ruling race, it is nevertheless possible even now, in spite of an extremely scanty supply of works of art, not only to recognize a specifically Akkadian art, quite distinct from the earlier Sumerian, but to observe several phases of development within its short duration. This is no accident but in accordance with the spirit of the early Akkadians, who totally rejected the static, and for whom

all existence was a continuous state of change, a perpetual evolution. Unlike art in Sumer, the main problem of Akkadian art is not so much the conflict between transcendentalism and nature as the release of objects from their rigid state of being into the freedom of becoming and happening. The attitude to life of this expanding, empire-minded race of men expressed itself most happily in the representation of movement.

a The Sargon phase

On more than one occasion in the ancient Orient, the founding of a dynasty and the creation of a new state structure transformed the intellectual and political world around it and immediately a new form of art was born. This does not quite seem to have happened with the great Sargon of Akkad, judging by what we can tell from the Akkadian art in our possession. In any case the victory stele[224] (Pl. 125), containing the portrait of Sargon identified by inscription and of which only scanty fragments have been found in Susa, constitutes no absolute break with relief of the Ur I Period. It is the immediate sucessor to the Stele of the Vultures of Eannatum of Lagash, both in its subject-matter and general layout. Perhaps a fragment,[225] on which there is a scene of enemies imprisoned in a net (Pls. 126, 127), belongs to the Sargon stele; in which case its relationship to the Stele of the Vultures would be increased even more; yet, on the other hand, clear indications of a new development should not be overlooked. Sargon is shown standing, or on a throne, under a sunshade, as the Great King at the head of his soldiers. The warrior striking the prisoners in the net is no god but Sargon himself, as the action takes place in front of an enthroned divinity whom we can recognize as the warlike Ishtar because of the shoulder symbols, the barely-preserved maces. The tufts on the clothes of the warriors, of Sargon himself and of the goddess look like darting flames and their contours are moulded plastically. They show none of the interior line-drawing which the Sumerians of the Ur I period used, but are more like the tufts on the dress of Ebih-il (cf. Pl. 66). These details suffice to indicate the changed standing of King Sargon in the structure of the state, as well as the rejection by the Akkadian sculptor of rigid, lifeless forms. A statue from Lagash, now in the Istanbul Museum,[226] is the counterpart to the enthroned goddess. On the other hand the seated figure of a goddess[227] (Pl. 128), which has an Akkadian and an Elamite inscription provided by Puzur-In-Shushinak, has post-Akkadian tufts resembling Sumerian ones and it may have been made in a later period, the Third Dynasty of Ur.

Two male statues from Mari may still belong to the early Akkadian and therefore to the Sargon phase. The stylization of the tufted garments with collars on these statues is carried further than in Sargon's time and approaches the style of the typically Akkadian so-called ruched or flounced dress.[228] Both figures represent a worshipper with a sacrificial lamb in his arms, a figure we recognize in scenes illustrated on many Akkadian cylinder seals and in a statuette from Susa[229] (Pl. 129), which unfortunately has been badly damaged. The garment of this statuette very much resembles the Sumerian dress in style, yet its head is unmistakably Akkadian, with the emphasis on the long skull and noble profile, with a delicately aquiline nose.

b   The Enheduanna – Manishtusu phase

In order to piece together the pattern of art during the second generation of the Akkadian dynasty, the generation of Sargon's daughter, the divine bride Enheduanna at Ur, and Sargon's two sons, Rimush and Manishtusu, we have only a few fragments which are inscribed and some statues in the round and reliefs related to them by their style.

The limestone relief of Enheduanna[230] has a votive inscription on one side and a libation scene on the other; although it is in pieces it enables us nevertheless to form an idea of the technique of relief, the pictorial composition and the dress of this period. Enheduanna's dress is a flounced garment of several layers of ruches which are cut off horizontally, while the tufts on the layers are vertical and wavy, like those on the dress of the man from Mari who was carrying a lamb (see above), and they are of equal

length throughout. On her head she has the thick padded turban which we have met before, as early as the Ur I Period, in the votive tablet from Ur (Pl. 116). Enheduanna's two attendants have been made a little shorter than her. Thus strict isocephaly has not been observed, and the individual figures have been arranged freely, in loose formation across the pictorial surface (Pl. 130).

There are three heads from statuettes of women which we should like to include in this section on the grounds of their external appearance as well as the expression of their inner nature. All three show a refinement of sculptural technique, an animation and a certain charm of expression which is quite unlike the numerous older Sumerian female heads, such as those from Eshnunna (see above). Taking just the external features into consideration the alabaster head,[231] with its heavy padded diadem on the wavy hair, comes closest to the portrait of Enheduanna in the relief. This alabaster head was found unstratified in Ur (Pl. 131). The little diorite head[232] (Pl. 133), which was found in the house of the divine bride at Ur, in the *Gigparku*, has a sharper, more austere appearance. In spite of its miniature dimensions, it radiates an inner majesty which, together with its completely un-Sumerian physiognomy, suggests it had an Akkadian origin. The third little female head, which W. Andrae had already assumed to be Akkadian, came from the ashes at the Ishtar Temple, Level G, at Ashur[233] (Pl. 132). The hair on this head was probably drawn up into a chignon, as it was on the last head, and bound with a broad – though flat – diadem, but it is covered with a cap. It probably does not, therefore, represent a *nin-dingir* but is more likely to be a high priestess of Ishtar. In any case both in style and quality it is the equal of the two heads from Ur which have just been described.

The same phase of the development of Akkadian art which produced the relief of Sargon's daughter on the disk from Ur (Pl. 130) also produced three more stelae bearing reliefs, which were discovered in Lagash, Susa and Southern Iraq. The fragment of the stele[234] from Lagash (Telloh), which is rounded at the top and has reliefs on both sides, still has the horizontal division into friezes, an arrangement constantly used in all earlier Sumerian relief (Pls. 134,

135). The battle scenes, however, which are the only subject on this stele, differ from those on the Stele of the Vultures inasmuch as they show individual fights, never a general battle. Here again the figures, like those on the disk of Enheduanna, are of varying heights and are set far apart on their background. The dress of the warriors, however – long slit skirts of finely pleated material or a kilt with a length of material draped crosswise over the breast, coming down to the kilt – their weapons and their manner of fighting are all new since the Sumerian age. But what really distinguishes this stele from the Stele of the Vultures is the variety and freedom of the movement of the bodies. Unfortunately no king is named in the inscription, but it has always been considered that this stele must, on stylistic grounds, be older than Naram-Sin's victory stele (see p. 51 below), and yet on the other hand it is clearly later than the Sargon stele from Susa (see p. 47). It must therefore belong to the second Akkadian generation, that of Enheduanna and Manishtusu.

Two fragments of a stele, recently acquired by the Baghdad Museum[235] (Pls. 136, 137), belong to the same level of development. One only has to compare the kilt and its crossed shoulder sashes. In this stele every detail of the naked bodies of the prisoners is carved with particular care.[236] This may have been easy to achieve when carving the soft alabaster of this stele, but then so much the more must one admire the skilful carving on the very hard diorite of another fragment,[237] which also depicts battle scenes (Pl. 138): this came from Susa and has been in the possession of the Louvre for a long time. It is a masterpiece of relief and in it the sculptor has combined the most exact observation of nature with a pronounced feeling for harmony, and has also succeeded in conveying an inner tension.[238]

The second son of Sargon, Manishtusu, seems to have had a considerable number of life-size diorite statues, both of standing and seated figures, erected in different cities of his kingdom.[239] In Susa fragments of statues were found bearing his legends, and a later Elamite king, Shutruk-Nahhunte, had subsequently had inscriptions carved on them in order that they might be re-erected as victory memorials. From these inscriptions it can be assumed that he had

removed the statues from Akkad and Eshnunna. On the other hand, in view of their style, we can safely assign a large number of the fragments of diorite statues from Ashur to Manishtusu's reign. They confirm what is becoming steadily more evident – that the Akkadian ruler was increasingly active in Ashur (cf. p. 46 for what we said about the Old Palace at Ashur). Manishtusu's interest in the city of Ashur is also shown by the existence of a spear-head[240] dedicated by one of his officials, which was found in the Ishtar Temple. The torso of a life-size statue of Manishtusu from Susa[241] (Pl. 141) reveals more than most works of art the complete change of spirit from the Sumerian to the Akkadian world. Unfortunately the upper part of the body and the head are missing. For the first time in the history of the Near East we are no longer considering a statuette but a large statue of a standing figure. The dress no longer consists of the tufted material usual in the Ur I period, but of a closely woven woollen material with a short fringed border along the selvedge of the weft and fringed tassels on the side of the warp threads. However, it followed the previous fashion in that it is thrown over the left shoulder like a rectangular drape, and then wound round the lower part of the body several times and finally the upper edge is rolled into a pad round the waist and tucked in at the back.[242] Whereas the Sumerian tufted dress turned the human figure into a lifeless block, here the draped material falls into long, diagonal folds, rippling like water over which a wind is blowing. The play of light and shade on these folds transforms the dead mass of the stone into a scene of the most vivid movement, such as had never been achieved by Sumerian sculptors, nor had they even attempted it.

The second statue of Manishtusu[243] (Pls. 139, 140), also life-size and made of diorite, came from Ashur, where it was found unstratified. W. Andrae would like to attribute it, like the Old Palace at Ashur, to the great opponent of Hammurabi, Shamshi-Adad I. But we consider this is not justifiable because of the dress itself, which is alien to the Old Babylonian epoch, and because of the style in general. This work is also a torso, but it lacks only the head, hands and feet. The material of the dress seems to be a very light one, because where there is just a single layer of it over the left arm, the shoulder and the back, the limbs of the body look as if they were showing through. The girdle is also less padded than that of the last statue. However, the arrangement of the clothes is just the same as on the standing figure from Susa. The waves of the folds show only slightly, but in principle they are the same as on the standing statue, and as on another statue from Susa,[244] of which only the lower part has survived. This shows the feet inside a small niche, and stands on a round base decorated with relief (Pl. 142). The statue from Ashur is of interest because it shows how muscles were treated. All Sumerian sculpture in the round seems diagrammatic in comparison, even though the shoulder blades of this statue are carved in a more schematic manner, like small round shields. There were several statues of this kind at Ashur, as is shown by another torso of an upper part of a body, which has been assembled from countless fragments of stone found at the same place[245] (Pl. 143). This fragment, on which the arm and chest muscles have been even more successfully rendered, is very close in style to the statue from Ashur which has just been described. The dress with the wide girdle, the position of the arms and the necklace of large pearls are the same on both works. In the storerooms of the Louvre there are also fragments of a vast seated statue of Manishtusu which Shutruk-Nahhunte had taken from Eshnunna to Susa, and of a standing figure with his dress leaving the knee free, and of a carefully carved throne[246] (Pls. 144, 147–149). They are proof that the sculpture of Manishtusu, made in a uniform style, had spread over the whole country. The stylization of the fringed tassles appearing on one fragment from Eshnunna[247] so resembles that on the torso from Akkad that one can only believe both statues must have actually come from one and the same workshop.

Akkadian sculpture in the round seems to have achieved dynamic plasticity most successfully in the form of a seated figure[248] made out of a kind of bituminous stone. This was discovered in Susa and has been exhibited for many years in the Louvre, where it has astonished the connoisseurs of ancient Oriental sculpture (Pls. 145, 146). The effective way in which the muscles have been emphasized in this seated fig-

ure, with its inner and external mobility, seems to anticipate Greek characteristics. The sinews and the muscles on the chest and back have a parallel, however, in the torso from Ashur (Pl. 143). The rear view, on the other hand, has its counterpart in the figure of a man fallen to the ground shown in the upper register of the relief on a fragment of a stele from Susa (Pl. 138), and this can therefore itself be dated from the Manishtusu period. In spite of the incompleteness of the material available to us, sculpture in the round from the period of Manishtusu reveals the structure of the human body beneath the skin and dress – for the first time in history and in contrast to Sumerian art. The skin and dress no longer hide the body's structure but merge into it, and in so doing display its inner strength.

c   The Naram-Sin – Shar-kali-sharri phase

It has only been possible to identify a few pieces of sculpture in the round from the period of the third Akkadian generation, the period of Naram-Sin, the son of Manishtusu. The attribution is certain in the case of a fragment of a statue base[249] inscribed with the name of Naram-Sin, though only the two beautifully carved feet of this have been preserved (Pl. 152). The technique of the sculpture is outstanding. With a much less well preserved surface, but of more interest in the history of art, a fragment of the upper part of the body from a diorite statue bears the votive inscription of a scribe, Sharrishdagal, who had dedicated the statue of the divine Naram-Sin to a goddess, NIN.NE.UNU. Naram-Sin appears here in a garment which until now has generally been described as neo-Sumerian, but which seems in fact to have existed in the Late Akkadian Period[250] (Pls. 150, 151). A rectangular cloth covers the chest and the entire left arm, of which only the hand remains free. The cloth is not fastened on the left hip but under the right shoulder, where the folds are clearly modelled. Even more clearly than on the Manishtusu statue from Ashur (Pls. 139, 140) the shape of the body of this statue of Naram-Sin is visible through the material, so that the breast has an almost feminine appearance. We find this, however, also in the reliefs of Naram-Sin. It is greatly to be regretted that the head of the statue is missing. How the physiognomy of Naram-Sin would have been portrayed in sculpture we can only learn by looking at reliefs.

On a fragment of a relief which reached the Istanbul Museum[251] from the district of Diarbekr (Pl. 153), Naram-Sin is shown in the long flounced garment, like that already seen on Enheduanna. The fine pleats of the flounces have only been sketched as wavy lines: the material, however, is so thin and clinging that here again the curve of the breasts can be noticed through it. The softly moulded right arm could also be mistaken for a woman's were it not for the beard and the inscription. There are heavy bracelets on both arms. The king is holding in each hand the shaft of a weapon or of a sceptre, both unfortunately broken in half. The face has been very damaged, but it still displays a striking resemblance, in all the details of its features, and in the complicated style of the hair and beard, to one of the most important of all Akkadian works of art, the life-size bronze head of a king[252] (Pl. 154), discovered in Nineveh. This head is the only witness, but a sublime one, of a highly developed Akkadian metal sculpture which had completely mastered the high art of toreutics, from hollow casting to the finest chasing. Even though it is not a portrait in our meaning of the word, it enables us to gaze at the face of a prince from the great and heroic ruling house of Sargon, which had transformed Sumerian culture in accordance with its own genius. We cannot identify with absolute certainty which member of the family it represents, but the bronze head is comparable, feature by feature, with the portrait of Naram-Sin on the relief in Istanbul, if one overlooks the cone-shaped cap in the latter. In both, the hair-style round the forehead is composed of three elements, one above the other: a band of flat segments of a circle, a flat diadem and, above that, a plait of hair wound round the head and tapering towards the front. On the neck, in contrast, the heavy chignon is patterned like a woven mat. In both works the long pointed beard is divided into three parts and stylized like that on the diorite head from Telloh (Fig. 38):[253] flat little curls round the upper and lower lips, side whiskers consisting of

Fig. 38 Diorite head from Telloh
(After: DC, Pl. 21, 1)

three rows of curled ringlets and the actual point of the beard itself, made up of long wavy strands arranged together symmetrically.

The most mature Akkadian work of art, and the one which also expresses the Akkadian spirit the most completely, is the Stele of Naram-Sin[254] (Pls. 155, 156), with which he celebrated his victory over the Iranian border tribe of the Lullubi, and to which Shutruk-Nahhunte later added a long second inscription, after he had taken it as booty to Susa. This memorial, in spite of its ruined condition, still holds a special position among the works of art of ancient Near Eastern relief. It consists of a slab of red limestone, tapering towards the top, about 2 m. high and 1 m. across at its widest point, with only one side cut in relief. The stele was erected by Naram-Sin in Sippar, the city of Shamash. Great stars, which have eight points and beams of rays, fill the top peak of the pictorial surface and probably symbolize the heavenly divinities. Whether these stars were connected with Shamash cannot be stated with certainty. It is clear from the inscriptions that the scene is intended to celebrate the victory of Naram-Sin over the mountain people, the Lullubi. This is carried out in an arrangement which has nothing in common with that of a similar theme presented by Eannatum on the Stele of the Vultures (Pls. 119, 120), and it also differs from the compositional division of a battle sequence into many individual fights, following each other, such as those we saw on an earlier Akkadian stele (Pls. 134, 135). That still had horizontal friezes arranged in separate registers, like the narrative scenes introduced earlier by Sumerian relief. The overriding principle of all Akkadian art – that of movement – now, with Naram-Sin's stele, spreads from the representation of the individual figures into the actual main composition itself: in the storming upward movement of the victors, in the retreat of the enemy, this movement carries all the figures irresistibly along with it, and the landscape itself, for the first time pictured in the real sense, becomes part of this dynamic composition. The four lines one above the other representing the ground rise like waves, diagonally from the bottom left of the picture up to the right at the top; on the right there are trees and the whole scene is crowned by a conical mountain-peak. At the top of the pass Naram-Sin, the divine hero in the horned helmet, armed with bow, axe and arrow, and surpassing by far his warriors in height, can be seen stamping on the fallen enemy. His figure is made the centre of interest, it forms the focal point of the whole composition, through which everything else – the ascent and the retreat – gain their meaning and purpose. In its violence the powerful, dramatic movement threatens to burst out of the framework of the little sandstone slab. In this relief for the first time the inner grandeur of the Akkadian attitude to life – storming heaven itself – manages to express itself effectively in monumental form. It was this scene which a later prince, probably a king of Sumer and Akkad – perhaps Shulgi – had carved upon a wall of rock at the gateway to Asia, to commemorate for all time his victory over the Lullubi[255] (Pl. 157).

The development of this great period of Akkadian art, divided here into the three generations, is borne out by the *glyptic* during the same period, in the very numerous Akkadian cylinder and stamp seals still surviving. Now that these have been collected, arranged and presented systematically,[256] one can appreciate that engraving during this important period of art followed the same course in style as that taken by contemporary major art.

It is quite true that no single one of the many Akkadian cylinder seals can be linked by inscription to the founder of the dynasty, Sargon the Great, yet we know of good examples of Akkadian glyptic from the period of his daughter, Enheduanna, of his son, Manishtusu, his grandson, Naram-Sin and his great-grandson as well, Shar-kali-sharri: indeed, we have even recently discovered a seal impression bearing the name of a servant of the last Akkadian king, Shudurul.[257]

The development of the very first phase of Akkadian glyptic, belonging to the beginning of Sargon's reign must lie between the very last stage of glyptic in the Ur I Period – i. e. the phase which produced the impressions of Lugalanda and Urukagina of Lagash – on the one side and the period of Enheduanna or Manishtusu on the other. But as both these periods are known to us, we feel justified in connecting with Sargon of Akkad a group of seals, which because of their style and iconography come between the two periods just mentioned.[258] The cylinder seal of Adda, the steward of Enheduanna,[259] has on it a frieze of figures which is still completely in the Sumerian tradition. Only the plastic quality of its modelling and its more relaxed composition, together with certain details of costume, distinguish it from the seals of the Ur I period. On the other hand, another official of Enheduanna, Kukudug (?),[260] has a seal of a type which is already truly Akkadian. On an impression from his seal, found at Ur, we meet very early on the typically Akkadian breed of cattle, the arna buffalo with its great curved horns.

It must have been during Enheduanna's lifetime – that is, during the first generation after Sargon – that the first great transformation in style in Akkadian glyptic took place. It was this change which we saw in Enheduanna's disk, if we compared it with the Victory Stele of Sargon: under Manishtusu, Enheduanna's brother, sculpture in the round showed that a similar step forward was taken by major art during the same period.

The development of glyptic during Manishtusu's reign, which cannot have been very remote in time from his sister Enheduanna, is at present harder to recognize than the development of the sculpture of statues during his reign.

An *ensi* of Susa, who held office during the period of Manishtusu, Ishpum (= TIS. SUB), is named in the legend of a seal impression from Susa. It belongs to a group of cylinder seals which R. M. Boehmer (op. cit., Pl. XXVIII) has combined together under the heading 'Akkadian II'.

On this a row of gods, fighting each other in pairs, resemble somewhat the warriors on the probably contemporary limestone stele from Lagash (see p. 49; Pls. 134, 135). The motif of the fight, particularly the seizing of an enemy by the beard with the left hand in order to hit him with a mace held in the right hand, is employed continuously on the cylinder seals of the phase Akkadian II[261] and on the stele from Lagash. The latter must accordingly belong to the second Akkadian generation.

How far the style used in glyptic under the third generation of the Akkadian dynasty – in the reigns of Naram-Sin and Shar-kali-sharri – had travelled from that of the early Akkadian phase can be seen from a series of cylinder seals, the legends of which contain the names of these kings,[262] as well as from the impressions from Telloh with the name of a Lugal-ushumgal, governor in Lagash under Naram-Sin and Shar-kali-sharri[263] (Pl. M 4).

Akkadian glyptic employed simultaneously two principles of composition, one being a free, disengaged arrangement, and the other a connected one. The appearance of a highly developed seal of this period in connected composition is displayed in a classic manner by the seal of Ibn-Sharrum, a scribe of Shar-kali-sharri, from the de Clercq collection (No. 46)[264] (Pl. F 1). Above a broad band symbolizing a river between mountains, two mighty arna buffaloes stand with raised heads, their backs to each other and in mirror-like symmetry. Each is about to drink from a vessel gushing water, held towards each of them by a kneeling, naked hero (with his head *en face*). The space between the horns of the animals is filled in with an inscription in eight compartments. The whole impression presents a complete, ornamental design, in a connected style, and yet free of the rigid compression into a fixed space of the Sumerian

epoch, and forming a classic union of picture and writing. How far Akkadian glyptic has risen in this impression above the rigid compression of the 'figured band'! And the Akkadian seal-cutter happily sought out new variations in this connected style[265] (Pls. F 2–3).

Yet during this same period there were other cylinder seals where, as on the great Victory Stele of Naram-Sin, they managed to arrange the figures across the pictorial surface in such a way that a real effect of space was obtained. Belonging to this group is the scene of a ceremony which, according to the attached inscription, represents a priest in front of an enthroned woman, Tudeshshar-libish, the king's favourite. This scene, on a seal impression from Telloh,[266] takes place in the open air, which is indicated by a conifer placed by itself on the pictorial scene (Pl. M 4). It is possible to fix a date to this impression because it contained the name of Lugal-Ushumgal and a notice from the period of Shar-kali-sharri. The persons represented, identified by the accompanying inscriptions, are the 'Beloved of the King', a magician-priest Dada and a female servant. Tudeshshar-libish, in the shape of her body and in her bearing, reminds one in every detail of the statuette dedicated by the scribe Sharrishdagal for Naram-Sin (cf. p. 51; Pls. 150 and 151). Is this the figure of a woman after all, or of Naram-Sin himself? The composition of these little scenes in glyptic seldom suggests movement in the same way as does the Victory Stele of Naram-Sin now in Paris (Pls. 155, 156), even when they have freed themselves completely from spatial compression.

A few hunting scenes from the Late Akkadian Period have the lines of the ground shown as long waves, similar to those on the Naram-Sin stele, and allow men and animals to storm across the pictorial surface[267] (Pl. F 7).

However, the most important contribution of glyptic to our knowledge of Akkadian art is not in its form but its subject-matter. Only occasionally, up to the end of the Ur I Period, had the seal-cutter included in his repertoire of pictures the great gods of the pantheon, and if they were included, it was only in an offering or libation ceremony in front of a divinity. But in the Akkadian Period we see everywhere engraved scenes taken from the mythical world of the great gods, whose deeds and misfortunes were probably being recorded in epic songs at that time. It is true that we have not actually got any such epic song from the Akkadian Period, and know only of versions made in later periods, by which time they were probably already greatly altered and in canonized form. So it is not surprising that it is only with great difficulty that we can identify some of the scenes from Akkadian cylinder seals with episodes of the later epic renderings of the myth: the one which seems the most certain is probably the flight of Etana to heaven[268] (Pl. F 6). The most famous of all epic poems, however, and the most widespread in the Ancient Orient, the Gilgamesh epic, did not feature at all amongst them. Yet the basic theme of the Gilgamesh epic,[269] the fruitless struggle of a hero to obtain eternal life, had probably become the principal subject of all Akkadian epic poems. They were either concerned, like the epic poem of the creation of the world, with the shaping of the world by a younger generation of gods battling against the older generation and against the original Chaos, or – like the poem of the deception of Ea, the god of Eridu, by Innin, the goddess of Uruk – were later aetiologies of historical events, in this instance the transference of leadership from Eridu to Uruk.[270] The epic poem is pessimistic as regards man and his hope of eternal life. If man in Sumerian times, like the whole of creation and existence, was part of the cycle of death and life, then the official Akkadian attitude was that the great gods, when ordering the world, had retained life for themselves and apportioned it to man each according to his respect for the gods. Only heroes could strive for more, but they too finally all fail, like Adapa, Gilgamesh and Etana. That this thematic cycle was taken up by the seal-cutter must surely be because of the importance of its content rather than for the stylistic possibilities of the individual motifs on a small cylinder seal.[271] A question which forces itself into the forefront is whether large-scale relief in the Akkadian Period also adopted this epic material, and whether glyptic was thus only an imitation of the major art, a question which cannot at the present time be answered owing to a paucity of examples of relief. One could easily imagine some of the compositions of myths and epics now preserved for us on cylinder seals presented in the form of large reliefs. On a cylinder seal[272] made of lapis lazuli, scarcely 3 cm. high, which was dug up in Kish (Pl. F 4), there is a scene showing the victorious fight of three gods against five others, and this is carved with so much freedom and vitality, and with such an inner splendour in its conception, that the theme would seem to be more suitable for rendering in monumental dimensions. Equally the greeting of the sun-god in the moment of his ascent of the Mountain of the Underworld by his sister, the winged heavenly Ishtar, by the god of the life-giving waters, Ea and by the latter's Janus-faced visir Usumia on the one side, and by Ninurta as an archer, the conqueror of the bird Zu, on the other – all this one would have liked to have seen as a wall-painting on a grand scale rather than as a scene on a cylinder seal, such as exists in fact in the British Museum[273] (Pl. F 5). A lion, the symbol of death and the underworld, is attached to Ninurta, the hero among the gods, who vanquishes the evil bird and delivers him up to the god Ea once more, while on the other hand a bull, a symbol of life since the Protohistorical Period, is attached to Ea. Near Ishtar the plant of life is growing from the Mountain of the Underworld. It is unlikely that this epic-mythological theme would have been confined to the minor art of glyptic during the Akkadian Period. If we possessed only some of their monumental works, Akkadian art would be seen to have surpassed even more clearly than is the case now, both in style and content, all art which had preceded or followed it in the Near East.

E THE SUMERO-AKKADIAN REVIVAL
(Ur-Baba of Lagash to Sumu-abum of Babylon)

As the strength of the Sargonid Dynasty and its army became exhausted, the wild tribes of the Guti, who had threatened the empire ever since the reign of Shar-kali-sharri, poured down from the Iranian mountains towards Akkad, laying waste cities and temples and seizing power for themselves. Only the southern part of the country remained largely unscathed, and it was there that, after the collapse of the Akkadian empire, the Sumerian revival began, closely linked to the Sumer of the pre-Akkadian period, while in the north of the country the Gutian kings continued to try and build a form of empire. The renaissance of old Sumerian concepts and forms in religion, politics and state administration was probably most genuine – in the period before the victory over the Guti and their expulsion by Utu-hegal of Uruk – in the city of Ningirsu (Telloh) under the *ensis* Ur-Baba and Gudea. It reached its culmination however, under the kings Ur-Nammu, Shulgi, Amar-Sin and Shu-Sin of the Third Dynasty of Ur,[274] though it cannot be denied that the old Akkadian elements more and more became part of the neo-Sumerian culture, and because of this it would be better if we described the works of art from this period of the state of *Sumer* and *Akkad* as belonging to a 'Sumero-Akkadian' revival. It was to continue until the arrival of a new wave of Semitic nomads, the Canaanites, penetrated the population of the country to such an extent that in many cities foreign princes, Elamites or Canaanites, were able to seize power. The two new dynasties in Isin and in Larsa, both Canaanite in origin, who to begin with shared control of the country, at first carried on with the outward forms of the Sumero-Akkadian civilization. It was not until the foundation of the Kingdom of Babylon by the Canaanite Sumu-abum that we can speak of a distinctive Old Babylonian culture, and therefore of an Old Babylonian art.

1 The Guti and Art

It is not possible to identify the Guti themselves by archaeology. W. Andrae has conjectured that there was some building at Level F of the Ishtar Temple at Ashur[275] which can be attributed to the Guti, as it alone had foundations of quarried stones. But since then other stone foundations have been discovered

elsewhere, which clearly did not originate with the Guti. In this connection one only has to think of the great stone architecture at Tell Chuera in North Mesopotamia, which was begun in the ancient Sumerian period and which may possibly be connected with the Hurri of the third millennium but not with the Guti.[276] Seals have been found at Eshnunna, which H. Frankfort would like to attribute to the Guti.[277] Their subject-matter is Akkadian and their appearance so indeterminate that we cannot glean any positive indication about style from them.

It is not possible to decide whether the Guti were powerful and numerous enough to have affected the Sumero-Akkadian population biologically, and perhaps even intellectually. The physiognomy of the new type of man, who was different from all his Old Sumerian and Akkadian predecessors, and who dominated pictorial art under Gudea (see p. 62) may – as far as one can tell – possibly be connected with the Guti. But this cannot be proved. The fragment of a statuette, inscribed with the name of one Laasgan, the son of Asmatien, would seem to represent a Gutian if, as Landsberger thinks, these names are Gutian. The costume indeed shows a certain peculiarity, but the face has unfortunately not survived. The fragment was excavated at the palace in Mari.[278]

2 Architecture during the Sumero-Akkadian revival

The magnitude of the building activity during the Sumero-Akkadian revival, both in the number and size of the buildings, is almost too much to comprehend. In all cities of any consequence, in Eridu, Lagash, Uruk, Ur, Nippur, in the cities of the Diyala region, in Ashur, Mari and North Mesopotamia, there arose not only individual temples but extensive and complex sacred precincts, the unifying purpose and historical development of which can only be more or less understood if, by examining the most important buildings of the period systematically, we attempt to understand the characteristic features and outward style of these buildings as an expression of their inner meaning. In doing so one can proceed from the simple to the complicated, from the lower to the higher, from building material to the planning of buildings and their artistic design.

a Temple building

The basic element of building was still the mud-brick, which was only baked into a hard brick when needed as a protective casing or for drainage. The shape of the brick resembled that of the Akkadian Period and varied from a square to a half square. Its dimensions, however, are in general smaller: its length scarcely exceeded 40 cm. In contrast to the stamped inscriptions of the Akkadian Period, the bricks at this time were once more inscribed by hand, as, for instance, the bricks found at Telloh for Ur-Baba, Nammahni and Gudea. In his inscriptions the latter relates how the measurement of the bricks for the Temple of Ningirsu was dictated to him in a dream by a divinity. Thus the basic element of building had in itself a cult-magic significance. The *foundation figures* were also related to magic: these were the successors to the so-called 'peg figures' known to have been used in Sumerian architecture from the Mesilim Period onwards, though they now slowly changed their shape, in spite of the unchanging nature of the fundamental belief on which they were based – that of the banning of evil by the peg.

Under Ur-Baba and Gudea there appeared the first foundation figures in bronze, in the shape of a kneeling, long-bearded god with a great crown of four horns, who is driving the nail-shaped peg into the ground with both hands[279] (Pl. 160). An example of this figure can be seen on the relief of a governor of Susa, Puzur-In-Shushinak by name, at the end of the Akkadian Period[280] (Pl. 158). From the reign of Ur-Nammu onwards the kneeling god was replaced by a man (or a woman) carrying a builders' basket on his head, and even by Ur-Nammu's period the nail has been omitted[281] (Pl. 159).

The two fundamental achievements of architecture during this period are, firstly, the true 'ziggurat', the artificial high podium for the temple of the city god

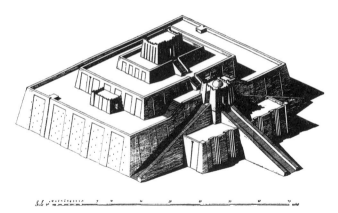

Fig. 39   Reconstruction of the Ziggurat of Ur-Nammu at Ur (After: UE 5, Pl. 72)

which, with an almost square ground-plan and a height of 20 to 30 m., may have sloping or graduated exterior walls, and secondly, the type of temple building erected on level ground with a *broad cella* – at least, we have no evidence of this from earlier periods.

The best preserved ziggurat from the Land of the Two Rivers is that of the moon-god Nanna at Ur[282] (Pl. 161). It owes its good state of preservation to the thick casing of baked bricks with which Ur-Nammu had had the core of the building covered[283] (Figs. 39, 40). The four corners were orientated to the four points of the compass, and the casing is arranged in niches and flat buttresses. The central stairway, lying at right angles to the north-east side, probably led straight up to the highest platform, on which the actual High Temple was built. The side stairways join the main stairway on the terrace of the first stage, and then lead off separately onto the second stage of the tower.

The temple tower of Innin at Uruk[284] (Pl. 162), built like that of Ur-Nammu at Ur on top of older terraces, was simpler than that at Ur (Fig. 41). Yet here the casing was not made of baked bricks but of stamped, sun-dried bricks. The outside walls were not stepped back but were provided with flat buttresses. The construction of the brickwork is even now easy to see: between the layers of sun-dried bricks there are, at regular intervals, layers of rush matting to ensure an even structure. In the high levels the mats are replaced by reed straw. In addition, interspersed right through the core, there are horizontal channels in which there are reed ropes as thick as a man's arm. These probably served to anchor the outside walls against the pressure of the weight of bricks from inside.

The ziggurat at Warka covers a square surface with sides of about 56 m. The height of the core must have been about 14 m. This was crowned by the actual High Temple, of which Loftus in the middle of the nineteenth century could still see traces.

Even today it is difficult to decide whether the artificially built ziggurat of the neo-Sumerian period is also the expression of a new religious cult concept or whether the ziggurat in the form it is known to us since the reign of Ur-Nammu is merely a formal sublimation and canonization of what had earlier arisen naturally – in the course of the renewal of a temple over the centuries, as with the Anu ziggurat at Uruk or the earlier Sumerian temples at Eridu – namely, the raising of the main shrine on a high podium. As Ur-Nammu built his ziggurats at Ur,

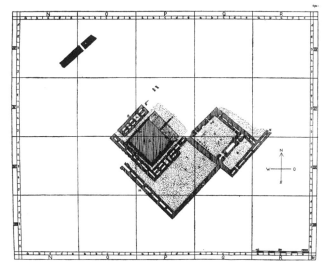

Fig. 41 Plan of the Innin Ziggurat at Uruk (Warka)
(After: H. J. Lenzen, *Die Entwicklung der Zikkurat*, Pl. 9)

Uruk, Eridu and other cities on the same site where earlier the high terrace for the main temple lay, it is reasonable to assume a religious tradition rather than a break in the development of the religion. If, however, such a tradition did exist, then we may also link the form of the ground-plan and the layout of the interior of the early Sumerian High Temple (the 'White Temple', and the temples at Eridu and Tell 'Uqair, see Figs. 4, 5, 6: pp. 5–6) with the report made by Herodotus about the temple on the ziggurat in Babylon at a later, post-Babylonian period, in order that we may evaluate the significance of a ziggurat. All the ruins mentioned have a cult building with an inner room in which there was a sort of stage or platform built near one of the shorter walls, of a size well suited to serve as a resting place. In addition, in the middle of the room, there was always a form of table for sacrifices, built of brick. According to Herodotus 1, 181 the temple on the ziggurat contained, as its main cult requisites, a couch and a table, and this would correspond very well with the platform and the sacrificial table. Herodotus reported that the Sacred Marriage between Marduk and his chosen bride took place in the temple. In accordance with this we may identify the temple on the ziggurat, or at least a part of it, with the so-called *gigunu*, which is often referred to in

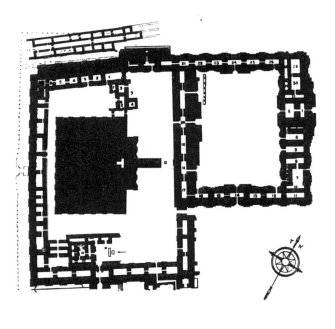

Fig. 40 Plan of the Ziggurat of Ur-Nammu at Ur
(After: UE 5, Pl. 72)

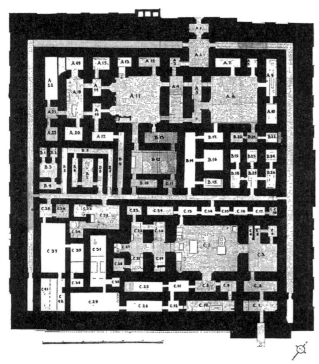

Fig. 42   Plan of the Ningal Temple in the 'Gigparku' at Ur
(After: AJ 6, Pl. XLIV)

form of temple where door, forecourt, broad antecella and broad main cella, with a niche for the throne, are all arranged on one axis as a succession of rooms through which the supplicant is led by the hand of his mediator with a certain inevitability towards his goal, the enthroned, divine lord. Our best example of this neo-Sumerian method of building, of monumental size, is the so-called Ningal Temple in the *Gigparku,* the cloister of the royal spouse of the god in the main shrine of Nanna at Ur[286] (Fig. 42). The temple which King Amar-Sin had built for the god Enki in the harbour area, the south-eastern part of the city of Ur, is more moderate in size but essentially the same[287] (Fig. 43): the broad cella, and the ante-cella lying in front of it, equally broad, form a rectangular block, with its entrance through the centre of one of the long sides, on the central axis of

the cuneiform texts as the place at which it was customary to hold this marriage festival, and this again would explain why, on the bricks out of which a ziggurat was built at Choga Zambil near Susa by an Elamite king of the second millennium, a *kukunnum (= gigunu)*[285] is mentioned as part of the High Temple.

Ever since the Protohistorical Period two religious concepts had permeated and increasingly linked together the earthly cosmos of the Sumerian state and the heavenly powers; on the one hand the ritual of a Sacred Marriage between the goddess (or god) and the king (or priestess), and on the other the progressive anthropomorphism of the principal gods through their assimilation to the concept of the king as earthly Lord who might only be approached with the aid of an elaborate court ceremonial. If the ritual of the marriage between man and god finds its highest architectural expression in the ziggurat, towering towards heaven, equally the conception of god in human form as a world ruler graciously receiving his supplicants finds its expression in that particular

Fig. 43   Plan of the Enki Temple of Amar-Sin at Ur
(After: AJ 10, Pl. XXXVII a)

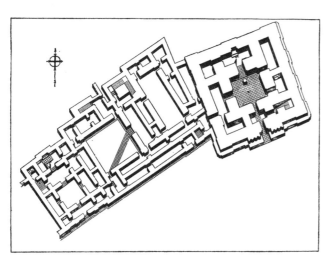

Fig. 44 Shu-Sin Temple of Ituria and complex of Ilushuilia at Tell Asmar
(After: OIP 43, Pl. I)

the whole complex. The entrance is flanked by towers on both sides. In this temple the niche for the image of the enthroned god probably lay in the inner rear wall of the cella, on the main axis of the whole building, but we can no longer identify it. A rectangular encircling wall, with side rooms built into it, surrounds the central complex. It forms a rectangular forecourt in front of the cella, and the forecourt is approached through an antechamber lying on the main axis. This emphasis on the axis is deliberate, and so is the sequence: gatehouse, forecourt, antecella and cella. Everything leads towards the niche containing the throne.

The representation of the supreme gods as human beings, a Sumerian concept, during this period of the neo-Sumerian-Akkadian revival, is met half-way by the ancient Akkadian concept of the deified king, and so it followed that the temples built for the kings of Sumer and Akkad – who were attempting to create a unified culture as the expression of a unified kingdom – could no longer be told apart from the temples built for the gods.

At Eshnunna a governor, Ituria, had a temple built[288] for his deified overlord, King Shu-Sin of Ur, with the same components – gateway building set in the encircling wall, forecourt, cella and niche – as the temples of Ningal or Enki at Ur (see above). Only the antecella is missing (Fig. 44).

b Palace building and the concept of kingship during the Sumero-Akkadian revival

In many cases the difference between god and king was becoming very slight: for instance, a prince, himself not deified, Ilushuilia, the son and successor of Ituria at Eshnunna during the reign of the weak suzerain, Ibbi-Sin of Ur, added a complex of buildings to the governor's palace at Eshnunna, situated to the west of the Shu-Sin temple,[289] which is an exact copy of the temple for Shu-Sin, and this was probably used for the audiences which Ilushuilia would have granted to supplicants led ceremoniously before him. Only the walls are thinner and the rooms rather smaller.

However, this palace of the governor of Eshnunna was primarily an administrative centre rather than the expression of the concept of kingship. Its residential and administrative quarters actually consist of a group of buildings round a courtyard situated to the east of the audience chamber group, with an imposing, elongated oblong hall, from which a door on the south-west side led into the court. Access from the street into the courtyard was in complete contrast to that obtaining in the audience chamber group built by Ilushuilia, inasmuch as the courtyard could only be reached by a circuitous route through a small entrance hall, and thence through long narrow corridor-rooms and a wash room.

The kings of the Third Dynasty of Ur, who were endeavouring to maintain the Sumero-Akkadian dual tradition in their kingdom of Sumer and Akkad, not only had royal temples in the tradition of the Sumerian broad cella temple, but, at the same time, seem to have continued to apply the Old Akkadian building concept of a world emperor's palace, at Ur itself; the large building at Ur to the south-east of the *Gigparku* which, in the inscriptions on the paving stones in its courtyard dating from Shulgi's reign, is identified as the palace of Ur-Nammu and Shulgi, called the *Ehursag*[290] (Fig. 45), in its general arrangement shows a resemblance – even though its excavated ground-plan may still be far from complete – to the two Akkadian palace buildings known to us already, those at Ashur and Tell Brak (see above, Figs. 36, 37).[291]

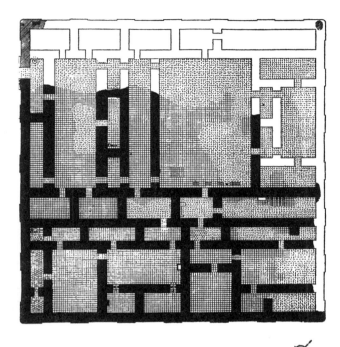

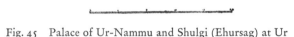

Fig. 45   Palace of Ur-Nammu and Shulgi (Ehursag) at Ur
(After: AJ, p. 382, Pl. LVII)

If one ignores the thickness of the walls the ground-plan of the *Ehursag* at Ur and Naram-Sin's palace at Tell Brak are actually in principle identical. Both cover an area which is surrounded by a perimeter wall, planned as an approximate square and consisting of a main courtyard group with several ancillary courtyard groups beside it. The interior can only be reached through a single gate, with an entrance hall within the encircling wall, and thence from court to court. Both palaces give the impression of being a state building rather than a royal residence. Ur-Nammu and Shulgi probably conducted the actual affairs of state in the *Ehursag,* because here there was less room for audiences and performances of a royal or cult nature.

c   Royal tomb building

We can understand how complicated the concept of monarchy had grown during the period of the neo-Sumerian-Akkadian revival if we examine one particular branch of architecture, royal tomb building. This had, for the first time in Sumero-Akkadian history, assumed monumental proportions, and, in contrast to Egypt, it never again in the Near East regained them: the archaeologist Woolley found the tombs of the Third Dynasty, from Ur-Nammu to Amar-Sin,[292] not far away from the *Ehursag,* to the south-east of the great Nanna shrine and almost exactly at the place where centuries earlier the pit graves of the First Dynasty of Ur had been made – with only slight architectural pretensions but nevertheless filled with the sensational funeral equipment of the royal retinue and its luxurious gifts. The tomb buildings of the Third Dynasty, which can be dated by the inscribed bricks of Shulgi and Amar-Sin, still give the impression, even today, of being important buildings, with their niched walls clean and sound, built of baked blocks set in bitumen, and the vaulted rooms of the tombs and the stairways (Pl. 163). But these are not ordinary graves, nor even ordinary royal graves, because above all they express a fundamental concept of Sumerian culture – almost certainly a very old one, namely the idea that the dead king (who in life had so often, as the personification of the royal shepherd Tammuz, participated in the ritual of the Sacred Marriage with the goddess Inanna) must after death again be freed from his grave, i.e. the Underworld, in order to receive, in a special house, the honours due to him and the sacrificial offerings.[293]

The reports made by Woolley on the tombs in all the three areas of the mausoleum (Fig. 46), on the main building as well as on the two annexes, which are in fact only smaller versions of the main group, have made it quite clear that these tomb buildings were made in several stages in accordance with the ritual of the funeral ceremony:

1 The laying-out of the underground vaulted tombs, and the steps leading to them.
2 The bricking up of the tomb doors after the burial and
3 The erection of a temporary superstructure so that the gifts for the dead could be put in front of the tomb doors, on the steps and in the gallery.

4 The building of the final superstructure in the form of a more or less richly decorated dwelling-house, with bases for statues and altars for libations and burnt sacrifices.

The particular nature of this superstructure is apparent from its very unusual ground-plan (Fig. 46). This has clearly nothing in common with the ground-plan of a broad cella type of temple, such as that built at Eshnunna by Ituria for the worship of Shu-Sin, the deified suzerain (see above, p. 59 and Fig. 44) but is far more like the ordinary Sumerian dwelling-house of the animal-pen type, in which the main feature is the inner courtyard containing the pen, with rooms round the courtyard which are, in contrast, of only secondary importance, built on to the inside of the protective wall. All the rooms open onto the courtyard and are connected by it. That this is no ordinary secular dwelling-house is clear, however, because of the width of the rectangular enclosing wall, built with flat buttresses and with its corners rounded, and also because of the towers on each side of the entrance which are decorated with stepped niches. A walled pedestal stands in one of the corners of the courtyard, and its presence is difficult to explain except as a pedestal for the image of the dead man, who would now, after his death, live in this sacred house. In the rooms situated over the actual tombs there were complicated libation arrangements built for the presentation of funerary gifts.

5 An opening to the tombs by means of a narrow slit in the wall above their doors
6 Filling of the tomb-shaft with clean, white earth and concealment of the entrance to the tomb steps.

Woolley's observations, on which this rough outline of the building sequence of the tombs is based, were repeated so often in the different parts of the whole layout that they can be accepted unreservedly: but in order to assess their true significance one must surely replace Woolley's acceptance of a robbery of the tombs during the carrying out of the building operation with the interpretation arising from a study of the findings, that there was an intentional opening of the tombs and removal of the dead man into the dwell-

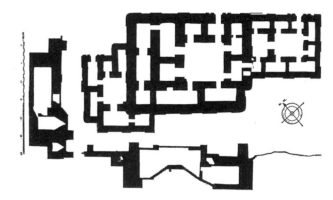

Fig. 46 Plan and cross-section of the Royal Tombs of the Third Dynasty of Ur (After: MJ 22, Pl. XXIX)

ing-house built over the tomb. It is only in this way that the layout of these buildings can be endowed with the deep meaning which is inherent in their very essence by reason of the Sumerian concept of kingship. It is at present difficult to identify among the buildings known to us structures comparable with the Royal Tombs of the Third Dynasty of Ur. The only analogy is provided by part of the famous palace at Mari, which was built, as we shall see later when we examine the wall-decoration, long before the period of Zimrilim, a contemporary of Hammurabi. The south-eastern buildings of the palace, which were situated at its highest point, form a group with Room 148 as its centre, and this is surrounded by Rooms 136–138 and 146, 147, 149 and 150, 209, 210 and 212, arranged in the form of a Babylonian courtyard house, similar to the courtyard house above the tombs of Shulgi and Amar-Sin.[294]

The main room, No. 210, which Parrot called a 'sanctuaire', that is, a temple, on the grounds that its entrance had towers with niches, is actually an inner room situated on the courtyard. Rooms 149 and 150 (named 'chapels' by the excavator), which have a valuable heavy wooden door dividing them, contain a podium built in two stages one above the other, and this can be recognized by the circular recess on its upper surface as the companion piece to the libation arrangements in the tombs of the Ur III period at Ur. The statuettes of Laasgan and Idi-ilu, of which fragments were found as foundation deposits, partly in particularly well-made boxes in

Room 149, may be remnants of the statuettes of these two rulers which may have stood on a pedestal before they were shattered and buried.

Though by this time the architecture of the Sumero-Akkadian revival had become formalized and eclectic in many respects, yet in the remnants of its mighty temples, palaces and tombs, excavated with so much care, it provides those who care to understand and study it with an imposing statement of the Sumero-Akkadian concept of god and king. Nowhere else have the sources of Sumerian and Old Akkadian culture mingled so well as in the architecture of the kingdom of Sumer and Akkad.

3   Art during the Sumero-Akkadian revival

a   *Sculpture in the round*

Large statues from the period after the Old Akkadian dynasty and before the founding of the Old Babylonian dynasty were amongst the earliest of the archaeological discoveries which led to the scientific reconstruction of Sumerian civilization. In the years following the end of the last century L. de Sarzec excavated numerous statues of Gudea at Telloh, which now fill a large room at the Louvre. Their discovery created a revolutionary source of information in the field of ancient Oriental art. These statues of the greatest *ensi* of Lagash,[295] some of which are life-size, some seated and some standing, today are seen as part of a centuries-long chain of development, and now that their long inscriptions have been read and translated, they have become monuments both in the history of religion as well as in the science of language. As works of art they do not achieve the intellectual quality of the Mesilim Period nor the human warmth of many works from the Ur I Period. Technically they are a continuation of the major sculpture from the Old Akkadian period, above all externally as far as material and dimensions are concerned. In no statue of Gudea, however, has diorite, that 'stone from the Land of Magan', been moved and animated by the same inner restlessness and

burning desire for action sometimes shown in the period of Manishtusu. One only has to glance at one of the figures of Gudea[296] (Pl. 165), to sense in this statue almost a rejection of the Akkadian spirit. These portraits, in spite of their continued use of the type of dress worn by Naram-Sin, are not the expression of an expanding world-empire but rather, as the personification of prayer, they strive for the state of rest inherent in the block of stone itself, and to express the static immobility which had earlier been the keynote of the little figures of worshippers produced during the First Dynasty of Ur. Probably this is also why Gudea particularly favoured diorite for his large statues, and he expressed this feeling in an inscription on Statue B (= 'Architecte au plan')[297] (Pl. 167): 'This statue has not been made from silver nor from lapis lazuli, nor from copper nor from lead, nor yet from bronze, it is made of diorite . . .' For Gudea diorite was not as it was for Manishtusu, a means of showing that even this hardest of materials could be employed to express movement, the concept dominating all art at that time: now it was a symbol, provided by nature, representing everything that was immutable, an example of the eternal in creation, a symbol in accord with the spirit of the Sumerians as early as the First Dynasty of Ur, and which the *ensi* of Lagash, following the collapse of the Akkadian empire, wished to adopt once again as their own attitude to life. This too explains the suppression of plasticity in these mighty figures, owing to their surfaces being covered in extensive cuneiform inscriptions,[298] and this was also the reason for the conspicuously plump massiveness of most of the Gudea figures, with their heavy-looking heads sitting practically neckless on their shoulders[299] (Pl. 170). In view of the undoubtedly high level of technical skill with which they are made, this tendency can scarcely be considered as only resulting from the difficulty in working a hard stone. The small figure of Gudea in Copenhagen,[300] which is dedicated to Geshtinanna, is made of steatite, a completely soft stone, yet it has just as four-square an appearance as most of the others.

The canons of sculpture in the round had in fact been evolved in all their essential features before the time of Gudea, during the period of his father-in-law, Ur-Baba, the real founder, of the true neo-Sumerian revival. A statue of Ur-Baba (Pl. 164) standing in a plain dress, reveals a compact, muscular man, his right shoulder free of his robes, both hands clasped in prayer before his chest, his back covered by a long inscription.[301] It is clearly based on sculpture from the Ur I Period, an art-form which was illustrated for us by the statues of Lupad from Lagash or Kurlil from Al 'Ubaid (see Pls. 106, 108). But the statue of Ur-Baba also anticipates all the sculpture of Gudea, although – because its head is missing – we cannot be quite sure about either the physiognomy or the head-covering and hair-style of the Ur-Baba statuette.

We should not overlook the anthropological character of the sculpture of Gudea's time, a feature differing from everything that we know of the Near East, shown by certain statues of bald-headed men,[302] which in view of their resemblance to heads of Gudea in relief, can only be ascribed to him (see below, p. 67). In particular, the so-called 'White Head' in Berlin (Pls. 168, 169), seen in profile, is not like the 'Near Eastern' type of man from Sumer nor the 'Oriental' Akkadian. Yet to read into this an influence of the Guti would merely be an assumption.

The statues of Gudea do not only have the name-cartouche of the man dedicating them, such as those on some of the older Sumero-Akkadian figures in the round: the extensive inscriptions with which most of their surface is covered list the achievements of the prince for the benefit of the gods, achievements for which he hopes to obtain from them a promise of life.[303] From these inscriptions we are able to discover the meaning of these statues: they are not just like-nesses, portraits intended to preserve the memory of a man for posterity, rather are they a magic substitute for the man who dedicated them, which then them-selves received a life of their own through the cere-mony of the 'mouth-opening', and have their own name and require their own sacrificial gifts, so that they may ceaselessly serve the god to whom they are dedicated.[304] They too represent the tendency which permeated all the Eastern world, towards the yearn-ing for life and for its preservation.

The long series of stone statues of Gudea, standing and seated, enable us – if we examine them all care-fully – to recognize variations of style in the individ-ual works. These variations cannot be explained as

due only to the existence of several different work-shops, but more probably arose from a gradual change in the intellectual atmosphere, in particular from a diminution of the purely Sumerian aspect of the revival and a stronger renewal of the old Akkadian ideas and forms. This is, therefore, a development which had started in Lagash itself as early as the period of Gudea and which then grew stronger in the realm of Sumer and Akkad under the kings of the Third Dynasty of Ur. In the cities of the Diyala region, in Mari and Ashur, the Akkadian tradition was from the start stronger than the Sumer-ian, and this was soon evident there in its influence on art.

Although to a modern observer the numerous statues of Gudea may well seem rather tedious, be-cause they are invariably very heavy and clumsy, yet there is no greater contrast than that which exists be-tween the small seated statue in the Louvre – the only one with its original head, excavated at Telloh[305] (Pl. 170) – and the figure dedicated to Gudea by a High *Gala* Priest, Namhani, which is now in the Harvard Semitic Museum.[306] Unfortunately the head of the Harvard Museum statue is missing, and its surface badly preserved. But it shows clearly enough a widely divergent style: the dress is shorter and leaves more of the legs free, the proportions are more extended, the folds are more rounded. However, of greater importance is the lifelike rendering of the musculation of the back, under the clothing, to a degree only equalled by the Akkadian sculptors. We cannot at present be sure whether the man who dedicated this statuette was the same Namhani known to us elsewhere as the second son-in-law of Ur-Baba in addition to Gudea, but we can probably assume that the figure was made at the end of Gudea's life, thus anticipating a style which we shall meet again in figures of Gudea's son Ur-Ningirsu. One cannot find a more beautiful example of this way of por-traying muscles than on the back and right upper arm of the statuette of Ur-Ningirsu in the Berlin Museum (VA 8790)[307] (Pls. 171–174). A comparison of this with the rear view of the seated figure of Gudea in the Louvre is conclusive and makes it immediately obvious that plasticity in sculpture underwent an important transformation during the period of Gudea.

Akkadian influence was not limited to style. By Gudea's period sculpture had already made use of pictorial motifs which originated in the world of Old Akkad and not of Old Sumer. There is, for instance a diorite statuette of Gudea which reached a private collection as a result of a tomb robbery[308] and although its style is not particularly remarkable, it shows Gudea holding an aryballos vase in both hands in front of his chest, an arrangement usually only employed for divine persons. The base of the statuette has also been decorated all round with this symbol of life, probably a symbol of Akkadian origin, as it does not appear to have been of any significance in art prior to the Akkadian Period.

There is a scene in relief on another statuette of Ur-Ningirsu[309] (Pls. 175, 176), the son of Gudea, now in the Louvre: this shows several kneeling figures of captive enemy, carrying gifts, beneath the feet of the statue, indicating a new interpretation of the prince-concept, from the Sumerian to the Akkadian attitude, from the figure of a supplicant to that of a conqueror.

Only insignificant remnants of statues of the kings themselves from the Third Dynasty of Ur have survived in comparison with the particularly large numbers of statues of Gudea of Lagash. We have only fragments of a statue of even the most powerful king of the dynasty, Shulgi.[310] But if we take into account everything which we can attribute to this period from Ur, Lagash, Mari and the cities of the Diyala region, we are able to see in these also the same change from the purely Sumerian to a more Akkadian aspect of the revival.

One of the best preserved standing figures, made of black stone, is still completely in keeping with the spirit of the neo-Sumerian revival of Ur-Baba and Gudea: it was found in Room 65 of the Palace at Mari and according to its shoulder cartouche is of the *shakkanakku* Ishtup-ilum of Mari[311] (Pl. 177). The block-shaped figure, with his arms and hands pressed in close, the plain robe with no folds and simple hatched borders, scarcely emerges from the hard stone. It is related in spirit to Lamgi-Ma'ri, the king of Mari from the period of the First Dynasty of Ur (see Pl. 84). It has, however, the flat headband, joined diagonally on the left side, like that worn by some women in Lagash in the Gudea period (see Pl. 184). This statue

represents the style of the phase of Ur-Baba and Gudea in the series of statues from Mari.

If any statues of Ur-Nammu, the founder of the Third Dynasty, had survived, they would have been more or less in the style of this period. But our earliest examples of statues in the round of kings of the Third Dynasty of Ur, apart from foundation figures, are two fragments, both from Lagash, which are possibly of Shulgi, the second ruler of the dynasty, and a third fragment from Ur. The latter (Photo Iraq Museum)[312] (Pl. 178) somewhat resembles the portraits of Ur-Ningirsu in the modelling of the naked parts of the body (Pls. 171–176). A fragment from Lagash of a statuette of Shulgi,[313] because the robe is open at the front to reveal the carefully modelled left leg, reflects clearly the Akkadian style of stressing the plastic qualities of both body and attire.

Another work from Lagash,[314] dedicated for the life of Shulgi by Halalama, daughter of Lukagalla, looks really more like a man than a woman. Like the statue of the *shakkanakku* Idi-ilum of Mari (Pls. 179, 180),[315] it shows that clothes in the period of Shulgi were draped in the fashion of Manishtusu, with the same sort of tasselled border. Consequently Idi-ilum would have been a contemporary of Shulgi.

We are not in a position to judge sculpture in the round under the later kings of the Third Dynasty of Ur (Amar-Sin, Shu-Sin and Ibbi-Sin) on the evidence of statues of these kings themselves, because virtually nothing of them has survived. But we can form an approximate idea of their nature with the aid of some statues of governors in Mari and Eshunna, who can be placed in the period towards the end of the Third Dynasty of Ur. First among these comes a pair of statues which must have come to Babylon in some way as booty.[316] On one of these two statues could be fitted a head which had already at an earlier date reached the Berlin Museum via the art trade[317] (Pls. 181, 182). Both statues have inscriptions which, where the writing has not been chiselled away, record one Tura-Dagan, a *shakkanakku* of Mari, and his two sons, Puzur-Ishtar and Milaga.[318] They may be dated from the reigns of Amar-Sin and Ibbi-Sin.

Both statues are of a man standing in a cloak in an attitude of prayer. They differ from each other hardly at all, only in the execution of certain details of the fringe on the seams and in the style of the hair on the beard. The stylization of the seam tassles is old Akkadian, which we have seen already on the statues of Shulgi and Idi-ilum. The greater emphasis on the deification of the ruler who is represented by the statue – through the adding of two horns on the edge of his cap – must reflect old Akkadian influence; they form an analogy to the horns on the helmet of Naram-Sin himself on his victory stele in the Louvre (Pl. 156). If one compares the back view of the statue of Puzur-Ishtar from Babylon[319] with the back view of Ishtup-ilum, the increasing influence of Akkad on sculpture in the round in Mari is just as evident as it was when we compared the transition from the statues of Ur-Baba and Ur-Ningirsu. Only when there was a revival of the old Akkadian spirit could the combination of body and clothes endow the stone with so much life, as is shown in this statue of Puzur-Ishtar.

There is a limestone figure in the Louvre[320] which is one of the statues in the round which were brought to Susa from Eshnunna as booty. It was attributed to the *shakkanakku* Ur-ningizzida of Eshnunna by Jacobsen on account of the inscription,[321] and in time and style it is very close to the statue of Puzur-Ishtar but it does not achieve the latter's excellence.

Women from the neo-Sumerian period are represented by a few smaller statuettes but, apart from details of feminine attire, do not add anything really new to the history of sculpture. They are of women related to the *ensis* of Lagash, Gudea, Namahni and Urgar. The best of them (Pl. 184)[322] has no inscription. The profile of this woman shows the same anthropological type which we met for the first time in the so-called 'White Head' (Pl. 168) and is evidence that this was not just limited to a single man. This woman too has nothing about her to suggest the Sumerian or the oriental. She must be from another ethnic stock. Her mouth and nose are identical in shape to those on the 'White Head'.

This female type, together with the statues of Gudea, represents the specifically neo-Sumerian revival; one cannot detect in them anything to suggest an Akkadian influence – neither in their clothing, the long dress, the shawl with its double row of tassels,

and the flat hair-diadem, nor in their spirit or physiognomy.

This influence seems much more likely in another example of a female statue from this period, a seated figure which originally may have been excellent but which has been spoilt by modern restoration. It is of a divine bride from the shrine of Nanna in Ur. According to the inscription it is a portrait of Enannatuma, the daughter of King Ishme-Dagan of Isin, who had rebuilt completely the *Gigparku*, the cloister of the Divine Bride at Ur[323] (Pl. 183). The *nin-dingir* Enannatuma who dedicated this diorite statue to the goddess Ningal, the wife of Nanna, for her life, had herself portrayed as a goddess, in a long pleated dress, with both shoulders covered. Provided one can assume as certain the existence of a padded diadem holding her hair together, she appears in this statue – coming at the very end of the period of revival, between the old Akkadian and the old Babylonian periods, and immediately before the founding of the First Dynasty of Babylon – in precisely the same attire as that of Enheduanna, daughter of the great Sargon of Akkad shown in the relief on the disk from the *Gigparku* (see Pl. 130). In this, at least as far as her external appearance is concerned, she clearly resumes the connection with the old Akkadian tradition.

b Bas-relief and other two-dimensional art

i Relief

The sadly damaged remnants of relief from this period from Ur-Baba to Sumu-abum, which we know either in original or just from written descriptions, also reveal the same two-fold aspect of the revival in the kingdom of Sumer and Akkad that we had already noticed in its architecture and sculpture. Again this was based on the twin roots of Sumero-Akkadian culture. Even the kind of objects which bore the relief followed inherited patterns: votive plaques with a central hole were the most widespread type during the Mesilim Period, the cult stone vessels decorated with relief originated in the period of Sumerian Protohistory, as did the stele, though this seems to have been given its classic shape (the elongated rectangular slab with the rounded top) only during the reigns of Eannatum and Naram-Sin. In the old Akkadian period the votive plaque was given a frame of two padded rolls, of which we have already seen fine examples from Lagash.[324] Gudea retained these frames, even though he only used this ancient type of relief-bearer to illustrate his favourite presentation scene[325] (Pl. 185). Occasionally, however, as well as using the same external form to carry his relief, he also carried on the tradition of the early Sumerian religious motif, as when, for example, we find on a votive plaque an episode from the cult festival of the Sacred Marriage[326] (Pl. 186). On the other hand one is sometimes reminded of the old Akkadian feeling for style, and capacity for symbolism, as on a fragment of a votive plaque which now only has the picture of a single bull but which must once, as in ancient times, have shown an entire procession of animals being led to sacrifice.[327]

For cult purposes Gudea had stone vessels made of the most varied type and size, decorated with scenes in relief which were probably related to their use.

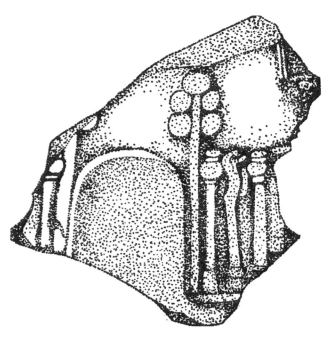

Fig. 47   Fragment of stele showing a row of stelae and standards, from Telloh
(After: G. Cros, *Nouvelles Fouilles de Tello*, Pl. X I)

He had his steatite libation vessel[328] decorated with the symbol of his protector god, Ningizzida, and with a pair of twining erect snakes (Pl. 187), placed between two Mushhush dragons, feathered composite creatures which can be traced far back into Sumerian Protohistory and closely connected with various chthonic divinities such as Ninazu-Tishpak, Ningizzida and Marduk. The symbolizing of life, in the form of a globular vessel from which water poured in streams and which was carried by, amongst others, goddesses in female form, sometimes winged, soaring down from heaven – this is surely a primitive concept from old Akkad.[329] Gudea used it imaginatively as the subject of a relief on a huge stone basin, in which cult water was stored in the temple. Parts of this exist today, reconstructed from countless small pieces, in the Istanbul Museum[330] and the Louvre (Pl. 188).

We have, however, lost the principal works of relief, in spite of painstaking attempts to reconstruct them. There are the stelae, over three metres high, several of which were erected on a walled platform near the temple cellae in the great courtyards of the main sanctuaries. Traces of the platforms have been identified in the debris of the Eanna Sanctuary of Uruk[331] and in the Nanna Sanctuary of Ur,[332] and hundreds of pieces from a Gudea stele excavated by Cros at Telloh were also connected with the remains of sub-structures of brick. One of its pieces actually has a picture showing how the stelae and standards of the gods were arranged in Telloh[333] (Fig. 47).

After the statue in the round the stele was the main medium for the *ensis* and kings of the revival on which they could present in an enduring pictorial form their plea for a prolongation of life and its presentation to the divinity. Like the statue, the stele – as bearer of this cult function – was given its own name. If the main emphasis of a statue in the round was on prayer and immortality, the main theme of a stele was rather a pictorial account of the services rendered to the gods. In this the stele as conceived by Gudea is related directly to the stele of the old Sumerian *ensi* of Lagash, and above all to the Stele of the Vultures of Eannatum. It is therefore not surprising that Heuzey and Parrot, in their attempt to reconstruct a complete stele of Gudea from the hundreds

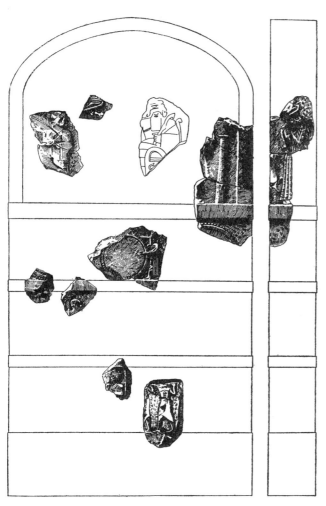

Fig. 48   Stele of Gudea from Telloh. Reconstruction
(After: A. Parrot, *Telloh*, p. 183, Fig. 37)

of fragments (Fig. 48),[334] have arrived at a form of monument which shows the closest relationship to the Stele of the Vultures: an elongated, rectangular slab of stone, rounded at the top, placed end up and covered with several friezes, one above the other, which continue all the way round the slab. Probably the curved space at the top of the stele was always given over to a scene of the prince presenting a sacrifice, in front of the god for whom the stele was intended.

The fragments stored in the Near Eastern Department of the Berlin Museum (Pls. 189, 190), which were assembled to form the curved space at the top of a stele of Gudea, as originally published by E.

Meyer,[335] actually belong to two stelae. Not only does the curve of the border ridge on the right near the small subsidiary god not fit in with the curve of the rest of the upper ridge: but near the right edge of the main fragment – which shows a scene of Gudea led by his protector god Ningizzida and a herald god – a wide stream of water, poured from a pitcher, is still intact and this must have been originally held in the hands of the enthroned principal god to whom Gudea is being presented. We can reconstruct this main scene easily with the help of an impression from a seal of Gudea[336] from the Louvre (Pl. N 1). Do other fragments in Berlin, such as the two-faced head of Usumia, the visir of Enki, or the god in the chariot drawn by sheep,[337] also perhaps belong in this presentation of Gudea before Enki, the great God of Water (Pls. 191–193)? The curved space at the top of the stele of Gudea reassembled from the Cros fragments (see Fig. 48) would probably have once again shown Gudea sacrificing in front of another principal god, Ningirsu. All the scenes on the stele dedicated by Gudea to Ningirsu are – as far as one can tell from the reconstruction – of purely cult significance (worship, procession of standard-bearers, procession of musicians, gift-bearers, transport of building material [?]). At any rate it cannot at the present time be proved that Gudea ever took the field like Eannatum, as the champion of the rights of Ningirsu. But the exact counterpart of the Gudea stele, the great stele of Ur-Nammu, which L. Legrain in Philadelphia has reassembled from countless broken splinters[338] (Pl. 194) collected in the *edublalmah* of the Nanna sanctuary at Ur, probably had as its subject-matter only the cult functions of the ruler as temple-builder, bringer of peace and builder of canals. It can be seen how closely related are the ideas underlying the revival in Lagash and Ur, just from the actual relief on the curved space at the top and in the upper registers of the Ur-Nammu stele. The angels pouring heavenly water hover over Ur-Nammu with their gushing vessels, on the front side as well as on the back. Ur-Nammu is shown as he is about to make a libation in front of his principal gods. If we remember that the main inscription on the back of the Ur-Nammu stele[339] carefully lists all the canals dug by the king (that is to say, his provision of water of life for the country), we can understand how here the general theme was presented to the observer in the uppermost reliefs of the stele, with its five registers divided between the two sides, each three metres high. The pictorial matter of the main scene used by Ur-Nammu is the same as that employed by Gudea: a libation in front of high gods, blessing by winged goddesses pouring water. It is true the cult episodes depicted on the two great stelae of Gudea and Ur-Nammu differ to some extent in their content but the purpose of the subject-matter is the same in both cases. The stelae not only resemble each other in their subject-matter, their style is completely analogous. Both adhere to the old Sumerian practice of dividing the pictorial surface into several continuous registers placed one above the other, framed and divided by raised bands. There is no indication that the entire surface of the monument was ever covered by a whole composition, as had occurred but once only in the earlier stele of Naram-Sin. The similarity in style is not, moreover, limited only to the division of the surface and the arrangement of the picture. It appears in all the details, of which we need only mention a few examples: compare the bald, shaved servant assisting Ur-Nammu to carry his building tools[340] (Pl. 195) with the bald Gudea on a fragment from Lagash[341] (Pl. 196) or a detail of the Ur-Nammu stele showing the arrangement of a robe[342] (Pl. 198) with the rendering of a robe on a statue of Gudea[343] (Pl. 197). If one places a drummer from Ur-Nammu's relief (Pl. 199) next to a drummer on a vessel from Lagash[344] (Pl. 200), one sees that not only are their clothes the same but they are both wearing the same calotte-shaped hair-style, also worn by Gudea's son, Ur-Ningirsu. Moreover, the gods and goddesses on both stelae look as if they had been chiselled by the same hand, down to each hair and each pleat of their flounced clothes[345] (Pls. 201, 189). The sculptors of Gudea and Ur-Nammu who carved these two reliefs must have been very closely in touch with each other – and they could not have been widely separated in time.

An interesting new development occurs in relief as it did in the sculpture in the round during the period from Ur-Baba to Sumu-abum, with the more marked introduction of old Akkadian styles and concepts.

This must have happened at least as early as the period of Shu-Sin, in view of what we have recently learnt from a clay tablet, published and discussed by Dietz Otto Edzard, from the Hilprecht Collection (2009) in Jena.[346] It contains copies of inscriptions and epigraphs which once formed part of a victory stele of King Shu-Sin of Ur. According to these inscriptions the king must have been shown on the stele with his commander-in-chief. They mention that the commander-in-chief is stamping with his foot on the conquered enemy, the *ensis* Indasu of Zabshali. This provides evidence that during Shu-Sin's reign the old Akkadian motif of the conqueror, which we first met with Naram-Sin, reappears in relief on a stele from the period of the revival. Thus, even as far as the motif is concerned, this removes the last grounds for assigning the relief on the rock near Darband-i-Gawr, which has been described already, to Naram-Sin[347] (Pl. 157). This must be one of the most convincing proofs of the strength of the Akkadian renaissance at the time of the kingdom of Sumer and Akkad. We shall soon discover further confirmation of the effect of precisely this conqueror motif when we come to examine the glyptic of the period (see below).

ii Glyptic

We possess cylinder seals, or impressions from cylinder seals, from both the founders of the neo-Sumerian revival, from Gudea as well as Ur-Nammu. Their subject-matter is the presentation, by an intermediary, of a worshipper to a god or a deified king, which was also the favourite theme in relief. We have already made use of an impression of this sort in order to reconstruct, with its help, the Berlin Gudea relief (Pls. 189, 190). On an actual cylinder seal from the Morgan Library in New York[348] Gudea is shown in his usual robe but with a beard and a calotte hair-style like those otherwise first worn by his son Ur-Ningirsu (Pls. 171–174); he is being led by an interceding goddess dressed in the simple, long pleated robe to an enthroned goddess in the flounced robe (Pl. G 1). This theme had already been used in glyptic in the Akkadian period[349] but it became almost the distinctive mark of the period from Ur-Baba to Sumu-abum. During the revival the scene of the presentation to a deified king was favoured more and more[350] (Pl. G 2–4). Like the royal temples with the broad cella, such as that built for Shu-Sin of Ur by Ituria, governor of Eshnunna (see above, Fig. 44), this scene was the expression of the concept of kingship which had developed during the period of the kings of Sumer and Akkad. Yet the old Akkadian concept of kingship, of a warlike conqueror of all evil in the shape of dragons, wild animals and national enemies, an idea of which Naram-Sin's stele was the most powerful illustration, did not die out. This still continued side by side with the presentation scene as part of the development of neo-Sumerian glyptic. The increasing dominance of Akkadian influence over glyptic clearly began during the reign of Gudea's son, Ur-Ningirsu, and that of Ur-Nammu's successor, Shulgi, as we can see from the seal impressions on the clay tablets in the Louvre, which can be dated in that period.[351] They can scarcely be distinguished from Akkadian cylinder seals, either in their subject-matter (battle between naked hero or a bull-man and an arna buffalo or a winged lion-dragon), or in their style (angular position of arms!). That the increasing domination of glyptic by Akkadian influence must have been complete by the reign of Ibbi-Sin is made particularly clear in the seal of Ilushuilia of Eshnunna, on which he described himself as the first independent king and Ruler of the Four Regions of the World (Pl. N 2).[352]

iii Wall painting at Mari redated

No wall painting from the period of Gudea, the kings of the Third Dynasty of Ur and the Isin-Larsa period has so far been recorded in archaeological literature. In my summary *Altvorderasiatische Malerei*, which was published a few years ago, I myself made no reference to any example of painting from this period. This was because all the wall paintings excavated in Mari were discovered when the huge palace there was unearthed and consequently – more or less as a matter of course – they were considered to have originated in the last great period of this palace,

namely in the reign of Zimrilim, the last great king who had lived and ruled there. But Zimrilim was one of the great opponents of Hammurabi of Babylon. Accordingly all the wall paintings from Mari were dated in the Old Babylonian period, shortly before the thirty-fifth year of Hammurabi's reign when the city of Mari was finally destroyed. André Parrot, who discovered these valuable remains, in his book *Sumer*[353] also suggests the eighteenth century B.C. as the date of all the painting at Mari. In the publications on the findings of the excavations in Mari the paintings were rightly assigned a volume to themselves.[354] In this all the fragments of the paintings are listed according to the various places inside the palace where they were found, and then carefully described, reconstructed in their mutual relationship, interpreted, their artistic merit assessed, and compared with wall paintings from Alalakh and Crete. Also the variations in the technique of the painting and of the wall plaster on which they were painted were discussed.

The palace at Mari is a vast complex where building most probably went on for centuries,[355] and the sculpture found there also came from different centuries,[356] some at any rate dating from a considerably earlier period than that of Zimrilim. There would thus seem to be no reason to take it for granted that all the wall paintings, which were found in many different parts of the palace, came from the period of Zimrilim. Once one rids oneself of the assumption that they all date from Zimrilim, it only remains to examine their content and external appearance, to compare them with other works of art from Mari and from other sites known to us already, and then to assign them a place in the development of art in Mari.[357]

The so-called 'Investiture of Zimrilim'

Once there has been a query about the dating of the wall painting from Mari, this obviously also applies to the best known and most complete work, the so-called 'Investiture of Zimrilim'[358] (Fig. 49a) on the south wall of Court 106, to the right of the entrance to Room 64. The content and style of this very important work of ancient eastern painting will be discussed later but here it is sufficient – in order to obtain a chronological fixed point – to establish its dating in the period of Zimrilim, and this has now fortunately become possible with the help of new discoveries in Mari itself, in the field of glyptic, namely with the new impressions and cylinder seals which must once have belonged to a high official of Zimrilim.

The so-called Investiture of Zimrilim is a wall painting which was painted immediately above an ornamental plinth directly on a mud plaster coating, in contrast to the extensive second group of wall paintings on the same wall of the courtyard, which were painted on a thick white gesso. These stretched round the walls of Court 106, about two metres in height. The actual Investiture[359] shows a prince in a big robe with a double fringe and with a tall, oval hat. He is standing with his right hand raised in greeting, facing to the right in front of a goddess in the long slit dress. She has her right foot pressing on a recumbent lion, her left arm hangs down and she is holding a sickle sword in her left hand, and with her other hand she is holding out a staff and ring towards the king. She can be recognized as the warlike goddess by the symbol rising high from each of her shoulders, the mace between two axes. The horns on her divine crown can still be seen, drawn in profile, like the horned crowns of all the other divinities appearing in this painting: the interceding goddesses in flounced dresses, the subsidiary god in the diagonally cut dress and the water goddesses appearing in the space below the actual investiture scene.[360]

The supposition that the king in this great painting actually is Zimrilim (to whom the warlike Ishtar seems to be handing over royal power symbolized by the ring and staff) is supported by a newly published seal impression, which a high official serving Zimrilim, called Mukannishum, had put on several clay tablet envelopes.[361] For our purposes the most important of these seal-impressions of Mukannishum, the superintendent of the Palace at Mari, is that which shows the conqueror scene[362] (Pl. N 3), of unmistakable Old Akkadian origin, and which we also showed earlier to have been used for Shu-Sin and Ilushuilia. The king – it can only be Zimrilim, because Mukan-

Fig. 49 a   Reconstruction of the wall painting 'Investiture of Zimrilim' in the Palace of Mari
(After: Hirmer-Strommenger, Fig. 34)

nishum describes himself as the latter's servant – is trampling on his enemies in battle, while the winged Ishtar protects his rear and an interceding goddess stands before him in an attitude of greeting. Although Ishtar is here shown with wings, yet it must be the same goddess who is offering him the ring and staff in the Investiture scene. The identity of the two kings, on the Mukannishum seal impression and in the investiture is, moreover, abundantly clear from the similarity of all the details of their attire. So, on the Mukannishum impression, although the king is in battle he is wearing a robe with the double border of rounded tabs, and at the back a band hangs down from his neck to the hollow of his knees: he is also wearing the same tall, oval head-gear.

Whereas the gods in the wall painting of the so-called Investiture are all wearing the two- or four-horned crown drawn correctly in profile, this is not the case on the Mukannishum impression, where, as on all earlier works of art on a flat surface, the horned crowns are shown *en face*, even when the face is in profile. In the next chapter, however, we shall find a notable advance in Old Babylonian art in the treatment of perspective in two-dimensional art – namely that when the gods' heads were shown in profile their horned crowns were also shown in profile – and this advance can in all probability be dated at the end of Hammurabi's life (for the Code of Hammurabi, his most important relief, and the earliest datable relief, which uses this relief-technique, can scarcely have been made until the last years of Hammurabi's life).[363] Because the Investiture of Zimrilim employed the same method for presenting horned crowns, while Mukannishum's seal does not, we might conclude from this that the painters of the Investiture had studied the contemporary art in Babylon well and conformed to it but that the stone-cutter, on the other hand, had not. However, as we shall see later in other Old Babylonian glyptic too, it is difficult to find a crown illustrated in the same way as that in which the crown of Shamash is presented on the Code of Hammurabi. Probably the seal of Mukannishum is somewhat older than the Investiture of Zimrilim and the period of Hammurabi. The investiture scene would fit in best in the period between the two conquests of Mari by Hammurabi, in the thirty-third or thirty-fifth year of his reign, whereas Mukannishum probably belongs to the years before the first conquest of Mari by Hammurabi. Exceptionally in this instance, therefore, we are for once dealing with a date of an ancient eastern work of art which can be limited to within a few years.

What relationship do the remaining wall paintings at Mari have with the painting of the Investiture which we have just considered?

Bull brought to sacrifice

On all four sides of Court 106 the walls were covered with a thick gesso on which there were extensive paintings applied with a uniform technique: ornament and figures were outlined in black, with the surfaces coloured either with the white of the plaster or ochre which varied from brown to orange. In the main this results in the colour scale black-white-red, common since ancient times. But occasionally blue was also used. An attempt has been made to reconstruct individual figures and scenes, more or less related, from the hundreds of small scraps of painting salvaged from the debris.[364] The most important of these fragments are those which form a large picture of sacrificial bulls, of which a piece was found still *in situ*. A smaller piece, now in Aleppo[365] (Pl. 202), shows a servant going from left to right, leading a bull on a rope, with a ring through its nose. While the man is facing to the right, he is turning back to the left and leaning his left forearm on the bull's mouth and forehead. The animal's horns are covered with metal points, and a large crescent moon with a swastika hangs between them. The servant is noteworthy for his half-length kilt, over which is wound a plaid-like piece of material with fringes of rounded tabs. The whole dress is held in by a narrow girdle. His headgear looks like a large wig or a soft felt cap with a double headband. His black beard is trimmed short. This work cannot be separated from another, whose theme, technique and style of coloured drawing are all the same[366] (Pl. 203). Here a male figure – so tall that he towers above the two registers which lie one above the other – is shown marching with his right arm swinging out, leading a procession of several temple servants towards an objective[367] which must originally have been on the right but of which nothing has survived. In this scene very little can be seen of the sacrificial bull, but like the one just described it too was decorated with a crescent moon on its forehead, which the painter, as in the first picture, again showed front view on, with the head of the bull in profile. This was completely contrary to the new style which appeared after the Code of Hammurabi and in the Investiture of Zimrilim, for artists then no longer tolerated a crown to be shown *en face* above a head drawn in profile. This suggests that these two groups of wall paintings on gesso are from a somewhat earlier period than the Investiture of Zimrilim. It is possible that we may yet be able to establish the historical position of these groups of paintings with greater accuracy by examining the clothes of the individual figures, and especially those of the tall leader of the sacrificial procession, who is probably a king. The attire of this king at first seems rather complicated but it is actually the same as that seen on the man leading the bull, who was described above: a knee-length kilt under a plaid made of material with a border of rounded tabs, held by a narrow girdle. The only difference is that this time the dress is enriched by the doubling of the oval tab border and the girdle is triple and decorated with lotus blossoms; also the first servants are wearing a neck chain with a round medallion. U. Moortgat-Correns has already pointed out[368] the similarities of this dress with that of Shamsi-Adad I on his victory stele, which reached the Louvre from Mardin. Clay tablets recently found in Shemsara[369] in northern Iraq have shown that this stele really does belong to Shamshi-Adad I, as E. Forrer originally suggested (Pls. 204, 205). It is true that Zimrilim also had material with a double row of rounded-tab fringes on his robe, as we have seen already, but he did not wear a girdle, which seems to have been characteristic of the West Semites. On the other hand the dress of Shamshi-Adad I on the Mardin stele has a girdle like that of the royal leader of the procession of the sacrificial bull in Mari, as well as other details of dress: the draping of the plaid with the double fringe on the thigh and the lotus-shaped ends of the girdle. The medallion is worn by Shamshi-Adad as well as by the lower-ranking men leading the bull to sacrifice in the Mari painting. Thus, by examining different details and reassessing them, we have been led to connect this second group of wall paintings from Court 106 at the Palace of Mari with Shamshi-Adad I of Ashur, the great, somewhat older adversary of Hammurabi of Babylon; consequently we may well assign them to the former's son, Iasmah-Adad (= Iasmah-Addu), governor of Mari. Indeed, in all probability, we can identify the royal leader of the procession as Iasmah-Adad himself. But if such an identification is correct, then Iasmah-Adad must have had Court 106 decorated right round with a complete sequence of wall paintings of about two metres in height,[370] and somewhat later, after Iasmah-Adad had been overthrown, Zimrilim had the legitimacy of his accession to the 'Throne of his Father' docu-

mented by the application of the wall painting of the so-called Investiture scene at ground level on the south wall of the same Court 106.

Wall paintings in the Audience Chamber (Room 132) in the Palace at Mari

A third group of wall paintings was found in a room of another courtyard complex, the so-called Audience Chamber, which could be reached from Court 131 by a semi-circular open stairway. The west wall of this long rectangular room once had extensive wall paintings. These have been reconstructed from countless tiny fragments salvaged from the rubbish by Parrot and his colleagues, and after an immense amount of work they were assembled into a scene which, though not indeed verified in every detail, was quite plausible if taken as whole[371] (Fig. 49b). They were not, like the last group, painted on a layer of gesso but direct on the mud plaster of the wall, like the Investiture painting in Court 106. The colour scheme consists of black, white and reddish-brown ochre, the old trio of colours from Sumerian pottery and

Fig. 49b Reconstruction of the wall painting from Room 132 in the Palace of Mari
(After: A. Parrot, MAM 2, *Le Palais, Peintures murales*, Pl. XVII)

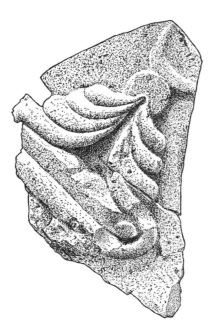

Fig. 50 Fragment of the Ur-Nammu stele with horned crown, from Ur. Redrawn
(After: MT XVIII 82)

wall painting. Blue, and more especially green, are missing. Only yellow still occurs.

This reconstruction has produced a composition of which the scenes are divided into five friezes, placed one above the other.[372] Perhaps it is not just due to blind chance that, after careful reassembly from countless fragments, this wall painting – like the two stelae of Ur-Nammu and Gudea described already – forms a scene composed of five friezes, without there having been any contact between the modern restorers. After all, the general theme of the wall painting in Room 132 – or as much of it as has survived – is in its essence the same as that in the upper arched pictorial area and the second frieze of the Ur-Nammu stele, and similarly many individual shapes and material details in this wall painting lead us in our search for comparable dated elements back to Gudea and Ur-Nammu, indeed, back as far as the Akkadian Period.

Exactly as on the Ur-Nammu stele, in the painting in Room 132 a king is shown at the festive sacrificial ceremonies in front of the principal divinities of the country, assisted by interceding goddesses and ministering priests. Whereas the subsidiary scenes portray battles or a procession of tribute-bearers on a smaller scale and on narrower friezes, the king is shown on the third and fourth friezes in the central part of the painting, dressed in the flounced robe, with a brimmed cap and a long rectangular beard like that of Ur-Nammu (see Pl. 194). He is pouring a libation from a beaker, of which the shape is similar to that of the Ningizzida beaker of Gudea, into two large vessels with pedestal bases. These are similar to those which, during the period of Ur III, usually contained branches and were placed in front of the seated gods. In this painting too they are in front of a principal god enthroned on a mountain summit, and behind him his animal-attribute is standing – a large black bull with a heavy dewlap. The god's robe is in a bad state of preservation. He is wearing on his head a flat crown (with two horns) under a round disk, and over the disk there is a crescent moon. This crown has only one parallel – that shown on a fragment of the Ur-Nammu stele[373] (Fig. 50). In the frieze above that of the principal god, there is a scene portraying the worship of the principal goddess of Mari, the war-like Ishtar, whom we can recognize because of the mace and axes on her shoulders. She is wearing the usual flounced dress of the Ur III period, and the interceding goddesses who are attending the king resemble so closely in every detail of their physiognomy, hair-style, necklace and dress an interceding goddess on a corner of the Gudea stele excavated by Cros at Telloh[374] (Fig. 48) that the painting in Room 132 at Mari cannot be very far from the time of Gudea: the theme of the painting, the god's crown with the crescent moon, as well as the libation vessels with high pedestal bases, all point to the same conclusion. The horned crown, with crescent moon above the disk, could even be old Akkadian in origin,[375] as indeed could the simple, chequered, box-shaped seat of the goddess in the painting from Room 132 at Mari.

If subject matter and factual details suggest that the large wall painting in the Audience Chamber belonged to the period of the Sumero-Akkadian revival – that is, to the period of the governors Tura-Dagan, Puzur-Eshtar and Idi-ilum of Mari – then we also find these dates corroborated if we compare details of clothing in this painting with those on the so-called Investiture of Zimrilim or on the group of the Iasmah-Adad paintings. In the painting in Room 132 there is no plaid with the single or double fringe of oval tabs, no girdled dress, no medallion worn on a neck chain. More significant, there are no horned crowns of gods and goddesses shown in profile above a face in profile, as they were in the Investiture scene. On the contrary, they are completely like the horned crowns shown *en face* on the reliefs of Gudea and Ur-Nammu. There can, therefore, no longer be any doubt that, in the wall painting of the Audience Chamber, we have an example of neo-Sumerian painting, which helps us to bridge the large gap that had existed hitherto in the development of this form of art between the Jamdat Nasr and the Old Babylonian periods. This is a conclusion of basic importance, as it not only suggests that painting in the neo-Sumerian period had followed the same path as the other branches of art – relief and sculpture – within the whole course of Ancient Mesopotamian art, but it also prevents us from assigning all the wall

painting discovered in the Palace at Mari to the eighteenth century B.C. – that is, to the Old Babylonian period. On the contrary, this conclusion compels us to differentiate carefully between the various phases in style which spread over several centuries: moreover, with their help we may conclude that the wall paintings in Room 132 and parts of the palace round Court 131, which cannot logically be separated from the Audience Chamber, are the work of the neo-Sumerian revival and not from the period of Zimrilim.

Taking everything into consideration, the palace at Mari does in fact offer us the possibility of following the development of Ancient Mesopotamian painting through three phases:

1. the neo-Sumerian revival,

2. the Canaanite-Old Assyrian epoch, under Shamshi-Adad and Iasmah-Adad, and

3. the Canaanite-Old Babylonian phase during the period of Zimrilim and Hammurabi.[376]

II Old Babylonian Art

(The art of Ancient Mesopotamia during the period
of the Canaanite First Dynasty of Babylon)

In the previous chapter on the art of the Sumero-Akkadian revival, when considering the wall paintings discovered in the Palace of Mari we had to distinguish those which belonged to the period of Gudea and the Ur-Nammu dynasty. To do this we also had to examine the later painting, from the period of Zimrilim and Iasmah-Adad, the son of Shamshi-Adad I: that is, the two groups of painting from the so-called Old Babylonian period, which we count as starting with the foundation of the dynasty of Babylon by Sumu-abum and which was given its greatest political-cultural expression by the creative personality of Hammurabi of Babylon. For only a short period, but with far-reaching consequences he was able to create a united kingdom, in which political and military power was in the hands of the Semitic Canaanites, who had slowly, for centuries, penetrated the whole Sumero-Akkadian area, from Aleppo to Larsa, from the Mediterranean coast to the Iranian border mountains.

The paintings on the walls of Court 106 in the Palace of Mari are a good example of the ability of the Canaanite people to come to terms in their own way with the age-old tradition of art in the Sumero-Akkadian mother country. In spite of their great willingness to adopt and continue the ideas and forms of the Sumero-Akkadian revival, we cannot fail to recognize their own individual character in contrast to the cultural inheritance which they had adopted. It was only this which has made it possible to differentiate so clearly and with such conviction the painting in Audience Room 132 from those on the walls of Court 106 and to attribute them to the Sumero-Akkadian tradition of the period of the Third Dynasty of Ur.

It is true that the painting of the Investiture of Zimrilim, in its pictorial formulation of the concept of kingship in ancient Mesopotamia and of its relation to the higher world of the state pantheon, has taken over many inherited elements, but they are combined and carried further in what was undoubtedly a new manner. Even though this painting is not superior in quality to that in Room 132, yet it widens the scale of colours used and even, like the sculptors in the reign of Hammurabi, makes use of the latest discoveries in the field of 'perspective'.

It now remains to decide whether the significance of the wall painting at the Palace of Mari can be attributed to a special predilection or to a special talent, or whether the other branches of art – architecture, sculpture and relief – during this Old Babylonian period, and particularly under Hammurabi himself in Babylon, also evolved their own idiom for their own concepts. We must make this attempt, even though we ourselves realise that the sources for the history of Old Babylonian art are even more inadequate than those for the Old Akkadian. It is sad that the many decades of German excavations in the capital city of Babylon have produced only meagre material dating from this period, because the city of Hammurabi lay below the water-table. The results of American, English, French and Iraqi excavations in the provincial cities formerly governed by important rivals of Hammurabi are, therefore, of even greater importance.

A ARCHITECTURE

1 Cult building

The question which must interest us most, when we consider buildings of this period, is whether there was a special form of cult building: that is, were there special types of temple ground-plans in the Canaanite level in Mesopotamia, or can one at least recognize that they decisively changed the old type of Sumerian temple? We can indeed ask this question but we cannot answer it with certainty on the basis of the evidence at present at our disposal.

The sanctuaries, large and small, excavated so far are few and isolated. Their findings have not yet all been published in their definitive form by those excavating them, which makes it harder for us to form a final opinion on them. Also we have to differentiate between the central region of the Sumero-Akkadian civilization – which was later to become the central region of the Babylonian-Assyrian civilization – and the actual Canaanite region, in which one should perhaps include Alalakh (Tell Atchana) with its im-

Fig. 52   Plan of the Dagan Temple at Mari
(After: Syria 41, p. 6, Fig. 1)

portant monuments from the period of Yarimlim, the contemporary of Hammurabi.

We have only a few cult buildings at our disposal in the region of classical Ancient Mesopotamia. Their basic outlines can be surveyed quickly. The design of the main sanctuary of the Assyrian national god, as it must have appeared during the reign of Shamshi-Adad I, the somewhat older rival of Hammurabi and of Zimrilim of Mari, can only be examined with the help of the foundation walls unearthed in the excavations of the German Oriental Society[1] (Fig. 51). From these we can gather that the god Ashur had a sanctuary at the highest point in the city, its foundations very limited in size owing to the naturally restricted space available, and that this was composed of a central courtyard complex and several forecourts, laid out at different levels. Unfortunately the original shape of the cella cannot be established, because by themselves the foundation walls which have survived are not enough. We therefore do not know whether the cella of the Ashur Temple was part of a so-called 'bent axis' type of temple or of some sort of a long house temple. A thousand years later Sennacherib altered the cella of the Ashur Temple into a truly Assyrian temple, combining a long cella with a wide antecella. We shall discover the origin of this type of temple later towards the end of the Middle Assyrian period. It has no bearing on the Canaanites of the Second Millennium.

At the Dagan Temple in Mari[2] (Fig. 52) we can still find no evidence of a Canaanite type of temple with a long cella, since so far no clear signs of a

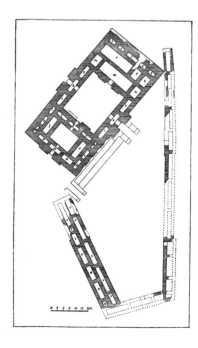

Fig. 51   Ground-plan of the Ashur Temple of Shamshi-Adad I at **Ashur** (After: WVDOG 67, p. 16, Fig. 2)

sanctuary have been recognized in its unusual format, and it cannot be compared with any other temple. Moreover we have recently felt ourselves unable to go on supporting the latest evidence for the existence of a long cella temple in the Old Babylonian period which had seemed to be suggested by a side cella in the shrine of the goddess Ishtar-Kititum in Neribtu (= Ishchali) in the Diyala valley, built by the powerful ruler of Eshnunna, Ipiq-Adad II. It will only be possible to come to a conclusion when a definitive report of this important shrine has been published. Its plans as they appeared in a preliminary publication seem partly to contradict each other.[3]

The shrine in Neribtu (Fig. 53), a vast layout of a complex nature, planned as a unity, the best surviving example of cult architecture from the period of Hammurabi, displays many features in its general plan which resemble those of the Ashur Temple of Shamshi-Adad I in Ashur. But the execution of the plan at Neribtu was not handicapped by the prescribed building site as at Ashur. Like the Ashur temple, the shrine of Ishtar-Kititum has at its southeast end a large forecourt, lying at a lower level, and reached through a huge gateway. From the court, steps lead to the actual Kititum Temple, which occupies the western end of the whole complex, and here one reaches a large forecourt which, as it has its own entrance, wide antecella and wide cella, all lying on

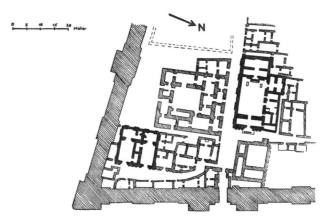

Fig. 54 Plan of the Large Temple and the Small Double Temple at Tell Harmal
(After: Strommenger-Hirmer, p. 85, Fig. 31)

the one axis, clearly represents a development of the temple of the Sumerian revival. The architect of the Old Babylonian period probably did not himself have to introduce the strict sense of order typical of Akkad, which we consider is reflected in the arrangement of several courtyard systems each with its own sacred cella, all within a rectangular, enclosed area, planned and executed with symmetry, because this sense of order had already been clearly expressed in the architecture of the kingdom of Sumer and Akkad during the Third Dynasty of Ur.

In Shaduppum (= Tell Harmal),[4] the administrative centre of a district of the kingdom of Eshnunna, founded and developed during the Old Babylonian period, the spirit pervading the architecture in the actual shrine of the city-god began to affect all parts of the settlement, even in the ground-plans of both temples, the large one and the smaller double one (Fig. 54). Both temples still retain the broad cella inherited from the Third Dynasty of Ur, and this form of temple was to remain for centuries, to the reign of Nebuchadnezzar II, as the typically Babylonian form of cult building. In both temples the cella still had an annexe like a sacristy, and both halves of the sanctuary were arranged in an interlocking symmetry, a peculiarity of the ground-plan, in which one may perhaps detect the somewhat playful formality characteristic of the period.

The so-called Audience Chamber of Naram-Sin of Eshnunna occupies a hitherto unexplained place in

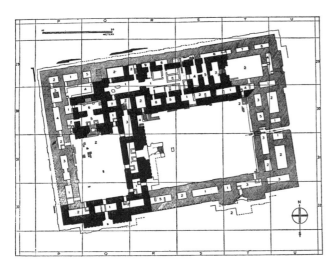

Fig. 53 Plan of the Ishtar-Kititum Temple at Ishchali
(After: OIC 20, p. 77, Fig. 60)

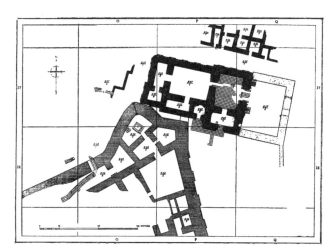

Fig. 55   Plan of the 'Audience Chamber' of Naram-Sin of Eshnunna
(After: OIP 43, p. 101, Fig. 87)

tecture arising from the special concept of kingship of the Old Babylonian period?

2   Palace building

We have information – even if of a provisional nature – about a whole series of palace buildings from the Old Babylonian period of Mesopotamia. The most important monument, the Palace of Hammurabi in Babylon, is again missing, and other palaces – that of Shamshi-Adad I at Ashur, the Palace of Nur-Adad in Larsa, of Singashid in Uruk, and also the palaces of Ibalpel I and Ipiq-Adad II – have only been excavated in part or published in a pro-

the history of Old Babylonian architecture. Naram-Sin, like the later kings of Eshnunna, had himself deified and perhaps for that reason bears the name of one of the great Akkadian rulers.

The explanation of the ground-plan of this building creates some difficulties. It conforms to no known type of cult building. Yet the walls throughout are covered with unmistakable evidence of its cult character, the so-called niche decoration[5] (Fig. 55). But it cannot possibly be considered to represent a temple for the worship of Naram-Sin on the lines of the temple for Shu-Sin at Eshnunna (see above, p. 59). On the other hand the architectural feature of the niche is really unnecessary for an audience chamber, as the excavators point out. And the whole Naram-Sin building is equally unsuited as a real temple for the land-god Tishpak, for whom a tiny subsidiary chapel had been provided in the building, in which a fragment of a stele inscribed with his name was also found. Basically it consists merely of a broad rectangular room with its entrance in the centre of one of the broad sides: in front of this lies an almost square forecourt, enclosed by a wall. The only buildings resembling this are the cult buildings in Syria and Palestine, that is, in the actual Canaanite region,[6] and later in Ugarit and Alalakh.[7] Have we here in the Diyala region a Canaanite development in archi-

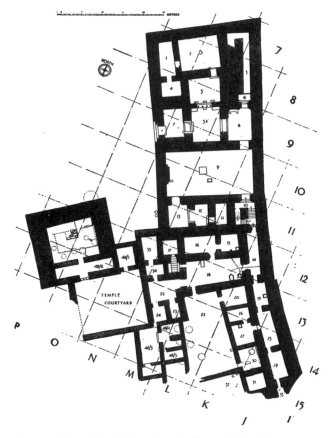

Fig. 56   Plan of the Palace of Yarimlim at Tell Atchana
(After: L. Woolley, *Alalakh*, p. 92, Fig. 35)

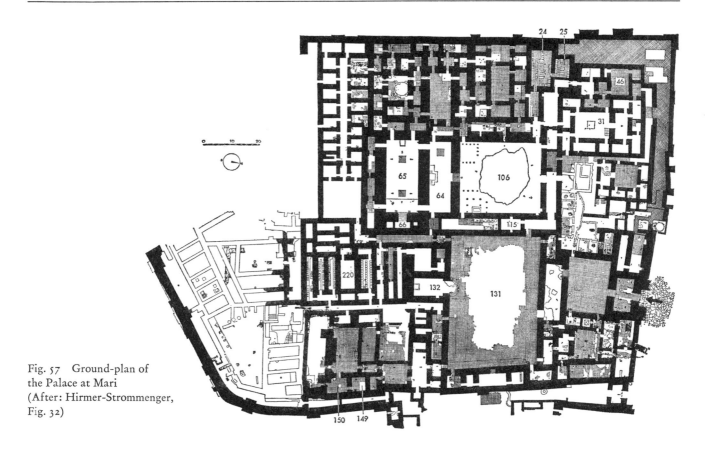

Fig. 57   Ground-plan of
the Palace at Mari
(After: Hirmer-Strommenger,
Fig. 32)

visional manner. Consequently for the time being the problem of what the Canaanite dynasties of the Old Babylonian period achieved in this field is also difficult to solve.

It is true we know part of the palace of King Yarimlim from Level VII at Alalakh[8] (Fig. 56). Owing to its closeness to the Canaanite homeland, it must express the concept of a Canaanite palace more accurately than the buildings in Mesopotamia which have just been listed. Many individual features of this building show a strong Aegean influence, such as the emphasis on the portico, with rooms supported by pillars, the orthostats covered with gesso and painted like frescoes.

When the final report has been fully published it may be possible, in the case of the Palace of the Kings of Eshnunna, to follow the changes in style which occurred in the course of the transition from the Third Dynasty to the period of Ipiq-Adad II, i.e. from the Sumerian to the Old Babylonian periods; yet here it remains probable that the palace of the

period of the Third Dynasty of Ur exercised a strong and lasting influence.

One of the greatest building undertakings of Ancient Mesopotamia, the Palace at Mari[9] (Fig. 57), could have provided us with our best source of information about palace building in Hammurabi's period, if it really were the palace of Zimrilim, as it has been called, – that is, if it had actually been planned as a whole and built as a unity by Zimrilim of Mari, the contemporary of Hammurabi. Then it would also be a record of the Canaanite kingdom in Ancient Mesopotamia. But our remarks on neo-Sumerian architecture outlined earlier, as well as on the painting in the Palace of Mari, have shown that large parts of the palace must have been built at the time of the Kingdom of Sumer and Akkad, and that in consequence these parts cannot be used as evidence in judging Canaanite achievement on its own in the field of architecture. The largest complex of rooms, round Court 131, with the Audience Chamber and its semi-circular, free-standing steps, must have been built centuries before the period of Hammurabi, for the wall paintings in it belong approximately to the period of Ur-Nammu, and this also applies to the block round Room 148, the house over the vaults: the fragments of the statuettes of Idi-ilum and Laasgan, which were found there, point to the Third Dynasty of Ur, and the so-called 'Head of a Warrior with a Chin-piece'[10] (Pl. 206), discovered on the steps between Rooms 148 and 210, has only one parallel, a figure in the wall painting in the Audience Chamber, which itself originated in the Third Dynasty. We consider that the wall paintings found on the walls of Court 34 in the so-called royal residence originated in the reign of Iasmah-Adad, the son of Shamshi-Adad I of Ashur (see above and below, pp.72 and 83). It is possible that the entire royal residence belonged to this period and was consequently Old Babylonian. However, this royal house has the ground-plan of a typical courtyard house, traditional in Ancient Mesopotamia, and is thus not specifically Canaanite. Besides, the architectural layout of the second large courtyard complex in the Palace of Mari, Court 106 (which was decorated from the time of Iasmah-Adad on with a series of wall paintings in exactly the same style on a thick white gesso, and which, somewhat later, had the Investiture of Zimrilim painted on its south wall) points to the tradition of palace building of the ancient Land of the Two Rivers, reaching back at least as far as the Kingdom of Sumer and Akkad. Ilushuilia, the son of Ituria, rebuilt the palace of the rulers of Eshnunna in such a way that its central area, with the throne room, shows the same sequence of rooms as that in the Palace of Mari – through Court 106, the Throne Room 64 and behind this, the greatest room in the whole palace, Room 65.[11] This architectural concept, pervading the most important and typical central part of the Mari palace, seems therefore equally not to have been specifically Canaanite, but had already been foreshadowed by the Kingdom of Sumer and Akkad. Therefore we can scarcely be far wrong if we take the Palace of Zimrilim to be a building in the Sumero-Akkadian tradition rather than as an example of a building exclusively Canaanite. We find this opinion confirmed when we compare it with the palace which the father-in-law of Zimrilim, Yarimlim,

King of Aleppo, had built in Alalakh. Yarimlim was one of the most powerful kings in the Near East during the period of Hammurabi: in contrast to the classical culture of Mesopotamia which, at just this phase of the First Dynasty of Babylon, was in the act of reaching a new peak of achievement, he shows himself completely independent in the ground-plan of his buildings and in their individual parts, as well as in the use of particular features in the elevation (orthostats, pillars etc.). Mari, however, which had grown over the centuries on the Middle Euphrates, was too far from the native source of the Canaanite kingdom to be able to escape from the influences of the age-old Sumero-Akkadian centre of culture, and yet again was not near enough to that centre to assume the intellectual leadership as Babylon was able to do under the Canaanite Hammurabi.

B SCULPTURE AND PAINTING

1 Glyptic art

Until a few years ago the minor art of the stone-cutter and the folk-art of the terra-cotta relief were the only – and indirect – sources available to us when we tried to visualize the subject-matter and style of the major arts (painting, relief and sculpture in the round) which presumably existed in the Old Babylonian period. The numerous cylinder seals and their impressions on the clay tablets, which in many cases can be dated fairly accurately, even made it possible to follow the organic development of Near Eastern art during the First Dynasty of Babylon,[12] from the period of its rise, through its prime to its final decline and decay. If the great significance of Hammurabi's ascendancy did not appear to be so clearly reflected in the glyptic known a few years ago, this source material has lately been much modified by the important new discovery of seals at Mari.[13]

If we attempt to evaluate the artistic significance of Old Babylonian glyptic by studying the chronological classification,[14] soon we come to the same conclusion as that we should obtain by reading the relevant sections of the reports on seal impressions on the dated clay tablets of the period: the Old Babylonian cylinder seal makes an immediate impression of coming from a debased branch of art, where quantity greatly exceeds quality. Even those fairly numerous seals inscribed with the name of a prince rarely suggest anything approaching a mastery of style, or anything which can be compared with the best in glyptic from another age. And even the subject-matter of glyptic in the Old Babylonian period differs noticeably from that of the previous age of the Sumero-Akkadian revival, though the enrichment of the seal-designs affects the main scenes less than it does the secondary scenes and the motifs used to fill spaces. The stone-cutters of the Old Babylonian period continued to use the two main themes of the revival period: the introduction and the worshipping scene, together with the conqueror motif of Naram-Sin, although the gods being worshipped and the victorious heroes and kings are always new, and though too a whole cycle of new magic symbols based on the religious world of the Canaanites are employed to fill the pictorial surface (Pl. G 8). Anyone seeking a deeper understanding of Old Babylonian glyptic has to try to comprehend the most important scenes and components of scenes not previously recorded, the new kinds of gods, the mixed creatures like the sphinx, the lion-dragon, the god on the bull, the god-king as warrior, the suckling cow, all of which are perhaps Canaanite in origin, and must follow their development. A first requisite is a detailed iconography of the types of gods in the foreground of glyptic during the First Dynasty of Babylon; the so-called Amurru, the god with the shepherd's staff[15] (Pl. G 6), the 'god-king as warrior', the naked Ishtar and the warlike Ishtar with the double-lion mace, the god with the lightning and the god on the bull, the little man with bent knees, as well as many new magic symbols – flies, masks, scales, a comb and many others, largely still not interpreted.

The classical introduction scene from the period of the revival which showed a worshipper led by an interceding deity before an enthroned supreme god seems to have been increasingly simplified during the course of the Old Babylonian period, when the enthroned god was changed into a standing one, and was finally omitted altogether: now all that remained was the interceding goddess in the long flounced dress and the legend, of two or three lines, of the owner of the seal[16] (Pl. G 7).

A sub-division of Old Babylonian stone-cutting does, however, form an exception in the particularly high quality of its technique. It employs scenes from the age-old Sumero-Akkadian 'figured band', which had survived into the period of the Third Dynasty of Ur, the hero with the six loops of hair, fighting the lion, and the naked hero with the bent knee overpowering a bull[17] (Pl. G 9–11). The detailed work on piece VR 467 is of an unsurpassed delicacy on the hard surface of ironstone. Of clearly Akkadian origin is the naked hero with six loops of hair, pressing with his knee into the back of a lion, and so is the winged lion dragon with the legs and tail of a bird of prey. On the other hand the upright, crouching position of the ox being attacked by a lion from behind is strange. This motif has a parallel in the Old Elamite cylinder seal of the Early Proto-historical Period, but there is no obvious link between that and Old Babylonian art. Only during the period of the First Dynasty of Babylon can we find workmanship so good in the stone-cutting of western Syria. This makes one wonder whether this sub-group of a different style of Old Babylonian glyptic does not in fact express a specifically Canaanite feeling for form, although in general the Canaanite influence on Old Babylonian art seems to have been predominantly of a thematic nature. The merging of typically Canaanite with Sumero-Akkadian subjects and styles does not seem to have happened uniformly everywhere or in a similar manner in the various areas of Old Babylonian culture – Larsa, Isin, Babylon or Ashur, in the Diyala valley, Mari or Alalakh. Probably the traditions of the different centres of the Land of the Two Rivers were too varied and too unequal in strength for a Canaanite imperial art to be imposed from a high level. Hammurabi's kingdom was of too short a duration – and the technical possibilities for excavating the kingdom's capital too unfavourable – for us to be able to form a clear idea of the art of stone-cutting under the great king himself, purely from the glyptic which has survived. The original seals bearing legends with the name of Hammurabi provide nothing much above the average Old Babylonian art. Moreover no seal relating to the great kings of Assyria – from Shamshi-Adad I or the district of Rim-Sin – shows any exceptional feature. Nor do the impressions of seals on the texts on clay tablets in the Louvre, originating in the period of Hammurabi, testify in any way to the grandeur of these rulers. Our conception of the development of glyptic in the Old Babylonian age will, however, be somewhat different if we turn to the cylinder seals and impressions newly found in Mari, which belonged to Zimrilim, his wife Shiptu and several of his high officials. They provide us with a new image of the content and style of Old Babylonian glyptic. In fact, they show us the difference between Canaanite glyptic in the Ancient Mesopotamian tradition, on the one hand, as Mukannishum, the Superintendent of the Palace, practised it[18] (Pl. N 3) – his seal has a picture of Zimrilim as a conqueror in battle, trampling on his enemies with the help of a winged Ishtar; her wings are perhaps the only alien element in this picture, which otherwise stems from the Old Akkadian tradition – and on the other hand the more Canaanite-Syrian features exhibited by a seal belonging to another official of Zimrilim, Ana-Sin-taklaku[19] (Pl. N 4). As far as subject-matter is concerned, one should note here an unusual innovation in the form of a second interceding goddess, and a partly bare figure of a dancing woman carrying a tambourine on her left elbow, as well as the Syrian diagonal dress of the fighting god and the strange padded garment wrapped diagonally round the worshipper, who is presenting an ibex as a sacrifice. The technique of the glyptic is outstanding. These seals from the world of Zimrilim of Mari show that the Canaanite stone-cutter in Mesopotamia had learnt by then to combine traditional motifs in a new way and to renew and revitalize them with elements of west Syrian-Canaanite origin. At the same time they show that in the glyptic too the development of art during the Old Babylonian period reached its highest point under Hammurabi or his immediate contemporaries.

Perhaps we may yet succeed through future excavations in discovering seals belonging to Hammurabi himself, which will be of the same high artistic quality as the seals of Mukannishum and Ana-Sin-taklaku from Mari.

2   Wall painting

As we were able earlier in the book, in the chapter on the art of the Sumero-Akkadian revival, to date the wall paintings in Room 132 of the Palace of Mari in the period of the Third Dynasty of Ur, this section of the paintings from the Palace is therefore omitted from our survey of Old Babylonian art. The remaining paintings in this great building are, however, sufficiently numerous and important to give us an idea not only of the state of painting in Zimrilim's reign, that is, during the same period as Hammurabi, but also in a somewhat earlier phase, which should be related to Shamshi-Adad I and his son Iasmah Adad (= Iasmah Addu) (see above, p. 80). This wall painting, the oldest from the Old Babylonian period

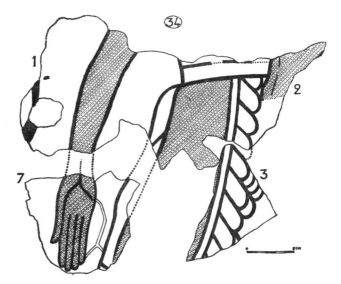

Fig. 58   Fragment of a wall painting (an army leader) from Room 34 in the Palace of Mari
(After: A. Parrot, MAM 2, *Le Palais, Peintures murales*, p. 9, Fig. 7)

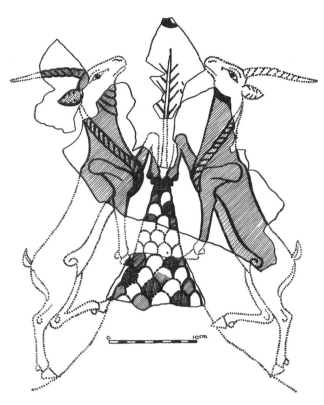

Fig. 59 Fragment of a wall painting with he-goats from Court 106 of the Palace at Mari
(After: A. Parrot, MAM 2, *Le Palais, Peintures murales*, p. 28, Fig. 23)

purely cult theme (Pls. 202, 203): Iasmah-Adad cannot have used this theme only on the walls of Court 106 because the fragment from Room 34[21] (Fig. 58), which forms part of the actual residence of the king, is from a figure in the same dress as the great leader, in the same movement, with the same swinging stride, and with the same hand movement. In addition to this cult motif Iasmah-Adad's artists introduced other subjects. As well as the cult scenes there were paintings of myths. An outstanding example of this is the fragment, heavily restored but well authenticated, with the scene of two he-goats on each side of a tree on a mountain top[22] (Fig. 59). The painters of this epoch not only used cult or mythical themes, but also had to glorify the concept of kingship. A broken fragment, picked up at the base of the west wall of Court 106[23] (Fig. 60) instead of by the south wall like the other, seems to have on it a picture of the king or of a high-ranking officer in a garment of which the seams were finished with the double border of rounded tabs, and with a short sword stuck in his belt: the blade with its knob hilt is just projecting from the sheath. The girdle end decorated with blossom is also preserved. The figure of the armed king must surely be part of a military scene. Thus painting under Iasmah-Adad must also

known to us, may also possibly contain an Old Assyrian element, though admittedly it is in a damaged condition, because it was originally placed high up on the walls, but its technique, especially in the rendering of the white layer of plaster which received the colours, was better than the technique used earlier or later, and what is most important, it is possible, in spite of the shattering of the murals, to obtain an idea of the thematic repertoire of this type of painting, which shows that the artist even at that period understood how to distribute one whole composition over the four walls of a large court or several rooms, and yet keep it together.[20]

The best-known pieces from the Iasmah-Adad phase are the two fragments, probably originally part of one scene, showing a great procession with sacrificial bulls, headed by the king himself as priest (see above, p. 72). They are the best examples of a

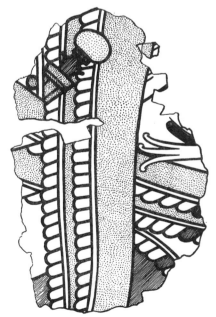

Fig. 60 Fragment of a wall painting with a dress and short sword, from Court 106 of the Palace at Mari (After: A. Parrot, MAM 2, *Le Palais, Peintures murales*, p. 42, Fig. 35)

have included scenes from the life of the commander-in-chief. If one visualizes the painting on the four walls of Court 106, and considers its pictorial content and inter-relationship, one is reminded involuntarily of the decoration on the four walls of some Late Assyrian palace courts (see below p. 130). Do the roots of Assyrian wall relief reach back to the period of Shamshi-Adad I?

There is scarcely anything new to say about the scene on the so-called 'retable' from Room 46 of the royal residence.[24] However, the painting can probably be assigned to Iasmah-Adad, because of the place in the palace where it was found. Is it actually a wooden frame over which some sort of tapestry was stretched? If so, it is of special importance, as it would be the first evidence of the existence of any kind of panel painting in the Ancient Orient, as opposed to the usual wall painting. Also the division of the pictorial surface into smaller compartments would be of interest, because of its resemblance to the treatment of the pictorial surface of the main scene in the wall painting dating from the Zimrilim phase in the Palace of Mari, the so-called Investiture of that king (see above, p. 70).

As we unfortunately only have this one wall painting in Mari from the reign of Zimrilim himself, we cannot come to a final conclusion on the painting technique, the range of subject-matter and the composition of the picture during this particular phase of Old Babylonian painting, though we have already noticed differences in the layer of plaster, in the colour scale and in the method of rendering the god's crown in profile, as between the wall painting under Iasmah-Adad and that under Zimrilim, and we have made use of these differences to compile a chronological sequence for the groups of paintings in Mari (see above, pp. 69 ff.).

Whereas the extensive friezes of Iasmah-Adad, with their varied themes – which included myths (tree + two goats + mountain), cult ceremonies (procession with the sacrificial bull), and the glorification of the king (man with sword in the blue robe and battle scene) – make use of the long row as the underlying element of its narrative art, the 'retable' from Room 34 and the Investiture scene seem to employ the enclosed and framed pictorial surface divided into small compartments, as the basis of their composition. When, as in the Investiture scene, the edges were bordered with tassel-shaped ornaments, probably imitations of a carpet-fringe,[25] the painting became a painted substitute for a textile pictorial carpet. Possibly the so-called 'retable', which belongs to the Iasmah-Adad phase, also represents a wall-carpet, which at one time stretched over a wooden frame, would have been used as a wall decoration. The difference between the two phases of Old Babylonian wall painting, that of Iasmah-Adad and that of Zimrilim, would therefore have depended more on the enlargement of the colour scale and a refinement of perspective rather than on subject-matter or composition.

In this way Zimrilim's artists drew closer to the relief sculptors of Hammurabi of Babylon than to their predecessors in Mari, the painters of the son of Shamshi-Adad I, King of Ashur.

3 Relief

Even if, like Goetze, we wished to redate the relief from Mardin (see above, p. 72; Pls. 204, 205), which we have already discussed and utilized to date a group of wall paintings in the Palace of Mari, and if we wished to attribute it to Dadusha of Eshnunna rather than to Shamshi-Adad I of Ashur, we should still not arrive much before the first years of Hammurabi for this relief, which is possibly the oldest relief instigated by a Canaanite prince in Mesopotamia. It is important, inasmuch as it enables us to recognize that, up to the beginning of Hammurabi's reign, the history of Old Babylonian relief did not amount to much more than a contribution of a few facts and material details primarily derived from the native costume of the Canaanite. Also the workmanship of the Akkadian-based conqueror motif, which shows the victor putting his foot on the body of his falling enemy, and equally the scene of the shackled prisoners on the rear side of the relief plaque, seems very stiff and provincial.[26] The rapid progress of Old Babylonian relief is then all the clearer if we compare this with the few examples which can be assigned to the period of Hammurabi himself.

There is a fragment of a stele in the Baghdad Museum which was found on the ground at Ishchali[27] (Pl. 207). It is scarcely possible to give it an exact date from the place where it was found, but the upper levels at that place cannot be far removed in time from Hammurabi.[28] The scene is of a worshipper standing in a long robe in front of Shamash, who is in a slit dress with his right foot forward and must have been holding something in each hand. In the technique of its workmanship – particularly in the contrast, probably intentional, between the very plastic rendering of the naked right leg and the quite flat dress over the left lower part of the god's body – the scene is much more lively and more skilful than the relief from Mardin. The noticeably high relief of this work perhaps suggests the period of Hammurabi himself, as we shall now see.

It is almost a miracle that chance has preserved at any rate two works of art from the entire stock of relief originating in the actual reign of Hammurabi. In fact only one of them is of real significance in the history of Old Babylonian art, and it is also a work of basic importance to the entire history of culture in Ancient Mesopotamia. This is the stele of diorite which is inscribed with the famous Law Code of the ruler. If we possessed only the other relief, the fragment of a stele which has been in the possession of the British Museum for decades[29] (Pl. 208), Hammurabi's name would scarcely merit a mention in the history of art. This has a Sumerian inscription, several lines long, and arranged in two parts, one above the other, which informs us that an official, Iturashdu, had dedicated it to a goddess for the life of Hammurabi.[30] Next to this inscription there stood once the figure of the king, viewed in profile looking to the right and lifting his right hand in worship. The surface of the relief has been so badly damaged that only parts of the face and upper body can still be recognized. Of the kings' face we can only distinguish faint traces of the powerful, delicately shaped but fleshy nose. The beard is clearly divided into two parts, that on the chin and the part on the chest. The latter consists of irregularly waving, vertical strands which taper slightly towards the bottom. The cap has a

much smaller brim than that of Gudea or Ur-Nammu, and leaves half his neck hair and ear free. Over his chest the dress had a diagonal fastening edged with a tasselled border, running from the right armpit to the left shoulder, and this left the whole, very slender right arm clear. The ruler was wearing a double necklace made of small and large pearls, and on his right wrist he wore a bracelet of two padded rolls. It is no longer possible to see whether the material of his dress was lifted from the right lower side and laid over the right forearm. Even when one takes its very poor state of preservation into consideration, this relief shows no particular skill in its carving, such as would have been worthy of a man like Hammurabi.

It is quite a different matter with the relief which fills the semi-circle formed by the top of the stele of the codex. This stele was originally erected in Sippar, the city of the sun god, and was then taken away in the Second Millennium by an Elamite king, Shutruk-nahhunte, as booty to his capital Susa, where it was discovered at the beginning of this century during the French excavations[31] (Pl. 209).

Its subject-matter of no particular interest, this picture of the greatest of the Canaanite rulers in front of the enthroned Lord of Light and Righteousness impresses every observer by its simplicity. Whoever studies the style of this relief with sufficient care must see in it a milestone in the long history of Ancient Mesopotamian art, comparable in importance in the history of art with works like the Stele of Naram-Sin or the torso of the statue of Manishtusu. It is sufficient to gain for Hammurabi himself a special place in the field of art, in addition to his significance in the history of literature, politics and law, which lifts him far above the great circle of the other Canaanite rulers in Ancient Mesopotamia.

We do not know if there was a fairly long passage of time between the Stele of Iturashdu and the Codex of Hammurabi, because we cannot date the former with sufficient exactitude within the life of Hammurabi. All we know for certain is that the Law Code originated in the later years of the king.[32] The difference in power of expression between the stele of Iturashdu and the relief on the Law Code, where Hammurabi is shown advancing in greeting towards his enthroned god, must be attributed to that same extraordinary creative genius and personality which inspired the poetic language used in the prelude to his code on the stele. There is no factual difference in the details between the figure of Hammurabi on the British Museum stele and his figure on the Code – bearing and attire, dress and brimmed cap, neck and arm ornaments, all are the same – but only in the plasticity and above all the inner vitality which is revealed by the modelling, and these are completely new. The modelling of the right forearm on both figures should be noted. This plasticity, related in spirit to that of Old Akkad, is also that which, since the Ur III period, has produced the completely new stylization of Hammurabi's robe in his Law stele. Nowhere else – not even with Gudea or the statues in the round of the Third Dynasty of Ur – can we find a similar treatment of folds (and incidentally these do not arise from the movement of the body) like the folds we see on the right side of the king's dress. Nowhere else does the material of the dress fall in such curved lines or mass in deep grooves and thick rolls, as it does over his left forearm. This should be compared with a relief on a stele in the Louvre[33] (Pl. 210), on which a prince from the earlier Sumerian period of revival is making a libation in front of an enthroned god. In the latter the material of the dress is completely without movement, utterly flat.

But the unique merit of the relief on Hammurabi's Code is not based only on this new ability to portray folds. It is also due to the rendering of the horned crown and beard of Shamash, and in essence as in all bas-relief it is less a question of style as such than the ability, fundamental to all two-dimensional art, to blend three-dimensional reality with a two-dimensional image. Ancient Mesopotamian art, like all 'pre-Greek' art, indeed like Egyptian art, remains throughout at the level of 'imaginative' art, i.e. in general it does not understand how to deceive the eye with an illusion of three-dimensional space on a two-dimensional surface, a technique generally called perspective.[34] Only when the artist has realised that the world of perception, felt by man with hand and seen by his eyes, is fundamentally an image of actual reality, a way of reflecting existence, can he strive in his art-form not merely to portray a symbol of things

independent of their incidental shape, but rather to capture reality in a copy, which the eye can recognize as an image. We must assume that the spirit of Hammurabi was approaching this stage when we see definite attempts at perspective suddenly appearing during this period. These attempts may be connected with the personality of Hammurabi himself or at any rate with his circle of friends, as they cannot be shown to have existed anywhere else in the Near East. The relief as such is in itself a form of two-dimensional art, but now with the Law Code of Hammurabi it moves from bas-relief towards sculpture in the round, and this is made clear in many features, particularly in the faces, the hair-style of the god and his crown, which practically stand out from the surface of the relief as though sculptured in the round. The sculptor is creating a completely new precedent, however, a first step towards perspective, when he no longer places the horned crown *en face* above the god in profile – as had been the custom since primitive times, and which was still the custom in the epoch preceding the Old Babylonian period, and indeed was still the custom even at the beginning of the First Dynasty of Babylon – but instead shows the flat top, the main part of the crown, surmounted by a circular disk, in profile, and similarly shows just four horns in profile instead of four pairs of horns from in front. We may regard these early attempts, which perhaps at first may seem rather unimportant to a modern observer, as symptomatic for the actual period of King Hammurabi, since it cannot yet be established in scenes like, for example, that on the seal of Queen Shalurtum, the wife of Singashid of Uruk, a daughter of Sumulailu of Babylon,[35] who lived only a little earlier. The same endeavour seems to have been behind the foreshortening of the dimension of depth in the god's beard. The horizontal waves of the long beard, which stretches down in an elongated rectangle over his chest, are no longer shown completely horizontal, as a purely frontal aspect would require, and like those, for example, on the similar stele in the Louvre (Pl. 210),[36] but actually run slightly diagonally from the bottom left up to the right, as though viewed from the side and foreshortened.

We may allow ourselves to consider these characteristics just outlined (the method of moulding the folds with plasticity, the raising of the relief until it seems almost to stand away from the pictorial surface, the portrayal of the horned crown in profile when the head is in profile, and the first beginnings of a foreshortening to achieve perspective) as characteristics typical of the relief originating in the period of Hammurabi in the narrowest sense, as we cannot yet find them occurring before his reign.

If we then go on to examine the terra-cotta relief so characteristic of the Old Babylonian period,[37] we can only find a few examples where the sculptor made any attempt at perspective. The best analogy with the head of Shamash and its horned crown is provided by the figure of a god on a terra-cotta plaque discovered at Khafaje on Hill B (= Dur Samsu-iluna). This has a mythical scene showing gods fighting, and it is of great importance[38] (Pl. 211): using a powerful knife, the god is cutting the body of a female demon into two halves: her head, with its Cyclops eye and ring of light-rays, is shown full-face, though her arms are tied behind her back and the upper part of her naked body is shown completely in profile. The god's great crown with its horns is the exact counterpart of that of Shamash. If the site of Dur Samsu-iluna may be used as proof of its age, this terra-cotta shows that the same level of style as that achieved under Hammurabi was at least maintained and even carried further under his son.[39] A second terra-cotta relief, which examination of the stratum suggests may be linked with Samsu-iluna,[40] has nevertheless a horned crown *en face* above a head in profile. Also the well-known Burney relief[41] (Pl. 212), a work of the highest quality, employs exactly the same relief technique which, as in the Code of Hammurabi, is really striving towards complete plasticity, and the horned crown of the goddess, who is winged and has the claws of a bird, can easily be recognized as identical in every detail with that of Shamash, except that the motif of a head *en face* affords no opportunity for a crown in profile.

By Hammurabi's reign the borders between relief and sculpture in the round are beginning to become indistinct, as we can see in the Burney relief – amongst others. Therefore in our endeavour to understand fully the sculpture of the Old Babylonian period,

and particularly the sculpture from the more limited period of Hammurabi within the Old Babylonian period, we may also be able to rely on relief for guidance.

4 Sculpture in the round

In complete contrast to the earlier period of the revival, when by and large only figures of worshippers were produced, the few surviving examples of Old Babylonian plastic art form a source-material which is heterogeneous in its technique and its content, and incomplete from the point of view of the history of art: portraits of gods and humans, individual figures and groups, made of stone and metal. Consequently at the present time there is no possibility of establishing a continuous stylistic sequence of standing and seated figures during the Old Babylonian period, with the help of a chain of homogeneous works, as was possible for earlier periods. Rather for the time being we can only try to gain a few fixed points in Old Babylonian sculpture, and in particular in that from the Hammurabi period in the narrow sense of the word. Indeed, to accomplish this we shall have to use every chronological method available to us: inscriptions, place of discovery, and its stratum, as well as an analysis of styles. It cannot be an accident that amongst the Old Babylonian statues in the round which have been found, scarcely any still show the old type of the Sumerian worshipper figure or that of the Old Akkadian conqueror. The last examples of these, the booty taken from Eshnunna to Susa – amongst which was the figure presumed to be Ur-Ningizzida of Eshnunna[42] – seem to form the final stage of a centuries-old tradition in Mesopotamia, only carried on reluctantly by the Canaanites.

The oldest of the Canaanite statues in the round, its period fully authenticated by an inscription, is the so-called 'Statue Cabane', the chance discovery of which at Tell Hariri gave rise to the excavations of the old city of Mari, with such far-reaching consequences. The inscription[43] states that Iasmah-Adad, the son of Shamshi-Adad I, had the figure made and brought to the centre of the city as an offering for Shamash. The statue itself is unique in the history of Ancient Mesopotamian art and has neither a predecessor nor a successor[44] (Pl. 213). Only comparable are the figures of the Hittite mountain god in relief and in the round.[45] It consists of the naked upper part of the body of a man on a conical base, which can be recognized as a mountain on account of its scale pattern. The two parts are joined by a wide girdle. The beard, which hangs far down his chest, has the same symmetrical and stylized curls as those on the much older portrait of the *shakkanakku* of Mari, Puzur-Ishtar, from the period of the Third Dynasty of Ur (see above, p. 65; Pls. 181, 182). This type of beard is therefore a characteristic feature, employed in Mari throughout the centuries. Perhaps Iasmah-Adad's statue of Shamash has also retained a slightly archaic appearance, but in any event it represents an earlier phase than that of the relief of Shamshi-Adad from Mardin, the wall paintings of Iasmah-Adad in Court 106 at Mari, Zimrilim's sculpture in the round, and certainly than that of Hammurabi.

The second example of a figure of a god from the Old Babylonian period is that of a statue which has become famous; it is of an almost life-size woman in a flounced dress and a simple crown with horns, and it was found in the Palace of Mari in several pieces, at the foot of the podium in Room 64, though its head was found near the basin in Court 106[46] (Pls. 214, 215). A water-jet must actually have flowed from the *aryballos*-type vase which she is holding in front of her in both hands, as a channel was found drilled inside the body of the statue. The whole object represents a transformation into three-dimensions of the water divinities who formed an important element of the great wall painting, the so-called Investiture of Zimrilim, which Zimrilim had put on the south wall of Court 106 (see above, p. 70). One might conclude from this related theme that the statue should probably be assigned to the period of Zimrilim. The statue is obviously quite in the old Sumero-Akkadian tradition, both in its theme and style. But it also deviates from that tradition in many

of its details. Whereas the flounced dress has been copied from it, the bodice made of wide bands of cloth crossed diagonally, covering the upper part of the body, the rounded tab fringes on the edges of the sleeves, and the association of the heavy hairstyle with two huge horns are not Ancient Mesopotamian in origin but would seem rather to be specifically Canaanite. On the other hand, the two heavy loops of hair, lying on each shoulder on either side of her face, link the figure with that of Shamash on Hammurabi's Code of Law and with some other Old Babylonian figures. It cannot be denied that the sculptor has found his own distinctive expression in the difficult language of sculpture in the round, and it emphasizes his own individuality in contrast to the weight of tradition. He has combined grandeur and delicacy in the modelling, and yet retained a feeling for elegance and tenderness in his drawing, as when he expresses on the surface of the dress the flowing and spurting of the water by his engraving of the waves, accompanied by fish, with the dress ending in volutes. His art approaches closer to the spirit of Hammurabi than did the Shamash figure of Iasmah-Adad.

The series of statues in the round from the Old Babylonian period concludes with a pair of bronze statuettes from Ishchali. One is of a god in a long flounced dress trailing a sickle axe from his right arm; the god is stepping with his left foot on a ram lying in front of him. The other is of a goddess seated on a simple stool, who is holding with both hands in front of her breast a vessel from which water is gushing[47] (Pls. 216, 217). Both deities have four faces and therefore were probably a pair. Both can be dated from their place of origin[48] to the period of Ishchali, that is to say, in the period of Old Babylon, yet they have several details which seem Canaanite-Syrian. The god, whose four faces are to a large extent made more plausible with the aid of his beard – and this, by the way, has the same arrangement of curls as that of the Shamash statue of Iasmah-Adad – resembles the so-called Amurru on the seal of Abishare[49] (Pl. G 5) so closely that it may be a representation of Amurru himself: and the seated goddess of the water of life, herself the counterpart of the water-goddess from Mari (Pls. 214, 215), is wearing a cylindrical hat consisting of a flat cap with horns and a high cylinder with an altar or temple façade drawn on it. This hat must have some connection with the head-dress habitually worn in Syria by goddesses,[50] so that both the theme and style of this pair of statuettes from Ishchali allow us to recognize for once something of the true Canaanite element, which played a decisive part in forming Old Babylonian art.

In the well of the court of the Ishtar Temple at Mari a fragment of the bust of a woman was found: it is of steatite and in dress and style it is so unlike all the earlier statuettes from the Ishtar Temple that Parrot thinks it can probably be dated to the beginning of the Second Millennium.[51] It is difficult to decide whether this bust still belongs to the period of the revival, as the 'Manishtusu tassels' on her shawl may indicate, or whether it should be assigned to the Babylonian period, which would fit in better with the long pendant hanging down her back like a pigtail. In any case it seems to be the portrait of a princess and not of a goddess. The style of the tassels is identical with the tassels on the robes of several of the male statues from Eshnunna. The heavy necklace and bracelet with padded rolled borders are familiar to us from the Old Babylonian period.

The pigtail-like pendant, which serves as a counter-weight for the necklace, appears again in a very similar form on an outstandingly well-made fragment from a group statue[52] (Pls. 219, 220), which has been in the Louvre for years, and it would therefore not seem reasonable to place the two works of art – the bust from Mari and this double group – far apart in sequence of time. There is scarcely another work of art from the ancient oriental world which expresses so vividly the rustling flow of the delicate material as the back of this pair of goddesses, with their arms round each other and both clasping the *aryballos* vase. The work is touched with an appreciation of beauty otherwise rare in Ancient Mesopotamia. This must be the real reason why, although it had no inscription and no known place of origin, it was dated to the Akkad period. Yet the theme, which we have already met at Mari and Ishchali, as well as the details of dress (the pendant down the back, the fish in the water waves, the bracelet with padded

rolls) suggest it should be dated to the period of Hammurabi.

If at the present time when dating a work of art we hesitate between the Old Akkadian and the Old Babylonian periods, it shows how greatly the latter period represents the culmination of the Old Akkadian renaissance, which we saw in its beginning during the reigns of Gudea and Ur-Nammu.

We have grounds for attributing to the time of Hammurabi himself two further bronze statues in the round from Larsa, which are individual both in their motif and technique: one is the worshipper,[53] about 20 cm. high on a rectangular base, which has a relief showing the same scene carved on its longer side, a kneeling figure worshipping in front of an enthroned god. An inscription in Sumerian informs us that this was dedicated by a certain Awil-Nannar for the life of Hammurabi of Babylon and for his own life to the god Amurru. The covering of the face and hands with beaten gold foil is striking. It recalls Canaanite-Syrian bronze figures made in a similar way. As this unusual feature is repeated on a second bronze work of art from Larsa,[54] it is possible to attribute both works to the same period. It is true that the three ibexes, which in this case are placed standing quite upright on their hind legs, fit freely into the iconography of ancient oriental art, yet the manner in which they are standing is unusual – on a high base with votive water basins supported by small human (or divine?) figures. The animals' faces are once more covered in gold foil, and the small human figures in silver foil (Pl. 218).

Although these examples of Old Babylonian toreutic are linked with Hammurabi of Babylon by their inscriptions, yet their artistic qualities do not help us to learn anything about the character of the greatest king of the Old Babylonian period. Perhaps we may obtain this in the end more easily by a critical examination of the style of some more or less neglected fragments: such an examination may show us that during the period of Hammurabi, who had created once again, temporarily at least, a great Near Eastern empire, sculpture in the round not only portrayed gods, as it has sometimes seemed, but also expressed the concept of kingship, as it had in earlier periods. If we really had a statue of Hammurabi himself, then it would have differed in style as clearly from the figures of the rulers directly preceding him (from about the time of the Isin-Larsa dynasties), as the relief on the Codex differed from Shamshi-Adad's relief from Mardin. Amongst the various standing and seated statues of rulers which reached Susa from Babylon as booty, there only seems to be one work to which this applies, namely the seated statue in the Louvre[55] (Pl. 221). Like the Code of Law of Hammurabi it is made of diorite and it differs from the other statues in the round from Eshnunna[56] firstly in that the usual stylized fringes on the old Manishtusu pattern are missing. But not only negative evidence identifies this figure: positive proof as well draws it close to Hammurabi, granted that one can compare a statue in the round with a relief. The scene on the stele of the Law Code where Hammurabi is greeting Shamash is truly, line for line, the two-dimensional version of the seated figure we are considering now. Both are completely motionless, the one standing, the other seated. Yet the robe of both shows a few strongly pronounced folds on the right side of the body, where the material is lifted, and it hangs down from the left wrist in a few thick folds. In both, the material at the bottom on the left is pulled back and comes to a point next to the end piece of the material shown as forming a right-angle. The thick bunched-up material running slantwise from the right armpit up to the left shoulder is arranged identically in both instances into three rolls. The bare parts of the body, the right shoulder and arm, are completely similar. If the city name on the seated figure (of which only a fraction of one character has survived) has been read correctly as Eshnunna, it may well be a seated figure set up by Hammurabi after he had destroyed the city. This seated figure, so unlike all the other statues from Susa, can only originate from Hammurabi, whose relief was equally individual. Once one has put forward this hypothesis, however, immediately one is obliged to complete this unique seated figure with the help of a head, just as unusual in style, from Susa.[57] This head, made of diorite (Pl. 222), the so-called 'Old Hammurabi', with its facial features lined by work and spiritual grief, half the picture of a king and half a portrait, leaps across the frontiers of the age-old art-form. Only on quite

isolated occasions and to a slight degree did the sculptor of the ancient Near East include anything of the personal character of the man he was portraying, in addition to the symbolization of the concept of kingship or the cult-religious purpose of his work – and then hardly ever with such emphasis. Was this attempt born out of the same intellectual attitude – the discovery that the external shape is formed by its inner character – which led the sculptor of the Law Code stele to introduce the beginnings of perspective? The beard shown on ancient oriental figures is obviously not shaped by their inner being, but it is also clear that its shape has not been arrived at by sheer chance. The style of the beard-peruke was probably based on the strict rules of the hierarchy, so that it may not be without significance that there is the same beard on both fragments of statues, the head and the seated figure from Susa. The beard was long and reached down to the chest on the seated figure which was found without its head: it is symmetrical and divided down the centre into two sets of four, stylized long strands like ropes. The two groups of strands are incised symmetrically with diagonal grooves. The chin beard on the head consists of several rows of spiral curls, of which only barely the beginning of the bottom row was preserved on the seated figure. On the head, the 'Old Hammurabi', on the other hand, the same division of the beard – above into spiral curls and below into long 'rope' strands – can still be seen quite clearly. This would suggest that both works represent the same individual. Our whole argument, for assigning both the seated figure and the head to the reign of Hammurabi himself, receives its strongest support if a statement by M. Pézard and E. Pottier (in the second edition of the *Catalogue des Antiquités de la Susiane*, Paris 1926, under Nos. 58 and 463 respectively) is correct. In this an inscription of Hammurabi's (No. 463) is linked to the seated figure itself (No. 58). This, in fact, can only be possible if the material of both the fragments is the same, namely diorite. But the material of No. 463 is cited as basalt (perhaps by mistake?)

Literary, legal and historic sources of the Old Babylonian period have for a long time made it seem likely that the reign of Hammurabi itself was indeed the political and cultural culmination of the centuries-long transformation of the Sumero-Akkadian civilization into a Canaanite-Babylonian one. Now this has been fully confirmed by our careful examination, sifting the archaeological remains of the same period and arranging them according to style, by the new discoveries of glyptic from Mari originating in the period of Zimrilim, Hammurabi's contemporary, by the new appraisal of Hammurabi's Law Code as a record of the style of relief in his period, with its introduction of perspective and its movement towards high relief, as well as by the survey of the statues in the round and portraits actually from Hammurabi's reign. The Kingdom of Babylon seems under Hammurabi to have found in its art the means to express itself in a way which suited it, even as centuries earlier in the same field the Old Akkadian kingdom of Sargon has succeeded in doing. Unfortunately the duration of this period of Hammurabi's rule was even shorter than that of the Old Akkadian. Just as the splendour of the Old Akkadian period in southern Mesopotamia was threatened with almost repeated regularity by a new invasion from Iran, the invasion of the Guti tribes, so, as early as the reign of Samsuiluna, the first powerful assaults by the Kassites trying to force their way towards Babylon from the Iranian border mountains had to be repulsed. The succession of the First Canaanite Dynasty was still maintained, but with Hammurabi's death the strength of the Canaanites was also extinguished, and with them the cultural influence of their empire died too.

In the period from about 1700 to 1500 B.C. an ethnic and spiritual change took place in the Near East which placed in jeopardy all that the Sumerians and the Semites had created during the course of a thousand years and brought completely fresh new races, such as the Hurrians, the Hittites and the Kassites into the centre of world politics.

Until that day towards the end of the sixteenth century when the city of Marduk was stormed and laid waste by a barbarian from Anatolia, King Mursilis of Hattusas, the remaining works of art from the Kingdom of Babylon at first unmistakably show signs of spiritual exhaustion, and yet at the same time there are traces of a new world, the world

of the northern mountain peoples, of whom some had – or had previously had – contact with the Indo-European races of Central Asia, which until then had not played any part in the leadership of the Near East. Unfortunately we have fewer sources of information about this period than about almost any other, earlier or later. If it were not for the glyptic, no information of any significance would exist about art, either its subject-matter or style. But as during this period too, sealed business documents and the engraved cylinder seals used for them did not quite come to an end, we have been able with their help to form at least a general view of the motifs used and of some of the features of style of stone-cutting towards the end of the First Dynasty of Babylon.[58] There seems to be a complete lack of new ideas. The Old Babylonian types of gods and magic symbols were carried on and copied, using the same stale subject-matter and style forms. The blurring of the forms was helped by the seal-cutter making use of the drill, the great enemy of precision work, and everything was turned into drilled chains and drilled

Fig. 61   Terra-cotta relief plaque with naked dancing girls, Baghdad. Redrawn.
(After: JEOL, Part 2, No. 8, p. 725, Pl. XXXV)

rosettes: hats became balloon caps and the god with the 'ball-staff' comes into the forefront (Pl. H 1–4).[59] A noticeable feature towards the end of the Old Babylonian period is the tendency to exaggerate the height of the human figure. This is common in glyptic and the easiest to date. This peculiarity also enables us to assign to this period as an exception, but with considerable probability, other small works of art which do not belong to glyptic. For instance, in the Iraq Museum in Baghdad there is an unusual relief on a circular plaque made of baked clay.[60] On the circular pictorial surface two naked women, probably dancers, are standing on a base line: their bodies show the typically Late Canaanite proportions of exaggerated length. Between them are two dwarfs playing lutes, while to the right and left, and above the lute players, there are figures of squatting and standing apes looking on (Fig. 61). The dancing scene was a common theme on the large group of Old Babylonian terra-cotta reliefs.

But probably the most beautiful object amongst works of art surviving from the end of the Old Babylonian period, and the most significant as far as its style is concerned, is a marble disk from Babylon (VA 5933).[61] This small work of art is also a circular plaque (Pl. 223) decorated with a deeply incised pattern, and therefore regarded as a casting mould similar to the terra-cotta moulds which were dug up in the Palace of Mari in such large numbers.[62] It follows that it may not be a coincidence that the picture on the marble disk greatly resembles that on one of the moulds from Mari.[63] Although on the clay mould there are only four naked heroes arranged as a swastika symbol and incised on the circle of the pictorial surface, here on the marble disk there are five naked heroes, altogether more decorative and probably also with symbolic meaning: their heads have six curls of hair and are shown *en face,* and their bodies are interlaced to form a magic pentagram. Not only their beards are unusual – widening towards the base and rendered in great detail – but also the balloon-shaped hair-style and the small round side curls. The exaggerated length of the limbs is here used so skilfully by the artist as part of the ornamental composition that they scarcely seem unnatural.

III Middle Babylonian (Kassite) Art

(Art in Babylon during the period of the Kassite supremacy until Melishihu II)

The Kassites ruled Babylon for several centuries after the overthrow of Babylon by the Hittite Great King, Mursilis. Their origin and early history, as well as details of their progress through Iran – particularly through the province of Luristan, where historians in antiquity still located them – are even now not clear, nor is the relationship of their own language with Indo-European.[1] The long duration of their dynasty (about four to five centuries) stands out in sharp contrast to the uneventfulness of their history. No archaeological monument of Kassite origin dates back beyond the fifteenth century B.C., neither buildings nor works of art, wall paintings nor seals.

A ARCHITECTURE

The earliest information we have of buildings which are really Kassite is linked to the kings Karaindash (1420–1400 B.C.) and Kurigalzu I. Neither shrank from initiating building within the perimeter walls of the two most revered shrines in the country: in Eanna, the sacred precinct of Inanna at Uruk, a centre of Sumerian culture for centuries, and in the shrine of Nanna at Ur. The building of Karaindash, the construction of which the king recorded with pride on his baked bricks,[2] though only a modest undertaking in comparison with the vast complexes erected there during previous centuries (it is a minute little temple for the goddess Innin, situated in the north-

east of the ziggurat), is all the same a special achievement in which everything is truly Kassite – the ground-plan and the elevation, the inner character and the

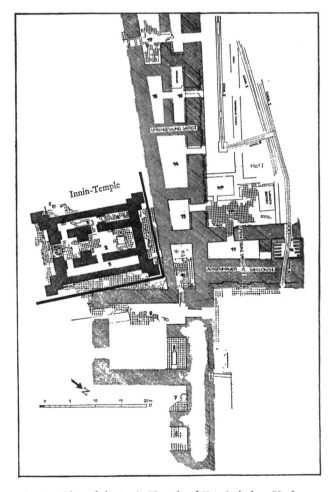

Fig. 62   Plan of the Innin Temple of Karaindash at Uruk (After: UVB 1, Pl. 10)

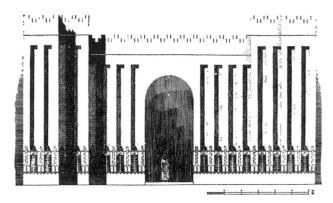

Fig. 63   Reconstruction of the south-eastern façade of the Innin Temple at Uruk
(After: UVB 1, Pl. 16)

outward appearance[3] (Fig. 62). Nowhere else do we know of a similar rectangular 'long house' temple. The entrance is situated on the axis of the temple, in one of the shorter sides which forms the front. The cella with its pronaos is not accessible directly from the gate and forms the heart of the building, flanked on each of its long sides by a corridor-like annexe. The four corners are built out rather like bastions. On the north-west wall, a platform was placed in the inner, rear part of the cella to hold the cult image. This ground-plan is quite unlike all the other ancient oriental ground-plans in that it has no inner courtyard. The building is a free-standing monument and the exterior could be walked round and admired, similar to a Greek temple. The elevation of the small Inanna temple of Karaindash is no less unusual. J. Jordan, the man who excavated it, has reconstructed the building with a vaulted entrance gate in the south-east side, and with its exterior walls decorated with niches in the manner customary for cult buildings[4] (Fig. 63). Entirely new, however, is a base, two to three metres high, made out of modelled baked clay bricks, pressed out of a mould. Parts of these bricks, which had been completely shattered, were reassembled fairly easily in the museums of Baghdad and Berlin. They form the oldest examples of Kassite architectural sculpture, as they come from the beginning of the fifteenth century. They provide us with the best evidence we have of the independence and originality of Kassite building principles, as well as of Kassite art (Pl. 226).

The reconstructed moulded bricks form a frieze of two rows of deities which stand in wall niches, facing outwards: a mountain god, identified by the scale pattern on his coat and cap, alternates with a river goddess, identified by her pattern of waves. It was also possible to reconstruct the *aryballos* vases with water streams flowing from them, as well as the row of mountains, represented by semi-circles[5] (Pls. 227, 228). Further traces of similar sculpture used in architecture were found at Ur, there too probably the work of Kassite builders,[6] and at Nippur,[7] in the Kassite palace of Dur-Kurigalzu,[8] in the art trade,[9] and even at Susa.[10] However, these all come from a later period than the reign of Karaindash, and it is highly probable that it is he who should be credited with the innovation. We may therefore attribute to the Kassites in general a far-reaching independence, a break with the tradition of a thousand years of Sumero-Akkadian and Old Babylonian art and architecture. For the Kassite moulded brick reliefs are sculpture which is actually used as part of the architecture, and the Sumero-Akkadian-Babylonian spirit would have been averse to anything of that nature. Moreover, the moulded brick was a real component of building construction, even though it had the

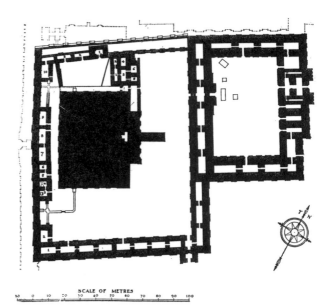

Fig. 64   Plan of the Nanna Shrine at Ur, replanned by Kurigalzu
(After: UE 5, Pl. 72)

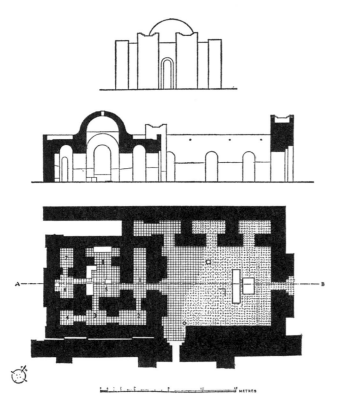

Fig. 65   Plan of the Ningal Temple of Kurigalzu I at Ur
(After: UE 5, Pl. 73)

appearance of sculpture, and it never loses its architectural merit. Even when it appears as a sculpture in
its own right – unlike, say, a mosaic made of inserted
cones or a fresco painted on plaster, it never serves
just as a cover for the real wall of mud bricks and the
structure of the building. The Kassite relief made of
moulded bricks is not a screen to hide the tectonic
forces, like a wall carpet, but is in itself a means of
architectural expression. This indeed represents an
artistic innovation of such basic significance – at least
as far as architecture is concerned – that it alone
would be sufficient to give the Kassite race a distinctive and special place, even though in the long run it
failed to establish itself everywhere within its Mesopotamian surroundings.

The second great patron of building amongst the
Kassite kings was Kurigalzu I. It was he who at the
beginning of the fourteenth century pulled down the
shrine of Nanna at Ur right to its foundations, in
order to rebuild it[11] (Fig. 64). There Kurigalzu has

visibly attempted – with an enormous expenditure of
energy – to free his building from the weight of an
architecture hemmed down by tradition. He built a
new dwelling for the wife of the Moon God, the
Temple of Ningal[12] (Fig. 65), for which he probably
did not use an older pattern. His ground-plan is so
alien that we can barely interpret it; and also the so-
called *Edublalmah* (which means, more or less, 'the
house for hanging up the exalted tablets'), where
Kurigalzu did a great deal of building, causes us some
difficulties, in spite of the inscriptions which have
survived. But it is of importance in the history of
Kassite architecture, both because it contains a vast
door with barrel vaulting, preserved to over three
metres in height, and because of the fact that Kurigalzu had the shrine built on a platform,[11] a kind of
raised *kisu* (Figs. 66, 67). The latter may have served
the desire to raise the building up out of its profane
surroundings. The barrel vaulting, a technique in
itself known in earlier periods, for the first time in
the *Edublalmah* was given a certain aesthetic significance.

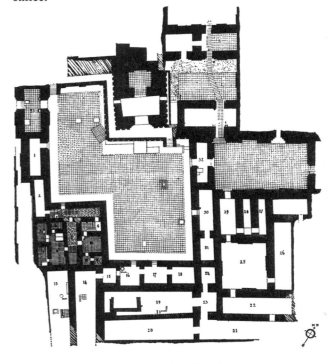

Fig. 66   Plan of the *Edublalmah* of Kurigalzu I at Ur
(After: UE 8, Pl. 48)

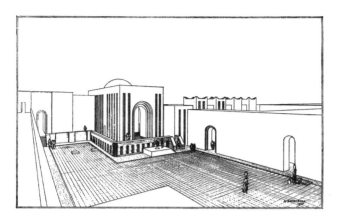

Fig. 67   Reconstruction of the *Edublalmah* of Kurigalzu I at Ur
(After: UE 8, Pl. 51)

Kurigalzu I is probably also the founder of the
residential city of the Kassite kings, situated outside
Babylon, a few kilometres west of Baghdad, on the
site of modern 'Aqar Quf, with its still impressive
ruins of a ziggurat. After F. M. Th. Böhl had again
pointed out the urgent need for it to be excavated,[12]
this was actually carried out during the years 1942–5
by the Baghdad Directorate General of Antiquities
under the supervision of Taha Bakir and Seton Lloyd[13]
(Fig. 68), but the first dig, the aim of which was to
lay bare a Kassite settlement, was unfortunately
never finished.

The place has revealed a curious extended, almost

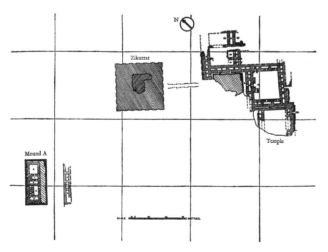

Fig. 68   Ground-plan of the hill at 'Aqar Quf (Dur-Kurigalzu)
(After: Iraq Supplement, 1945, Pl. I)

snake-like plan, which was necessitated by the terrain.
Apart from the ziggurat which, as a typical Sumerian
cult building, conformed entirely in style to the
tradition of Ancient Mesopotamian architecture,[14] the
excavations actually revealed only buildings of unique
character which can only, therefore, be considered
as Kassite: while what remains to-day of the ziggurat
stands at approximately the centre point of the whole
ruined area, the so-called Temple lies to its south-

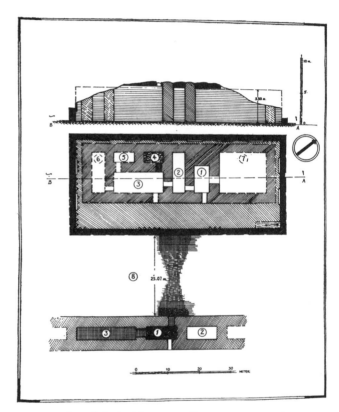

Fig. 69   Plan of the building on Hill A at Dur-Kurigalzu
(After: Iraq Supplement, 1945. Pl. II)

east, Hill A to its west with its massif of mud bricks,
and further to the west Tell Abiad and the remains
of the palace building. They all possess special features. Even the so-called Temple to the east of the
ziggurat has nothing one could consider as its core,
like the cella of a temple. On the contrary it seems
to be a square or rectangular court surrounded by
suites of rooms. The building inscriptions found there
refer to Enlil and Ninurta as the Lords of the House
of the Gods, to Ninlil as the Mistress of the House of

the great Lady of Heaven, and to Enlil as Lord of the Great Whole *(E-U-gal)*. Probably these names should be attached to individual courtyard-systems within the whole complex.

The central court, *E-U-gal*, with a large gate on its north-west side, was fully excavated. To its south it was bordered by a court, *'E-sag-dingir-re-ne'*, of which the south-east wall with its entrance gate seems to form the boundary of the whole sanctuary. To the north there are two more groups of buildings round courts.

The 'Central Tower' of mud bricks remains an entirely unresolved problem: it lies between the central and northern courts, only divided from them by narrow passages. It is clear that this tower is not a second ziggurat, as the excavators at first thought, because somewhat further to the west on Hill A a similar tower of mud bricks was found, and on it the remains of the foundations of a building which must originally have stood upon the tower[15] (Fig. 69). This possibly expresses a similar desire to raise a cult building on a platform, like the one we noted in the *Edublalmah* of Kurigalzu at Ur.

Finally, in addition to its temple architecture, Dur-Kurigalzu has provided us with its own form of palace architecture, in the most westerly part of the ruins, the so-called Tell Abiad. The palace complex consists of a central area A, a circle of surrounding court groups B–G, and a later annexe H[16] (Fig. 70). The central area is formed by a large court, 64 × 64 m., with groups of rooms lying on three of its sides. Each of these groups consists of a long rectangular room or corridor, surrounded on all sides by small rooms. If the corridor was roofed over, it would seem likely that its elevation was raised like a basilica to obtain light, as otherwise the only opening is a gateway onto the court. Because of the court's tremendous length of 64 metres, this gateway must have just looked like a slit in its façade. The stairway chambers situated at each corner of the north-eastern complex formed the ascent to the tower-like corner bastions, and these, together with the unbroken façades of the courtyard must have dominated the appearance of the whole palace complex. The eastern corner of the complex served purely domestic functions: here the arrangement consists of narrow passages from which

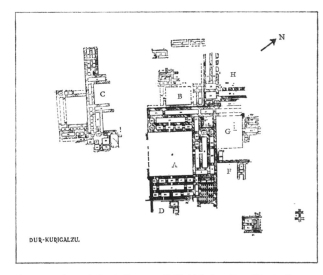

Fig. 70 Plan of the Palace on Tell Abiad at Dur-Kurigalzu (After: Iraq 8, Pl. IX, Fig. 1)

vaulted cellar-like rooms branch off on both sides[17] (Fig. 71).

A tower of mud bricks, found by the excavators to the south-west of the great court, must have been an important area in the palace. It resembled the terrace inside the temple complex on Hill A, except that the tower has not yet been fully explored. A peculiarity of Kassite building technique is the way in which the various groups round the courtyards were not placed next to each other, with a common outside wall, but were built in a loose arrangement

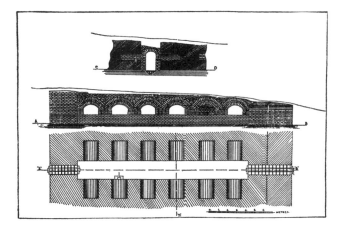

Fig. 71 Plan and section of store-rooms of the Palace at Dur-Kurigalzu
(After: Iraq Supplement, 1945, Pl. XVI)

with no clearly indicated pattern. At first one gets the impression that the individual courts were not built at the same time, but one after the other. However, one can see that this was not the case from the reports of the excavations, except that the so-called Annexe H was in fact erected later than any of the other parts. It was not possible to carry out a surface excavation *in extenso* at Dur-Kurigalzu, on account of the vast expanse of the buildings. The excavators were therefore limited to several soundings in depth, in order to obtain a picture of the palace's development.[18] A comparison of these deep excavations showed that the central area and the rooms directly round it were divided into four levels (I–IV), of which Level I was in three sub-divisions (a-c). Annexe H lay at a much higher level than the central area. Thus the building H was built later and only became an integral part of the whole complex at a later date.

It is difficult to assign the different levels to their correct historical period even though several objects with inscriptions were found in the building strata, for not every inscription was found in its original place: far more often it had been used again.

Nevertheless one inscription has the name Kurigalzu, probably of the first king of this name, and also the name of the palace, *E-gal-ki-shar-ra* (= palace of the land of the totality). The fact that building stratum I can be linked with the late Kassite king Marduk-apal-iddina I (1176–64 B.C.) is of particular importance, because Annexe H, in which important wall paintings were discovered, lay directly on rubble which must be contemporary with Level Ic. Therefore Annexe H and its paintings must have originated towards the very end of the Kassite period, perhaps as late as the Isin II dynasty.

Even today the archaeology of the Kassite period is like patchwork. It is true that in the last thirty years completely new information has come to light concerning its architecture – varying from the actual ground-plan of the temple to the palace building and the arrangement of a royal residence, from barrel vaulting to the creation of a real architectural sculpture in the moulded bricks, but much still remains shrouded in mystery and we can ascertain neither its origin nor purpose.

One fact has been established: architecture in Babylon from the period of the Kassite king Karaindash, in spite of its link with tradition, received a completely new appearance, which can only be due to its Kassite character. Even if this new appearance lost the clarity of its features during the course of the first millennium, yet one should beware not to underestimate or even fail to recognize the achievement of the Kassite race.

B SCULPTURE AND PAINTING

Our knowledge of Kassite art has not quite kept pace with our knowledge of the architecture, but here again we have learnt to value Kassite achievement. The few works of art of which we do know enable us to perceive the fundamental change from the Sumero-Babylonian world to that of the Kassites, even before we have examined them individually in detail: for they belong throughout to a new category of art-form. From the Kassite period onwards we may look in vain for the figure of the worshipper, of which whole series were bequeathed to us from the Third Millennium; similarly the two main media for relief, the votive plaque and the victory stele, also seem to have disappeared. In their place the moulded brick relief makes its appearance in Babylon as part of architectural sculpture, the significance of which we have already noted. No less important – indeed for a time it was almost synonymous with the term Kassite art – was the so-called *kudurru*, which recorded a grant of land and was shaped like a stele, and this became the most important vehicle for relief.

1 The few remaining examples of sculpture in the round

Only very little Kassite sculpture in the round has so far been traced: at present the existence of this major art can only be presumed on the circumstantial evidence of a series of diorite fragments with the remains of a carefully chiselled Sumerian inscription of Kurigalzu.[19] Unfortunately they prove nothing but the existence of a seated figure of this king and add nothing about the details of its style. On the other hand a male head[20] (Pl. 225), about half life-size and made of terra-cotta, does tell us something about the individuality of their sculpture in the round. Its expression has been made even more lively by painting in vivid black and red. It is true that we know of too few works for comparison, to be able to speak of a typically Kassite work of art, but as this head was found in the ruins of the Kassite royal residence it can hardly have originated in another period of art. The sculptor who, with such a sure touch, made the hyena figure[21] (Pl. 224) from Dur-Kurigalzu, also employed the same methods to achieve realism.

Kassite supremacy seems to have lasted for several centuries in Babylon, yet all we possess in the way of sculpture in the round is too scanty for us to be able to follow its development. We shall still not succeed in this even when we come to examine the far more numerous examples of two-dimensional art, of wall painting, of reliefs on the *kudurrus,* and at best only partially in glyptic.

2   Wall painting

Kurigalzu had carried on in his palace the age-old tradition of wall painting, a tradition which we last examined during the Old Babylonian period at Mari. Its technique had not changed a great deal. Painting was still in the old colour scale black-white-red on a thick mud plaster or occasionally on gesso. In the older parts of the Palace at Tell Abiad, in Levels I–IV, only geometrical patterns were at first used as decoration. However, during the very last Kassite period, in the reign of Marduk-apal-iddina, we find figure painting which is different both from the Old Babylonian as well as from Middle and Late Assyrian painting. A row of striding men, probably officials, entering and leaving the palace on business, are shown together on a rectangular pictorial surface which is surrounded by an ornamental border and was always found in doorways. The pictures look

like tapestries put up to protect the wall and the edges of the door, since they stretch round the door.

These paintings in Annexe H show two types of figures: the first is a bare-headed figure dressed in a long robe, with a *tania* (headband) holding together his long hair which hangs far down his back: he has a long beard very similar to that on the terra-cotta head described above[22] (Pl. 225). The second type of figure (Fig. 72) is wearing a long tunic with a girdle (as well as a sash with fringed borders in front and at the sides, and inside the girdle). On his head he is

Fig. 72   Wall painting of male figure from Dur-Kurigalzu (After: Iraq 8, Pl. XII; = Moortgat, *Altvorderasiat. Malerei,* p. 38, Pl. 14)

wearing a tall fez-shaped hat, tapering towards the top. He has a broad squat body. Their heads seem to sit directly on their shoulders as though they had no necks. If one compares these figures, which almost certainly belong to Marduk-apal-iddina's reign in the late Kassite period, with the elongated deities from the Inanna Temple of Karaindash during the early Kassite period, one must ask oneself whether the complete contrast in the proportions of the human body which has taken place during these two and a half centuries is the result of an inner development in the Kassite attitude to style, or whether it is not the Middle Babylonian-Kassite race itself which has changed, due to the continually increasing strength of Aramaic influences. This question will have to be considered later when we are dealing with the origin of Late Babylonian art.

3   Relief

No other form of art is as closely linked to the Kassite character as the large group of the so-called *kudurrus*. Like the Caillou Michaux[23] in the Paris Bibliothèque Nationale, they are amongst the first works of art from the Ancient Near Eastern culture and history to become known in Europe. They have very little in common with the idea of boundary, which is inherent in their name *kudurru* and which links them in the mind to the hermae of antiquity. Their real legal and historical significance depends more on the very full text in cuneiform script which generally covers the major part of their surface, than on the religious-symbolic or mythological-historical reliefs, which are executed in a very artistic manner.[24] The texts make it clear that the *kudurrus* were official charters of grants issued by kings and high officials, to proclaim publicly in the form of a stone stele that which had probably been deposited in the temples in the form of an inscribed clay or metal tablet with the same content, namely the granting to a particular person, official, priest or temple of a particular piece of land, together with the remission of certain taxes and the imposition of certain duties. Thus the *kudurru* is a record of the feudal power of the

king, who in accordance with the land practice of the mountain peoples could dispose of land and property, and could endow his worthy followers with it, although he could also hand it over to the gods and their servants, the priests and priestesses. How far removed this is from the period of Sumerian Proto-history, when the *ensi* and the *lugal,* the king, held all land from God for administration! But the difference is probably a nominal rather than an effective one. The form of the charter expressing the power of the Kassite kings, the shape of the *kudurru*, remained the same as that used to proclaim their power by kings ever since the period of early history. The *kudurru* had the same shape as the stele, on which previously an *ensi* from the period between the Jamdat Nasr and Mesilim Periods had recorded a grant of land, on the so-called small *kudurru* from Larsa.[25] The stele was originally an elongated block of stone placed upright, and carved only slightly, which sometimes became a slab rounded at the top – as under Naram-Sin and Eannatum – but also became obelisk-shaped, as it had already under Manishtusu and did once again under the Assyrian kings. The Kassite kings used both shapes concurrently for their *kudurrus*. That the *kudurru* was an expression of the concept of kingship and its power is demonstrated (on the one hand) by the fact that Shutruk-Nahhunte, who conquered the Kassites in the twelfth century B.C., took the trouble to remove such a large number of them to Susa as booty. The fact that later, in Assyria, there were no longer *kudurrus* but 'obelisks' decorated with scenes of figures illustrating royal deeds underlines the different attitude of the Assyrians towards kingship, in contrast to that of the Babylonians and also of the Kassites.

Already by the Middle Babylonian-Kassite period the monarchy in Babylon refrained from any expression of its military, warlike or even its mythical-heroic character, in contrast to the Assyrian monarchy, which increasingly transformed itself into a political ideology. This difference had as a result the absence of any Middle Babylonian war annals or narrative Kassite reliefs: it also conditioned the purely religious-mythological nature of the most important group of reliefs from the Kassite period, of all the reliefs which the *kudurru* has preserved for us.

The relief-work on all the *kudurrus* has not as yet been assembled systematically and examined by archaeologists. Only when this has been done shall we be able to assess properly its subject-matter, style and its eventual development during the course of the Kassite supremacy, as well as the actual individual examples of Kassite relief.[26] We consider that at the present time the oldest example of the *kudurru* art-form from the Kassite period is the clay one in the British Museum,[27] which has on it the name of King Kurigalzu. However, this has no pictorial relief on it, and amongst the numerous *kudurrus* in the Louvre,[28] found during the excavations in Susa, the great majority are works from the Late Kassite period, particularly works from the reigns of King Melishihu II and of his son Marduk-apal-iddina, so that we have only a one-sided view of the history of the *kudurru* relief. Towards the end of the Kassite period, in the twelfth century, all the various styles of Kassite relief, early and late, were being employed at the same time. This was probably the most highly developed phase of the *kudurru* relief, both in its subject-matter and style, and thereafter, during the Late Babylonian period, there was only a faint echo of this art-form.

The subject-matter of the *kudurru* was never really self-sufficient, like for instance the narrative relief on the Assyrian obelisk (see below): it seems to have remained to the last subordinate to the text of the endowment charter, either to the whole text or to part of it, and in particular to the ritual oath which was added at the end of the charter for its protection. Although it is generally not possible to identify the deities named in the oath as the special protecting powers or amongst the symbolic emblems shown on the relief of the *kudurru*, yet there is no doubt that these signs were present to make the *kudurru* a numinous monument, so that to harm it, wholly or in part, would mean committing a sacrilege. The need to place the charter of the grant under the protection of as many divinities as possible, by adding their abstract symbolic emblems, assumes in the first instance the development of such emblems, which had their origin in earlier centuries. Perhaps in the Kassite period this need coincided with a turning against the idea of presenting gods in human form, which we might infer from the canonization of the epics and the moralizing selection of them in the literary field.

Nowhere else in the long history of ancient Near Eastern art has the iconography of divine symbols been employed to such an extent and so systematically as it was on the *kudurru* of the mature Kassite period, when it was also often provided, for purposes of identification, with appropriate annotations.[29] This iconographic picture-language of the *kudurru* relief is fundamentally not so much the artistic expression of religious ideas as an attempt in iconographic form to crystallize the theological speculation on the polytheistic pantheon of the Second Millennium B.C. It was no longer considered sufficient to find a suitable abstract symbol for the predominant nature of a divine personality, which had evolved over the centuries. Now it was also important to indicate the complex character of the gods, as in something like the goat-fish, and to explain their hierarchic position in the theological system and their bearing upon the various spheres of the cosmos. It is true that we cannot as yet understand all the theological and speculative intricacies of this iconography: however, a particularly fine work – such as the *kudurru* on which Melishihu II had inscribed a charter in favour of his son Marduk-apal-iddina[30] (Pl. 229) – presents us on its front side with an entirely comprehensible canonized system formed by the metaphysical powers ruling the cosmos. In five rows of friezes, arranged horizontally one below the other, the whole Kassite pantheon is represented in symbols, from the astral gods of the highest heaven down to the chthonic powers in the deepest underworld, in accordance with both the theological system and the hierarchy. Anyone damaging or altering the text of the charter would offend the divine pantheon. The pictorial part of the *kudurru* may be regarded as a reinforcement of the oath in the text, while on a second stone, erected by Melishihu for his daughter, the relief seems to be an illustration of the grant itself[31] (Pl. 230). In this Melishihu is shown leading his daughter by the hand to the enthroned goddess Nana. The goddess, in the divine robe hallowed for centuries, the flounced dress, and the new style cylindrical 'feather crown' on her head, is enthroned on a seat shaped like a temple, which is placed on a base with lions' legs. She is holding out both hands in greeting to the king, who is wearing a long girdled robe with bands crossing over his chest, and to his daughter, carrying her harp on her left arm. A tall thymiaterion is in front of the goddess and above her hover the three celestial emblems, Sin, Shamash and Ishtar. Since Nana, the high goddess, is in this instance represented on the charter in a completely anthropomorphic form, other divine symbols have probably been dispensed with. In its subject this *kudurru* for Melishihu's daughter is a return to the age-old Sumerian introduction scene, though the squat proportions of Melishihu's body are already like those of the painted wall figures from the period of his son in Dur-Kurigalzu, and thereby it also shows a strong Aramaic influence.

The symbolism of the pictorial language and the relief of the Kassites reached the height of their development shortly before the eclipse of the dynasty in the twelfth century, in a group of *kudurrus* where the shape of the stele itself seems to have a symbolic significance. The elongated, rectangular block of stone, placed upright, was no longer merely given a square cross-section; now the surface of the whole block of stone was carved in such a way that it had the form of a citadel protected by towers and battlements or of a fortified palace. The simplest example of this group is in the British Museum,[32] and it has on it the text of a charter of Melishihu. A fragment of another from the same category originated in Susa[33] (Pl. 233). The wall crowned by battlements between the three towers at the corners of the structure can be easily identified. But the most important part of this work is the remainder, unfortunately scanty, of a mythological scene in relief, barely preserved on the frieze above the citadel. In this relief there is a boat with a flat keel and a prow from which a dragon's head juts out, its tongue protruding; from the boat three shafts rise, which seem to be standards, and they too have similar dragons' heads fastened horizontally on top. We can probably identify the dragon head with Mushhush, the snake dragon – he is also linked with Marduk, amongst other gods – and from that we can also identify the god Marduk himself as a human figure, crowned by a tall cylindrical cap and dressed in a long garment reaching down to the ground, seen possibly on the point of going for a journey in his sacred boat.

By far the most important example of this last group of *kudurrus,* and at the same time the finest example of Kassite relief, in its subject-matter and style, even though we only understand so far a small part of the pictorial language of its symbolized mysticism, is a stone which had a large space left on it for a lengthy charter, but which was, however, never finished. This is the so-called 'Unfinished *kudurru*' from Susa, now in the Louvre, and in spite of its unfinished state Shutruk-Nahhunte did not hesitate to remove it as booty to Susa (Pls. 231, 232).[34] We know that the citadel protected by towers was not just intended as a copy of some fortified place but in itself was of great symbolic significance, because it rests on a giant snake which encircles the bottom of its foundations, while another, similar snake has twined itself round the summit of the stone, with a recumbent bull in its centre. The lower snake has the same two pointed horns on its head as Mushhush, the animal which represents Marduk and several gods of the underworld. Thus the citadel has its foundations in the world round which the river of the underworld flows. Its summit, however, is surrounded by the counterpart of that river, the celestial Oceanos (?), and is crowned by the celestial bull (?). Between the foundations and the summit of the citadel the spheres of the cosmos appear symbolically in different parts of the great structure and also as the beings shown there: from the waters of the deep rise the walls and buttressed turrets of the world. The walls were designed to carry ordinances of the King, the Lord of the World, in carefully prepared lines. Lying between the top of the crenellated towers of the citadel of the world and the spheres of the celestial bull and the celestial water are two pictorial friezes, separated from each other by dividing borders. The upper register, into which the head of the celestial serpent hangs down, and its frieze, is entirely filled with the well-known abstract symbols of the supreme gods, such as we have been able to study more easily already on the display side of the *kudurru* for Marduk-apal-iddina (Pl. 229). This is the sphere of the celestial gods, the summit of the pantheon. The second pictorial register, the most interesting part of the whole relief even though it is the hardest part to interpret, relates to a sphere between heaven and earth over which a paradisiac peace reigns between the heroic humans and the desert animals. In an artificial garden created by plants in great tubs are five men, dressed in half-length kilts, with bows and quivers on their backs, and a woman in a long flounced dress, all dancing and making music together in a cult procession. As though charmed, lions, ibexes and wild goats follow the clash of the cymbal and the music of the lutes.

Where is the source of this theme, which we shall only meet once more in the world of the ancient Near East, on two of the most splendid works of Late Assyrian wall relief of Ashurbanipal (see below, Pl. 283)? From where did the artist of our Late Kassite *kudurru* take the Orphean concept of the overcoming of wild animals by the power of music, of the peaceful victory of good over evil? Did this idea exist as early as half a millennium before Ashurbanipal in the Land of the Two Rivers. Did the Kassites find it in Iran?

The significance of this undoubtedly important *kudurru* in the history of thought certainly surpasses its aesthetic qualities. The transformation of a stele into a symbol of the whole cosmos divided by divine plan into spheres has admittedly been a success, and the various zones of superhuman life have been expressed in mythical scenes, but the quality of the sculpture itself, the force of its style and the structure of its composition never rise above mediocrity. There is no text to help us date the 'Unfinished *kudurru*' but the general design and all the details of its pictorial components show so many similarities with the other charters of land grants of Melishihu II that it may probably be assigned to this Late Kassite king. Whether the art of this late period was already showing clear signs of a decay in style or was still at the height of its development is difficult to decide with any certainty because of the inadequate supply of Kassite major art available to us. We can get a better idea of the development of this art with glyptic.

4 Glyptic art

In recent years a careful examination has been made of glyptic as such and for its connection with the glyptic of the Mitanni-Middle Assyrian area during the period from the Old Babylonian decline to the Second Dynasty of Isin, that is, to the neo-Babylonian period.[35] This has enabled us to observe how, in the fifteenth century, at the time of the architectural sculpture of Karaindash, glyptic began for the first time to free itself from the tradition of Old Babylonian art. In the fourteenth century we found the stone-cutters still using the exaggeratedly long figures which had been particularly popular during the decline of the First Dynasty of Babylon.[36] The legends were given increasingly more space on the cylinder seals and extended into long prayers, while the symbolism which we encountered in the relief of the *kudurru* only developed slowly. Divine symbols only occupied a moderate space. The Old Sumerian theme from the circle of Inanna and Tammuz, which the mountain people were soon to renew, appeared in subsidiary scenes on seals by the reign of Burraburiash[37] (Pl. H 5–7). It was only in the next stage of development, during the fifteenth to fourteenth centuries, in the reigns of Kurigalzu II and Nazimaruttash, that Kassite glyptic reached its full peak, in subject-matter and style, although we have only a few fragments to prove this.[38] But there are some impressions on a few clay tablets from Nippur, with their texts dated during the reigns of Kings Kurigalzu II and Nazimaruttash, which – in the richness of their pictorial composition and the natural freedom of their execution and style – show a clear reaction against the abstract symbolism and the strict stylization of the early Kassite period. Their counterpart in Kassite major art of the fourteenth century is missing from our stock of works of art found so far; we lack relief during the period of Kings Burraburiash and Nazimaruttash, and glyptic is unfortunately only partially a substitute (Pl. N 5–7).

IV Assyrian Art

A OLD AND MIDDLE ASSYRIAN ART
(Second Millennium B.C.)

1 Old Assyrian art

Assyria, the country on the Tigris to the north of Jebel-Hamrin (= Ebih), had been a Sumero-Akkadian province during the Third Millennium. In the first half of the Second Millennium the Assyrian people struggled for a very long time and with very great determination to avoid being absorbed by the Canaanites, who slowly extended their rule over the whole of the Land of the Two Rivers. Indeed, under the dynasty of Ilushuma and Erishum Assyria seems also to have tried to free itself from the leadership of the south in cultural matters. The princes of Ashur not only founded their own trading stations in Anatolia, from which they obtained essential raw materials, but Assyrian state law also operated in these cities of resident aliens, oaths were sworn on the sword of the god Ashur, only the Assyrian calendar was known and the years were named in the Assyrian manner after eponymous officials, the so-called *limus:* not only was the cuneiform script written with special strokes there, but a special orthography was used also.

In the realm of art and architecture we have not obtained sufficient material from the excavations at Kültepe and Ashur for the period of the Ilushuma-Erishum dynasty to enable us to identify their specifically Assyrian features. We cannot do this even in the glyptic – although we have many cylinder seals and even more seal impressions, on the so-called Cappadocian clay tablets from Kültepe.[1] Thus, at the present time, it is still impossible, among the great quantity of themes and formal elements shown by the so-called Cappadocian glyptic (Sumerian, Akkadian, Old Babylonian, Syrian and their own local work), to identify with certainty those items originating from the capital city of the Old Assyrian kingdom, from Ashur itself. It is nothing more than a conjecture, if we consider the few cylinder seals found in excavations in Ashur which are now in the Near Eastern Department of the Berlin Staatliche Museen[2] (Pl. J 1–4) to be examples of specifically Old Assyrian glyptic, rather than glyptic acquired by Assyrian merchants in Anatolia and then put into their graves when they were buried in their native city. If this supposition is correct, then the bull with the three-cornered object on its back, as shown by seal VR 505 (Pl. J 1), may possibly symbolize a god originating in Assyria and brought by Assyrian merchants to Cappadocia. Equally the pointed hat, which one can see on seal VR 508 (Pl. J 3) and the incisions on the figures on seal VR 516 (Pl. J 4) might be features originating in Assyria or adopted by Old Assyria in common with Anatolia, from an earlier folk level. If that were really the case, then in fact it would be easier to understand why the seal of the greatest of the Old Assyrian kings, Sargon I of Ashur,[3] can scarcely be distinguished in style from a so-called Cappadocian seal.

After the collapse of the Ilushuma dynasty, when Assyria finally yielded to the pressure of the Canaanite race, and the city of Ashur, under the leadership of the great rival of Hammurabi, Shamshi-Adad I, became a centre for this new Semitic society, the various buildings and works of art produced there must have been connected with this society. However, a great deal of what the excavator W. Andrae had thought he could assign to the great Shamshi-Adad I has, since then, been shown to be older, and this applies to architecture as well as to art. So, for example, following the final publication on the palaces and houses in Ashur, it has become clear that the first arrangement of the so-called 'Old Palace'[4] dates from the Akkadian period. Because of this it can tell us nothing about the architecture of the period of Shamshi-Adad I. And the many fragments of diorite, of valuable sculpture in the round which W. Andrae wanted to assign to this king,[5] belong to the period of Manishtusu (see above, Pls. 139, 140, 143).

On the other hand we may still attribute to Shamshi-Adad I one work of art, the only large relief which had been credited to him for a long time, though this attribution was also from time to time disputed: the stele from Mardin, which has been in the Louvre for many years[6] (Pls. 204, 205). Its obverse shows a triumphant ruler placing his foot on a conquered enemy, while the reverse only displays some men, possibly also enemies, in strange garments with the 'rounded tab' fringes which are generally a West Semitic characteristic.[7]

The theme of the victorious ruler was probably never chosen by Hammurabi, the Babylonian adversary of Shamshi-Adad I, to decorate a stele. This, for the first time, introduces a difference between the Assyrian and the Babylonian concepts of kingship, even though both countries were ruled by Canaanites. Hammurabi included in his concept of kingship the image of himself as the bringer of peace, an image developed in the Gudea period, whereas Shamshi-Adad I included the image of himself as the conqueror of all evil, an image which had last been chosen by the Akkadian period as its main theme. Should the stele from Mardin, however, originate from Dadusha of Eshnunna – as A. Goetze has suggested on the grounds that the name of the month *Makranum* occurs in its inscription[8] – then it uses the same triumph motif which is also attested for Tishpak, the god of the region Eshnunna, illustrated on an impression from the period of King Ilushuilia.[9]

2 Hurri-Mitanni and Middle Assyrian art

Of quite exceptional importance for the future of Assyrian and Near Eastern art generally was the flooding of northern Mesopotamia by the expanding Hurrians and their leading Aryan ruling caste, the Mitanni, following the collapse of the Canaanite supremacy during the second third of the Second Millennium. Assyrian art during the period from the decline of the Hammurabi dynasty to about 1400 B.C. cannot be separated from Hurrian-Mitannian art. At that time the authority of the Mitanni extended from the Zagros mountains to Palestine and most of Assyria was also included within their kingdom. Although the Assyrian race later overcame both the political supremacy and the racial domination of the Hurri-Mitanni, yet it is probably reasonable to conclude that the Assyrians, from the fourteenth century onward, brought to fruition, politically and culturally, all that the Hurrian people and the Mitannian kingdom had been striving to achieve. The dark age between the death of Shamshi-Adad I and the political rebirth of Assyria in the fourteenth century, under Eriba-Adad I, included at least three and a half centuries of dependence under Babylonian supremacy, but equally and to a greater extent, under that of the Hurrian-Mitannians, and recently a certain amount of evidence has come to light which would suggest that there was a complete transformation of Assyrian art and architecture during this period. For instance, architectural records show that the older Sin-Shamash Temple in Ashur may be the work of King Ashur-nirari I[10] (1516–1491 B.C.), that is to say, a work from the period directly after the collapse of the Hammurabi dynasty, Ashur having become a vassal state of that dynasty immediately after Hammurabi had conquered Shamshi-Adad I.

It is also the period during which the rise of Mitannian supremacy began.

The ground-plan of the first Sin-Shamash Temple cannot be linked to any other older or contemporary temple in the Near East. It seems to represent something which, for the first time, is specifically Assyrian, unless it goes back to a Hurrian source not yet known to us. It forms an elongated rectangle with its entrance on the north-west side, fortified by several monumental, graduated towers[11] (Fig. 73). The gateway is situated exactly on the axis of the north-west side: the rectangular centre court is reached through a wide gatehouse. The two parts of the double shrine are situated symmetrically to the south-west and north-east of the court, and each consists of a wide antechamber and a long cella, and thus it forms the exact prototype of the later Assyrian temple of the First Millennium. For instance, the resemblance with the Nabu Temple at Khorsabad (see below, p. 147) is such that there too the annexe rooms are arranged round the cella in the same formation as in this Sin-Shamash temple of Ashur-nirari I. It seems extremely probable that the older Sin-Shamash temple in Ashur is also the first example of a specifically Assyrian type of temple; with a court, wide ante-cella and long main cella. All that we know of Hurrian-Mitannian architecture, the remains of buildings in Nuzi and Alalakh from the period of the great Mitannian king Shaushatar,[12] provides no evidence to prove that this temple ground-plan is Hurrian-Mitannian.

The shape of the Ishtar Temple (Level A) in Nuzi had scarcely changed by the reign of King Shaushatar from the arrangement prevailing there in the much older levels, going back as far as the Akkadian period (GA. SUR), and it cannot therefore be considered to be purely Hurrian-Mitannian.

On the other hand, in the Palace of Niqmepa at Alalakh (Tell Atchana), which is dated by inscriptions, like the whole of the Level IV there, in the great Mitannian period of King Shaushatar, there is a part which could be the prototype of the so-called bīt hilāni, which we shall meet again later, both at Tell Halaf in northern Mesopotamia and also in the Assyrian royal palaces after Tiglathpileser III. This consists of an elongated rectangular room with a

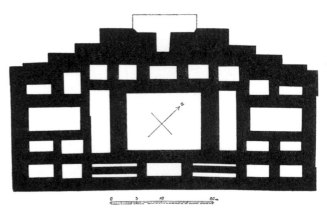

Fig. 73   Plan of the first Sin-Shamash temple of Ashur-nirari I at Ashur
(After: W. Andrae, *Das wiedererstandene Assur*, p. 100, Fig. 44)

pillared porch in front of one of its long sides, and inside a hearth and – in some instances – a podium along the short wall. Sometimes a free-standing stairway leads up to the pillared porch[13] (Fig. 74). Therefore it is possible that the so-called bīt hilāni, which was of importance from the middle of the Second Millennium, is a Hurrian-Mitannian element in Near Eastern architecture.

We may have been able to detect the beginnings of a truly Assyrian form of cult building up to the period of Shaushatar, in the Sin-Shamash temple of Ashur-nirari I: but we are not in the same fortunate position as regards Assyrian palace building, which expressed the Assyrian concept of kingship – a concept of the utmost importance for everything in Assyria – because the oldest royal palace known to us now with the truly Assyrian features of the mighty complexes in Kalakh, Nineveh and Dur-Sharrukin only dates from the thirteenth century B.C. The final publication on the palaces at Ashur[14] (Fig. 75) informs us that the remnants of the stone wall foundations excavated there are in all probability part of a palace which Adad-nirari I had built at the beginning of the thirteenth century. Its ground-plan differed from that of an older palace on the same site mainly in that it no longer had its various courtyard groups enclosed by a clearly defined perimeter wall definitely designed in advance, but by entirely irregular perimeter walls lying at right angles to each other, with the result that the whole layout was divided into

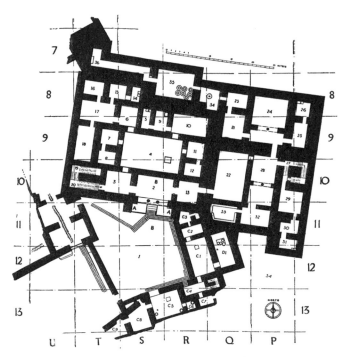

Fig. 74 Plan of the Palace of Niqmepa at Tell Atchana
(After: L. Woolley, *Alalakh*, p. 115, Fig. 45)

two courtyard complexes, one group round the entrance court (= *bābānu*) and another round the residential court (= *bītānu*). In this way, as early as the thirteenth century, the Palace of Adad-nirari I (1305–1274) displays the basic characteristics of the Assyrian royal palace, but it is not sufficiently old to provide clear evidence that the Assyrian palace building, like the Assyrian cult building under Ashurnirari I, had acquired its own particular form even before the achievement of independence from Mitannian supremacy, and that it was built independent of Mitannian influence. This would be of even greater importance, because we have found a palace at Nuzi[15] built by a governor under the Mitannian king Shaushatar (about 1450 B.C.) (Fig. 76). It enables us to make a comparison between Mitannian and Assyrian palace architecture, even though it is only partially preserved, so that its original layout can only be conjectured. It is certain, however, that it is not the type of building inside an encircling wall planned in advance, but is more of an arrangement on the lines of Zimrilim's palace at Mari (see above,

p. 79), which had to conform with the requirements of its site, and grew gradually in a shape which fitted these requirements. The whole complex was surrounded by a strong perimeter wall, which had niches and buttresses at certain places on both its interior and exterior faces. Two large courts were placed near each other but not on the same axis. Probably the main entrance of the building was at its north corner. Through this one reached first the more northerly of the two courts, which may have served as a reception court: benches against the walls probably served as seats for waiting visitors. Lying crossways to the south-west of this court was an oblong room with a hearth. This room also acted as a way through to the inner court. This great inner court also had an oblong room to its south-west, preceded by a colonnade, and this too was only the antechamber of an even larger oblong room with a hearth and a platform at one of its short sides. Someone standing at the entrance could see the platform behind the hearth, and this seems to have been the place for the lord of the house. We should not forget that there were also oblong rooms placed crossways and furnished with an altar and podium in the Assyrian palaces of the First Millennium (North-West Palace at Kalakh, Dur-Sharrukin or Til Barsip, see pp. 129, 146, 140). One cannot, therefore, reject out of hand

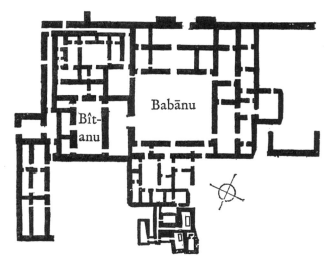

Fig. 75 Plan of the Palace of Adad-nirari I at Ashur
(After: WVDOG 66, Pl. 4)

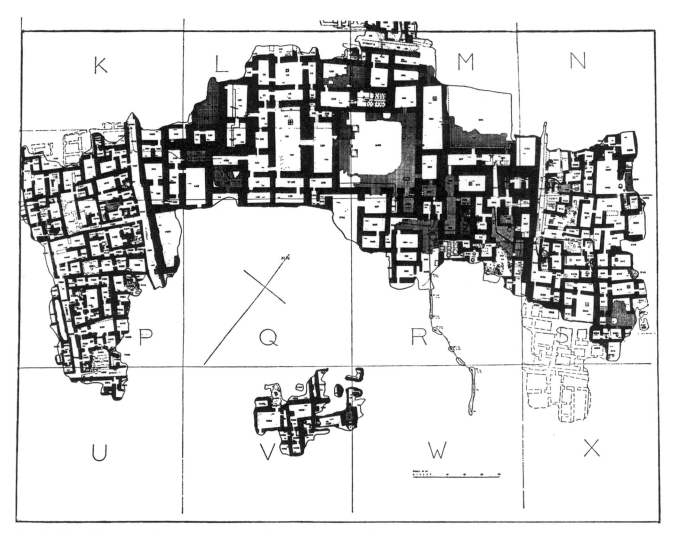

Fig. 76   Plan of the palace of the governor under Shaushatar, at Nuzi (After: F. Starr, *Nuzi,* Plan 13)

the possibility that Mitannian royal palace building may have exerted a certain influence on Assyrian architecture. In any case, the Palace of Adad-nirari I at Ashur resembled the governor's building at Nuzi in its general plan, as well as in the shape of its individual rooms more than, say, it resembled the nearly contemporary palace of the Kassite king Kurigalzu I at Dur-Kurigalzu (see above, under Kassite architecture, p. 97).

Assyrian art too was transformed completely during the fifteenth and fourteenth centuries. While at first in the fifteenth century it was still clearly under the influence of the Hurrian-Mitannians, in the four-

teenth century it was laying the foundations of a style which was the basis of the great achievements of the Assyrian stone-cutter in the thirteenth century and the monumental wall relief of the Late Assyrian period. This process of freeing the Assyrian pictorial language from the ties of Hurrian-Mitannian control, a process which was so decisive in the history of all Near Eastern art, can only be understood and reconstructed with difficulty at the present time, because only now is the supply of works of art at our disposal being slowly enriched by occasional new discoveries or by improved historical interpretations of our archaeological sources. How can we assess the relationship between Middle Assyrian and Hurrian-Mitannian art, when our knowledge of the major arts of the Hurrian people and of the Mitannian state rests on such a fragile base of works and knowledge, as is still the case even to-day?

Even with the American discoveries in Yorgan Tepe (Nuzi) which produced countless new finds for the history of art and architecture during the period of the Mitannian state[16] – in addition to a huge treasure of clay tablets: with Mallowan's explorations in the heart of the Hurrian region, in the Khabur and Belikh area:[17] Woolley's excavations in the western peripheral city of the Mitannian state, Alalakh (Tell Atchana):[18] the achievements of Claude Schaeffer in Ugarit (Ras Shamra), also important for our knowledge of Hurrian-Mitannian art: and finally, the explorations of the Oriental Institute of Chicago and of the M. Freiherr von Oppenheim Foundation in Fakhariya near Raselain[19] and on Tell Chuera:[20] in spite of all these we have still discovered no great work of art or architecture from a central, major city of the Hurrian-Mitannian state. All that we have discovered in the realm of temple and palace building comes from the peripheral regions and has a provincial character. Art, its subject-matter and form, is still best represented by the so-called Kirkuk glyptic. As yet we only possess fragments of the other categories of Hurrian-Mitannian art – sculpture in the round, relief and wall painting – and can only reconstruct them partially by using our imagination.

Several studies have been made in recent years of Hurrian-Mitannian glyptic and its relationship to Middle Assyrian glyptic.[21] The most recent[22] examined the many seal impressions we have found on the numerous clay tablets from the business archives in Nuzi and Ashur. These have not only shown us the extent of the repertoire of themes used by the Hurrian-Mitannians, but also have the advantage that we can date them fairly accurately, as they have been found on dated documents. During the fifteenth century B.C. the themes and styles fluctuated between Hurrian and Assyrian. A stone-cutter in Ashur uses an interweaving band to create a number of metope-like pictorial surfaces which he has then filled with individual masks (Pl. N 8).[23] His work is under the spell of the same motif as that used by the wall-

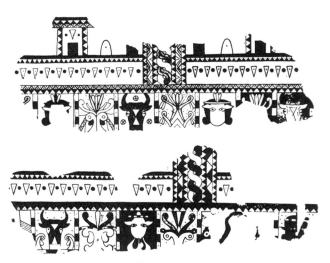

Fig. 77 Fragments of wall paintings from the governor's palace in Nuzi
(After: A. Moortgat, *Altvorderasiatische Malerei*, Pl. 15, p. 39)

painter to decorate the door lintels in the governor's palace at Nuzi[24] (Fig. 77). The latter has painted in the metopes a tree of life, a bucranium or a Hathor-like mask, in all of which it is possible to trace Syrian or even Egyptian elements. This intermingling was well suited to a state which, like the Mitannian state, had extended its rule within a short space of time over a wide region, between the Tauros and the Zagros. The bucranium – an age-old symbol used as early as the chalcolithic age on Tell Halaf ceramic – was stylized in Nuzi in a very characteristic manner, with its individual components strongly geometrized. The bull's head looks like a combination of several geometric symbols. The geometrical abstractions which dominate the style of this wall painting can also be seen on another animal mask,[25] modelled with plasticity, which was excavated at Alalakh in the Palace of Niqmepa. Skilfully carved out of white Dolomite limestone, its natural features have been rendered in such an extreme, abstract way that this work can only be identified by the curved horns, which are also the only grounds for calling it a ram (Fig. 78). One could easily imagine this stone mask as a wall decoration in the manner of the painted masks at Nuzi. Moreover, in Nuzi itself a ram's head made of limestone[26] was found which is close in style to the stone object from Alalakh (Fig. 79). The related

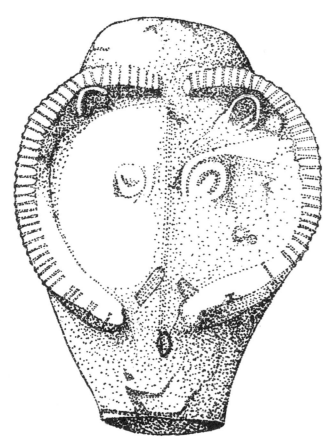

Fig. 78 Animal mask (ram's head) from the Palace of Niqmepa
at Tell Atchana. Redrawn
(After: Woolley, *Alalakh*, Pl. XLV)

in their appearance as any from Nuzi or Alalakh. And what is even more important is that this Kirkuk style was not limited only to the small objects of glyptic but was equally apparent in the works of art produced by the sculptor in stone and the goldsmith.

In Ugarit (Ras Shamra), at the northernmost point on the Phoenician coast, where the most varied cultural streams met and mingled and where, according to the evidence of many texts, there was a large population of Hurrian-Mitannian origin, it is not improbable that Hurrian-Mitannian art-motifs were used at the same time as those of Egypt and of the Hittites. The bull hunt from the light, two-wheeled war chariot drawn by a horse, which decorates the round frieze on the bowl of a gold plate[30] (Pl. 234), doubtless owed its inspiration to the influence of the Mitannian world, where this kind of chariot originated, even though the men seem to have the physical characteristics of the indigenous Canaanites.

style of these two works, which were both found in border areas on the extreme periphery of the Mitannian state, one in the east and the other in the west, enables us to presume the existence of an essentially unified Mitannian art. This unity, as we have recently learnt, prevailed in the realm of myths and epics from the Near East through Phoenicia far into the Aegean-Greek world;[27] this is confirmed not only by a similar dispersal of the so-called Kirkuk glyptic[28] and of the so-called Nuzi ceramic[29] (Fig. 85), but the unity of the Mitannian-Hurrian art is indicated even more clearly in places where the Hurrian spirit and the Hurrian style had been able to penetrate into alien surroundings, like Ashur, Kalakh or Ugarit. It is already noticeable that even in the fourteenth and thirteenth centuries B.C., at Ashur itself there were many documents impressed with seals just as Hurrian

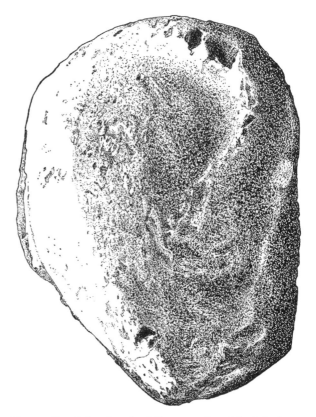

Fig. 79 Ram's head made of limestone from Nuzi. Redrawn
(After: F. Starr, *Nuzi*, Pl. 112 A)

Fig. 80   Stone lion from the tomb building (temple?) of Idrimi
in Tell Atchana. Redrawn
(After: L. Woolley, *Alalakh*, Pl. XLIX)

The statue of Idrimi from Alalakh[31] (Pl. 235), a
vassal of the Mitannian King Baratarna (= Shuttarna), also shows a combination of Syrian and
Mitannian-Hurrian features. The seated figure in
stone of this king stood in a sort of temple at Alalakh,
probably a tomb building, where it had been erected
as an ancestral image and received the worship due
to it, in the manner of the Hittite images in their
E. NA. In the long inscription on the seated statue
Idrimi tells of his participation in battles at the side
of the Mitannians against Hittite minor princes. Of
Shuttarna we know that he was burnt after death,
like the Hittite kings,[32] and the tomb statue probably
had a function as a cult image of the dead man
connected with the burning of the corpse,[33] a branch
of sculpture which had remained unknown in the
Sumero-Akkadian world. Idrimi is wearing a robe
recalling the Syrian robe with its padded roll, like
those we have seen on numerous Syrian cylinder
seals and bronze statuettes,[34] though on this occasion
the padded roll has been flattened down into a mere
ornamental border. Idrimi's hat also recalls the
pointed oval hats of the Syrian kings and gods. But
the style and character of this statue make an impression of an abstract, divorced from nature, and in
that it approaches the art-style of the animal masks
we have just described. The small moulded frit figures
from Ras Shamra[35] look so unlike nature that they
are almost caricatures, and their external appearance,
because of the frit material and because of the plank-

like shape of their bodies, calls to mind the figures
which, like older sacred objects, were buried in the
later Ishtar Temple of Tukulti-Ninurta I.[36] Though
some of their features are very Syrian, these too may
have originated in Ashur during the period of the
Mitannian supremacy. In the deliberate flattening of
all their shapes and the plumpness of their heads,
rising neckless from the chest, the two occupants of
the chariot in the small group from Ugarit resemble
the seated statue of Idrimi. This same geometrical
abstract style is, moreover, used again in two lions
which decorate the string-board of the stairs in the
same building of Idrimi[37] (Fig. 80). It is difficult to
think of other works of art comparable in style. If
some day these are proved to be Hurrian-Mitannian,
then they will in some way form part of the small
group of decorative objects which, apart from glyptic,
we can consider as part of Hurrian-Mitannian art.
To this group belongs a fragment of grey-white marble found in 1950 during the English excavations at
Nimrud (Kalakh)[38] (Pl. 237), which is part of a
libation bowl in the form of a hand and forearm,
similar to the many later examples made of steatite.[39]
Although the object is only 7.5 cm. wide, its decoration is important in the history of art during the
Second Millennium because its subject-matter and
style are quite clearly connected very closely with
illustrations on the Kirkuk glyptic. Running above
the finger tips of the hand, and not separated from
them by a base-line is a frieze which is parallel to
the edge of the vessel. It contains animals lying down
(lions, goats, birds): some of them have their legs
tucked in beneath them and their heads bent back, but
all of them have the same emphasized, circular eyes.
All the details of their features as well as the composition of the scene are typically Hurrian, in a way
we have met already in the glyptic from Nuzi and
Arrapkha (Kirkuk). However, even now, several
decades after its rediscovery, the best example of
this style is still the so-called cult relief which, broken
into countless fragments, was recovered from the
well in the main temple at Ashur[40] (Pl. 236). On an
almost square plaque made of a stone resembling
alabaster, and almost two-thirds life-size, there is
the anthropomorphic figure of a mountain god, facing
to the front, as are the two smaller river goddesses

shown on each side of him. All three are wearing a long garment on the hips and a cap shaped like a calotte. The god's robe and cap are decorated with the usual scale pattern, the symbol of the mountain, and those of the goddesses with the wavy lines of water. The goddesses are holding two *aryballos*-shaped vases from which water is flowing, while the god is holding two branches, each with three fruiting spurs. The goats are floating in mid-air with no ground line, nibbling at the fruit. Owing to the marked *en face* appearance of the deities, the unreal relationship in size of the figures and their placing as if in space free of gravity, the scene has a distinctly supernatural character. But mountain gods with vegetative features certainly did not originate in the classical Sumero-Akkadian cycle, but from the north of the Near East. The Hurrian-Mitannian gods lived on mountain peaks, and inevitably one cannot help thinking that the cult relief must have originated in Ashur during the time of its foreign occupation by the Hurrians, and then when the Hurrians had been overthrown, the relief was broken up by the Assyrians and thrown into the well of the Ashur temple. It would seem likely that it represents the image of the god Ashur himself, the Lord of the Ebih mountain, portrayed in the Hurrian manner. It has sufficient points which show it to be Hurrian, such as the balloon-shaped cap of the god, the circular eyes of the goats, and above all the composition of the picture with no base lines beneath the figures. So the relief from the well in the Ashur Temple at Ashur is a rare proof of the existence at one time of Hurrian-Mitannian major art, and at the same time its ruined condition suggests an explanation for the almost complete disappearance of this art. How great must have been the influence of the Hurrian-Mitannians over the Assyrian people during the fifteenth century B.C. if a truly Hurrian cult relief could be put up in the main shrine of the principal god in the Assyrian capital! And how great was the achievement of the Assyrians who, in the course of one century, directly they had succeeded in gaining political independence, transformed their alien tutelage into an inner enrichment, and indeed were able to produce a new major art out of the tensions of this fateful period of their history.

3   Creation of an individual Assyrian style in the fourteenth century B.C.

From the sources for the political history of Assyria shortly before and shortly after 1400 B.C., we know that the Assyrian kings of that period were merely vassals of the Mitannian Great King, of not much more importance than the kings of Arrapkha and Alalakh. It was only during the reign of Eriba-Adad I (1390–1364 B.C.) that Assyria threw off the Mitannian yoke and under his successor, Ashur-uballit I (1363–1323 B.C.), it took the place of the Mitannian state in North Mesopotamia and became the rival of the Hittite kingdom and of Egypt under Akhnaton. The Assyrian king changes from vassal to 'brother' of the Pharaoh. The political rise of Assyria was reflected accurately in the surviving art which has been handed down to us in the seal impressions on the legal documents of this period, excavated in Ashur.[41] As examples of a minor art they can only provide us with an incomplete reflection of the major arts of that period, but they are equally subject to the general course of the thematic and stylistic development of Assyrian art, as were relief and painting. The seal of Ashur-nirari II (1424–1418)[42] is quite in keeping with the humble political status of the Assyrian kingdom at that time. It is true that the composition of the Ashur-nirari seal (Pl. O 1), in its arrangement of the numerous figures which fill its pictorial surface (humans, animals and composite creatures), shows a certain tendency towards division of the field into registers, one above the other, and into antithetic groups placed side by side (Pl. J 5). These were features still entirely lacking in the well-known Mitannian seal of King Shaushatar (about 1450 B.C.): yet, at the same time, the composition of the Ashur-nirari seal is governed by the principle of weightless space, represented by the absence of base lines, which is a typically Hurrian characteristic. In addition, the individual motifs (such as the beast of prey or composite creature with raised forepaw, or the fighting hero in short kilt and a helmet with a long ribbon) show such a remarkable similarity between the two seals that the Assyrian seal, which is the later one, must be derived from the older seal –

that of Shaushatar, and from all the Kirkuk glyptic. Not only was Ashur-nirari II a vassal of the Mitannian kingdom: Assyrian art of his period was also under the influence of the Hurrian-Mitannian supremacy. On the other hand, Assyrian glyptic from the period of Eriba-Adad and Ashur-uballit (1363–1328) shows that this influence had been thrown off.[43] The tendency to overcrowd the pictorial surface with countless figures, and also the 'floating' effect in space, both disappear: the scene was now limited to a few figures and arranged in a tight design, symmetrical or antithetic, built up to form, as it were, a heraldic picture and often with a legend attached of three to four vertical lines enclosed in a box (Pl. O 2–4). This style, with its bias towards a formal design, was probably necessary in order to remedy the lack of a stylistic pattern which marked the art of the previous period. But nevertheless it too yielded to a more relaxed Assyrian idiom in glyptic as in other categories of art during the course of the fourteenth century. This inner freedom in the development of the art-form, which corresponded to the outward expression of political emancipation, and which during the thirteenth century led to a flowering of Near Eastern art in general, had, we have only recently realized, already started in the fourteenth century.

Seals (with scenes of a lion pulling down an ibex from the rear, at the foot of a 'sacred tree' growing on a rocky hill, or of a bird of prey swooping down on a bull as it approaches a tree) no longer show anything of the forced regularity of design and composition of the glyptic of Eriba-Adad: they give an impression of complete mastery of the free disposition of the pictorial elements, within the given space. But both these seal impressions mentioned[44] probably originated in the fourteenth century as they are on clay tablets which come from a hoard discovered intact, and this itself can scarcely be dated later (Pl. O 5, 6).

A small, original cylinder seal made of lapis lazuli, with a scene of a suckling goat beside a tree, has a theme and style very close to these seals of the fourteenth century[45] (Pl. J 6). It was found in a tomb which came to light in a Middle Assyrian stratum in Ashur,[46] and its excavator, W. Andrae, considered

it must belong to the period shortly before or shortly after Tukulti-Ninurta I. Yet the seal's style clearly indicates a date earlier than this king, actually in the fourteenth century. This is borne out by the other objects discovered in the same tomb. These consist in the first place of unguent jars made of native Assyrian alabaster, their shape closely resembling similar Egyptian jars, from El Amarna, originating in the fourteenth century, the period of Akhnaton.[47] Many of these alabasters are decorated with figures, incised or in relief. One vase with a flattened oval body on an attached pedestal base has an elaborate palm-tree on both sides, between two leaping bulls (Pl. 238). Another, reconstructed from countless small pieces[48] (Figs. 81, 82) has the figure of Ishtar (Shaushka?) on each side. She is shown with four wings, *en face* and wearing a polos: the lower part of her body is naked[49] (Pl. 239). Although the shape of the first alabaster receptacle suggests Egypt, the figure of Ishtar on the second is like that of a bone statuette from Hurrian Nuzi, which can probably be dated still in the fifteenth century[50] (Pl. 240). It came from the cella of the Ishtar Temple at Nuzi and represents the same type of goddess with a naked pubic area – although, unlike the figure on the alabaster vase from Ashur, it has no wings.

The ivory objects found in the same place tell us more than the lapis lazuli cylinder seal or the alabaster jars from Tomb 45 in Ashur, concerning the origins of Assyrian art during the fourteenth century B.C., for they too point to the period. Beside the incredibly rich ornaments belonging to the two latest burials in the tomb, they provide the most valuable information about the kind of people who were buried there, particularly in the absence of any weapon – only some ivory combs and an ivory pyxis. The pair can scarcely be man and wife[51] but were most probably two of the high priestesses from the nearby Ishtar Temple.

Both a comb[52] (Pl. 241; Fig. 83) and the cylinder-shaped pyxis are extensively decorated with drawings incised skillfully and with precision: these are the oldest examples of a fully developed art of a truly Assyrian character. The engraver has utilized the upper part of the frame, above the comb's teeth, to make a double picture using the front and the back,

Fig. 81   Fragment of two alabaster vases, one showing a palm-tree, the other a winged goddess, from Tomb 45 in Ashur (After: WVDOG 65, p. 139, Fig. 164)

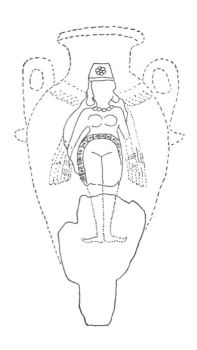

Fig. 82   Fragment of an alabaster vase with nude figure of Ishtar, from Ashur (Drawing by U. Moortgat-Correns)

and has enclosed the whole picture in a border. In this way the scenes on the front and back consist of two wide rectangular compartments, which are nevertheless connected by their subject-matter and together form one frieze. In the frieze there are seven human figures, probably all female, of which the first figure, on the left-hand side, is facing to the right to receive the other six, who are facing to the left. As far as one can tell, in view of its damaged condition, all the figures are wearing a long girdled garment reaching to the ground, and this is decorated with embroidery in horizontal stripes. They are all wearing a cylinder-shaped crown on their heads, possibly the so-called Feather Crown. Three date palm-trees drawn from nature, with date panicles and suckers, divide up the women's procession. Led by a priestess with a long cape hanging down her back, and accompanied by a harp player, the women are walking in a festive procession, bringing bunches of fruit, chains and garlands of flowers to the principal figure, the one with her profile facing to the right, who is probably Ishtar herself. If this figure

is not that of a woman, but is male, then the procession would be moving to the king, and the priestesses could be the so-called *naditu* priestesses, similar to those we have already met much earlier in Ur and Uruk. Unfortunately the ivory is so cracked that many of the drawing's details are now hard to decipher, yet we can sense in all these damaged engravings the same artistic spirit which was to reappear in the bas-relief on the alabaster wall slabs of the Late Assyrian palaces, in the ninth to the seventh centuries B.C. Particularly admirable is the way in which, even by the fourteenth century, the alternation of human figures and trees has been used in the frieze to create a rhythmic pattern out of the pictorial elements. This effect already foreshadows the art of pictorial composition which was to become one of the greatest achievements of the Assyrians.

Less remarkable in its composition, but with its linear rendering of life-giving nature all the more impressive, is the frieze (enclosed in the old Near Eastern manner, between two bands of rosettes, one above and one below) on the exterior surface of the

Fig. 83 Scene on ivory comb from Tomb 45 in Ashur. Redrawn
(After: WVDOG 65, p. 137, Fig. 163 a, b)

ivory pyxis from Tomb 45[53] (Pl. 242; Fig. 84). The
motif – of an animal walking and a tree – is known
to us already from glyptic. Here it is repeated twice
and varied: a larch tree, with a shrub beneath it and
two cocks in its upper branches, alternates with a
palm with date panicles. Two crows sit in the
palm's branches, goats nibble at the rosette blossoms.
The sun is shining in the firmament. The Middle
Assyrian engraver understood the art of omission,
even better than many other artists. Yet each engraved stroke is a pictorial language filled with some
cultic or religious meaning. The tree shown on the
pyxis is important, because it has a clear parallel in
the painting on a large potsherd of the late Nuzi
type[54] (Fig. 85), and this confirms its dating to the
fourteenth century. By alternating palm-tree and
conifer the painted potsherd from Ashur is, incidentally, a forerunner of the famous *paradeisos* scene
on the wall reliefs in the garden room of the Palace
of Ashurbanipal in Nineveh.[55]

One may well hesitate to date another group of
ivory fragments from Ashur, with detailed engrav-

Fig. 84 Ivory pyxis from Tomb 45 in Ashur. Redrawn
(After: WVDOG 65, p. 135, Figs. 161/162)

ings, because many of their features suggest the
fourteenth century, while others seem almost identical with those appearing on the glyptic of the
thirteenth century. Many years ago W. Andrae tried
to arrange a series of these fragments together and
he published his findings[56] (Pls. 243, 245). The little
ivory plaques, 3 to 5 mm. thick, must have been
inlaid in some utensil, possibly something made of
wood, decorated with an engraved frieze about 22 (?)
cm. wide, enclosed at the top and bottom by engraved bands decorated with rosettes, similar to those
on the pyxis from Tomb 45. All the separate pictorial
elements are still easily recognizable: a god with his
lower body in the shape of a mountain, aryballos-
like vases from which broad streams of water are

Fig. 85 Painted potsherd with trees from Ashur
(After: B. Hrouda, Die bemalte Keramik des 2. Jahrtausends,
Pls. 2, 3)

flowing, a palmetto, a pomegranate tree and, finally,
a series of winged bulls. Probably the water vessels
were connected with the mountain god and the
winged bulls with the trees, but one can no longer be
quite certain how the figures were arranged within
the frieze. Obviously the idea behind this work is
closely linked to the cult relief from the well at Ashur
(see above p. 111 f.; Pl. 236), to the brick reliefs in the
Karaindash Temple at Uruk (see p. 94 f.; Pls. 227, 228)
and to Middle Assyrian glyptic. The palmetto in the
ivory engraving has a near counterpart in an alabaster from Tomb 45, but on the other hand the
pomegranate is like that on a seal impression, not yet
published, on a clay tablet from Ashur.[57] In this the
pomegranate is introduced into a scene of a fight be-

tween a hero and a winged horse with a filly, which recalls related scenes on stone carvings from the thirteenth century,[58] and the hoard of little ivory plaques found in the North-West Terrace of Tukulti-Ninurta I in Ashur may be confirmation of this dating. The somewhat clumsy rendering of the winged bulls does not seem in keeping with the fully developed art of the thirteenth century, so it may be wiser after all to assign these ivories to the four-teenth century, in which they would be closer to the ivory engravings from Tomb 45.

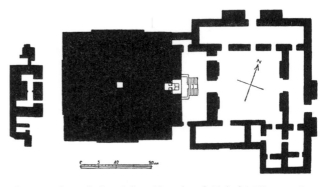

Fig. 86 Plan of the Ashur Temple of Tukulti-Ninurta I at Kar-Tukulti-Ninurta
(After: W. Andrae, *Das wiedererstandene Assur,* p. 92, Fig. 42)

4 Middle Assyrian art at its summit in the thirteenth century B.C. (Adad-nirari I, Shalmaneser I and Tukulti-Ninurta I)

The political and cultural fulfilment of all that Assyria had wished to achieve after throwing off the Hurrian-Mitannian yoke was brought about in the thirteenth century under its three great rulers, Adad-nirari I, Shalmaneser I and Tukulti-Ninurta I. The results of the excavations in Ashur tell us this much – even though they only recovered an insignificant fraction of the buildings and works of art: even though a project undertaken in conjunction with these excavations at Ashur, the exploration of the residence at Kar-Tukulti-Ninurta (founded by the most headstrong of all Assyrian kings a few kilo-metres north of Ashur), was not carried through to its conclusion: and even though – in spite of all the labours of the British for many years around the ruins of the city of Kalakh (Nimrud), founded by Shalmaneser I as the capital of his kingdom – so far almost nothing in the Middle Assyrian levels there has been examined.[59]

The three great rulers just referred to were also great patrons of building: this we know partly from building inscriptions,[60] even in places where the buildings have largely vanished. Though only scanty remains still exist, yet they are mostly of basic importance in the history of Assyrian architecture.

At the so-called 'Old Palace' at Ashur, begun in the Akkadian period, work was constantly carried on by numerous kings in the course of centuries to preserve and renew it,[61] and this was the case in the Middle Assyrian period as well. But it is probably no coincidence that a particular phase of this building can be confirmed as belonging to the first great period of the Assyrian kingdom by means of brick tiles bearing the name Adad-nirari I, used as paving in the central main court. Although the excavators could only find slight traces of the ground-plan dating from the reign of this king, yet it was so original compared with all the older building and was so individual that it must surely have been in-spired by a new upsurge of Assyrian royal might, such as that which actually took place in the thir-teenth century B.C. for the first time. Not only is it new, but it is a precedent for the future[62] (Fig. 75). What Preusser[63] has written so conclusively on the appearance of the Adad-nirari palace is more or less applicable to all later Assyrian royal palaces: 'that the palace of Adad-nirari I on three of its sides has no straight, continuous façade but has a very irregular arrangement of projections and recesses . . . These projections and recesses of the Adad-nirari building, even looked at very superficially, already show the most marked rejection of the traditional design pre-vailing throughout the centuries, which had com-pletely straight façades . . .' As in most of the Late Assyrian palaces, there was already a vast gate-house with two fortress-like towers and a group of monumental rooms forming a so-called *bābānu*, a gate-house complex leading to the central courtyard. Next to this, there is in this palace too a wide rectangular room, probably the throne-room, which is particularly remarkable because of its dimensions and the thickness of its walls: a very wide door leads into this from the courtyard. In addition to all this, here again there are other courtyard complexes – amongst them a residential group, the so-called *bītānu*. We cannot doubt that this Adad-nirari building in the thirteenth century B.C. represents the prototype of Assyrian royal palaces.

From the greatest king of the thirteenth century, Tukulti-Ninurta I, there are not sufficient remains of palace building either at Ashur or the new residential city of Kar-Tukulti-Ninurta[64] for us to draw

A = Antecella
B = Aššuritu-Cella
C = Dinîtu-Cella

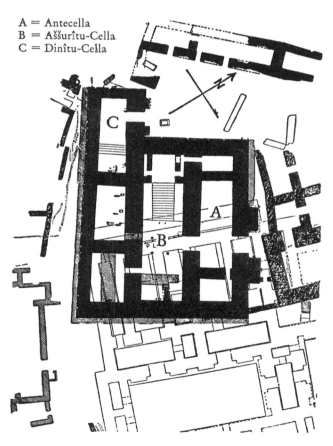

Fig. 87 Plan of the Ishtar Temple (Ashuritu and Dinitu) of Tukulti-Ninurta I at Ashur
(After: W. Andrae, *Das wiedererstandene Assur*, p. 109, Fig. 47)

any conclusions from them on Middle Assyrian palace building. On the other hand the achievements of this ruler in cult building can be traced more easily. These, however, express the self-willed personality of Tukulti-Ninurta rather than a clear-cut stage in the history of Assyrian architecture. Probably intentionally, the king copied Babylon at Kar-Tukulti-Ninurta when he added a typically Babylonian temple to the north-east side of the ziggurat of Ashur, the principal god of the kingdom. This had the classical layout of the courtyard house and a wide cella typical of Babylon[65] (Fig. 86). In his texts he also copied Babylon, since they are written in a language strongly influenced by Babylonian. Long before Tukulti-Ninurta's reign Ashur-nirari I had already created the truly Assyrian type of temple in the Anu-Adad-Temple at Ashur (cf. above, p. 107), when he used a wide ante-cella. And when Tukulti-Ninurta rebuilt the Ishtar Temple at Ashur, the oldest cult building in the city, he either did not want to follow the Assyrian design in the ground-plan or he was not able to carry it out.[66] He forsook the age-old tradition of building by pushing the temple away from its former site and turning it round 90°. However, he did in fact retain the ancient form of ground-plan of a temple with a 'bent axis', a feature employed as early as the Sumerian period, in the two cellae. These he dedicated to Ishtar in her main guise – that of the so-called Assyrian Ishtar (Ashur-itu) – as well as in a subsidiary role (at present not understood) as the so-called Dinitu (after a city Din?)[67] (Fig. 87). All the temples with a 'bent axis' from the previous period, i.e. all the temples in which the cella consisted of a long rectangular room with its entrance at the end of one of its long walls, are basically temples of the court-house type. They all have an inner court, with all the other, less important parts of the temple adjoining it. But the Ishtar Temple is not like this. It is an enclosed, covered complex with an antecella and a main cella. The latter contained a niche for the sacred image on a platform built against one of the short sides. A stairway of sixteen steps led up to this platform. The Dinitu cella is an integral part of the whole building laid out on the same pattern as that of the main cella, only smaller. The whole building is a free-standing monument,[68] of which the exterior was also designed to impress the onlooker (Fig. 88), rather like the small Innin Temple of the Kassite King Karaindash at Uruk (cf. p. 93). We have no evidence of the existence of a figured decoration on its exterior walls, similar to those on the Karaindash building.

Our knowledge of Middle Assyrian building, both temple architecture and palace building, is very incomplete at present owing to insufficient exploration. However, it does not seem probable that architectural sculpture and wall painting, the media in which building and art in Assyria combined to make their greatest reputation, had been developed to any great extent as early as the thirteenth century. The remnants of a figure of a lion, approximately life-size, which Preusser[69] believes he can link to the Middle Assyrian phase of the Old Palace at Ashur, could in fact be from a sculpture flanking a gateway, but the pieces are too slight for one to assess their style in relation to the history of architectural sculpture in the thirteenth century. At most they are evidence of the existence of this branch of art at that time.

We know rather more about the wall painting of this great period, thanks to a few fragments of painting on stucco from Kar-Tukulti-Ninurta, where they were found on the north and south sides of the palace terrace[70] (Fig. 89). They are frescoes in which only four colours were used – white, black, red and blue. The pictorial motifs are placed on metope-like pictorial surfaces and framed by ornamental bands, so that they look like an architectural panel – like the wall paintings at Nuzi and Alalakh, the two Hur-

Fig. 89   Wall painting from the palace terrace at Kar-Tukulti-Ninurta
(After: A. Moortgat, *Altvorderasiatische Malerei*, p. 40, Pl. 16)

rian-Mitannian outposts. The pictorial composition in the different compartments also appears Hurrian:[71] they show two antithetical gazelles standing on branches which spread out from a palm-tree to the right and left. This resembles the way in which goats were shown floating above branches on the Hurrian relief found in the well at the Ashur temple (see above, Pl. 236).

Whereas wall painting in the thirteenth century thus appears quite conservative in its colouring, composition and the arrangements of its surfaces, painters on pottery seem to have followed the trend of the period in every way. A great number of potsherds were collected during the excavations at Kar-Tukulti-Ninurta in the area of the palace: these had figures painted on them in black, red or brown on a light clay background.[72] They can be dated fairly precisely in the Tukulti-Ninurta period because of the site where they were found. Two or three sherds from the pottery room[73] belong, in their technique and style, to the same group of ceramics. It is interesting to note how the art of the stone-cutter and that of the painter was already during the Middle Assyrian period very much a unity independent of its different material and technique.[74] Only such a unity in the expression of an art could enable the unusual stylizations of trees and of animal movements to be rendered in an identical manner in two so dissimilar crafts as glyptic and pottery painting.

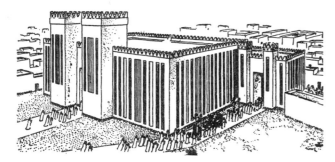

Fig. 88   Reconstruction of the Ishtar Temple of Tukulti-Ninurta I at Ashur, as seen from the north
(After: W. Andrae, *Das wiedererstandene Assur*, p. 110, Fig. 48)

When W. Andrae published his *Farbige Keramik aus Assur* he must still have been in doubt about the curious painted potsherd which he reproduced in Plate 5 a of his book – as to whether it was a picture of a bull leaping up or sinking to its knees. Since that time Assyrian glyptic of the thirteenth century has been explored further with the help of the seal impressions found on clay tablet documents from Ashur,[75] and it is now one of the glories of Assyrian – especially Middle Assyrian – art, but at that time it was still shrouded in darkness. But once one has seen in the glyptic of the thirteenth century the beginning of an almost mannered rendering of a four-footed animal, leaping in a mountainous landscape covered with trees in such a way that one of its hind legs is thrown high in the air with its outstretched tail,[76] one realizes that the contemporary pottery painter was employing the same pattern of movement[77] (Fig. 90). The rosettes also look as if they came from the same school of art: they consist of up to thirty long petals, growing wider at the ends, and in the thirteenth century they appeared on sherds as well as on cylinder seals.[78] They form part of the sacred tree,[79] a feature characteristic of the period.

One of the most important achievements of Assyrian art, the narrative pictorial frieze (without

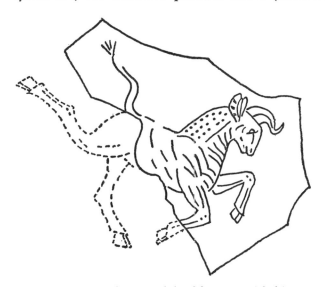

Fig. 90   Fragment of a painted sherd from Kar-Tukulti-Ninurta. Reconstruction
(After: *Vorderasiatische Archäologie, Festschrift Anton Moortgat*, p. 172, Fig. 6)

which neither the wall relief nor the wall painting of later periods can be imagined), the pictorial counterpart of the literary royal annals, seems to owe its inception to the thirteenth century, to the period of Tukulti-Ninurta I. Two objects of a quite different kind have reliefs which support this conclusion. One is the fragment of a lid of a jar, a circular black disk of marble,[80] which was found at Ashur on the northwest side of the New Palace, and therefore must belong approximately to the period of Tukulti-Ninurta (Pl. 244). The fragment, clearly part of the lid of a circular jar, on account of the hole made to take a clasp, bored in its upper edge, was decorated on the outside with a garland of rosettes. Although this lid belongs only to a minor art, yet the subject-matter and style of the relief on its upper surface make it a major work of art. The circular field provided by the lid did not induce the sculptor to adapt the pictorial arrangement of his theme – an episode from a royal war campaign – into the round space available. He preferred to create at least two, and possibly three pictorial registers, one above the other, by means of a horizontal band running across the pictorial field. The top register clearly had to have a domed upper edge like that on many stelae. Within this semicircle he has composed a scene of great artistry: the king is shown turning to the right, attacking an enemy who is collapsing to his knees. The king is trampling him down with his left foot, seizing him by the scalp with his left hand to cut off his head, with his sword in his raised right hand. The tip of the right foot of the conquered man is exactly at the centre point of the horizontal band, which forms the base line of the relief. Whereas the face of the man beaten in battle still appears distorted by pain, death has already softened away the tensions in the faces and limbs of his comrades-in-arms lying round him. The lower picture, only partially preserved, still shows a man in a fez-like cap, probably the king, and probably holding a drinking-vessel in his right hand, standing in front of two horses, having just descended from his chariot, in which a high official, also wearing a fez cap, is swinging a spear. All the details – the harness of the horses, the hair-styles, the hands and feet, the muscles and the action, have been carved with care. The ability to master a theme as a whole and at the same time, in every detail, is revealed here right at the beginning of the art of Assyrian relief, in a scene full of visible movement.

Two other reliefs of Tukulti-Ninurta I are equally important for the history of the origins of the narrative frieze. These are on the fronts of two so-called symbol pedestals, that is, supports for divine emblems. Both works[81] (Pls. 246, 247) illustrate the same subject, the king portrayed as a worshipper in front of the symbol of the god to whom the particular pedestal was dedicated – Nusku, the god of light, or Shamash, the sun god. Nusku can be identified by the inscription on one of the stones;[82] Shamash must be hidden in the symbolic standards with wheel-like emblems on top, which are being held erect by two heroes, both with six curls of hair, one on each side of the king. In both works the dynamic character of the true Assyrian, allied to the Old Akkadian spirit, breaks through the rigid restraint of the immobile, almost static composition. In the first, the sculptor has not so much shown the king as a worshipper, but has depicted the act of worship in two successive phases which he has united in one picture.[83] In the second, he has combined the strict symmetry of the main scene with the wave-like rise and fall of an episode, apparently warlike in theme, carved on the plinth of the stone, which is decorated with a pictorial frieze, the oldest known in Assyria.

Static or dynamic composition – that dominating problem in the great art of Assyrian wall relief throughout later centuries – had clearly already occupied the attention of the sculptor of the thirteenth century.

However, it is glyptic which in the thirteenth century B.C. has bequeathed us the most beautiful examples of the spirit of the Middle Assyrian artist, who was able to confine his passionate inner freedom within the restrictive limits of form which he himself had chosen.[74, 75]

The cylinder seals of this period only provided a pictorial field measuring a few square centimetres and it was under these difficult conditions that the stone-cutter had to carve the miniature figures in negative relief from the hard stone, yet it was precisely this handicap which seems to have increased his technical skill and artistic capacity. Like the Greek coin-stamper the Middle Assyrian stone-cutter was compelled by the limits of space to exercise in his pictorial compositions the very greatest concentration in his figures, and to restrict himself to the essential, yet the smallness of the pictorial field did not detract from their inner greatness. The pictorial surface of the seals is small, but the feeling of space which it suggests to the observer is vast. It is the spaciousness of nature, a part of the cosmos itself. In it wild animals struggle for existence, a hero fights for mastery and order, demons and genii from another world struggle with each other. All is filled to overflowing with life and struggle, and yet the *horror vacui* of earlier periods is completely overcome. The wild animal grazes peacefully in the mountains, the birds perch in the bushes. In only a few periods of Near Eastern art has the sacredness of nature been felt so deeply and in even fewer has it been sublimated in a work of art with such effect[84] (Pls. J 7–8; K 1–5; O 7–8).

5   Decline of Middle Assyrian art

Almost three hundred years passed between the murder of Tukulti-Ninurta I, shortly before 1200 B.C., which marked the end of the greatness of Middle Assyrian art, and the conclusive establishment of Late Assyrian architecture and art in Kalakh (Nimrud) by Ashurnasirpal II. During this time the Near Eastern world had been ethnically and politically transformed. After Tukulti-Ninurta's death the migration of the 'Peoples of the Sea' overwhelmed Asia Minor and Syria, wiped out the Hittite kingdom, brought the Phrygians into Asia Minor, the Philistines to Palestine and pushed Egypt to the brink of ruin. At the same time the Aramaeans, the latest branch of Semitic nomads, began to infiltrate in increasing numbers from the Syrian steppes, eastward towards the Euphrates and across it. In the region of the North Syrian colonies of the Hittite kingdom, and in the region which had formerly been Mitannian, and in Babylonia itself in South Mesopotamia, no defence was strong enough against them. Only in Assyria a strictly disciplined, well-armed army in the service of a royal ideology based on religion, barred their way into the land of the Tigris and the Zab. In what seems to have been an almost ceaseless battle throughout several centuries, waged with blind rage, Assyria succeeded in avoiding being utterly absorbed by the Aramaeans, who had seized Babylon. Thereby Assyria succeeded at the same time in transforming its own small state first into a great kingdom and finally into an empire. As long as the struggle of the Assyrian people with the neighbours to the north and west continued – in the twelfth, eleventh and tenth centuries – they scarcely had sufficient time or strength to spare for great undertakings in architecture, sculpture or painting. Probably for this reason very few works of art have survived, even from the reigns of the greatest kings, during the period between Tukulti-Ninurta I and Ashurnasirpal II (about 1200–900 B.C.). It is true we are told something of the temple buildings in the inscriptions of several kings,[85] but the only important building from this tumultuous period is still the Anu-Adad Temple in Ashur, on which Tiglathpileser I and his father worked during the twelfth century, when they also carried out maintenance work on the Old Palace in Ashur. The emphasis on Anu (= El?) may even possibly be due to Aramaic influence.[86] But its ground-plan followed that of the older Sin-Shamash temple in Ashur (see above, p. 105).

While the Assyrians were conquering and absorbing the new influx of Aramaeans, not only was the god Ashur transformed from a local Lord of the Ebih mountains into a leader of the whole pantheon, but the Assyrian kings – who (even the greatest of them, Tukulti-Ninurta I in the thirteenth century) had been only the leaders of a great state, comparable with the Hittite king or the Egyptian Pharaoh – now had to put into practice the concept of Ashur as ruler of a world-empire. This transformation of the concept of kingship is the root of the difference between the Late Assyrian empire and the Middle Assyrian kingdom. The artistic output of Late Assyria, its architecture as well as its art, expresses this revitalized, wider concept of kingship and only by not forgetting this concept can we understand and assess the

problem which we must always bear in mind: this is, to what extent was this new concept of kingship rooted in Assyria and to what extent was it rooted in Aramaic elements of the Late Assyrian character? Though the Aramaeans did not share the Assyrian love of fighting, of conquest, yet they rather than the local Assyrian state had the expansive, ranging nature of the nomad, which found its best expression in the language of conquest. Only in this way can we understand why much of what distinguished Late Assyrian architecture and art from that of the earlier Middle Assyrian period originated in the remains of the Aramaic settlements on the Middle Euphrates and its tributaries, the Khabur and the Belikh, in Bit-Adini, Bit-Bahiani and the Hittite colonies in North Syria near Carchemish, which had become Aramaic in character, and at Tell Halaf near Raselain.

With such a profound transformation taking place as that undergone by Assyrian art during the period from Tukulti-Ninurta I to Ashurnasirpal II, obviously there was not only a change in the style of the individual shapes or a refashioning of the composition of the scenes, but also new branches of art were bound to arise in addition to the old: we need only name two of the most important – alabaster wall relief and the so-called obelisk. Yet we possess so few works of art actually from this period of strife and reconstruction, from 1200 to 900 B.C., that they are not sufficient to enable us to make a systematic survey, though they throw a little light on certain phases in the development of art, phases which do not always coincide with the more decisive personalities of the political history of the period, who again and again carried Ashur with them over periods of weakness, ever onwards towards its goal of world empire.

In all our collection of Assyrian works of art there is one which is a rarity, a bronze statuette published by León Heuzey many decades ago in his *Origines Orientales de l'Art*[87] (p. 265 ff.) (Pls. 248, 249), which had an informative inscription: 'To Ishtar, the great lady who dwells in E-gashan-kalam-ma (in) Arbela, to the great lady . . . for the life of Ashurdan, King of Ashur, his king . . . Shamshi-bel, the scribe of Arbela, son of Nergal-nadin-ahhi, the Scribe, for his life, his well-being and the well-being of his first-born son, a statue in bronze, weighing a mina, he dedicated it and brought it as an offering; the name of this statue is "Ishtar, my ear is turned towards you."'

This Ashur-dan was probably the first of his name, an important ruler in the twelfth century. The very slender figure in the narrow tunic, with a small elegant shoulder shawl and a belt with two straps across the shoulders, is as truly an Assyrian piece of sculpture in the round as is possible. It is entirely comprised in the basic shape of the pillar, conceived from a single viewpoint, its details incised with great delicacy. There is no trace here of Aramaic influence, which at that period was already very evident in Babylon, for instance in Dur-Kurigalzu.

From the eleventh century we possess another unusual work, somewhat later in date – the torso of a statue of a nude woman, cleverly chiselled in stone. No one would have assigned this to the same people or the same century had it not been for its conclusive inscription,[88] because it presents such a marked contrast in style to the varied series of Assyrian statues in the round known to us already – not only to the Ashur-dan bronze but to all the Assyrian sculpture in the round taken as a whole. This inscribed figure, bearing the name of King Ashur-bel-kala, the son of the great Tiglathpileser I, can be considered as possibly the most beautiful Assyrian rendering of the naked body. That it is an anthropomorphized image of Ishtar from Nineveh, which is where Rassam found it near her temple during the last century, is hardly a coincidence. Here for once the sculptor of the Ancient East was freed by the subject-matter itself from the convention of cloaking the body with a garment, and immediately one can see in the skill displayed in the modelling of this Assyrian nude of the eleventh century that the practice of masking the body was not due to technical incapacity but was the outcome of a mental attitude (Pl. 250).

The only other works of art we have from the end of the Second Millennium, from the centuries preceding and following Tiglathpileser I, the first Assyrian king to check the onslaught of the Aramaeans, are of more importance because of the novelty of their art-form than of any artistic merit. Owing to two fortunate discoveries, Assyrian glyptic of the twelfth century is well known to us[89] (Pls. K 6, 7; O 9, 10), and it clearly reveals itself, in both subject-matter and style, as an echo of the great Middle Assyrian stone-carving.[90] On the other hand the relief carved for Tiglathpileser I on a rock-face near the source of the Tigris is of historical value, and so is its inscription,[91] but the relief itself,[92] a portrait of the king, has scarcely any merit as a work of art. It is only of interest as the oldest example of this category of rock relief in the Assyrian realm, and its iconography is important because it shows the king still wearing the simple fez cap without the conical spike, i.e. he is probably wearing only the Assyrian and not the Babylonian royal headgear. Indeed he never described himself in his inscriptions as the King of Babylon. The kings following Ashurnasirpal I were the first to wear the double cap of Assyria and Babylon ('White Obelisk'), but Tiglathpileser is shown again with just the plain fez cap on a seal impression on the great vase with his inscription which was discovered in Ashur.[93]

And the other type of monument of significance in the development of Assyrian relief is represented now for the first time by a fragment dug up by Rassam at Kuyunjik (Nineveh), at the same time as the torso of Ishtar described above. This is the so-called 'Broken Obelisk', now in the British Museum, the broken-off two-stepped upper part of a pillar-like stele with a rectangular base. Its front has a scene in relief (Pl. 252), and to the right of this is an inscription in five columns of Tiglathpileser I or, more probably, of his son Ashur-bel-kala.[94] The history of this form of monument, misleadingly called 'obelisk', cannot be traced back to the Middle Assyrian period. They reached their height only in the middle of the Late Assyrian period; from Ashurnasirpal I in the middle of the eleventh century onwards they were the principal medium for Assyrian narrative relief, the first pictorial annals of the Assyrian kings. Here, with the obelisk of Ashur-bel-kala, the obelisk was at the beginning of its development and it just had a single pictorial field,[95] and the king's report was still confined to the inscription. But soon afterwards, perhaps thirty years after Ashur-bel-kala, the first pictorial annals were made – even earlier than the wall relief of Ashurnasirpal II in Kalakh (Nimrud): this was on a continuous pictorial frieze carved on an obelisk from Nineveh, the so-called 'White Obelisk' in the British Museum.

The White Obelisk in the British Museum, discovered by Rassam in 1852–3 at Kuyunjik, is a limestone block[96] (Pl. 251; Fig. 91), 2.90 m. tall, stepped at the top, finished roughly and with carving on its two narrow and two broad sides. It has an unfinished inscription of thirty-four lines, with a two-lined addition, and a relief frieze arranged in eight registers one above the other: these contain some very badly weathered scenes divided up quite haphazardly. Both the inscriptions and the relief scenes raise a variety of problems regarding chronology and style.

Rassam had already recognized the name Ashurnasirpal in the inscription and this caused him to attribute the White Obelisk to the well known king Ashurnasirpal II, the founder of the Late Assyrian kingdom. E. Unger was the first to assign the monument to the earlier King Ashurnasirpal I, in opposition to Landsberger, after he had re-examined the inscription as well as the relief. It would not seem possible to solve the problem of its correct date by philological means alone. But as we can now examine

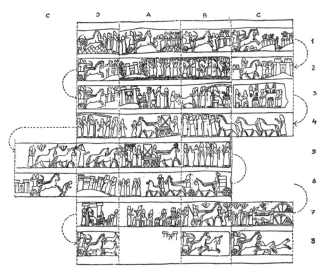

Fig. 91   Relief frieze from the 'White Obelisk' from Nineveh. Redrawn
(After: MAOG 6, Vol. 1–2, Pl. XVII)

the relief-work of Ashurnasirpal II in an incredibly rich variety of wall reliefs, particularly from his palace at Kalakh (Nimrud) (see below, p. 130), it ought to be possible for us either to assign the White Obelisk to this king or to decide to the contrary. A comparison can be carried out under three headings: 1) subject-matter, 2) composition, and 3) iconography and history of material civilization.

When one examines as a whole the pictorial themes presented on the White Obelisk[97] (warlike expeditions to the mountains, conquests of strongholds and cities, the offering of tribute to the Assyrian king, sacrifices in front of the temple, wild animals hunted on foot or from a chariot) it is immediately clear that these themes are basically the same as those used by Ashurnasirpal II for the first time in the throne room of his palace at Kalakh on wall-slabs decorated in relief, the so-called orthostats. Ashurnasirpal II combined the narrative relief with a stereotype extract from his annals, repeated on each slab, the so-called standard inscription. The White Obelisk also has a short text in cuneiform which Unger, probably correctly, considers to be related to the scenes on the relief. Yet the manner in which the sculptor divides up the given pictorial field of the White Obelisk, and the way in which he has arranged individual scenes on its sides, is so uncoordinated and has so little reference to any planned design that this factor alone makes it at once difficult to believe that any single artist or patron was responsible both for the White Obelisk and for the first historical reliefs at Kalakh (Nimrud). The arrangement of the Assyrian pictorial annals, the freedom of their design, their highly disciplined, rhythmic composition, is one of the strangest and most characteristic creations of the Late Assyrian period, which began precisely with Ashurnasirpal II. But the White Obelisk shows no sign of this. The sculptor of the White Obelisk had altogether no appreciation of the idea that the picture and the pictorial surface may be treated in a planned, regulated relationship, and that this relationship may be made the basis of the whole pictorial composition. Not even the eight pictorial registers which encircle the four sides of the White Obelisk, one above the other, have been drawn horizontally, nor have the bands which separate the pictorial friezes, nor do they keep to roughly the same height. An even more important feature is that even the sections of the relief which show the various individual scenes do not fit the divisions formed by the four display sides of the stone, i.e. the narrative pictorial frieze continues on round the corners of the stone, right in the middle of one of the figures reproduced in it – say, an animal – without any break in the composition. This makes us think that the White Obelisk can in no way be regarded as a work from the period of Ashurnasirpal II (cf. the composition of the Black Obelisk, p. 139, below).

For us to be able to make a comparison between the White Obelisk and the wall reliefs in Kalakh (Nimrud), the quality of the relief on the obelisk is too poor, apart from its bad state of preservation, and the execution of all the linear and plastic details is too careless for us to be able to recognize with any certainty the ductus of the outlines and the modelling of individual features, such as make up the particular stylistic character of a work of art. It is easier to carry out an iconographic comparison (i.e. a comparison between the various factual details – hair-style and clothing, representations of animals and plants, tools and weapons, chariots and furnishings etc.). Without being able in this book to make such a comparison in systematic depth, the following points represent a few of the evident differences of an iconographic nature between scenes with the same theme, shown on the White Obelisk and the reliefs from the period of Ashurnasirpal II respectively:

1) The hunting and war chariot of the latter is equipped throughout with a shield, often with a lion's mask in its centre, fixed to the back of the chariot body: between the front rail of the chariot and the tip of the shafts there is always a lozenge-shaped cover stretched across, probably as dust-protection for the occupants of the chariot. Both details, which were characteristic of the war chariots of the ninth century B.C., are completely lacking from the White Obelisk[98] (cf. Pls. 261–266).

2) The horses on the White Obelisk wear a head-decoration consisting of a rosette crowned by a bunch of feathers (register A 5, 6; D 8, C 8, D 2). With Ashurnasirpal II the harness-like head-decoration of the horses lies diagonally across their foreheads: they also, however, have feathers.[99]

3) Ashurnasirpal II in the Kalakh reliefs is always seated on a simple stool without a back-rest (cf. Pl. 259),[100] but on the White Obelisk the king always has a chair with a high back-rest (B 3, D 7).

4) Noticeable differences also exist between the renderings of plants and animals. The low shrubs with three branches, a rosette on each tip (pictorial register C 5), on the White Obelisk are meant to represent the landscape. They do not appear in the relief of Ashurnasirpal II. Combined with these shrubs are cattle, of which the skeleton and muscles are etched in an exaggeratedly sharp way. The animals look like bare carcasses, a feature that can be seen nowhere in the reliefs of Ashurnasirpal II. In this animal drawing the only feature in common is the musculature of the bull's hind legs, stylized in the shape of an inverted tulip (C 5). The action of the horses shown on the White Obelisk is unlike that in the ninth century. In particular, the animals are shown standing with all four legs on the ground, whereas in the Ashurnasirpal II relief they are already shown raising one foreleg (A 5)[101] (cf. Pl. 267). In this the White Obelisk seems to be from an earlier age than the reliefs of Ashurnasirpal II.

5) There is a clear difference between the White Obelisk and the reliefs of Ashurnasirpal II in the hair-style and clothing of the king and his officials. On the White Obelisk they are also all wearing the long smooth tunic, partly decorated with rich embroidery in vertical and horizontal bands. Sometimes a cloth is also laid over this but it is never, as in the ninth century, wound round the body in diagonal bands like a puttee. The head-dress of the king throughout is a fez-shaped tiara with a conical spike on it, i.e. unlike Tiglathpileser I, the king of the White Obelisk wore the cap of the Babylonian kingdom, as did all the Assyrian kings after Tiglath-pileser I.

But it is of particular interest to note that on the White Obelisk, several high officials in addition to the king are wearing the fez,[102] and this detail can also occasionally be seen during the period of Tukulti-Ninurta I[103] but never in the period of Ashurnasirpal II and later. Again, in the reliefs of Ashurnasirpal II the *turtan* alone wears a diadem and bracelets. Also the style of the hair and beards does not conform with the fashion of Ashurnasirpal II, when the officials were generally beardless, and the hair-styles on the White Obelisk are different from those on the reliefs of Ashurnasirpal II. In the latter, the heavy half-length neck chignon sticks out diagonally from the neck, in stiff parallel strands, whereas on the White Obelisk there is a long chignon, coming out of the fez in quite loose curls, as with Tukulti-Ninurta I.

The name Ashurnasirpal with the addition 'limu' given on the inscription of the White Obelisk from Nineveh leaves us no other alternative for the identity of its patron than one of the two Assyrian kings known in history by that name, Ashurnasirpal I (1047–1029 B.C.) or Ashurnasirpal II (883–859 B.C.). The differences outlined above in the rendering of numerous factual details between the White Obelisk and the wall reliefs of Ashurnasirpal II, preclude the choice of the great king of the ninth century, the founder of the Late Assyrian empire. Therefore we can only assign the White Obelisk to the first king of that name. Once this is done, its style will also conform to its place in time and history. The reliefs of the White Obelisk are the product of a period of decline in Assyria: with their careless, indifferent expression of form and their loose composition, they would be out of place under the great generator of Assyrian royal power, the final conqueror of the Aramaeans, Ashurnasirpal II, the true creator of Assyrian art. Ashurnasirpal I was – as the scenes on his White Obelisk show him – a true Middle Assyrian king, a *primus inter pares* who scarcely differed from his high officials and officers in all outward trappings. Ashurnasirpal II on the other hand – as we can recognize immediately in the reliefs from his Throne Room (p. 135, below) was a being of a higher, magical nature, who enjoyed respect as a supernatural being not only from his officials but also from other supernatural beings. And here lies the real division between the Middle and the Late Assyrian kingdoms.

B   LATE ASSYRIAN ART

1   The ninth century B.C. (Tukulti-Ninurta II – Shalmaneser III)

a   *Aramaic influence on Assyrian art*

How deeply even the Assyrians were affected by the Aramaeans during the first decades of the ninth century – particularly by the Aramaicised neo-Hittite principalities of North Syria and North Mesopotamia – has been revealed to us in a striking manner by a relief of Tukulti-Ninurta II, the father of Ashurnasirpal II (883–859 B.C.). This relief is on a basalt orthostat with an irregular, triangular cross-section: it was discovered recently at Tell Ashara (Terqa) on the Euphrates[104] (Pls. 254, 255). The short inscription incised in archaic cuneiform script describes the victory of Tukulti-Ninurta II over the Aramaic state of Lakē on the Middle Euphrates: on the relief the state of Lakē is represented symbolically as a large, coiling snake being destroyed by the god Adad who is shown swinging an axe high up with his right arm. The king's father, Adad-nirari II, is also shown watching the fight, and holding a staff in his right hand and two ears of corn in his left. The god's hair is rolled up in a neck chignon, and above this he is wearing the cone-shaped helmet with two horns projecting from his brow. He also has a band hanging down his back as far as his knees, like the Hittite gods – for instance, those on the reliefs in the North Syrian Sam'al (Zinjirli). The king's figure is carved in such a way that the proportions of his body are completely distorted, and here again there is nothing in the slightest Assyrian in his appearance, neither in his clothing nor his physique. If the art of Ashurnasirpal II, the son and successor of Tukulti-Ninurta II, had continued in the same direction as that of his father, the whole heritage of Middle Assyrian art would have been lost, and the art of the Near East would have been Hittite and Aramaic, serving Adad rather than Ashur.

However, in the course of his very long reign Ashurnasirpal II was able finally to break free of the Aramaeans, not only in military and political spheres but also in the field of Assyrian art and architecture. He not only cruelly suppressed the Aramaeans, but he also began to settle them on the borders of the Assyrian kingdom: indeed, his new capital, Kalakh (Nimrud) – founded by his ancestor Shalmaneser I near the confluence of the Zab and the Tigris – was built with the help of thousands of deported Aramaeans. It was there he celebrated in a magnificent festival of thanksgiving the completion of the first great Late Assyrian royal palace – the North-West Palace, the first monument of Late Assyrian art. Discovered by Layard in the last century, it has recently been explored further by Mallowan. Ashurnasirpal II gave an account of the holding of this festival in a long inscription on a special stele[105] (Pl. 253). This stele does not conform to the usual pattern as its rectangular shape is more like that of a clay tablet than that of the usual Assyrian royal stelae – a tall rectangle rounded at the top. Its entire surface is covered in cuneiform script, except for a recessed, almost square pictorial field on which Ashurnasirpal II is shown as a worshipper, with his staff and mace-sceptre, in front of the symbols of the principal gods of his pantheon: Ashur, Sin, Ishtar, Anu, Adad and the *sibitti*. The text of this inscription commemorating the building of the palace includes so many human details in contrast to the horrifying annals of the Aramaic wars, that one senses the intention of Ashurnasirpal II not only to use the Aramaeans as a labour force, but also to incorporate them as a special unit in the federation of the Assyrian empire. It seems probable that the Assyrian race had been penetrated by the Aramaeans, by their culture and their customs, to such an extent that even the most determined supporters of the Assyrian concept of kingship had to abandon any thought of exterminating them.

We shall see soon that it was probably not just as manual labour that the Aramaeans took part in the building of the first great Assyrian royal monument, the North-West Palace at Kalakh (Nimrud).

b The royal palace of Ashurnasirpal II, as a unity of architecture and pictorial art

The North-West Palace in Nimrud was built by Ashurnasirpal II in the sixth year of his reign, with the help of the Aramaeans he had conscripted. He then joined with them in a cult festival to celebrate the completion of the palace before sending them back to their homeland. The palace was actually excavated more than a century ago by A. H. Layard, who also published its plan[106] (Fig. 92), but this plan showed only a portion, though a central portion, of the palace of Ashurnasirpal II. If we want to interpret it correctly in its historical origins and significance, we must also take into consideration the additional parts and extensions discovered by the more recent excavations of Mallowan, and in particular the fact that a large rain wadi had eroded the northern wing in the course of time.

The plan of the latest excavations of the North-West Palace of Ashurnasirpal II, published in Volume XIV of the journal *Iraq* (Fig. 1 on p. 6 ff.), shows clearly that the building had not just one single large Inner Court (Y), as it seems from Layard's plan, but that, following entirely in the tradition of

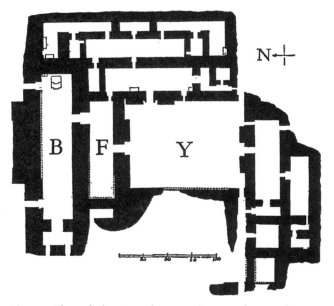

Fig. 92 Plan of the Layard excavations at the North-West Palace at Nimrud
(After: A. H. Layard, *Nineveh and its remains*, p. 42, Plan II)

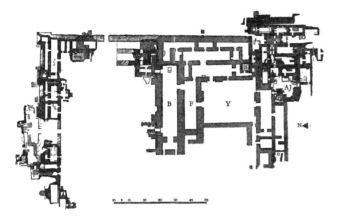

Fig. 93 Plan of the more recent excavations at the North-West Palace at Nimrud
(After: M. E. L. Mallowan, *Nimrud and its remains II, 1966,* Plan III)

the Assyrian royal palaces at Ashur (see above, p. 107, Fig. 75) built during the Middle Assyrian period of Adad-nirari I, it was made up of several groups of rooms, each group placed at right angles around a square or rectangular court and the groups themselves also at right angles to each other. A unified and regular perimeter wall, encircling the whole palace, was dispensed with (Fig. 93). This arrangement of the ground-plan makes the first Late Assyrian palace a building which is indeed truly Assyrian and a symbol of the Assyrian concept of kingship. But we should not overlook the other features which distinguish it from the Middle Assyrian building of Adad-nirari I. These do not appear in the arrangement of the rooms, or in the general relationship of the rooms and courts, but rather in the shape of the individual rooms themselves and their equipment, and in the design and use of the different courtyard complexes which together make up the whole building. In Layard's plan there is only a central court, Court Y, round all four sides of which are rectangular rooms, mostly arranged in two rows. Their dimensions vary considerably, from the monumental hall to tiny rooms. According to the latest excavations (which can be followed best by reference to the 1957 plan of Nimrud,[107] Fig. 94) the North-West Palace (Fig. 93) has, in addition to Court Y, another court to the north of this, largely destroyed by a rain wadi,

with the room complex ZT, and, to the south of Court Y, a third court, Court AJ, in the residential and domestic quarter. It is possible that there was yet another court to the east, also surrounded by its own complex of rooms. However this may be, it is already clear that the North-West Palace of Ashur-nasirpal II in Nimrud, in the composition of its ground-plan, conforms to a basic principle which created a precedent for Late Assyrian palace building: the division of the whole palace into two main sectors, the first round the forecourt or gate-court, the so-called *bābānu,* and the second, the heart of whole building, round the inner court with its reception and residential rooms, the *bītānu.*[108] In the North-West Palace the *bābānu*[109] comprises the northern courtyard, cut into by the rain wadi, and the 'Building ZT'; Layard's Court Y, with all the rooms surrounding it, forms the *bītānu.* The two courtyard systems are connected by the largest room in the whole layout, which is at the same time the most unusually shaped room – Room B, the throne room, the true centre of the whole palace. It is this room which, in addition to the division of the palace into the *bābānu* and the *bītānu,* represents the second characteristic feature of the Late Assyrian royal palace, for this feature was not present in the palace

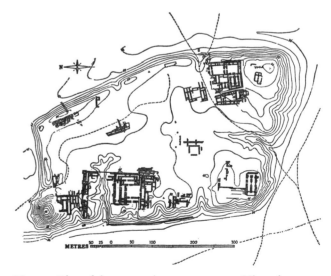

Fig. 94 Plan of the excavations up to 1957 at Nimrud
(After: Iraq 20, Pl. 13)

of Adad-nirari I in Ashur in the Middle Assyrian period – any more than the division of the palace into two areas, the forecourt and the inner court complexes.

Room B is not only much the largest of all the rooms, with a length of nearly 50 metres, but it is also a very elongated rectangle as its width is barely 10 metres across. Access to it from the northern forecourt was through two doors, one at its western and one at its eastern ends. Inside the room a vast, double-stepped platform was placed on its long central axis in front of the eastern transverse wall as a podium for the royal throne. On the south side of Room B and parallel to it was a smaller rectangular room (F), with a door in its south wall leading into the inner courtyard of the palace. The western short side of the throne room was connected to a small staircase building, which can be deduced by a comparison with several other Late Assyrian royal palaces. For it has already been established that there is a great resemblance between the ground-plan and general arrangement of the North-West Palace at Nimrud and those of the palace in the provincial capital Hadatu (= Arslan Tash)[110] (Fig. 95), which was probably built or renewed by Tiglathpileser III in the eighth century. F. Thureau-Dangin in his publication of the Arslan Tash palace has already drawn attention to the simplicity and clarity of this building, and he has interpreted the function of its individual rooms from details of their fittings (concave stone slabs with diagonal fluting and central cavities, stone slabs with rails for movable hearths in Room XXVIII, bedrooms and bathrooms, ramp to the roof). All these details are also present in the North-West Palace at Nimrud, and may therefore be identified and given the same interpretation as those in the palace at Arslan Tash.

The first great royal palace of the Late Assyrian period, the North-West Palace of Ashurnasirpal II at Nimrud, cannot be explained just as the normal development of the Middle Assyrian palace of Adad-nirari I. In the latter there is some trace of the division into the *bābānu* and *bītānu,* but there is no throne room connecting these two areas of the palace. No room in the Middle Assyrian palace at Ashur has the same fittings as either the Arslan Tash palace or

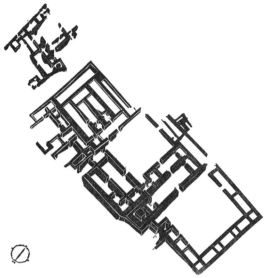

Fig. 95   Plan of the Palace with the *'Bâtiment aux ivoires'* at Arslan Tash
(After: F. Thureau-Dangin, *Arslan Tash,* Main plan)

the North-West Palace at Nimrud. Ashurnasirpal II can, therefore, have had no precedent when he created the Late Assyrian palace and it may be that the Aramaeans whom he had brought to Nimrud were expressing their own concept of building, which they had brought with them from the west, from their own homeland. Is the eighth century palace at Arslan Tash a provincial Assyrian copy of the royal palace built by the great Ashurnasirpal II as his new residence more than a century earlier? Or does it not, on the contrary, owe these special features (the features listed above, which it shares to such a marked extent with the Late Assyrian palace but which were, however, alien to the Middle Assyrian palace at Ashur) more to the Aramaic environment in which it developed? Hadatu was situated in the territory of one of the largest Aramaic tribes, in Bit-Adini, with whom the Assyrian kings had had to contend vigorously for a long time. And although too the great provincial palace at Arslan Tash was probably only built by Tiglathpileser III long after the North-West Palace at Nimrud, it was certainly not the first or oldest building erected there. Indeed, owing to the excavations of Thureau-Dangin and Dunand, we know its predecessor, a far more modest building, but with its basic features essentially the same, a building known as the 'Bâtiment aux ivoires', in which the now famous collection of ivory carvings was found.[111] This building lies outside on the eastern slopes of the Tell, partly washed away and also partly built over by the palace, and the level of its courtyard is 4.60 m. lower than that of the inner courtyard of the palace: it seems very likely that it was therefore built before the reign of Tiglathpileser III. In the publication on the excavations at Arslan Tash, on p. 42 ff., there is a thorough study of the striking and radical similarities in every detail between the 'Bâtiment aux ivoires' and the later palace of the Tiglathpileser period, those same features which it also shares with the North-West Palace of Ashurnasirpal II at Nimrud (division into *bābānu* and *bītānu*, throne room as connecting room between these two, stairway room next to the throne room, throne in a niche on the short wall, inset stone slab with central hole, access from the throne room through a room behind it to the inner court, residential quarters for the king and queen off the inner court, sometimes a bathroom, *liwân*-like small guard rooms on the inner courtyard). If the 'Bâtiment' is in fact earlier than Tiglathpileser III, it seems very likely that native Aramaic influences were at work, and these may well have been reflected both in the main palace at Arslan Tash and in all the building of Ashurnasirpal II at Nimrud.

Without taking such a hypothesis as proven, it may nevertheless be accepted that architectonic details do exist in the 'Bâtiment aux ivoires' which clearly do not stem from Assyria but rather from Aramaic-North Syrian-Hittite or North Syrian-Mitannian history. The clearest instance of this is the development of an ante-chamber with pillars, a portico, as the entrance to the main room from the inner court – as, for example, is shown by Rooms 1 and 2 of the 'Bâtiment aux ivoires'.[112] There is nothing really comparable in truly Assyrian architecture. On the other hand in North Syria something similar has already been recorded at Alalakh (Atchana) in the Palace of Niqmepa, the vassal of Shaushatar, in the middle of the fifteenth century, and also in the completely Aramaicised Sam'al (Zinjirli), where the Upper Palace has an almost identical arrangement.[113] The ante-chamber decorated with pillars is a building

concept native to North Syria/North Mesopotamia, and the most varied races contributed to it – Hurri-Mitanni, Hittites, Aramaeans and Assyrians: in its last stage of development as the '*bīt hilāni*' it was finally introduced into Assyria by Tiglathpileser III as an example of North Syrian-Hittite architecture. If Tiglathpileser III, who was really the architect of the transformation of the Late Assyrian state into an empire, considered it possible to introduce into his palace at Kalakh a *bīt hilāni* 'in the manner of a palace from the Land of the Hittites',[114] thus showing the great influence exercised by the architecture from the west over the Assyrian world, then it is reasonable to assume – bearing in mind all the similarities mentioned above between the North-West Palace and the architecture of Arslan Tash – that as far back as Ashurnasirpal II non-Assyrian new elements in world architecture had been borrowed by him when he first conscripted the Aramaeans. By doing this he showed that he had not only conquered the Aramaeans, he had also assimilated them politically and had thereby also given a new architectural form of expression to the enlarged concept of Assyrian kingship.

c Wall painting and architectural sculpture

The penetration of Assyria throughout the century by the North Syrian Aramaeans was of even greater consequence and significance for Late Assyrian art than it was for the development of Late Assyrian architecture. Never again in the course of its history was the Assyrian state offered such an opportunity for pictorial development as it was under Ashurnasirpal II after the physical and cultural absorption of the Aramaeans into North Mesopotamia.

Here everything came together: a half mythical concept of kingship rooted in a Near Eastern tradition thousands of years old, carried to a new peak by its overcoming of a very real historical problem, the incorporation of the Aramaic race into the Assyrian empire: the inclination and talents of the Assyrian for proclaiming to the world the achievement of the king in the service of his god in word and picture: the great skill in drawing, painting and modelling in clay and stone, already acquired in the practice of centuries. As early as the fourteenth to thirteenth centuries the Assyrian seal-cutters had shown how much they could express pictorially in the most limited space, and then in the eleventh century the sculptor of the first Ashurnasirpal had been given the problem of finding space for his pictorial annals which he arranged in pictorial friezes, four in number, one above the other, round an obelisk-like pillar. Now finally, in the North-West Palace at Nimrud, the great surfaces of the courtyard and the walls of the hall were placed at the disposal of the sculptors and painters for extensive, monumental wall paintings and wall reliefs, like a visual challenge for the product of their creative imagination. Ashurnasirpal II understood this challenge when he was building his new palace at Kalakh: when he had the throne room and the walls of the great palace adorned with rows of imaginatively connected paintings, reliefs and portal sculpture, he became the founder of Late Assyrian wall painting and architectural sculpture, in which Near Eastern art, just at the final phase of its development, was to achieve a supra-national significance for all time.

After Ashurnasirpal II great progress was made towards the unification of the Assyrian empire, the integration of the various political entities of the Near East, Ashur, Babylon, Urartu and the Aramaeans, with their previously diverse traditions, racial, linguistic and religious, reaching back to Sumer and Akkad, to the Hurri and the Mitanni. This integration was to continue until the reigns of Tiglathpileser III and Sargon II. If the works of art, architecture and pictorial art were to follow suit, they too would have to undergo a process of great intermingling: the aspects of the concept of kingship, built up in the course of history, ranging from the mythical-legendary to the just and vengeful defender of Ashur, could no longer be expressed adequately in *one* temple, *one* painting, *one* statue or *one* form of annals.

In the North-West Palace at Nimrud the various branches of architecture and art, including the building of temples and palaces and later of forts, sculpture in the round, relief and painting, were combined together to create an integration of architecture and pictorial art, in which the architectural coalescence of royal palace and divine temple as a higher cosmic unity finds its expression: painting and relief are not merely used to decorate vacant wall surfaces as the servant of architecture: on the contrary, sculpture in the round and two-dimensional art combine to create a new organic form of art, *architectural sculpture:* even the words and writing in the ornamental bands of cuneiform combine with the relief friezes to glorify the concepts of king and empire in the great pictorial annals.

And here again we find the contribution which must have been made to this by the Aramaeans and by their traditions built up out of Hittite and Hurrian-Mitannian elements.

In the same building, the North-West Palace of Ashurnasirpal II at Kalakh (Nimrud), where the ground-plan for the first time had a specifically Late Assyrian character, and yet at the same time was also related to the Aramaic buildings of the West, we find in Room B, the throne room already mentioned, the first grandiose example of Late Assyrian *architectural sculpture* and, of especial interest, the first example of a Late Assyrian wall relief devoted to scenes of the heroic and mythical aspects of the Assyrian monarchy. In Throne Room B, where the concept of kingship was enacted in great ceremonies, the entrances and exits were guarded by magical mixed beings made up of lions, bulls, humans and birds of prey, their bodies carved partly in relief on one of the stone blocks on the reveals of the gateways and partly as sculpture in the round projecting from the wall (Pl. 256).[115] This category of works of art – the 'lamassu', who were protection against evil spirits and guardians for the good spirits – has produced some of the most powerful works of Assyrian representational art.[116] They are architectural sculpture in the true meaning of the term, because they are not just sculptured wall decoration: the giant building blocks from which they were carved, partly as sculpture in the round and partly as high relief, still keep their essentially tectonic function as they support the brick walls above them and form the inside surface of the mighty gateways. One should not really describe Assyrian wall relief, which is clearly bas-relief on relatively thin slabs of alabaster, as architectural sculpture in the same way that one uses the term for the *lamassu*, nor should we refer to orthostats in this way, though it is often done. The stone blocks flanking the doorways are in fact building blocks placed on end, whereas the wall relief slabs are decorative slabs to protect the lower part of the walls of the hall and court and have no real tectonic function. They are actually wall painting transformed into stone, and this is further emphasized by their polychrome colouring, which has survived on many fragments (see p. 134). Late Assyrian wall relief cannot disown its derivation from Middle Assyrian wall painting such as that at Kar-Tukulti-Ninurta (see p. 118) and from the wall painting of the Old Babylonian period such as that in the palace at Mari (see above, p. 82). Perhaps the father of Tukulti-Ninurta I, Shalmaneser I, when he built Kalakh (Nimrud) as his residential city, also decorated his palace there with wall paintings: but we can find no conclusive evidence of architectural sculpture, neither sculptured doorways nor wall reliefs, in the Middle Assyrian period.[117] Architectural sculpture is a branch of art which – together with the pillared porch and the Late Assyrian palace ground-plan (throne room as connecting link between the *bābānu* and the *bītānu)* – had presumably been passed to the Late Assyrians by the Aramaeans of North Mesopotamia and North Syria. In the central regions of the land of the Hittites, portal sculpture with magical properties was familiar, even during the period of the great empire, and in Alalakh (Atchana) this same kind of portal sculpture was also used to flank the approach of a staircase, as early as the second millennium B.C. The orthostat as such is a familiar building element of true Hittite architecture, as, for instance, in Alaca Hüyük, where the building blocks were decorated with relief as early as the period of the Great Empire; and in the world of the neo-Hittite principalities in North Syria and Mesopotamia, soon to come under Aramaic influence, a special preference was shown for the technique of building with orthostats and for combining them with portal-sculpture and friezes of relief. The Aramaic cities stretch from Carchemish to Tell Halaf, and orthostats have been found in their ruins. In the more westerly cities the Aramaeans may have adopted the orthostats from the Hittites of

Anatolia, in the more easterly, above all at Tell Halaf, from the Hurrian-Mitannians, and then later transmitted them to the Assyrians at the time when the Near East was coming under Assyria.

How enduring this technique of building orthostats was, is shown by the fact that Tukulti-Ninurta II and his son, the great Ashurnasirpal II, in places where stone was not available had orthostat-like building blocks of baked clay made, which were then decorated with scenes in glazed painting. These also show how closely wall painting and wall relief were related in their purpose and origin. We have already examined the basalt stele of this same Tukulti-Ninurta (p. 125): it was found in the vicinity of Terqa and is quite in the style of the Aramaicised neo-Hittite region of North Mesopotamia. A series of similar brick orthostats from his reign, unfortunately in very poor condition, with enamel painting on them, were uncovered by the excavations at Ashur, the most southerly metropolis of Assyria, which was still very much under the influence of the Sumero-Akkadian tradition.[118] But Ashurnasirpal II himself also had painted brick orthostats used in the building of his palace at Nineveh. We also have a large number of fragments of these, thanks to the British excavations under Mallowan.[119] Both groups, those found at Ashur and those at Nineveh, are closely related in technique and style, and their subject-matter and form are both of importance in the history of Assyrian art. In Assyria not only were orthostats used in building, a technique which originated in the stone building usual in the mountains, but also when necessary a substitute orthostat was created and painted with glazed colours. It is more than likely that it was the Aramaeans of Northern Mesopotamia who transmitted this branch of art and architecture which they in turn had borrowed from the mountain peoples. The painted orthostats of Tukulti-Ninurta II, inscribed with his name, show interesting details from the events of his wars, and so did the orthostats of his son. For instance, there is an unusual scene showing the god Ashur as an anthropomorphic winged sun, bow in hand, in a sky heavy with rain clouds, intervening in a chariot battle.[120] One can sense a final influence from Middle Assyrian art, with its great sensibility for nature, and the symbolizing of the firmament as a winged sun, yet it also anticipates Ahuramazda, the supreme god of heaven of the Achaemenids, symbolized pictorially as the man in the winged sun. Even more unusual, if we can assume its attribution is entirely correct, is a scene showing Ashurnasirpal II with a crown in the shape of a fortified wall with towers and battlements: an officer with fans stands behind him paying ceremonial respects to the king, who has probably accepted a a small receptacle from a second servant.[121] We have countless pictures of Ashurnasirpal II but nowhere else except here is he wearing a long chignon of hair, tied at the bottom, and hanging down his back. The only crown of walls we know of is a later one, the head-dress of Ashur-sharrat, the wife of Ashurbanipal, on her stele from Ashur.[122]

Under Tukulti-Ninurta II, as under Ashurnasirpal II, the painter of the glazed bricks on the orthostat surfaces constructed his scenes carefully, but also arranged the orthostats on the wall into a regular pictorial frieze, by framing them between an upper and lower border consisting of a continuous ornamental band, generally of a band of chevrons. Fragmentary though this material is in relation to the history of Assyrian wall decoration, it should be recorded that the coating of the base of a wall with a row of orthostat plaques as part of a continuous narrative pictorial frieze was not created in the first instance by Ashurnasirpal II at Kalakh but by his father Tukulti-Ninurta in Ashur.

d Wall relief

However, Ashurnasirpal II not only occupied a special place in the political history of Assyria but also in Assyrian art. As far as we can tell today it is due to him that the Assyrian royal palace became, by the integration of architecture and pictorial art, an artistic unity rather than merely a building. Not only did he change from wall painting to wall relief in the interior decoration of the North-West Palace at Nimrud, but he had the pictorial art decorating the throne room presented as a whole, a unified manifestation of the Assyrian concept of kingship in both its aspects, half mythical-supernatural and half real and historical.[123] In doing this he created the point of departure for the progress of Assyrian art throughout the following two centuries.

i Subject-matter

The subject which the sculptors in Throne Room B had to try and express was just as complex as the nature of Assyrian kingship itself, developed over many centuries and evolved from age-old traditions. It was partly immediate and living, certainly to be experienced in its latest form by its contemporaries in the room itself, of which the architectonic form and pictorial decoration were designed for the great ceremonies of the royal cult: and yet, at the same time, it raised mythical and heroic undercurrents of which the origins reach back to ancient prehistory, an age of which the Assyrian of the ninth century B.C. would have had no clear understanding, and the significance of which may be easier to determine – if it can be understood at all – through archaeology, on the basis of an examination of works of art from the Sumero-Akkadian and Hurrian-Mitannian past. No one could doubt that the great figure shown reaching right to the top of the relief slabs on the walls of Room B is that of the king: his figure is repeated several times, seated or standing, always in the same attire, which was probably strictly laid down by ritual, a long tunic with a fringed shawl wrapped round it, and an imposing wig of hair and beard. He is seen accepting a libation in a bowl from men in similar attire, or being sanctified with magic and protected by winged men, either with human faces or with bird heads, using an *aspergillum* and a basin full of holy water. Not only could no one doubt but that this tall figure represents the king, but it is also unquestionable that the whole ritual scene pictured here actually was enacted in Room B on ceremonial occasions in order to present visually the mystical nature of the king and the central idea of his *mythos*. We understand why the *lamassu*, the magic animals guarding the gates, whose duty it was to prevent evil spirits entering this sacred room in particular, had to adopt supernatural forms. In this room then sat the king, the sacred symbol of all life, on a huge stepped podium in front of the niche in the eastern transverse wall. The whole width of the base of this wall was covered with a relief panel, three times larger than usual, in which the king was shown, in order to symbolize in a heraldic manner the essence of the Assyrian concept of kingship[124] (Pls. 257–259).

The centre of the relief, which is several metres wide, contains a tree in a highly stylized form, a form which had been increasingly expanded since the reign of Tukulti-Ninurta I. Its shape is abstract, ornamental and exaggerated, which underlines its mythical-transcendental significance to the observer. It is a symbol of mortal life, which, rooted in the earth, stretches upward towards the celestial firmament and the sun. From the right and the left the king, the same dedicated figure, mirrored twice in heraldic duplication, approaches the Sacred Tree in order himself to bless and protect it. This central scene is also flanked by winged genii who, as we saw above, protect the king's person. Nowhere else is the interchangeability of the king and the tree of life expressed so vividly as in this Late Assyrian relief. The theme of the Sacred Tree combined with the figure of the Royal Shepherd and the protector of life is a Sumerian concept which had never been lost in the Near East, from the beginning of the great culture of the Protohistorical Period around 3000 B.C. The royal shepherd, the mythical form of the king in Sumerian Protohistory,[125] typified in art as the 'man in the net skirt', is not only associated with plants, as the fountain of life, but he also takes the place of the sacred tree, so that in Late Assyrian rites the 'Tree of Life' received the same consecration as the king himself. However, the concept of the close association of the king with the preservation and renewal of life, originally a Sumerian concept, found its way for the first time into Assyrian art in a formulation which it had received during the period of the Hurrian-Mitannian supremacy: the particular popularity and widespread use of this formula is shown in the glyptic of the second millennium B.C., in the Kirkuk glyptic and also in Middle Assyrian glyptic after about the reign of Eriba-Adad. In the art of the neo-Hittite principalities in North Syria and North Mesopotamia – and particularly on the orthostat

reliefs there – the Tree of Life below a winged sun is as common as it was in Late Assyrian stone-carving. We cannot exclude the possibility that these pictorial formulae of the Assyrian royal myth came from there, and were borrowed by the Aramaeans after 1200 B.C. from the Hittites and the Hurrians, and then transmitted to the Assyrians. In any case we cannot find evidence of this theme in the Middle Assyrian period.[126]

Layard's excavations had already shown that whole rooms in the North-West Palace of Ashurnasirpal II at Nimrud had the base of their walls covered by relief slabs: these reliefs repeated the theme outlined above, either in its entirety or individual parts of it, in an almost monotonous fashion, like a litany.[127] And again in Room B, the heart of the palace building of Ashurnasirpal II, reliefs cover the greatest part of the available wall surface – not only the most important wall surfaces in the niche of the eastern, shorter wall, where the king's throne was placed, but also along the major part of the south wall. The outstanding new element in Ashurnasirpal's wall relief was, therefore, the extension of the theme, by an enlargement of the mythical aspect of the king, as well as scenes which relate to the second aspect of Late Assyrian monarchy – its heroic-historical character which, in the literary field, since the second millennium had produced the 'Letter to the God' as well as annals in epic and prose narrative style.[128] This aspect of the monarchy was also to remain of the greatest importance to Assyrian art to the end of its history. With this development, the sculptors of Ashurnasirpal II created an important precedent: in the south-east corner of Room B, as well as in its south-west corner, they employed a group of alabaster slabs to record a pictorial account of the king's great deeds in war and hunting, completely in the manner in which this aspect of Assyrian monarchy had already been illustrated on the White Obelisk of Ashurnasirpal I at Nineveh. Art in this way not only gained an enrichment of thematic material of importance, but was for the first time also enabled to express in monumental manner the Late Assyrian concept of kingship as a whole, in both architectonic and figurative form.

ii   Technique

Before this great example of an artistic unity combining several branches of art could be carried out, the right technique had to be found: was painting or relief to be the chosen technique for the wall surfaces available for decoration in the new palace? Ashurnasirpal decided to have the wall surfaces covered with alabaster slabs, and relief therefore became the main medium for Late Assyrian art, though painting was not excluded by this, since the wall reliefs were themselves polychrome coloured compositions,[129] so that wall painting and wall relief were fused into a new, typically Late Assyrian form of art. Though the question 'painting or relief' had been decided, the surfaces provided by the walls of the rooms and courts which were usable still had to suit the theme intended for them. In particular, in order that the historic-heroic aspect of the pictorial theme could be included in the whole display of wall decoration, a frieze had to be created, as long as possible, to correspond with the narrative flow of events. But the dimensions of the alabaster slab, derived from an orthostat, provided a surface suitable for a composition containing only a few figures, yet the representation of events and actions stretching over a longer period of time badly needed a ribbon-like pictorial surface, unfolding like a film. Ashurnasirpal's sculptors at Nimrud bisected the height of the wall slab, and thereby they not only obtained twice the length of pictorial register, but could also, without interrupting the scenes shown in bas-relief, insert the accompanying standard inscription from the annals on its own band between the two registers of pictures.

iii   Style

Though we owe it to Ashurnasirpal II that the Late Assyrian concept of kingship gave rise to the new artistic unity of art and architecture in the royal palace, yet this idea was essentially too varied, its origin too complicated, its form of expression too disparate, for this style to be able from the first to maintain its unity, let alone impose a rigid monotony.

It is true that Late Assyrian relief, no less than Middle Assyrian relief, remained an art of decorating flat surfaces, based on drawing, incised lines, and engraved outlines rather than on modelling or plasticity. Assyrian relief always remained decidedly flat, with emphasized bodily contours and linear infilling of details. Even in Assyrian sculpture in the round it is the surface, the garment, which stands in the forefront of artistic interest: the portal animals, of necessity partly three-dimensional, are really two profile views conceived at right angles and then combined as one. The pictorial surface in Assyrian relief almost never conveys spatial depth in perspective. Yet just this abstract pictorial medium, and its relationship with the individual scenes, in the relief of the Late Assyrian period became a quite individual and most effective element in art, its most important means of expression. The *structure of the scene*, the *composition*, became the determining factor in the development of style.[130]

Probably the greatest and most fruitful achievement of the sculptors of Ashurnasirpal II was that they recognized the artistic significance of pictorial structure at the right moment in the development of Assyrian art, and gave it preference over the stylistic development of individual figures. By using different pictorial arrangements they succeeded in rendering the great pictures of the mythical aspect of monarchy separate in their form from the pictorial annals of which the theme was more of a continuation of the pictorial narrative of the White Obelisk.

As we have already pointed out, the concept of the sacred tree, which together with the king had become the symbol of life, originated in ancient Sumer. It is a religious-political idea represented as a heraldic abstraction made up by a few pictorial elements – tree, king, ministering attendants, either human or mythical, as well as the winged sun. They do not represent a particular event, or the action of a particular king, but a symbol for the mythical aspect of kingship itself, divorced from space and time. *Heraldic symbols* for religious ideas had existed in the Near East before the Assyrian period, and were as old as history itself. Sumerian art in the third millennium had already developed them extensively, probably even earlier than the Egyptians, and with greater emphasis on the abstract, particularly during the Mesilim Period and the First Dynasty of Ur. They had at the same time paid attention to the framing of a regular pictorial field, and for the first time subjected their figures to the spatial discipline of the pictorial field, arranging them in a continuous sequence with the aid of symmetry, responsion, isocephaly and balance,[131] in order to remove them from the limits of space and time and to lift them above reality. In this case the sculptors of Ashurnasirpal II at Nimrud did not have to determine the surfaces themselves and their dimensions, nor their sequence. The orthostat technique which provided them with a series of wall slabs on the base of the hall and court walls, also provided them to a certain extent with the format and sequence of these wall slabs. The group of reliefs showing the mythical king, which take up the greater part of the walls in Throne Room B of Ashurnasirpal's palace at Nimrud, inherited from its Near Eastern predecessors not only the royal myth but also the abstract style of expression, the static symmetry and unending sequence, which the Late Assyrian sculptors had undoubtedly borrowed unaltered, instinctively choosing the right style for this mythical part of their theme.

It is all the more remarkable and informative that they should have acted quite differently the moment their task altered owing to the change in theme. Directly they were no longer glorifying the abstract myth – probably at the command of the king himself – and began to glorify the historical deeds of the ruler in the service of the state god Ashur, and had to describe these deeds in pictorial form, they not only created another sort of pictorial field by the division of the orthostat surfaces into two halves, one above the other, but also created a new style of composition, the rhythmically composed, epic pictorial narrative. And in this, and really only in this, lies the achievement of Late Assyrian relief. Epic pictorial reports of wars and hunting had existed to a greater or lesser degree in the ancient Near East from its memorable origins in Sumerian Protohistory, and the Akkadians had also played a considerable part in its development. Since the third millennium artists had employed the frieze, the pictorial band, and with the help of its sequence had indicated to the observer

the passage of time between the events illustrated. Sumerians, Akkadians and Assyrians, all had equated the sequence in time of the events portrayed with the sequence of the pictures illustrated (see for example, the Stele of the Vultures of Eannatum, the Limestone Stele from Telloh, or the so-called Standard from Ur, or the White Obelisk in the British Museum) without subjecting them to any particular order prescribed for purely aesthetic reasons. Even on the White Obelisk, erected in Nineveh by Ashurnasirpal I, the ancestor of Ashurnasirpal II (of which the subject-matter, country and period are all very close to those of the first truly Assyrian 'historical' wall reliefs in the throne room of the Palace at Nimrud), one can in fact find nothing which suggests a really planned structure of the pictorial friezes or of the scenes within the friezes. On the contrary, it would be difficult to name another Assyrian work of art which showed so little reflection and such poor planning of an artistically viable composition, in the apportioning of the pictorial surfaces provided by the monument itself to the scenes and individual figures shown by the sculptor. He did not even attempt to make his five pictorial registers, lying one above the other, of equal height. In all the illustrations on the obelisk one can distinguish scenes of different types – warlike, hunting and cultic – which must have been separated from each other in time, but it has not occurred to the artist to make these thematic segments of his narrative conform with the segments of the frieze provided by the width and depth of the obelisk. He not only continues the pictures round the corners of the obelisk, he even lets the body of a bull in the middle of a scene continue on round the edge of the monument. From such a haphazard, almost chaotic type of structure there is no transitional link with the new disciplined pictorial language of the sculptors of Ashurnasirpal II. They stand diametrically opposed, and one is puzzled where to look for the basis of such a change in style. To suggest here again that there was an Aramaic influence on the origins of this typically Late Assyrian relief would not in any case be supported by what we know of the art of the Aramaeans: it may be that for the division of the pictorial band into regular compartments of the length of a wall slab, i.e. an orthostat, one should look back generally to the orthostat technique itself, and if one does this one immediately comes across an Aramaic influence, even if indirectly, since the Aramaeans are considered to have taught this technique to the Assyrians (see above). But the new pictorial composition of the Late Assyrian wall relief is not confined to the division of the whole pictorial narrative into intelligible elements, i.e. into individual scenes and figures on lengths of frieze arranged coherently: a simple chain, a sequence of regular compartments still does not produce a true rhythm, as this only comes when a rise and fall are added to the beat, an accentuation, such as the regular interchange of long and short, and it is this that one actually finds in Nimrud under Ashurnasirpal II.[132]

The Sumerians also occasionally tried to add rhythm to a narrative pictorial frieze. Yet this rhythm would not have been suited to their nature and could only have been a *parallelismus membrorum*, i.e. the movement inherent in the action illustrated was stabilized and transformed into an equilibrium, a symmetry. It is interesting to proceed to compare the Sumerian composition of a pictorial theme with the way in which the same subject would have been composed by a Late Assyrian sculptor. To do this I shall use the back of the well known so-called Standard from the Royal Cemetery at Ur[133] (Pl. 260). The coloured inlays show us a scene arranged in strict symmetry, with the unnaturally large figure of the king in the centre, and two rows of men stretching quite far to each side of him – to his right, the conquered enemy being led towards him, to his left his warriors and chariot. The horizontal arrangement of the whole scene in the way of a balance expresses complete peace after battle.

The equivalent scene, of prisoners being delivered to the Assyrian King Ashurnasirpal II, can be seen on two of the wall slabs of war scenes in the throne room in Nimrud[134] (Pls. 262, 263). The entire episode – the procession of an entire row of conquered enemy led by the *turtan*, the Assyrian army leader, up to the king, who has descended from his war chariot, bow and arrows in hand, while the first of his followers holds a sunshade over his head as an insignia of rank – this entire episode again falls into

two halves, both in respect of subject-matter and composition, with the action of both coming together towards the centre. The king is coming from the left, in his war chariot with a charioteer and weapon bearers; the royal figure, crowned by a tiara and with a sunshade, reaches the top of the figured band. From the right the *turtan* approaches him, with a group of officers leading the prisoners in a procession which decreases in size. But now the main focal point in the row of figures on the frieze is no longer the king, who, when standing exactly at the centre was – so to speak – holding the beam of balance, the sign of a balancing equipoise: now the king is moved away from the exact centre of the whole scene, so far to the left that his feet, together with the head of the first enemy prisoner kneeling in submission, in *proskynesis* before him, form the lowest point in the row of figures. The way in which Late Assyrian relief has created here a completely new, ordered language of form – making a strongly accented sequence by means of a rising and falling flow of figures into an organized rhythm related to the picture's meaning – is, to my mind, very exceptional in the history of representational art, and it would be difficult to find anything comparable. An analogy which suggests itself is the ordered form of expression of the ancient Greek epic poems in hexameters, because, like the strict beat of the metrical feet, under the influence of the rising and falling the relief transforms itself into a truly aesthetic rhythm, in which the main accent does not lie precisely at the centre but is removed from it, to the third or fourth foot. That this picture of prisoners being delivered is not a single occurence, not just an accident, but an intentional, preconceived language of form of Late Assyrian art, produced from the depths of its being, is made clear in that we can see the same pictorial structure in other scenes, even though these are not arranged on two wall slabs but are either shorter or longer. The classical examples of a narrative relief scene from the Late Assyrian period in its most concise and rhythmic form, with its main accent moved away from the centre, is provided by the two wall slabs from Throne Room B, showing the well known chariot hunt of bulls or lions respectively, and the two scenes which complete the conception, depicting the libation of the king over the dead animals[135] (Pls. 264–266). In these, each scene consists only of a single width of wall slab, but it is also not difficult to perceive a similar rhythmic pictorial structure in the extensive war scene in Throne Room B: it records a great battle between Assyrian soldiers in chariots and on horseback against enemy foot-soldiers. This covers a frieze of four wall slabs[136] (Pl. 267), only in this composition on the four slabs the main accent of the movement shifts within the width of the slab, the unit of the composition, running from left to right. The whole battle is divided into four similar episodes on four similar sections of the frieze. The metrical foot remains constant, only the longs and the shorts are varied. Furthermore, two widths of slabs can be drawn together into a single unit by a slight shifting of a detail to an adjoining slab, across its dividing line. Thus, for example, slabs 7a and 8a become a single compositional entity when the chariot wheel from 8a is drawn back a little into slab 7a; or 9a is fused with 10a when one of the little bowmen, who are turning round to defend themselves, is similarly included on slab 9a. In these reliefs the principle which originated in the orthostat technique, the rigidly accented sequence, has become an aesthetic means of expression in the composition, a kind of poetic language: it raises the epic character of the king's heroic deeds, the subject of the illustration, above the level of everyday events. Here, for the first time in ancient Near Eastern art, a strongly organized idiom has been found which is suited to the dynamic flow of an action. We have still to see how this newly found pictorial structure from the Ashurnasirpal period transmits its own, self-created character in the following two centuries of Late Assyrian art, and how its final development, up to the end, heavily influenced – indeed, represented – the truly formative element in the style of Late Assyrian relief (cf. below the chapter on wall relief in Dur-Sharrukin, the South-West Palace of Sennacherib in Kuyunjik and finally, Ashurbanipal's reliefs at the same palace and in the North Palace at Kuyunjik).

The royal palace in the north-west region of the citadel in Kalakh as an artistic unity, with its own individual ground-plan and its own kind of wall-reliefs in two styles – heraldic-symbolic to express the numinous character of the monarchy, and rhythmic-narrative to record his battles for Ashur – these were the greatest achievements of Ashurnasirpal II in the field of architecture and art. These achievements would surely not have been conceivable except for the influence of his own unusual personality, and this is made abundantly clear by the course of the development of art in Assyria during the reign of his direct successor, his son *Shalmaneser III*.

e The Ekal-masharti of Shalmaneser III

Shalmaneser III was no longer a young man when he ascended the throne after the death of his father. With the help of a *turtan* who served him faithfully and relieved him of most of the labour of his ceaseless wars, he was able to maintain the power and extent of the state of Ashur, and even increase them. He turned the city of Ashur, the ancient religious metropolis of his people, into a powerful fortress, with bastions and protective walls, and monumental gatehouses in which he placed his image. Where he maintained or renewed temples, he acted in pious reverence for the old traditional forms of his ancestors and for their cultic customs.[137] He was as great a military leader as he was organiser of the imperial administration. From his reign we have the remains of huge temple buildings in Ashur and the best preserved obelisk, the Black Obelisk in the British Museum,[138] and also, from Mallowan's recent excavations, not only the door-fittings in beaten bronze from Balawat (Imgur-Enlil) with their very long pictorial annals, but also a building in Kalakh (Nimrud), the so-called *ekal-masharti*, which could be described as a fort, armoury, palace and arsenal all in one[139] (Fig. 96). But nowhere does one sense the *ekal-masharti* as a comprehensive work of art, nowhere is there an item which suggests superhuman deeds in a rhythmically composed pictorial language of artistic vigour. Shalmaneser's nature was that of a prosaic soldier, his palace at Kalakh (Nimrud) was a work of expedience, rather than a work of art, his pictorial annals from Balawat are only factual prose.[140] After Mallowan had organized excavations in Balawat in 1956 and

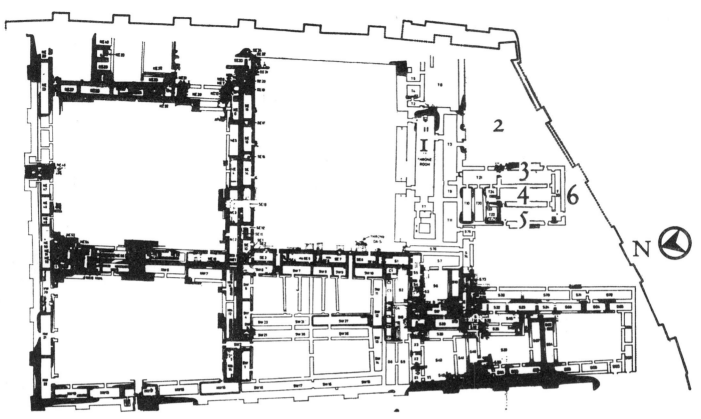

Fig. 96   Plan of 'Fort Shalmaneser' at Nimrud (After: *Iraq* 25, 1963, Pl. II)   (1 = Throne Room T 1, 2 = Courtyard T, 3 = T 27, 4 = T 26, 5 = T 25, 6 = T 28)

had also explored the Temple of Māmu there, he had the luck to find the bronze door-fittings, the counterpart of those discovered already in the eighties by Hormuzd Rassam in Balawat. Now we know for certain that these really originated in Balawat and not in Nimrud, as Budge thought.[141] The bronze reliefs of Shalmaneser, of exceptional importance in the history of culture, have lately been restored and reassembled as a whole by the British Museum[142] (Pl. 268). They certainly never decorated a door in the *ekal-masharti*, for they originated in the Temple of Māmu, but their slightly soulless and perfunctory character and their fine workmanship make them very close in spirit to the great arsenal of Shalmaneser at Kalakh and to the reliefs on the base of a throne found there, which dates from the year 851 B.C. On this the king is shown restoring the Babylonian King Marduk-zakir-shumi to his father's throne, under his care and in opposition to a rival.

The *throne base of Shalmaneser III* was one of the most important discoveries from the English excavations in recent years at Kalakh (Nimrud), under Mallowan's direction. Like the podium of Ashurnasirpal II in Throne Room B of the North-West Palace, the heart of the whole palace complex, this base was found in the throne room of the powerful arsenal built by Shalmaneser in the south-eastern corner of the city of Kalakh, still inside the city wall and attached to it. The excavators gave this arsenal the name 'Fort Shalmaneser'[143] (Fig. 96). Though this name does not cover all the functions of this building, yet it does reflect its essential character, and shows us how very much it differs from the North-West Palace, in spite of their many points of resemblance.

With the help of the latest excavation plans and the drawings of the reconstruction published in the *Illustrated London News*, it is possible to compare the *ekal-masharti* of Shalmaneser III with the North-West Palace of his father. The main features in the arrangement of the ground-plan of the North-West Palace, which we felt able earlier in this book to interpret as a new development by Ashurnasirpal II under Aramaic influence, were adhered to by Shalmaneser III in the *ekal-masharti*. In this too the whole arrangement is made up out of several courtyard complexes, of which the various functions can be identified throughout. Here again there is a courtyard which we can identify as the *bābānu*, with its main doorway on its north side, and a residential area – a *bītānu* – to the south. Once again there is a mighty throne room, T 1, which more or less acts as a bridge between these two main parts of the palace. Just as the ancient religious-cult metropolis, the city of Ashur itself, was transformed under the soldier Shalmaneser into a fortified place, so too his palace in Nimrud was turned into a huge arsenal for weapons, and there were not only quarters for his officers but also for his war-chariots and chargers, and store-rooms for his weapons and the booty from his conquests. It is true that Room T 1[144] is a replica in all its details of Room B in the North-West Palace of Ashurnasirpal, though with somewhat greater dimensions, but even here the military character of Shalmaneser has affected the character of the room. Shalmaneser's palace not only has a podium for the king's throne in Room T 1, but in addition, on the west side of the great south-west court, a second base for a throne was excavated, at precisely the place which seems entirely suitable for reviewing parades of soldiers.

To what extent Shalmaneser reflected the nature of the Assyrian kingdom is demonstrated even more clearly than in his buildings by the subject-matter and style of his pictorial friezes, largely narrative, of which we have a large number. We are led straight to the heart of the matter by the reliefs which decorate the outer surfaces of the throne base itself in Room T 1[145] (Pl. 269). Ashurnasirpal had left the huge stone block on which the base of the king's throne was placed, clear of any pictorial decoration. He had his throne on its stepped base placed in a niche on the eastern short wall of Room B, as if in the adytum of a temple cella, and then had the full length of the rear wall of this holy of holies (in front of which the king sat on his throne) covered with a relief slab which expressed in symbolic fashion the nature of the king represented as a vegetation god (see above, p. 132, Pls. 257, 258). In this relief the king is raised right up into the sacred sphere of the Tree of Life, crowned by the winged sun and protected by winged genii. Under Ashurnasirpal II the military achievements of the king are expressed quite modestly on a few narrative wall slabs (see above, p. 135, Pl. 267). Under Shalmaneser the pictorial decoration of the throne room is quite dominated by them: even the throne base, the sacred place of the enthroned king, carries three relief scenes, the content of which is fully documented by three notes, which show important events from three separate campaigns of Shalmaneser, referred to in his annals.

The front side of the projecting tongue of the great base block carries on its wide rectangular pictorial surface a scene of interest to history and the history of art, the pictorial account of the greatest political success of Shalmaneser III.[146] Standing beneath a panoply Shalmaneser, in his official attire as King of Assyria, is shown meeting Marduk-zakir-shumi, the Babylonian king, who is dressed in the curious Babylonian style which the Assyrian sculptor has clearly striven to reproduce exactly. In an otherwise unrecorded manner, which is pleasantly modern, they stretch out their right hands to each other, probably to confirm the treaty of friendship which they had just concluded. In the year 851 Shalmaneser III marched into Babylonia with his army, to protect Marduk-zakir-shumi against a usurper, his brother Marduk-bel-usati. He generously allowed Babylonia to keep its independence, and turned his overwhelming forces against Bit-Jakin, the Sea-land at the southernmost tip of the Land of the Two Rivers, by now completely Aramaicised, and exacted tribute from it. All the remaining reliefs also illustrate Shalmaneser's military power politics in the Near East and they cover all sides of the base in a metre-long frieze, even the re-entrant angles.[147] Two of the scenes show the payment of tribute, a theme common in Assyrian art and one used often by Shalmaneser himself in the bronze door reliefs. And there is no doubt but that one can detect a gradual exhaustion in

Shalmaneser's reliefs, a relaxing of the clarity of the contours, a coarsening of the drawing of the infilling, a poverty of subject-matter and of composition. The paralysis which was creeping over Shalmaneser's art can be perceived most clearly in the disintegration of the ordered pictorial structure. We have no wall slab amongst the works of art from Shalmaneser III, so not surprisingly we can scarcely find any trace in his reign of the influence of the orthostat-technique which, under his father, had led to a highly developed, rhythmic pictorial composition. Neither the metal-workers who made the bronze pictorial bands of Balawat, nor the stone-masons who decorated the outer surfaces of the throne base at Kalakh (Nimrud), could have had any sort of understanding of orthostat composition, nor was there any trace of a narrative wall relief anywhere in the *ekal-masharti* of Shalmaneser. Neither the pictorial bands from Balawat nor the frieze on the base of Shalmaneser's throne at Kalakh (Nimrud) reveal any artistic figure composition, nor do they show any understanding of pictorial structure used as a means of expression. In both, the figures on the pictorial frieze are placed side by side in a row, not in accordance with any artistic principle but at best to correspond with the passage of time during the events illustrated.

Nothing of Ashurnasirpal's artistic epic-rhythmic pictorial language survived under Shalmaneser III. Although on the Black Obelisk in the British Museum[148] (Pls. 270, 271) Jehu of Israel, the son of Omri – who is shown prostrate before Shalmaneser, in a wide rectangular pictorial field – is placed in such a way that the king is not the focal point of the composition, and does not form the centre of the scene but is standing just removed from the centre, nevertheless, it does indeed resemble the pictorial structure of the kind that we encountered in Ashurnasirpal's hunting scene, with a chariot and lions or bulls. But this was probably only the routine of an old stone-mason or just an accident. If anyone wants to appreciate the loss of quality in art as between father and son, he only has to place the picture of the delivery of prisoners from Shalmaneser's throne base next to that of the same subject on the wall relief slabs of Ashurnasirpal II in Nimrud (see Pl. 263). One should probably not use the same artistic

yardstick for the Balawat bronzes as for the alabaster reliefs, because of the difficulties of technique inherent in bronze work.

2 The eighth century B.C. (Late Assyrian wall painting and the Turtan Shamshi-ilu 780–752 B.C.)

Often – very often, and particularly in the Ancient Orient – the development of art runs parallel to the rise and fall of a kingdom and its standing in power politics. But there is a good example of the reverse in the period around the catastrophic year of the eclipse of the sun, 763 B.C. This was the period of three weak kings (Shalmaneser IV, 781–772, Ashur-dan III, 771–754 and Ashur-nirari V, 753–746), for whom the great *turtan* Shamshi-ilu of Til Barsip in reality administered the empire, and the immediately preceding decades of the Babylonization of Assyria, under the son and grandson of Shalmaneser III, Shamshi-Adad V and Adad-nirari III. This period shows us how a nation during a period of political decline, when all their material sources are dwindling, can create a form of art which gives the fullest expression to their inner being. The crumbling walls of the remnants of the palace at Tell Ahmar (= Til Barsip),[149] which Thureau-Dangin excavated with his colleagues Maurice Dunand, Cavro and Dossin, were decorated with very extensive remains of Assyrian wall painting, and this recently had, as it were, a rebirth through the publication of copies made by the painter Cavro, which had been stored in the Louvre for years.[150] Only fragments have been preserved, and we can only study the paintings by examining the modern copy of them, nor do we even know for certain whether the copy reproduces the antique colouring quite correctly, yet there are two aspects of the paintings which we can assess – the draughtsmanship and the composition of the scenes. And these represent two major achievements, the two features truly characteristic of Assyrian art in general, brought to perfection here at Til Barsip, in the Late Assyrian period.

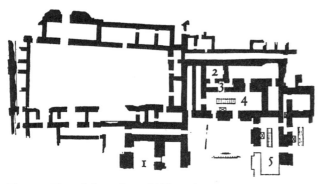

Fig. 97   Plan of the Palace of Til Barsip
(After: F. Thureau-Dangin, *Til-Barsip,* Album, Pl. B)
1 = Room XXII, 2 = Room XXVII, 3 = Room XXVI,
4 = Room XXIV, 5 = Room XLVII

The palace at Til Barsip (Tell Ahmar) in which these valuable Late Assyrian paintings were found, had been frequently renewed or rebuilt in the course of its long history, from Shalmaneser III in the ninth century to Ashurbanipal in the seventh, and undoubtedly the building of Shalmaneser, who conquered the town of Barsip, the capital city of the Aramaicised people of Bit-Adini and officially renamed it Kar-Shalmaneser, was preceded by an Aramaic palace building.[151] Yet the particular historical importance of this provincial palace lies not so much in its architecture, of which we have examples in the buildings of the great kings from the ninth to the seventh centuries, as in its wall painting, of which at least a major part throws a light on an exceptionally obscure period of Late Assyrian art, and in particular of Late Assyrian wall painting. Anyone who looks

carefully at the design of the ground-plan of the Til Barsip palace, from the drawings of M. Dunand[152] (Fig. 97), soon realizes that it belongs to the group of Late Assyrian royal palaces, the origins and furnishing of which we have already tried to describe in the chapter on Ashurnasirpal II and Shalmaneser III in the ninth century B.C. in Kalakh (Nimrud) (pp. 125 ff.). We can obtain new information of the progress of Assyrian art by examining firstly its wall paintings, and then in particular those found in Rooms XXIV and XXVI. They differ so clearly and unmistakeably in style from the paintings in Rooms XXII and XXVII, i.e. in the rooms which originate from a later renovation of the palace under Ashurbanipal, that they themselves cannot have originated in the reign of that king. Their dating and artistic merit have been examined carefully by Thureau-Dangin in Chapter II B ('Les peintures du Palais') of his above-mentioned publication of the excavations.[153] This is done in an exemplary way, making careful use of all the technical details and of information provided by the history of art. On pp. 45, 46 he amends his earlier opinion,[154] to which A. Parrot also subscribed,[155] that the pictures from Rooms XXIV and XXVI originated in the period of Tiglathpileser III: '*Certains faits sont difficiles à expliquer si elles (i.e. les peintures) sont contemporaines de ce roi. Ainsi les soldats sont coiffés d'un casque à couvre-nuque dont les sculptures assyriennes, notamment celles de Teglathphalasar, n'offrent à ma connaissance aucun exemple. Les fourreaux des épées sont généralement munis à la partie inférieure de la garniture à double*

Fig. 98   Wall painting frieze of royal audience, from Room XLVIII of the Palace of Til Barsip   (After: A. Parrot, *Assur*, Fig. 113)

Fig. 99   Wall painting frieze of royal audience, from Room XXIV of the Palace of Til Barsip   (After: A. Parrot, *Assur*, Fig. 112)

volute, si commune au temps d'Assurnâsirapal et de Salmanasar, mais dont par la suite on ne trouve d'exemple que sur la stèle de Saba'a qui représente Adad-nirari III., sur un relief de Nimroud, qui selon toute probabilité, représente Teglathphalasar, sur une stèle d'Arslan-Tash qui figure le dieu Adad et semble dater également du règne de Teglathphalasar, enfin sur les reliefs de Khorsabad ... elles ont, notamment dans l'expression de la musculature, conservé quelque chose du style large et vigoureux qui caractérise les sculptures du IXe siécle. Il ne semble donc pas exclu qu'elles soient antérieures à Teglathphalasar et remontent, par exemple, jusqu'au règne d'Adad-nirari III.' That was precisely the period during which the influence of the great *turtan* Shamshi-ilu was paramount. He also had the inscription carved on the lions at the entrance to the north-east door in Til Barsip, in which he makes a report of his victory over the Urartian king Argistis I without mentioning the name of his royal master.[156]

It may be possible to explain in this way a fact which would otherwise be difficult to understand. Namely the two rooms XXIV and XLVII provide the most important surfaces for wall painting, and both have the entire length of their walls covered with the same homogeneous scene, showing the presentation of conquered enemies.

In the painting in Room XLVII the enemy are being led by the *turtan* before the enthroned king, who can be identified clearly as such by his royal tiara with its streamers and cone spike[157] (Fig. 98). In Room XXIV on the other hand, the enthroned man seems to be wearing just a diadem[158] (Fig. 99).

And there is no beseeching enemy kneeling in *proskynesis* before him as in the other picture. *Shamshi-ilu has probably had himself shown on the throne, in the place of his master.*

In this palace for the first time, each of the four walls inside the room form a pictorial surface filled with only one homogeneous scene. If one thinks back to Throne Room B in the North-West Palace of Ashurnasirpal II in Kalakh (Nimrud), where the surface of the four walls included a symbolic-cult decoration behind the throne, and great scenes of the mythical Tree of Life with king and genii and finally a group of scenes of war and hunting, one sees how important a step forward has been taken, from the ninth century to the wall paintings of Til Barsip, in the composition of these great wall paintings. It is important to realize how consistently Assyrian art, although it was interrupted by outside events, was

Fig. 100   Fragment of a wall painting, with prisoners in front of a chariot, from Room XXIV of the Palace of Til Barsip (After: A. Parrot, *Assur*, Fig. 117)

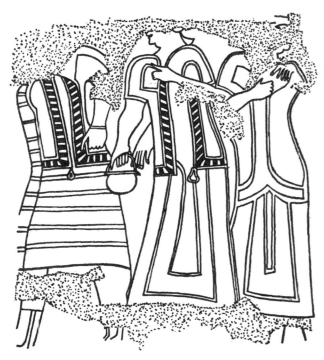

Fig. 101 Fragment of a wall painting of striding men, from Room XXIV of the Palace of Til Barsip (After: A. Parrot, *Assur*, Fig. 344)

able to continue its development undiverted: if the composition of great murals as one whole work – the apportioning of the different parts of a scene over the walls of a room – could still be developed further under weak kings like Ashur-nirari IV and deputizing officials like Shamshi-ilu, in a provincial palace such as Til Barsip, then this art of composition must have been more than just a phenomenon of the court, it must have been an expression of the artistic nature of the Assyrian people themselves.

The excavator F. Thureau-Dangin has for his part[159] already pointed out the achievement represented by the paintings of Til Barsip, taken as a whole: the quality of their drawing, their truly Assyrian ability to make an abstract design from the contour lines and the infilling, is no less remarkable. It is that which sets Late Assyrian wall painting apart from the alabaster wall relief of the same period, even though the colouring of both, the four colour scale (black, white, red and blue), is the same. Yet no alabaster relief, which must have been carved from stone by one or more craftsmen from a model designed

by an artist, can approach the vivid directness of the contours of the figures in the paintings of Til Barsip, which, as the excavators could see, had been drawn by the supervising artist himself and had then been altered while the work was actually in progress on the site and improved.[160] The two skills combined – the eye for the whole design and its arrangement on the walls of a whole room, its elevation as well as its width, and the capacity for expression in the sketched outline – produced in the wall paintings of Room XXIV at Til Barsip the classic maturity of Late Assyrian art[161] (Fig. 100, 101). It is therefore all the more necessary to point out that the orthostat technique and the rhythmic narrative style in composition of Ashurnasirpal II never appeared again in Late Assyrian wall painting.

3 The eighth century B.C. (Tiglathpileser III to Sargon II)

a Architecture and art of the Late Assyrian empire (745–705 B.C.)

If the politico-civic development of Assyria were a complete analogy to the development of Assyrian art, it would only be reasonable to look for the peak of Late Assyrian architecture and art in the period of the two great rulers Tiglathpileser III and Sargon II. In barely half a century they had brought the whole Near East under the rule of the god Ashur, organized it into an empire, administered it as a unity, and divided it into provinces ruled by governors, with the various races of the Near East largely integrated and in cultural matters strongly under the influence of Assyria, although with Aramaic as the vernacular. But the artistic development of the Near East was not quite in step with the course of its politics. When Sargon in 705 B.C. died on one of his campaigns, he had, it is true, completed his own residential city, a few kilometres to the north of Nineveh, of which the conception and the execution of its design may serve as the expression of the Late Assyrian-Near Eastern empire: but for Tiglathpileser III we have neither records of a building, nor reliefs, nor painting to correspond in the realm of art with the founding of the Near Eastern empire under Assyrian leadership. On the contrary, the quality of what has survived, more or less by chance, of works of art dating from Tiglathpileser, and what we can surmise from the drawings of excavators, does not seem quite at the same level as the work of his great predecessors of the ninth century even though new tendencies cannot fail to be recognized.

Tiglathpileser III lived mainly in Kalakh. He also built a large new palace there, as we know from his inscriptions, the so-called Central Palace on the Acropolis, intended to outshine the palaces of his forebears. However, not enough of it remains for it to take its place in the history of architecture.[162] More indicative of the mentality of Tiglathpileser III, and even more instructive for his views of the Assyrian empire and kingdom, is the inscription in which he describes how he built a *hilani* house, on the pattern of those of the Hittite princes in Syria. He not only considered himself King of Assyria but also, as Pulu, King of Babylon and probably of all the Near East, so that he was also the successor of the Hittite princes, and as such built himself a Hittite house.[163] In his desire to integrate the Near East, its politics and culture, in the provincial city of Hadatu (Arslan Tash) he built a city-gate building with portal-sculpture and orthostat reliefs all entirely in the local style (Assyrianized Aramaic-Hittite), and he even had the lions at the gate inscribed with his own inscription in cuneiform.[164] Indeed, this provincial, to a large extent somewhat rustic style of the North Syrian-North Mesopotamian principalities, which from the reign of Tiglathpileser III spread ever further throughout the Assyrian empire, probably also influenced the style of the wall reliefs of King Tiglathpileser III in his own palace at Kalakh (Nimrud).[165] The often rather clumsy individual figures, apparently drawn and chiselled by an unpractised hand, are the most noticeable thing about this style.[166] But as far as composition is concerned, it can be seen clearly, even with the fragments of the relief slabs, that the sculptors of Tiglathpileser III understood well enough on the one hand the rules of the rhythmic epic style created by Ashurnasirpal II

in his North-West Palace, yet at the same time in their desire to maintain historical reality, they also attempted to extend the pictorial surface upward and sideways – that is, they no longer regarded the wall slab surface as the basis of the composition – as was still very much the case in Tiglathpileser's orthostat relief at Til Barsip, as in the neo-Hittite principalities of North Mesopotamia between Carchemish and Tell Halaf. One cannot fail to recognize the close ties between the great wall reliefs of Tiglathpileser III (which even in the days of antiquity had been removed by Esarhaddon from the Central Palace in order to use them again in his own South-West Palace at Kalakh) and the wall reliefs of Ashurnasirpal II in his North-West Palace.[167] In both, the wall slabs are divided into two pictorial registers by a broad band along the centre, generally with an inscription on it, and the individual figures generally reach up to the top of the register. This was the same under Tiglathpileser III in the reliefs where he was not using a ninth-century motif – as, for example, when he used the conqueror motif, in which the king is shown putting his foot on the neck of a conquered enemy, like the Akkadian imperial ruler in his day.[168] Soon, however, a basic difference appeared between the ninth and the eighth centuries in the pictorial structure of the narrative relief. The sculptors of Tiglathpileser no longer understood the rhythm of the pictorial band. They attempted instead to make a factual pictorial report; they no longer wanted to present the mythical aspect of the monarchy but the history of its heroic deeds. To do that they needed to suggest real space, and therefore introduced landscape and other factual details, which now began to cross the borders of the individual wall slabs. Perhaps it is no coincidence that so far no picture dating from Tiglathpileser III has been found with the Tree of Life and genii. The sculptors of Tiglathpileser created a radical freedom of movement for themselves within the structure of the picture, which the painters at Til Barsip had not even felt the need to strive for. For them the orthostat unity did not exist. The sculptors of the eighth century abandoned the individual wall slab as the unit of composition. They began now to allow the individual episodes to spread from one slab over to another, and now the divisions between two slabs were allowed to pass through the individual figures of man and animal[169] (Pl. 272). But not only the vertical dividing line was now regarded as a hindrance to the artist, the horizontal base line also – either the bottom edge of the slab or the inscribed band – appeared as a curtailment of space. Under Tiglath-pileser III, therefore, we encounter again a pictorial structure with no base line, which reminds one of the primitive composition of the Hurrian-Mitannian period, around 1500 B.C. An example of this is the well known relief in the British Museum (118882) with the scene of two scribes counting booty, one an Assyrian and the other an Aramaean[170] (Pl. 272). The men, the animals and chariots are arranged here on so many different base lines that one is given the impression of a complete lack of order. The disintegration of the strictly ordered, rhythmic composition of the narrative pictorial bands, created so carefully by the artists of the period of Ashurnasirpal II, now seems complete. The last blossoming of Late Assyrian art, however, during the seventh century, will show us that this was not a final loss but a creative pause, which would finally lead to a further development on a broader base.

b The architecture of Sargon II (Khorsabad–Dur Sharrukin)

Though in contrast to Tiglathpileser III Sargon II (722–705 B.C.) gave back the high priests of the country their old privileges, in practice he completed his predecessor's political-military undertakings. Under his rule the Late Assyrian empire reached the peak of its power, and no one else has produced a more worthy monument of art for this empire and for its ruling power, the Assyrian kingdom. Like Tiglathpileser, he lived for several years in Kalakh, and there he restored the *ekal-masharti* of Shalmaneser III. Soon after this he moved to Dur-Sharrukin, his newly founded city about fifteen kilometres north-east of Nineveh, on the site of modern Khorsabad. In his royal citadel there, its huge dimensions outstripping all others, he demonstrated in the eyes of men an architectonic image of the

cosmos, and at the same time a symbol of his concept of empire. The Palace of Ashurnasirpal II at Kalakh (Nimrud) had already possessed – in addition to the *bābānu* and the *bītānu* and throne room, an important temple area for Ninurta and Bēlit-Māti, with a ziggurat and cella included in it: yet Dur-Sharrukin surpassed the earlier work in this respect too, even though it was clearly modelled on it.[171]

The next point one notices about Dur-Sharrukin is the great difference in the level of the various parts – city, citadel, temple inside the citadel, temple in the royal palace, ziggurat – they stretched like symbols towards the heavens from the earth below. Gradually, in the course of the two centuries from 900 to 700 B.C., the Assyrian kingdom had increased its size. It no longer included just the local area between the Tigris and the Zab, but the whole Near Eastern civilized world; its god Ashur had become the head of the world pantheon, as successor to Enlil. Dur-Sharrukin, unlike the North-West Palace of Ashurnasirpal II at Kalakh, was no longer just the expression of the Late Assyrian concept of kingship, of its character, magic and heroic; now it was the image of the world ruled by the Assyrian king with the help of the great gods, their functions and regions of power allotted according to hierarchy. The ordered world, the cosmos, was represented by the lowest of the city levels, enclosed within a fortified wall forming an almost equal sided square. One or two gate-houses in each side of the fortified wall form a link with the outside world (Fig. 102). The danger threatening from there, from the chaotic world outside, had to be warded off by the great genii, the portal-animals. The actual royal palace extended outside the city wall and at the same time formed its strongest bastion (Fig. 104). Was it intended to show that the king, here in his citadel, had to maintain order in the world against unknown evil forces? The actual palace of the king stands on its own terrace, reaching out to the north from the cosmos into the hostile outside world, and to the south into the world of order. From the level of the king's terrace one descended by a ramp into a form of citadel which constituted a transitional area between the world and the royal palace. It was surrounded by an inner defensive wall, with its own gate-houses (A and B). On the middle

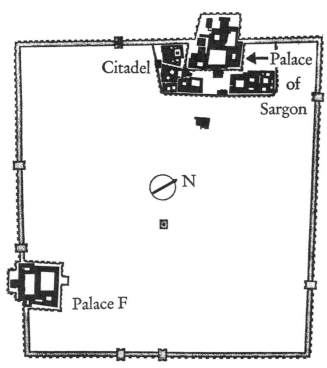

Fig. 102 Plan of Khorsabad after the later American excavations
(After: OIP 40, Pl. 69)

level of this citadel, to the south of the actual royal terrace, several cult and civic buildings were crowded together. The most important of these was the Temple of the god Nabu, the son of Marduk, the second greatest god of Babylon, who had been given a special place in Assyria as early as Adad-nirari III. Like the king's palace, the Temple of Nabu stood on its own terrace, and the two terraces met at the south-west and formed a connecting bridge. This was prob-ably also meant to indicate the link between the king and the world of the gods, and since Nabu is a chthonic god, between him and the chthonic region of the cosmos with which, ever since the Sumerian Protohistorical Period (Tammuz), the king had stood in a close relationship. The celestial region of the pantheon had its own temple area inside the king's palace, built immediately to the west of the palace perimeter wall, with the ziggurat as its highest point. The tension between the cosmos and the hostile world on the one side, and the chthonic and the celestial

regions on the other, through the king, would seem to be expressed beyond any doubt by this powerful architecture, and nowhere else can we find an equally clear parallel.

In this, on closer inspection, we can see increasingly clearly the connection with the older traditions of building, particularly now after the latest excavations of Mallowan at Kalakh (Nimrud). It is satisfactory that we can now recognize as truly Assyrian the temple cellae for Sin, Shamash, Ningal, Adad and Ea – in their ground-plans with the typical combina-tion of a wide ante-cella and a long main cella, and in their elevation with its glazed painted bricks on the front of the temple podium. Temples were being

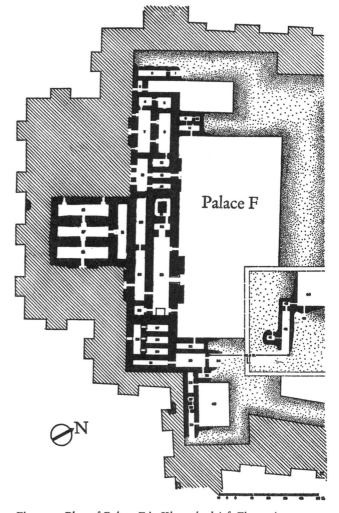

Fig. 103 Plan of Palace F in Khorsabad (cf. Fig. 102)
(After: OIP 40, Pl. 75)

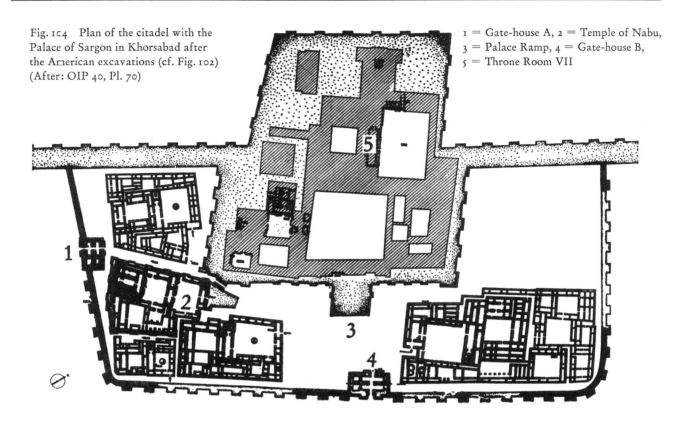

Fig. 104   Plan of the citadel with the
Palace of Sargon in Khorsabad after
the American excavations (cf. Fig. 102)
(After: OIP 40, Pl. 70)

1 = Gate-house A, 2 = Temple of Nabu,
3 = Palace Ramp, 4 = Gate-house B,
5 = Throne Room VII

built in this way by Assyrian kings for their gods as
far back as the second millennium B.C., and we need
no longer regard this important part of the palace in
Dur-Sharrukin as having been a harem. We now also
do not need to consider Palace F (Fig. 103) – the
second, smaller palace situated on the city wall at the
southern corner of the city like a second citadel – as
a palace of the crown prince now that, thanks to the
excavations at Fort Shalmaneser in Kalakh, we have
discovered that Sargon in this Palace F had copied
fairly accurately the *ekal-masharti* of Shalmaneser
in Kalakh, which had been used by him for many
years.[172] Therefore it was the royal arsenal, the military centre of the empire, where Sargon held his
army in readiness, as he had done earlier in Kalakh,
and where he could also store the vast booty from his
victorious campaigns. A great deal in the palace of
Shalmaneser III in Kalakh must have been dear to
him. The three doors in his throne room in Dur-
Sharrukin were probably taken from there, and
without the example of Shalmaneser III he would

probably not have decorated the outer surfaces of the
throne pedestal in Dur-Sharrukin with a frieze in
relief illustrating war scenes.[173] Even more instructive
for the history of Assyrian architecture would be a
clear connection between Fort Shalmaneser and Dur-
Sharrukin, because it would help us to understand a
very important part of the Palace of Sargon – namely
the complex of Rooms 1 to 8,[174] built on the terrace
on the north side of the palace. For this building
complex not only appears to be the same as that in
Palace F in Khorsabad,[175] but it also has a basic resemblance to the great Throne Room T 1 in the *ekal-
masharti* of Shalmaneser III (Fig. 96), that is, with
something built a century and a half earlier. To the
south, between the throne room and the city wall on
Courtyard T, there is a block of buildings in which
three long rectangular rooms lying parallel to each
other are connected by another room lying crosswise
to them (T 25 to T 28). This group at Kalakh from
its position, directly to the south and adjacent to the
Throne Room T 1, must have had a function con-

nected with the latter. In Khorsabad too the same group of buildings (1 to 8) is not far away from the great Throne Room (VII). One can reach one from the other internally. However, unfortunately the ground-plans in Kalakh and Dur-Sharrukin are not sufficiently clear to make the function of this curious section of the palace entirely intelligible. And this is still not possible when we refer to the wall reliefs in the small room 7, of which some at any rate have been preserved, because these only show episodes from the king's hunting, and from a drinking scene connected with it.[176]

Are we able to classify the royal citadel and city of Dur-Sharrukin as an architectural achievement of Sargon II on roughly the same level as that of the first great Late Assyrian royal palace, the North-West Palace of Ashurnasirpal II in Kalakh, an achievement on the scale of the political-military creation of the Near Eastern-Assyrian empire of the eighth century? If we can, we should probably limit this assessment to its architecture only. The furnishing of the courts, rooms and corridors with painted and carved works of art corresponds, it is true, in size to the vast dimensions of the building, yet the style shows no basic innovation in the execution of individual figures and the subject-matter no real intellectual growth over the pictorial imagery of Ashurnasirpal's time. In this book we can only compare the respective main features of the works of art of Sargon and Ashurnasirpal II, as we could scarcely review them in extenso, and even less describe them and examine them in detail. Only by doing this can one really understand the thematic and stylistic essence of Late Assyrian pictorial art during this great period.

In accordance with the usual practice since Ashurnasirpal II, a large number of the vast rooms, courts and corridors of the citadel of Sargon in Khorsabad are revetted with tall alabaster wall slabs several metres high, decorated extensively in relief. The content of the relief scenes also remained largely the same under Sargon as in the ninth century. They glorify the king on the one hand as a supernatural being protected by magic powers, in scenes such as those which would have taken place in the great festivals in the throne room, with cultic cere-

monial. On the other hand they show him as the conqueror overpowering evil, the enemy and wild beasts, as the hunter and commander-in-chief. In the first category Sargon, like Ashurnasirpal II in Kalakh, is again shown with the human figure reaching the full height of the wall slab, and the area of the slabs is still kept as the unit of the composition. We can now see this quite easily from the report of Gordon Loud on the later excavations made by the Oriental Institute of Chicago on Court VIII and the throne room in Khorsabad.[177] We still wonder whether in fact it is a procession of tribute bearers which is shown on the walls of Court VIII, or whether it is not in fact a picture of a festival, of the kind which occasionally took place in the throne room (VII) – because not only are the king's table, chair and foot-rest being carried by servants, as is shown in the publication,[178] but there is also scented water for hand-washing, the king's retinue appear, and probably presents are also offered. In style the figures in the relief (king, official, weapon-carrier, turtan, winged genius) have changed only in inessential details. From Sargon onwards the Assyrians wore a wig with their hair in a neck chignon which lay horizontally on their shoulders and back in a thick roll of curls. This is a useful guide when dating works, but it tells us nothing about the nature of art after Sargon. Of more significance perhaps is the appearance at this time, at the end of the history of the Ancient Near East – and in conjunction with those mythical composite creatures, the magic lamassu, to whom the protection of the important gates of the palace was entrusted – of an age-old mythical being, the man overpowering a lion (Pl. 275). Now he appears again and, moreover, in the habitual attire of the Assyrian King – shawl, hair and beard – though not always with the six curls framing his face. And it is true that the lion he is holding under his arm is not much larger than a domestic cat: but the connection in this context is such that he must be intended to represent the hero, the protector of the herd, who existed at the beginning of Sumero-Akkadian art, and of all Near Eastern art – the heroic form of the royal shepherd Tammuz, who had appeared in the reign of Ashurnasirpal II in his second guise, a vegetation god, with the Tree of Life.[179] With the primeval weapon, the crooked stick, in his right hand, here at Khorsabad he is standing between the gates of the throne room as a powerful *apotropaion* protecting the front of the fortress-like towers. With the four winged bull-men placed in each case at the four corners he forms an imposing and symmetrical pictorial group of gigantic dimensions[180] (Fig. 105).

In the second category of wall relief, the narrative scenes of war and hunting, Sargon again follows his predecessors closely, particularly Tiglathpileser III, though not so much Ashurnasirpal II, whose reliefs were used more by Sargon as models for the magic type of relief already described. Under Sargon, even more than under Tiglathpileser III, the sculptors attempted to 'historicise' the scenes of the kings' wars and hunting, i.e. to represent them as real events which had taken place, and presented against a background of real facts and landscape. These were often named in the texts (Musasir), whereas the scenes of war and hunting in the throne room of Ashurnasirpal II in the North-West Palace at Kalakh were still imaginary happenings in a half-mythical place out of this world. Under Sargon this identification is even on one occasion carried so far that a person is named, and that in one of his few new themes, the flaying of a disloyal ally.[181]

The 'historicising' of scenes of war and hunting had logically to be accompanied by an *increased naturalism in the pictorial field*. And this, moreover, had to lead to an increasing suppression of the original concept of the pictorial field as an abstract space. When, however, consciousness of the significance of the pictorial field as imaginery space vanishes, then the aesthetic effect of this space, of the so-called spatial discipline, on the pictures and their artistic arrangement, must also disappear. In this way, under Tiglathpileser III and Sargon, the rhythmic composition, created by Ashurnasirpal II on the basis of the orthostat-unit, disappears finally, or itself undergoes a form of naturalisation (see below, under Sennacherib and Ashurbanipal, pp. 150 ff.).

For the vast majority of his narrative pictorial reports Sargon, like Ashurnasirpal II and Tiglathpileser III, used two rows of friezes with a band of cuneiform between them.[182] The ribbon-shaped pic-

Fig. 105 Reconstruction of part of the entrance to the throne room (VII) in Khorsabad. Redrawn (After: OIP 38, Fig. 45 top).

torial field of these friezes was a means of expressing the passage of time, the sequence of events, rather than an indication of space. But in *Khorsabad* there are a few exceptions to this, when there seems to be a new feeling for space. One of these is a relief in two registers, illustrating a procession of tribute bearers dressed in furs and driving horses and camels. In this each man, his bearing and his movement, is shown in such an individual way, and the animals are arranged in such a marked echelon, that involuntarily one gets an impression of spatial depth. The flow of movement is so natural that no compositional design would seem to be present.[183]

The abstraction of the absolute pictorial surface was increased considerably under Sargon from the first, with the help of conventional symbols for 'mountain', 'water + fish', 'trees' for forest, whereby the surfaces were partially covered in order to indicate the location of the event. A good example of this kind of space suggestion, which probably cannot be established in wall decoration before Sargon, can be seen in the reliefs in the small room 7 inside the complex on the north terrace, the complex with three identical rectangular rooms, of the type we first found under Shalmaneser III at Fort Shalmaneser.[184] This wall relief has two pictorial registers divided by a horizontal band of cuneiform, and these illustrate the themes, associated together for thousands of years, of the hunt and the symposium, the drinking scene. Here again, as in the cylinder seals from the Royal Cemetery at Ur, the symposium is again shown in the upper registers. Not much of this drinking scene was discovered during the excavations of the Chicago Oriental Institute but Botta in the middle of the nineteenth century had still been able to see several of them. The hunt, the king in his chariot, his retinue on horseback, takes place in a coniferous wood, in which a small temple with pillars also appears by a lake. Wild birds teem in the trees, and already the attendants are shown carrying the dead creatures home. The human figures and the trees vary their size in a remarkable way and apparently with no plan, across the whole picture, so that Sidney Smith in his publication on the wall slabs, which were acquired by the British Museum[185] (Pls. 273, 274), has come to the conclusion that a kind of perspective is present, and this is indeed not impossible because the fact that the visual appearance of an object is dependent for its size on distance was known in the Ancient Orient in Sargon's day.[186] And although too the true vanishing line of perspective was still far from being found, yet the pictorial surface at Dur-Sharrukin is no longer an absolute aesthetic space with laws of its own, but is itself a substitute for real three-dimensional space, a copy, and this alone is of greater significance for all pictorial art than all the imposing, though often exaggerated, dimensions of the architecture as well as of the sculpture at Dur-Sharrukin.

4   The seventh century B.C. (Sennacherib, Esarhaddon and Ashurbanipal)

The Late Assyrian empire, i.e. the Near Eastern empire, a political-military creation under the Assyrian leadership of Tiglathpileser III and Sargon II, had been built up by the hard work of many generations since the 'El Amarna period'. After it had reached its peak it only survived a short span before its sudden collapse. Yet for art this short span was of particular importance because the Assyrian people and their kingdom experienced an inner change at precisely this final stage.

For a long time before this the Assyrians had not known how to reconcile their political relations with Babylon with their appreciation of Babylonian culture and religion. Sammuramat and her son Adadnirari III had already once before declared the Babylonian god Nabu to be the only god, and names

formed with Marduk, the principal Babylonian god, became increasingly numerous in Assyria. It is true that the Assyrian concept of kingship was once again personified so powerfully in Tiglathpileser III and Sargon II that the Empire suffered no harm. But Sennacherib must have come to the conclusion that his god Ashur had to take the place of Marduk, if Assyria were to be saved. In Ashur he built a New Year Festival House for his god like the *bīt akītu* of Marduk in Babylon: and yet he wrote his annals in good Babylonian and married a West Semitic woman, Naqi'a (Zakutu), who was certainly closer to the Aramaic-Chaldean-Babylonian character than to the Assyrian. But it was she who soon was to have the leadership of Assyrian policy in her hands: twice at least in moments decisive in imperial history she chose the successor to the throne. It was probably under her influence that Sennacherib allowed Naqi'a's son Esarhaddon (Ashur-aha-iddin = Ashur has given a brother) to be named as crown prince at a great imperial assembly, at which the elder brothers also had to take part, and at which he prudently also had his name changed to Ashur-etil-ilani-mukin-apli (= Ashur, Ruler of the gods, has appointed the son). In direct contrast to his father, Esarhaddon, even as crown prince, was very friendly with Babylon, and his first order was that the Marduk sanctuary in Babylon, which Sennacherib had destroyed, was to be rebuilt. This attachment to Babylon was not a characteristic only of Esarhaddon, apparently his whole family was noted for it. When Esarhaddon died on a campaign to Egypt, Naqi'a again intervened in the imperial assembly to ensure the succession for her grandson *Ashurbanipal*. In this she was successful after the Assyrian nationalist party had refused to acknowledge his older brother Shamash-shum-ukin – at least as king of Assyria – on account of his extreme friendship for Babylon. So Shamash-shum-ukin had to be satisfied with the royal throne of Babylon. This solution of the Babylonian problem, which in practice meant a division of the empire, must even then have dismayed the extreme Assyrian circles.[187] The historical significance of all these court intrigues (on which we have recently been so well informed owing to the discovery of the great tablets at Kalakh (Nimrud) of a treaty bearing the inscribed oaths of fidelity of the Median vassals and the official Assyrian state seals[188]) lies in the undoubted fact that by then the Babylonization of the Assyrian people had penetrated right to its heart, to the wielders of royal power. This can be seen most clearly in the last great Assyrian king, in Ashurbanipal (668–626 B.C.) himself. Even in his youth his grandmother Naqi'a probably realized that he was not only a good rider, hunter and bowman, but also a man of intelligence and highly cultured. Because at first he was not considered for the succession to the throne, he was trained to be a priest and a learned man. We owe to this training not only the library of cuneiform script which he had assembled with notable interest and energy, but we also owe to it those Assyrian works of art which, in their final mature ripeness of form, were imbued with a touch of classical beauty.

a Architecture

We meet the final transformation of Late Assyrian art in the two palaces built by Sennacherib and Ashurbanipal on the hill of Kuyunjik inside the ruins of Nineveh near Mosul, in the centre of the empire. The Tell Kuyunjik was not virgin territory like the site of Sargon's royal city but, like Ashur and Kalakh (Nimrud), was one of the oldest holy places on the Tigris, a shrine of the world-renowned Ishtar. For centuries the Assyrian kings had built temples and palaces there on a narrow building area. For a new building, an older one often had to make way. The exterior walls rose at places right above the steep slopes of the hill, over the Tigris.

Sennacherib left Dur-Sharrukin, the mighty new construction of his father, after the latter's death abroad. At first he settled in Ashur and then, from 701 B.C. on, he built a new palace on the southern point of *Kuyunjik*, the 'palace without a rival', as he himself described it in a long inscription,[189] and this should not be understood only in an aesthetic-technical sense: it is neither larger than Dur-Sharrukin nor was it a building organism which, like Dur-Sharrukin, served a variety of functions of the state and monarchy. It was probably never regarded, as Dur-Sharrukin was, as a symbol of the cosmos, but, unlike

all the Assyrian royal houses since Ashurnasirpal II, it was really built in accordance with a new ground-plan design[190] (Fig. 106). Layard had worked on the building as an excavator only during two expeditions (1845–47 and 1849–51) and the later explorations of Ross, Rassam, King and Campbell Thompson produced only supplementary information and amendments, so that until now the disposition of the South-West Palace of Sennacherib has been revealed to us only in a fragmentary way. Moreover, because the excavations of Layard and his publications were, in the truest sense of the term, pioneer work of Near Eastern archaeology, we are able to make only a very limited and provisional assessment of this building, and particularly of its position and significance in the history of architecture.[191] Only one statement is certain – and even that is a negative one – and can be verified, even though we understand so little of the layout of the palace we are considering: the ground-plan of the Late Assyrian royal palace, known to us from the time of the North-West Palace at Kalakh (Nimrud) of Ashurnasirpal II (in which

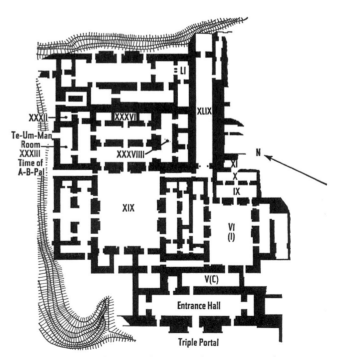

Fig. 106 Plan of the South-West Palace at Kuyunjik
(After: A. Paterson, *Assyrian Sculptures*, Supplement to plates)

the *bābānu* and *bītānu* are linked by the throne room, with a podium for the throne, a stairway room, libation slabs and movable hearth) cannot be identified with what we know of Kuyunjik. The South-West Palace of Sennacherib is, it is true, still made up out of courtyard complexes – that had been usual from the Middle Assyrian palace of Adad-nirari I (above, p. 107), but the room arrangements grouped round the courts were completely different in shape and function from the Assyrian palaces already known to us. Moreover, it is very difficult to recognize and define a positive planning principle, as against our negative statement, behind the design of the South-West Palace of Sennacherib. A general characteristic feature governing the entire design of the South-West Palace as a whole might perhaps be described as its *permeability*. The room complexes are not merely all accessible from one side but from several, often from all sides, and this applies to the courts as well as to the rooms and the corridors. And this is connected with the remarkable fact that the palace – at least as much as we know of it at present – did not merely have *one* entrance façade, but at least three, to the north, south and south-east. Both the main façades, including that on the south side which bordered direct onto the steep embankment of the Tigris, were provided with a vast *triple portal*, with towers and portal-animals, and this led into a wide rectangular room, which again is itself surrounded by smaller rooms, at its sides and rear. There is however, nothing to suggest that this space was more than an *entrance hall*. Through *Room V* at the rear of the northern entrance-hall complex one can reach *Court VI* and, indirectly, *Court XIX*. The latter was, in a way, the heart of the whole design because it is enclosed by the most important group of room arrangements. These groups of rooms, which are all arranged following the same ground-plan design, form the cells out of which the whole ground-plan design of the palace is composed: several (two to five) long rectangular rooms, which could again be subdivided along their length into several smaller ones, were combined into one building block of which the two opposing long walls were furnished with a triple portal, with towers and portal-animals, smaller than but entirely resembling the main portals. In

this way each of these complexes was accessible from all sides and they remind one of the structure in front of the palace, with Rooms 1–8, on the northern terrace of Dur-Sharrukin (Khorsabad). This building also had triple portals on two of its sides and it could be passed through in every direction. We first encountered this curious feature in the ground-plan design of the *ekal-masharti* of Shalmaneser III in Kalakh, and it reappeared yet again under Sargon in the smaller *Palace F*.[192]

So far it has not been possible to ascertain the reason for this layout design in Assyrian architecture. But nevertheless we now recognize that it had had a longer history, extending at least from the ninth into the seventh century.

Off Courts VI and XIX of the South-West Palace we find four building blocks following this pattern, the smallest (IX–XI) to the south of Court VI, and by far the largest between the south portal of Court XIX and the steep banks of the Tigris.[193] In the North Palace of Ashurbanipal (Fig. 107) we can no longer trace the layout of a triple elongated rectangular block, although in other respects there are probably features in that palace which resemble those of the South-West Palace, in particular the *long corridors or ramps*. The walls of these were particularly suitable for connected, long narrative wall reliefs of the heroic and memorable deeds of the ruler. In the *part plan of the North Palace* one can

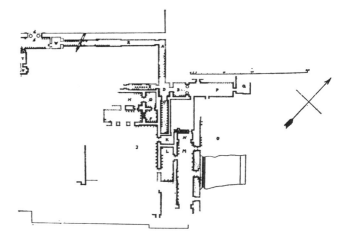

Fig. 107   Plan of the North Palace of Ashurbanipal at Kuyunjik (After: B. Meissner – D. Opitz, *Studien zum Bīt-Hilāni im Nordpalast des Assurbanapli zu Nineve*, Pl. I)

still identify a large, long rectangular room, as for example on the west side of the so-called *Great Hall* (O), which is probably a court, and this room can be reached from the court through a *triple portal*, following the pattern repeated so often in the South-West Palace of Sennacherib. But here too the rectangular *Room M*, the so-called Babylonian room, was probably not a *throne room* as in the ninth century and this shows the essential *change* not only of the *Royal Palace* but also of the *kingdom* itself. From the reign of Sennacherib onward the heart of the Assyrian palace is no longer the room in which the king, as in the reign of Ashurnasirpal II, came as a numinous, half-mythical being to receive the honours due to him, it is no longer the place where this concept of Assyrian kingship found its pictorial-symbolical expression in the architecture itself and in the great wall reliefs decorated with the Tree of Life and the genii. In the final stages of the empire under Sennacherib and Ashurbanipal the so-called mythical reliefs of the ninth century, which had been considerably in the majority in the North-West Palace of Kalakh, virtually ceased, while the category of reliefs showing the historic-heroic deeds of the king, which at the beginning, under Ashurnasirpal II, had formed quite a small minority of all the slabs, now on the contrary almost dominated the art of relief. If one examines the two royal palaces at Kuyunjik one gets the impression that they have not only lost their previous function as the heart of the mythical cult of kingship but that with their rooms accessible from all sides, their portals, corridors, ramps and courts, as well as their wall reliefs of the pictorial annals, they only serve to display the worldly-historical achievements of the king.

b   Art at Kuyunjik (The South-West Palace of Sennacherib)

In Sennacherib's South-West Palace at Nineveh (Kuyunjik), even more easily than at Dur-Sharrukin, it is very often possible to identify the events portrayed in the wall reliefs with specific places and times, and many are documented historically by legends. Often we can recognize in certain groups of

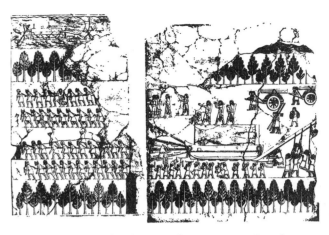

Fig. 108   Relief slabs showing the transport of a *lamassu*, from the South-West Palace at Kuyunjik
(After: A. Paterson, *Assyrian Sculptures. Palace of Sennacherib*, Pls. 27, 28)

rooms in the palace wall reliefs which portray an unified theme, a single campaign or a particular battle. Later, in the North Palace of Ashurbanipal even specific hunting episodes and specific combats of the king with wild animals were reproduced as an unified picture in a palace room. The reliefs are, therefore, no longer architectural sculpture in the precise sense as they were earlier, but there still remains throughout an imaginative link between the building itself and the wall relief: indeed, it looks as though the design of the South-West Palace was conceived for the purpose of displaying the wall-reliefs, i.e. as if its numerous rooms were built to carry the pictorial annals. And now there are no longer rooms containing the symbols of the numinous kingship of Sumerian and Hurrian-Mitannian origin as there were in the throne room of Ashurnasirpal II at Kalakh, with the tree of life beneath a winged sun. Now, on the contrary, all the deeds and activities of the king are pictured in the most realistic and historic form possible: all his battles against man and animal – and even the vast process of building the palace itself. The heavy drudgery undertaken by the conquered enemy in the transport of the gigantic protective genii, the human-headed winged bulls for the inside of the gateways, and in the moving of the mounds of earth for the foundations of the terrace[194] (Fig. 108) was portrayed on the sides of the great ramp (Room LI, north of XLIX) as well as in Court VI.

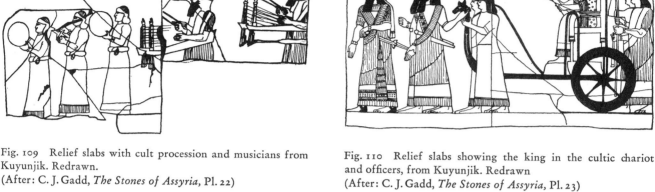

Fig. 109   Relief slabs with cult procession and musicians from Kuyunjik. Redrawn.
(After: C. J. Gadd, *The Stones of Assyria*, Pl. 22)

Fig. 110   Relief slabs showing the king in the cultic chariot and officers, from Kuyunjik. Redrawn
(After: C. J. Gadd, *The Stones of Assyria*, Pl. 23)

Besides the scenes of battle and victory in war and out hunting, the more peaceful events from the happier side of life were given increasingly more space under Sennacherib. As we have seen (above, p. 126), even the harsh Ashurnasirpal II had concluded the labours of building his palace by providing a great festival for the people, and perhaps something of the same kind has been recorded again in Sennacherib's relief in the ramp-room (LI) showing a procession of people coming home from the hunt, not only leading back the king's horses but also carrying with them the spoils of the hunt for the feast[195] (Pls. 276, 277).

Sennacherib also borrowed a new and peaceful theme from the cult of the great gods to decorate the walls of a ramp connecting his palace with the Temple of Nabu.[196] In this he showed a procession of warriors and musicians, male and female, probably picturing a cultic festival (Figs. 109, 110). He had the human figures shown taking up the entire height of the relief slabs, as the figure of the mythical king used to do in earlier periods, a figure which now no longer is seen. For at last the subject-matter of wall relief had changed to suit the change in the monarchy itself, just as the design of the royal palace has done. In a palace with no throne room, the king could no longer be shown as a royal shepherd and vegetation god. This aspect of the Assyrian royal myth only

appeared again, and in another form, in the relief of Ashurbanipal in the North Palace at Kuyunjik.

The most important feature changed by *Sennacherib* in the apogee of Assyrian wall reliefs was in the composition of the great battle pictures, which represent both the complete liberation and the final fulfilment of the rhythmic pictorial language created by Ashurnasirpal II in the ninth century at Kalakh.[197] The technical basis of composition during the ninth century, the orthostat slab and the horizontal frieze borders, had been abandoned much earlier, under Tiglathpileser III. For artists under Sennacherib the basis for a composition and its dynamic had been nature itself: the horizontal frieze division was often suggested by a path or a river, either wide or narrow[198] (Pl. 278). The most powerful and dynamic of these compositions, built up out of very realistic elements, is the battle scene of Lachish, in which a single vigorous movement from the bottom left of the picture, rising up to the top right, to the king enthroned on the mountain, dominates the whole scene and unites it.[199]

But nature is not only the source of the dynamic movement of these reliefs, but also of their peaceful patterns, and particularly, for instance, the long rhythmic rows of palms creating the background pattern of the confusing great procession of prisoners and men bearing sacrifices[200] (Pl. 279).

c The art of Ashurbanipal

Although we unfortunately do not know a great deal about the architectonic achievements of *Ashurbanipal*, we are considerably better informed concerning the *art* of his period, indeed, we are particularly well-informed, thanks to the two palaces at Kuyunjik and a few other remnants. We are even able to follow its various branches – outline drawing, wall painting, clay models and the carefully executed wall reliefs – through at least two different phases. In each work of art, however, we sense not only the high quality of the workmanship but beyond that an unmistakable touch of genius, suggesting an influence on the artists which can only have come from their patron, from Ashurbanipal himself. This is as apparent in the preliminary sketches which have survived as in the finished works when painted and modelled: in the scintillating brilliance of the drawing we can really find nothing from the pre-Greek era to compare with these pictures of riders and lions from Til Barsip, either in power of expression or sureness of touch[201] (Figs. 111, 112). Another work, equally typical of Ashurbanipal's period, in the richness of its detail as well as in the elegance of its line drawing, is the fragment of a clay relief from Ashur[202] (Pl. 280) with a picture of a rider: this is probably a sculptor's model. One only needs to place it beside the second model, which is also made of clay[203] (Pl. 281), to see at once the clear difference in style between these two, the same difference which separates the two kings Sennacherib and Ashurbani-

Fig. 112   Fragment of a wall painting from Til Barsip (Lion) (After: A. Parrot, *Assur*, Pl. 304)

pal. Because of the unusual shape of the rider's laced boots it is possible, now that B. Hrouda has made a comprehensive study of the details of the Late Assyrian reliefs at Kuyunjik,[204] to show that only one of the clay models should be attributed to Sennacherib, and not both as W. Andrae thought. The rider on the clay model is undoubtedly wearing a laced boot with an uneven, stepped upper edge, a feature typical of Ashurbanipal's reign, while Sennacherib's soldiers had laced boots with just a plain, straight edge.

Nowhere else does Ashurbanipal personally seem so westernized, so Aramaic in his constitution, though in purely Assyrian royal dress (shawl garment with rope girdle and double tiara) as on a limestone relief from Babylon, which has an inscription on it about the rebuilding of the temple of Marduk, *Esagila*. Dressed in Assyrian royal attire, Ashurbanipal himself is shown carrying a builder's basket on his head, in an age-old Sumero-Babylonian cult attitude[205] (Pl. 282). Certainly this *Babylonization*, which Assyria experienced under and through Ashurbanipal, involved no loss of its own character but led to an inner enrichment and fulfilment of the Near Eastern monarchy through a blending of the Assyrian and the Babylonian concepts of kingship. This inner enrichment was, moreover, not expressed only in Ashurbanipal's works of art. For the first time in

Fig. 111   Fragment of a wall painting from Til Barsip (Rider) (After: A. Parrot, *Assur*, Pl. 339)

the Ancient Orient there is in these works a serenity and harmony of form like that which the great Babylonian king Hammurabi wished to impart to mankind, when (as he wrote): 'he caused men to rest on peaceful meadows, he caused his beautiful shadow to fall over his city.' In quite similar terms Ashurbanipal speaks of his reign as if his kingdom were not just a fierce battle for Assyria, as if he had really introduced once again the happiness of the proto-historical era, a form of Golden Age: 'Like fine oil the four regions of the world were smoothly order-ed',[206] and lions paced through the vine and palm gardens of his palace in the wake of the singers, spellbound by the sacred strains of the cultic music of the lyres and harps[207] (Pl. 283). We have met this concept before, on a Late Kassite *kudurru*,[208] prob-ably dating from Melishihu: it seems as if here there were already Orphean images pressing westward. And when in the first year of his reign the blades and ears of corn grew so tall that men were still talking of them thirty years later,[209] Ashurbanipal must have felt himself to be the bringer of well-being and happi-ness, a feeling inspired by his very pious sensitive nature. Anyone reading his report on the building of the North Palace, the *bit-riduti*, in which he recalls his happy childhood,[210] must surely feel that Ashur-banipal was influenced not only by his head but also by his heart. He seems to have been very attached to the two houses in the citadel at Nineveh – the South-West Palace of his grandfather and his own house, which he only built after his 'favourite brother', Shamash-shum-ukin, had deserted him and had then perished miserably as a traitor in Babylon.

The architecture and reliefs of the two palaces at Nineveh represent Late Assyrian art at the final summit of its development, which directly preceded its abrupt collapse. These palaces are widely sepa-rated from each other historically. One is the work of Sennacherib, the other the work of his grandson Ashurbanipal. The former can be dated precisely by inscriptions in the first decade around 700 B.C., but the North Palace was built in the forties after the fratricidal battle between Sennacherib's two grand-sons had been resolved in Ashurbanipal's favour through the capture of Babylon. The whole of the palace in the south-west corner of Kuyunjik dates

from Sennacherib; its wall slabs also date from then, as they have his inscription on the back. It is more difficult, however, to apportion the reliefs on the wall slabs, found during the excavations, between Sennacherib and his grandson Ashurbanipal, because a large part of the reliefs in the South-West Palace of Nineveh originated under *Ashurbanipal*. We have known this for many years, from, amongst others, the inscriptions on the great relief in Room XXXIII showing Ashurbanipal's decisive and destructive battle against the king of the Elamites, Teumman, in the year 653 B.C.

A large part of the relief work there originated in the reign of Sennacherib himself (704–681 B.C.), the builder of the South-West Palace in Kuyunjik. Sen-nacherib had the central room of the whole palace, Room XXXVI, which according to the layout forms the heart of the whole place, decorated with one of the greatest battle scenes of the Late Assyrian period, the great composition of the Battle of Lachish in Palestine. The campaign took place around 700 B.C. Other large compositions carved by Sennacherib's sculptors have been found in Court XIX and in many other rooms, and these either record the build-ing of the palace or are scenes from battles in the Babylonian marshes.

It was decades later before Ashurbanipal con-tinued with the decoration of the South-West Palace. Hrouda has been able to show that the reliefs in Room XXXII came from a transitional phase. The first battle scene composed according to the design of his grandfather, the relief in Room XXXIII showing his victory over Teumman and the Elamite army (Pl. 284), cannot have been made before 653 B.C., the year in which the battle took place. We now have other clues which suggest that Ashurbanipal also had reliefs, made in his final style, erected in Court XIX and Room XXVIII.[211]

Ashurbanipal's reliefs in the North Palace must be somewhat later than those in the areas XIX and XXVIII of the South-West Palace, because the North Palace cannot have been built until after the defeat of Shamash-shum-ukin, that is, not until the forties. Consequently there is a gap of several years between them. It is therefore hardly surprising to find that they differ from each other quite considerably, both in subject-matter and style. The figures are now no longer distributed across the whole pictorial field to fill all the space, with great use of the so-called cavalier perspective but are greatly reduced in scale and are arranged in rows like friezes, which are divided by borders. In contrast to the relief of Sennacherib the compositions of Ashurbanipal were in this way imbued with a sort of intimacy, the quality found in a miniature, and they regained something of the rhythmic poetic pictorial language of the period of Ashurnasirpal. However, the world-renowned pictures of fighting animals in the North Palace surpass the art of relief of the ninth century, because the pictorial art of Ashurbanipal – the expression of the combined Assyrian and Babylonian concepts of kingship – to a large degree succeeded in overcoming the dualism which had both assisted and hindered classical art in the Land of the Two Rivers from the end of the Jamdat Nasr period and espe-

cially from the Mesilim Period. That is why Ashurbanipal's art can show us the world of wild animals spellbound by music in the *paradeisos* and the Sacred Marriage in the vineyard (Pl. 287). That is why when we look at the king's contests with lions, we are moved not so much by a sense of the conquest of evil than by pity for the tragic fate of the beasts[212] (Pls. 285, 286).

These scenes from the North Palace move all who look at them by their mature beauty, with an appeal which reaches beyond the limits of their own land. They form the natural conclusion of the classical art of Ancient Mesopotamia, a pictorial art expressing a concept of kingship which had been created by the artists of the Protohistorical Period out of the Tammuz myth, and evolved further by the artists of the Akkadian Period and by the Assyrian ideas of monarchy: all this found in a way its culmination and renewal under Ashurbanipal (Pl. 288).

V Neo-Babylonian Epilogue

Classical art in Ancient Mesopotamia began, as we have seen, as Sumerian pre-Akkadian Semitic art in the third millennium B.C., and reached its full strength in the Akkadian Period and under the kings of Sumer and Akkad during the Third Dynasty of Ur. However, after the Canaanite penetration of the population of Mesopotamia around 2000 B.C., in the second millennium, this art developed into a powerful growth but with *two* main branches, one Kassite-Babylonian and the other Mitannian-Assyrian. This second branch, the Assyrian, was nourished by an exceptionally active concept of kingship, which expressed itself very artistically in the great narrative pictorial art which was itself only a component of the Assyrian royal palace. The culmination and end of this branch came under Ashurbanipal. But the first great branch, the Kassite-Babylonian branch, which had grown away from the main stem of classical art, was often and over a long period overshadowed by the Assyrian branch, yet it never died away, even when the Assyrian empire and its kingdom finally collapsed as a political entity, at the end of the seventh century, under the combined pressure of the Babylonian Aramaeans – the so-called Chaldaeans – and the Iranian Medes. Under the Chaldaean ruling house of Nabopolassar and Nebuchadnezzar II, free from Assyrian pressure, neo-Babylonian power and cultural activity revived into what was truly an astounding renaissance, a second revival which in many respects renewed the link with the Babylonian culture and art of Hammurabi. This second branch of the classical art of Mesopotamia was based on an entirely different concept of kingship that had first appeared in the Late Sumerian period under the *ensis*

of Lagash, the kings of the Isin-Larsa dynasties and, above all, under Hammurabi of Babylon – the idealized figure of the defender of peace, the builder of temples. Now it is not the king's heroic battles but his pious deeds which count. That is also the reason why there are at this period no annals with texts glorifying the king's deeds in the Assyrian manner, no epic pictorial art. In this concept the king is regarded more as the builder of temples, so that in the Babylonian world – and also in this neo-Babylonian world – architecture moves into the forefront of royal activity, and, of course, temple building in particular.

Because the Babylon of Hammurabi lies below the level of the water-table, Koldewey was not able to rescue it despite years of excavating. It is therefore all the more important to examine the neo-Babylonian reflection of this second branch of the classical art of Mesopotamia, the monumental, sacred art of

Fig. 113 Perspective reconstruction of the Ishtar Gate
(After: WVDOG 32, Pl. 20)

Babylonia. It is, of course, the architecture of a later period but it contained two of the wonders of the world of its day – the Palace of Nebuchadnezzar with the hanging gardens he made for his Median wife, and, greatest of all, the shrine of Marduk, *esagila*, with its elevated temple, *etemenanki*, the Biblical Tower of Babel.

It is true that the excavators have not found much more than the ground and elevation outlines of these ruins, together with large areas of polychrome glazed bricks which could be pieced together. Yet anyone who takes the trouble to combine in his imagination the excavation-plans with the reconstructed coloured façades displayed in the East Berlin Museum can in this way form a picture of the great architecture of neo-Babylon as it must have appeared at the time of Nebuchadnezzar. At that time, too, it must have been displaying successfully to the world the sacred and royal character of Babylon, as it existed in the great classical period of Hammurabi.[1]

The Chaldaean patrons of building are not only successful in their interpretation of a royal sacred building and in the size of the building, and its variety – from a fortified building to a palace or temple – but above all they are successful in that they forged a link between the tradition which lies behind all their monuments and the history of the world. Whether it is the powerful city wall of Babylon,[2] or the Ishtar Gate[3] (Fig. 113), whether a small temple like the Ninmah Shrine[4] (Fig. 114) or a gigantic undertaking like the Esagila or the Entemenanki, all their buildings, in their character as well as in style, have their roots in the most ancient architectural history of the land and are all based on the early Sumerian mud-brick architecture of the Uruk Levels VI–IV (cf. Chapter I 3a pp. 9 ff.).

Ashurbanipal has recorded his study of Old Sumerian and Old Akkadian inscriptions, and just as he has clearly completed the historical circle of Protohistorical and later periods in his buildings – one need only recall his lion fights and the symposium scene in the 'vine garden' – so Nebuchadnezzar also has shown us the inner and external connections between his neo-Babylonian architecture and the Sumerian architecture of the Uruk Protohistorical Period. Whereas we can only trace the layout of the

typically Assyrian temple, with its combination of the long and the wide cella, as far back as the Middle Assyrian period, i.e. for a few centuries, it is not difficult in something like the typically neo-Babylonian layout of the temple of Ninmah[5] or of E-patutila[6] to return for thousands of years to the Late Sumerian period. Even in the *Gigparku* of the Nanna shrine in Ur from the Third Dynasty of Ur

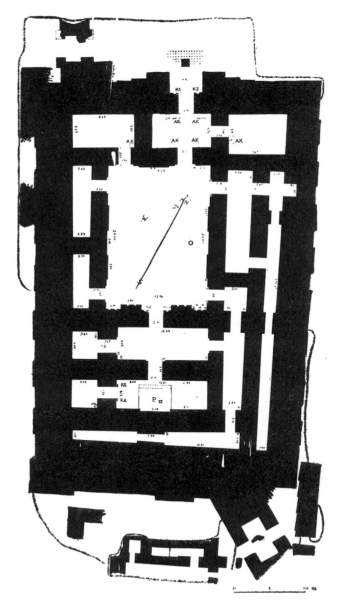

Fig. 114   Plan of the Ninmah Temple in Babylon (After: WVDOG 15, Pl. III)

the temple plan with a wide main cella and antecella already existed (see above p. 56).[7] But it was not only in the layout of the heart of its temple, the holy of holies, that neo-Babylonian architecture carried on the traditions of its history, but in the whole conception of the Marduk sanctuary of Nebuchadnezzar in Babylon (Fig. 115) – its complex of buildings round the courts and also adjoining the perimeter wall,[8] as well as in the ziggurat, the Tower of Babel – its meaning and shape were all derived from the great shrines of Sumero-Babylonian history, from the fourth and the third millennium B.C., and these can be seen best in Ur and Uruk as a result of the German and Anglo-American excavations.[9] The most splendid feature in the Marduk sanctuary of Nebuchadnezzar is probably its division into three, namely the temple at ground level *(esagila)*, the high temple on the ziggurat *(etemenanki)*, and the Temple of the New Year Festival *(bit akitu)* outside the city, which is probably to be sought on the other side of the Euphrates. This whole *Neo-Babylonian monumental sacred architecture* must be considered a continuation

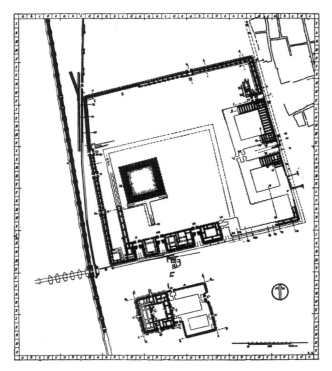

Fig. 115   Plan of the Marduk shrine Esagila in Babylon (After: WVDOG 59, Pl. 2)

of the Sumero-Babylonian tradition since it merely added a classical shape to the same religion.

This is probably not quite the same in the case of Chaldaean *Palace building*. The Babylonian concept of kingship – in contrast to the Assyrian – was actually never strong or assertive enough to provide a comparison with anything like the Late Assyrian integration of several branches of art in the royal palace in Kalakh from the period of Ashurnasirpal II. But although the neo-Babylonian Marduk sanctuary in Babylon differs from the Late Sumerian Nanna shrine mainly because of its dimensions, its monumental size, yet Nabopolassar and Nebuchadnezzar had notwithstanding made the Southern Citadel in Babylon into a royal residential, administrative and reception centre which is clearly quite unlike the Late Assyrian royal palace[10] (Fig. 116). It was not just the size of the so-called Southern Citadel (Südburg) with, in all, five courtyard complexes, which set the king's house apart from the ordinary house, it arose from the multiplication of the normal components of the ordinary dwelling-house.[11] The oldest parts of the neo-Babylonian Chaldaean Southern Citadel, built by Nabopolassar, can still be recognized in its 'West Court' in the same part of the whole Southern Citadel which later under Nebuchadnezzar was used as his actual royal residence. The other courtyard complexes, the main court, the middle court, east court and annexe court, had been built consecutively on a similar, but somewhat different ground-plan to suit the various needs of the kingdom.

Among the countless rooms of the palace one is particularly striking, the vast *Throne Room*, lying on the south side of the main court, a wide rectangular room designed to lie symmetrical to the axis, with three entrances from the court and a central, slightly recessed niche in the centre of the rear wall which was intended for the king's throne. While it is true that the king's throne room is quite different from a Late Babylonian temple cella, owing to the absence of the ante-cella, the main difference is that which makes it unlike the Assyrian throne room, where the king's throne was placed on a platform near the short transverse wall (see above p. 128). Even judging by the shape of the throne room, the ceremonies of the king's cult must have been quite different in Babylon from

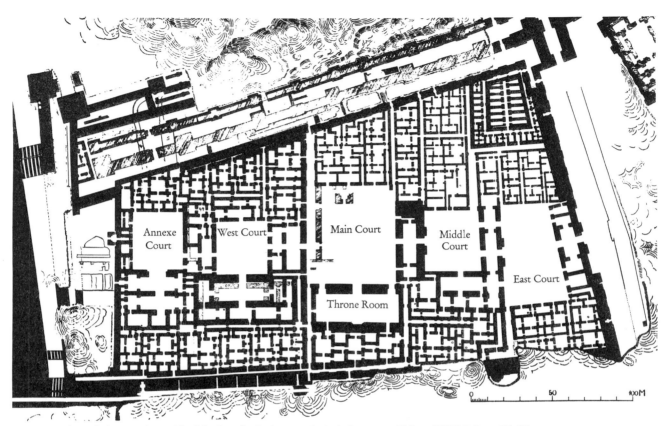

Fig. 116　Plan of the Southern Citadel of Nebuchadnezzar in Babylon　　(After: WVDOG 54, Pl. II)

those in Ashur, though in both regions of Ancient
Mesopotamia, Babylon as well as Ashur – precisely
because of their common origin in the Sumerian
Protohistorical Period in Uruk – the concept of
kingship was connected with the concept of life itself.
The decoration of the façade of the throne room
facing the main court, made of painted and glazed
bricks, suggests this very strongly: anyone standing
in the main court and looking at the façade, as it
appears in Koldewey's reconstruction, would be able
to look through the main central door at the king
enthroned in the niche[12] (Fig. 117). As the heart of
the whole layout, as it were, it would have been
encased in an enamel decoration which covered the
whole surface of the façade (Pl. 292). It is part of
one of the greatest compositions in glazed brick of
the neo-Babylonian period, and its symbolical-
decorative meaning is undoubtedly connected with
the concept of the neo-Babylonian kingdom. A long
row of stylized, slender trees with volute capitals

supports a continuous frieze of palmettes, and is
suspended above another frieze of lions pacing along
on a band decorated with rosettes. There can be no
reasonable doubt about the meaning of the whole
decoration: tree and palmette, symbol of life, as old
as Mesopotamian culture, suspended above the lions,
the symbol of the Underworld, from which life is
bursting forth. In the centre of this sits the king
enthroned, the protector and renewer of life.

We know of two other sites in the Babylon of
Nebuchadnezzar where similar examples of this
glazed painting can be found: in the so-called 'Processional Way' and in the Ishtar Gate, through which
the Processional Way had to pass to the world outside
the double city wall (Pl. 289). Here, on the walls of
the Processional Way, are more lions – again conceived symbolically – pacing above rosettes (Pl.
290). But on the walls of the Ishtar Gate we meet
two fresh symbols of life or death, the bull and the
mushhush[13] (Pl. 291). The bull, as the symbol of life

Fig. 117   Reconstruction of the façade of the throne room in Babylon
(After: MDOG 69, Fig. 2)

and the friend of man, had its origins in the oldest pictorial language of Mesopotamia.[14] In the same way the *mushhush* – i.e. the snake dragon, the attributive animal of the gods of the Underworld, Ninazu, Ningizzida, Marduk and Nabu – can also be traced back to the Protohistorical Period, if its meaning has an intellectual connection with the dragons with twining necks seen in the glyptic of the Uruk IV period.

Though their themes were very limited and in no way comparable in richness of ideas with the works of Late Assyrian relief, yet these examples of neo-Babylonian enamelled brick technique just mentioned form the peak of the artistic achievement of the Chaldaean kingdom, which is also the peak of art during the period of Nebuchadnezzar. Indeed, they simultaneously represent the final stage of the course of the Babylonian branch of Mesopotamian classical art and form an analogy with the technique of wall decoration evolved by the architecture of the Proto-historical Period. Thus these vast coloured surface decorations in enamelled tiles are the supreme expression of the tectonic spirit of Sumero-Babylonian architecture regarded as a whole, an architecture which does not express an inner structure but which, on the contrary, from the Protohistorical Period onward, has veiled the stresses and strains of a building by covering it with an ornamental skin. When the enamel brick technique appeared in Babylon

during the neo-Babylonian period, in the three building phases of Nebuchadnezzar (L. Koldewey, WVDOG XXXII Section), it had two variants: a completely flat, glazed and painted surface or a glazed relief. The relief pictures of lions, bulls and dragons are composed of moulded bricks,[15] of the kind we first encountered in Uruk, in the little Kassite Temple of Inanna built by King Karaindash (see above p. 93).[16] In all probability the neo-Babylonian building decoration has, therefore, at least some of its roots in the Kassite period. Of the second element, the glaze itself, we cannot trace the origins but there is no doubt but that glass and glazing achieved great popularity in Mesopotamia in the middle of the second millennium.[17]

It is essential for an historical appreciation of *neo-Babylonian building decoration* – in contrast to Assyrian architectural sculpture, to the *lamassu* on the door reveals and the epic wall-relief – to recognize the inner relationship between Sumerian cone mosaic and neo-Babylonian enamelled brick decoration. Both techniques leave undisturbed the mass of the wall, made of sun-dried bricks, and are in no way related to the structure of the brick building, but cover the exterior surface with an ornamental layer, earlier made of fired and coloured clay cones, later of painted or moulded and glazed bricks. Both form a protective coat for the building which is made of easily damaged bricks. They also manifest the symbolical and sacred powers, yet say nothing of the technical and structural forces which operate in the building itself.

Thus though neo-Babylonian architecture forms an historical unity with Sumerian architecture in the type of building and its layout, this is equally true of the decoration of its elevation. Just as Chaldaean architecture continued to use the Sumerian cella, complexes round the courts and perimeter walls, the ziggurat and the *bit akitu* – so it also transformed the wall decoration of the Sumerians, the cone mosaic, into a large enamelled painting, and then carried this through to its greatest development. Together the early Sumerian cone mosaic and the neo-Babylonian glazed brick wall-painting also form an historical unity, the unity of classical Sumero-Babylonian architecture and building decoration.

1. Niches decorated with cone mosaics from the pillar terrace at Warka. Baghdad, Iraq Museum

2. Half-columns decorated with cone mosaics in front of the pillar terrace at Warka. Berlin, Staatliche Museen

3–5. Fragments of gypsum statuettes, from Warka.
Height 12–15 cm. Berlin, Staatliche Museen

6, 7. Two statuettes of naked men in grey limestone. Paris, Louvre

8–10. Statuette of a naked man in grey limestone. Height 25 cm. Zürich, University

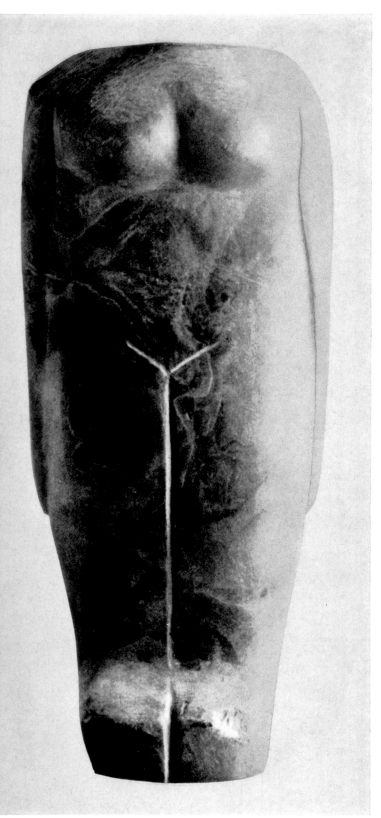

11. Statuette of a naked woman in greenish-grey stone from Warka. Height 19 cm. Baghdad, Iraq Museum

12. Statuette of a woman in white stone, from Khafaje. Height 11 cm. Baghdad, Iraq Museum

13. Upper part of a statuette of a man in grey alabaster, from Warka. Height 18 cm. Baghdad, Iraq Museum ▷

15, 16. Steatite cult vessel with figures in high relief. Height 16 cm. Berlin, Staatliche Museen

17–18. Alabaster trough decorated with reliefs, from Warka. Length 1.03 m. Berlin, Staatliche Museen/London, British Museum

◁ 14. Basalt stele decorated with reliefs ("Lion-hunt stele"), from Warka, Height 80 cm. Baghdad, Iraq Museum

19. Alabaster cult vessel decorated with reliefs, from Warka. Height 1.05 m. Baghdad, Iraq Museum

20, 21. Details from top frieze of the alabaster vase from Warka

22, 23. Head of a ram in bituminous limestone, from Warka. Length 14.5 cm. Berlin, Staatliche Museen

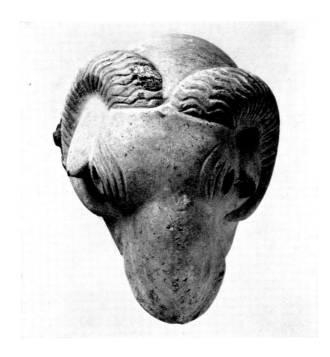

26. Head of a woman in marble
(alabaster?) from Warka.
Height 20 cm.
Baghdad, Iraq Museum ▷

24. Grey stone ewer decorated with shell-inlays, from Warka. Height *c.* 14 cm. Baghdad, Iraq Museum

25. Limestone figure of a bull with inlays and appliqué in silver and semi-precious stones, from Warka. Length 8 cm. Baghdad, Iraq Museum

27. Alabaster head from the Eye-Temple at Tell Brak. Height 17 cm. London, British Museum

28. Alabaster head, from Tell Brak. Height 9.2 cm. Aleppo, Museum

29. Foundation figure (Peg-figure), copper.
Height 13.5 cm. London, British Museum

30. Limestone slab decorated in relief ("Personnage aux plumes"), from Telloh.
Height 18 cm. Paris, Louvre

31–34. Limestone stele (Kudurru), decorated with reliefs from Larsa or Umma. Height 22 cm. New York, Metropolitan Museum

35. Limestone mace-head of Mesilim King of Kish, from Telloh. Height 19 cm. Paris, Louvre

36. Top of the mace-head from Telloh

37. Slate amulet in the form of a lion-headed eagle with inscription, from Khafaje. Length c. 25 cm

38. Mace-head decorated with four lions' heads in grey stone, from Tell Agrab. Height c. 7 cm

39–41. Fragments of figures for inlay in white limestone and slate, from Kish

42. Votive tablet in limestone, from Khafaje. Width 29.5 cm. Baghdad, Iraq Museum

43. Fragment of votive tablet in limestone, from Ur. Width 27 cm. Philadelphia, University Museum

44. Height 11 cm

45. Height 13.8 cm   46. Width 18.2 cm

44–46. Fragments of votive tablets in gypsum, from Fara. Berlin, Staatliche Museen

47. Fragment of votive tablet in limestone, from Susa. Width 13 cm. Paris, Louvre

48. Fragment of votive tablet in limestone, from Khafaje. Width 24 cm. Baghdad, Iraq Museum

49. Votive tablet in Limestone, from Tell Agrab. Width *c.* 17.5 cm. Baghdad, Iraq Museum ▷

50. Fragment of a foot from a bronze statue, from Tell Agrab. Width 8.4 cm. Baghdad, Iraq Museum

51. Bronze model of chariot from Tell Agrab. Height 7.2 cm. Baghdad, Iraq Museum

52. Bronze offering stand with naked man, from Khafaje. Height 55.5 cm. Baghdad, Iraq Museum

53. Bull's head in bronze. Height 22.9 cm. Berlin, Staatliche Museen ▷

54. Alabaster statuette of a naked man, from Khafaje.
Height 24.5 cm. Baghdad, Iraq Museum

55, 56. Limestone statuette of a naked, kneeling man carrying a vessel, from Tell Agrab. Height 10 cm. Chicago, Oriental Institute

57. Alabaster statuette of a man, from Khafaje. Height 30 cm. Baghdad, Iraq Museum

58. Gypsum statuette of a man, from Tell Asmar. Height 48.5 cm. Baghdad, Iraq Museum

60. Statuette of a man, with base decorated with relief in yellow stone, from Khafaje. Height 20.3 cm. Baghdad, Iraq Museum

◁ 59. Upper part of a gypsum statuette of a man, from Tell Asmar. Height 55 cm. Chicago, Oriental Institute

62. Upper part of a gypsum statuette of a man, from Tell Asmar. Height 72 cm. Baghdad, Iraq Museum

◁ 61. Upper part of a gypsum statuette of a woman, from Tell Asmar. Height 59 cm.
Baghdad, Iraq Museum

63. Limestone statuette of a woman, from Khafaje. Height 14.9 cm. Baghdad, Iraq Museum

64. Fragment of a breccia statuette of Idi-Narum, from Mari. Height 21 cm. Aleppo Museum

65. Inscription on shoulder of Ebih-il (cf. plate 66)

66. Seated statue in alabaster of Ebih-il, from Mari. Height 52.5 cm. Paris, Louvre ▷

67. Impression of a chalcedony (?) cylinder-seal of Sar-il, from Mari. Height 3.2 cm. Paris, Louvre

68, 69. Seated statue in gypsum of the singer Ur-Nanshe, from Mari. Height 26 cm. Damascus Museum

70, 71. Alabaster statuette of a man, from Tell Chuera. Height 17 cm. Damascus, Museum

72, 73. Alabaster statuette of a man, from Tell Chuera. Height 23.5 cm. Damascus Museum

74, 75. Alabaster statuette of a man, from Tell Chuera. Height 27 cm. Damascus Museum

76. Alabaster statuette of a man, from Khafaje. Height 23 cm.
Philadelphia, University Museum

77. Gypsum statuette of a man ("Konsistorialrat"), from Ashur.
Height 44 cm. Berlin, Staatliche Museen

78. Gypsum statuette of Itur-Shamagan,
from Mari. Height 92 cm. Damascus Museum

79. Gypsum statuette of Nani, from Mari. Height 46.4 cm.
Damascus, Museum

80. Gypsum statuette of a man, from Mari. Height 45 cm. Damascus,
Museum

81. Upper part of a limestone statuette of a man. Height 12 cm.
Paris, Louvre

83. Limestone foundation figure (Peg-figure) of Lugalkisalsi with inscription. Height 23.8 cm. Berlin, Staatliche Museen

82. Upper part of a limestone statuette of a man, from Warka.
Height 12.5 cm. Berlin, Staatliche Museen

84. White stone statuette of Lamgi-Mari, from Mari. Height 27.2 cm. Aleppo, Museum

85. Grey stone statuette of a son of Eannatum I of Lagash. Height 23.5 cm. Baghdad Museum

86. Golden cult head-dress from the tomb of Mes-kalam-dug at Ur. Height 23 cm. Baghdad, Iraq Museum

87, 88. Diorite statuette of Entemena of Lagash, from Ur. Height 76 cm. Baghdad, Iraq Museum

89. Limestone, from Tell Agrab. Height 12 cm

90. Gypsum, from Mari. Height 3.4 cm

91. Gypsum, from Mari. Height 14.9 cm

92. Gypsum, from Mari. Height 7.2 cm

89–92. Heads of female statuettes. Baghdad Iraq Museum

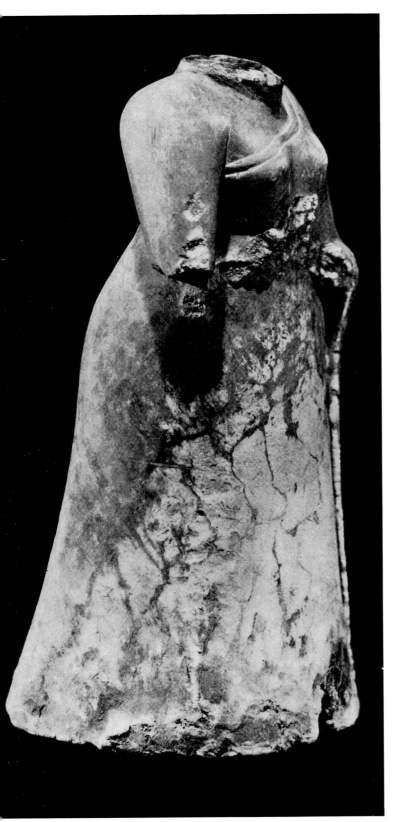

93. Alabaster statuette of a woman, from Khafaje. Height 30.8 cm. Philadelphia, University Museum

94. Marble statuette of a woman. Height 22.8 cm. London, British Museum

96. Alabaster statuette of a woman, from Mari. Height 23 cm. Aleppo, Museum

97. Gypsum statuette of a woman, from Mari. Height 17.1 cm. Paris, Louvre

98. Gypsum statuette of a woman, from Ashur. Height 45,5 cm. Berlin, Staatliche Museen

◁ 95. Seated statue of a woman in gypsum, from Mari. Height 36 cm. Damascus, Museum

99, 100. Gypsum statuette of a woman, from Telloh. Height 22 cm. Paris, Louvre

101, 102. Limestone statuette of a woman. Height 30 cm. London, British Museum

103. Seated statue of Dudu in grey stone. Height c. 39 cm.
Baghdad, Iraq Museum

104. Seated statue of a woman in gypsum, from Mari.
Height 19.3 cm. Paris, Louvre

105. Marble, from Khafaje. Height 15.4 cm. Baghdad, Irac Museum

106. Trachyte, from Al 'Ubaid. Probably representing Kurlil. Height 37.5 cm. London, British Museum

107. Limestone. Height 43 cm. Copenhagen, Ny Carlsberg Glyptotek

108. Diorite, Lupad of Umma, from Telloh. Height 40 cm. Paris. Louvre

105–108. Statuettes of squatting and seated men

109. Limestone, from Telloh. Height 40 cm. Paris, Louvre

110. Limestone, from Telloh. Height 45 cm. Istanbul, Museum

111. Limestone, from Telloh. Height 43 cm. Istanbul, Museum

112. Limestone, from Telloh. Height 23 cm. Paris, Louvre

109–112. Votive tablets of Ur-Nanshe of Lagash

114. Votive Tablet in limestone, from Telloh. Height 17 cm.
Paris, Louvre

115. Fragment of a basalt vessel of Entemena of Lagash.
Height 25 cm. Berlin, Staatliche Museen

116. Votive tablet in limestone, from Ur. Height 22 cm.
London, British Museum

117. Votive tablet of Dudu in bituminous stone, from Telloh.
Height 25 cm. Paris, Louvre

◁ 113. Silver and copper cult vessel of Entemena of Lagash, from Telloh. Height 35 cm. Paris, Louvre

119. Detail from the reverse of the victory stele

◁ 118. Obverse of the victory stele

118–121. Victory stele of Eannatum of Lagash ('Stele of the vultures') in limestone, from Telloh. Height after restoration 1.88 m. Paris Louvre

120. Detail from the reverse of the victory stele

121. Detail from the reverse of the victory stele

122. Limestone, slate and copper-plate. Height 22 cm. Baghdad, Iraq Museum

123. Shell, slate and copper-plate. Height 22 cm. Baghdad, Iraq Museum

124. Limestone, slate and copper-plate. Height *c.* 20 cm. Philadelphia, University Museum

122–124. Friezes with inlay from Ninhursag's temple at El Obeid

125. Fragment of diorite stele of Sargon of Akkad, from Susa. Height 50 cm. Paris, Louvre

126, 127. Fragment of diorite stele of Sargon (?) of Akkad, from Susa. Height 54 cm. Paris, Louvre

128. Seated statue of a goddess in limestone with inscription of Puzur-In-Shushinak, from Susa. Height 85 cm. Paris, Louvre

129. Limestone statuette of a man, from Susa. Height 48 cm. Paris, Louvre

130. Limestone disk decorated in relief of Enheduanna, from Ur. Diameter 26 cm. Philadelphia, University Museum

131. Alabaster, from Ur. Height 9.2 cm. Philadelphia,
University Museum

132. Gypsum, from Ashur. Height 7.2 cm. Berlin, Staatliche Museen

131–133. Heads from female statuettes

133. Diorite, from Ur. Height 8.3 cm. London, British Museum

134, 135. Limestone fragment (obverse and reverse) of a stele, from Telloh. Height 34 cm. Paris, Louvre

136. Height 21.2 cm

136, 137. Two fragments of an alabaster stele. Baghdad, Iraq Museum

138. Fragment of a diorite stele, from Susa. Height 46 cm. Paris, Louvre

139, 140. Diorite statue of a man, from Ashur. Height 1.37 m. Berlin, Staatliche Museen

141. Headless diorite statue of Manishtusu, from Susa.
Height 94 cm. Paris, Louvre

142. Headless white limestone statue of Manishtusu (?), from Susa.
Height 1.25 m. Paris, Louvre

143. Fragment of a diorite statue of a man, from Ashur. Height *c.* 48 cm. Berlin, Staatliche Museen

144. Fragment of a diorite statue of a man, from Susa. Paris, Louvre

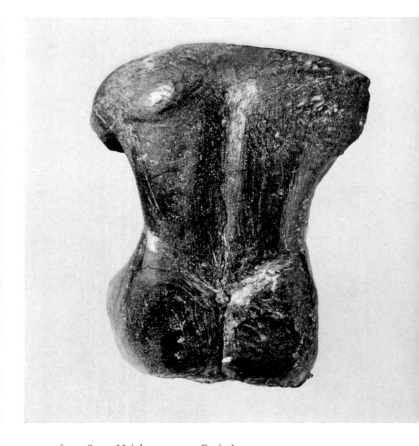

145, 146. Fragment of a seated statue of a naked man in bituminous stone, from Susa. Height 10.5 cm. Paris, Louvre

147–149. Three fragments of a seated diorite statue of Manishtusu, from Susa. Paris, Louvre

150, 151. Fragments of diorite statues with votive inscription for Naram-Sin, from Susa. Height *c.* 15 cm. Paris, Louvre

152. Fragment of a diorite statue of Naram-Sin, from Susa. Height 47 cm. Paris, Louvre

153. Fragment of a diorite stele of Naram-Sin, from Pir-Hüseyin. Height 57 cm. Istanbul, Museum ▷

154. Head of a bronze statue of Naram-Sin (?), from Nineveh. Height 36 cm. Baghdad, Iraq Museum

155. Victory stele of Naram-Sin in reddish
sandstone, from Susa. Height 2 m.
Paris, Louvre

156. Detail of the victory stele of Naram-
Sin

157. Relief, cut in rock, near
Darband-i-Gawr ▷

158. Fragment of relief in limestone with inscription of Puzur-In-Shushinak, from Susa. Height 57 cm. Paris, Louvre

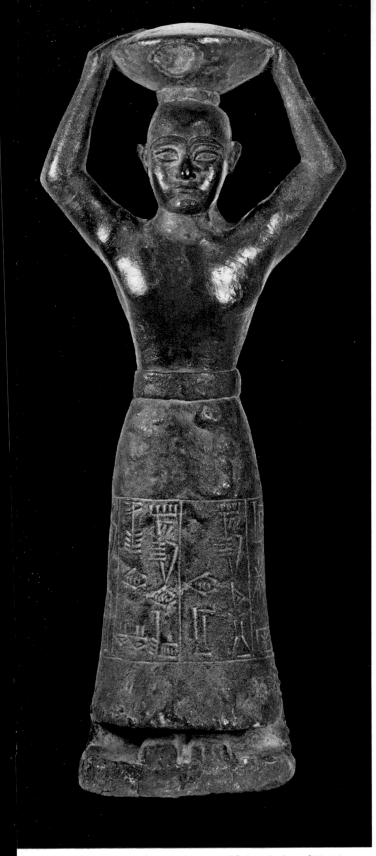

159. Foundation figure in bronze with inscription of Ur-Nammu. Height 33.5 cm. New York, Pierpont Morgan Library

160. Foundation figure in bronze with inscription of Gudea, from Telloh. Height 20 cm. Paris, Louvre

161. Ziggurat of Ur-Nammu at Ur

162. Ziggurat in the Eanna sanctuary at Warka

163. Entrance to a king's tomb of the third Dynasty in Ur

164. Diorite statuette of Ur-Baba of Lagash, from Telloh. Height 68 cm. Paris, Louvre

165. Diorite statue of Gudea of Lagash, from Telloh. Height 1.42 m. Paris, Louvre

166. Head of a diorite statue of Gudea, from Telloh. Height 24 cm. Paris, Louvre

167. Seated diorite statue of Gudea, from Tellch. Height 93 cm. Paris, Louvre

168, 169. Head of a male statuette in white limestone. Height 13 cm. Berlin, Staatliche Museen

171–174. Fragment of a statuette of Ur-Ningirsu of Lagash in steatite (?). Height 17 cm. Berlin, Staatliche Museen

< 170. Seated diorite statue of Gudea, from Telloh. Height 45 cm. Paris, Louvre

175, 176. Alabaster statuette of Ur-Ningirsu, from Telloh (?). Height 46 cm. Paris, Louvre

177. Statue of Ishtup-ilum (upper part) in black stone, from Mari. Height 1.52 m. Aleppo, Museum ▷

178. Diorite statuette of Shulgi, from Ur. Baghdad, Iraq Museum

179, 180. Steatite statuette of Idi-ilum, from Mari, Height 41 cm. Paris, Louvre

181, 182. Diorite statue of Puzur-Ishtar of Mari, from Babylon. Height 1.73 m. Istanbul, Museum / Berlin, Staatliche Museen ▷

183. Seated statue of Eannatum in diorite, from Ur. Height c. 20 cm. Philadelphia, University Museum

184. Fragment of a steatite statuette of a woman, from Telloh. Height 17 cm. Paris, Louvre

185. Votive tablet of Gudea in stone, from Telloh.
Height c. 45 cm. Paris, Louvre

186. Alabaster fragment of a votive tablet, from Telloh.
Height 11 cm. Paris, Louvre

187. Steatite pitcher of Gudea, from Telloh. Height 23 cm. Paris, Louvre

189. Height *c*. 70 cm.

189, 190. Limestone fragments of
two stelae of Gudea, both in
Berlin, Staatliche Museen

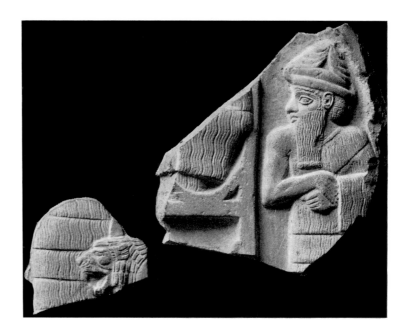

◁ 188. Fragment of a water basin of Gudea in limestone, from Telloh. Height *c*. 70 cm. Paris, Louvre

192. Width 15 cm.

191. Fragment of a limestone stele. Height 15 cm.
Berlin, Staatliche Museen

192, 193. Two fragments of a stele in limestone, both in
Berlin, Staatliche Museen

193. Width 21 cm.

194. Limestone stele of Ur-Nammu, from
Ur. Height after restoration c. 3 m.
Philadelphia, University Museum

195. Detail of Ur-Nammu's stele (plate 194)

196. Fragment of a limestone stele of Gudea, from Telloh (?). Height 24 cm. Paris, Louvre

197. Upper part of a diorite statue of Gudea, from Telloh. Height 1.25 m. Paris, Louvre

198. Detail of reverse of Ur-Nammu's stele (plate 194)

199. Detail of reverse of Ur-Nammu's stele (plate 194)

200. Fragment of a steatite vessel. Height 12 cm. Paris, Louvre

◁ 201. Detail of Ur-Nammu's stele (plate 194)

202. Fragment of a wall painting from the palace at Mari. Height *c.* 45 cm. Aleppo, Museum

203. Fragment of a wall painting from the Palace at Mari. Height *c.* 80 cm. Paris, Louvre

204, 205. Basalt fragment of a stele of Shamshi-Adad I (?) of Assur, from Mardin (?). Height 40 cm.
Paris, Louvre

206. Alabaster head of a warrior's statue, from the palace of Mari.
Height 20 cm. Aleppo, Museum

207. Fragment of a limestone stele, from Ishchali. Height 42 cm.
Baghdad, Iraq Museum

208. Fragment of a limestone stele with representation of
Hammurabi of Babylon. Height of the figure 15.2 cm.
London, British Museum

209. Top of diorite stele inscribed with the law code of Hammurabi, from Susa. Height of the picture area 65 cm. Paris, Louvre

210. Upper part of a limestone stele. Height 80 cm. Paris, Louvre ▷

211. Terra-cotta relief, from Khafaje. Height 12 cm.
Chicago, Oriental Institute

212. Terra-cotta relief. Height 50 cm. Norman Colville collection,
formerly Burney collection

213. Limestone statue of the god Shamash with inscription of
Iasmah-Addu ("Statue Cabane"), from Mari. Height 1.10 m.
Aleppo, Museum

214, 215. Statue of a water-goddess in white stone, from the palace of Mari. Height 1.50 m. Aleppo Museum ▷

216. Bronze statuette of a four-faced god, from Ishchali. Height 17.3 cm. Chicago, Oriental Institute

217. Bronze statuette of a four-faced goddess, from Ishchali. Height 16.2 cm. Chicago, Oriental Institute

218. Statue of a man kneeling in prayer with votive inscription for Hammurabi, in bronze, partly gold plated, from Larsa (?). Height 19.5 cm. ▷ Paris, Louvre

219, 220.
Limestone fragment
of a group of two
water-goddesses.
Height 29.7 cm.
Paris, Louvre

◁ 219. Obverse

220. Reverse ▷

222. Head of a diorite statuette of Hammurabi (?), from Susa. Height 15 cm. Paris, Louvre

◁ 221. Seated diorite statue of a prince of Eshnunna, from Susa. Height 88 cm. Paris, Louvre

224. Sculpture in the round of a hyena in terra-cotta, from Dur Kurigalzu. Height 7 cm. Baghdad, Iraq Museum

▽ 223. Marble disk decorated in relief (casting-mould?), from Babylon. Diameter 7.1 cm. Berlin, Staatliche Museen

225. Painted head of a male statue in terra-cotta, from Dur Kurigalzu. Height 43 cm. Baghdad, Iraq Museum

226. Reconstructed façade of temple

227, 228. Details of façade of temple

226–228. Moulded brick frieze from Inanna's temple built by Karaindash at Warka, in terra-cotta. Height 2.05 m. Berlin, Staatliche Museen

229. Limestone kudurru of Melishihu II, from Susa.
Height 68 cm. Paris, Louvre

230. Diorite kudurru of Melishihu II, from Susa. Height 90 cm.
Paris, Louvre

231. Limestone kudurru,
from Susa.
Height 54 cm.
Paris, Louvre

232. Upper part of kudurru (plate 231)

233. Fragment of a limestone kudurru of Melishihu II, from Susa. Height 49 cm. Paris, Louvre

234. Gold bowl decorated with reliefs, from Ugarit. Diameter 19 cm. Aleppo, Museum

235.
Seated limestone
statue of Idrimi,
from Alalakh.
Height 1.05 m.
London,
British Museum

236   ▷
Limestone cult relief
from the well of the
Ashur temple at
Ashur. Height 1.36 m.
Berlin,
Staatliche Museen

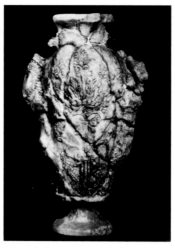

237. Fragment of a marble pitcher decorated
with reliefs, from Nimrud. Diameter *c.* 7.5 cm
London, British Museum

238. Alabaster receptacle decora-
ted with reliefs, from Ashur.
Height 15.8 cm. Berlin,
Staatliche Museen

239. Fragment of alabaster receptacle decorated
with reliefs, from Ashur. Height 15 cm.
Berlin, Staatliche Museen

240. Statuette of the goddess Ishtar in bone (?) (ivory?), from Nuzi.
Height 8.2 cm. Baghdad, Iraq Museum

241. Ivory comb with incised design, from Ashur.
Width c. 6 cm. Berlin, Staatliche Museen

242. Ivory pyxis and cover with incised design, from Ashur. Height 9 cm. Berlin, Staatliche Museen

243. Height of the mountain god *c.* 14 cm

243, 245. Ivory inlay frieze with incisions, from
Ashur. Berlin, Staatliche Museen

244. Fragment of a marble lid of a jar decorated with reliefs, from Ashur. Diameter *c.* 12.2 cm

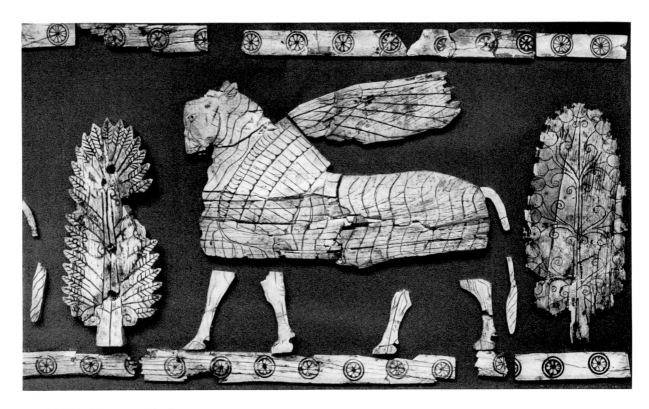

245. Height of the winged bull *c.* 22 cm

246. Altar of Tukulti-Ninurta I in gypsum, from Ashur.
Height 57.7 cm. Berlin, Staatliche Museen

247. Altar of Tukulti-Ninurta I in limestone, from Ashur.
Height 1.03 m. Istanbul, Museum

248. Obverse

249. Reverse

248, 249. Bronze statuette of Ashur-dan I (?). Height 30 cm.
Paris, Louvre

250. Limestone statue of a naked woman with inscription of Ashur-
bel-kala, from Niniveh. Height 94 cm. London, British Museum ▷

251. 'White Obelisk' of Ashurnasirpal I (?) in white limestone, from Niniveh. Height 2.90 m. London, British Museum

252. Upper part of an obelisk ('Broken Obelisk') of Ashur-bel-kala in granite, from Niniveh. Height of relief c. 23 cm. London, British Museum

253. Upper part of sandstone stele of Ashurnasirpal II, from Nimrud. Height 1.28 m. Mosul, Museum

254, 255. Basalt stele of Tukulti-Ninurta II, from Tell Aschara. Height 90 cm. Aleppo Museum

256. Alabaster statue of a winged human-headed bull ("Lamassu"), from Nimrud. Height 3.35 m.

257. Alabaster mural relief from the N.W. Palace of Ashurnasirpal II in Nimrud. Height 1.78 m. London, British Museum

258. Alabaster mural relief from the N.W. Palace of Ashurnasirpal II in Nimrud. Height 2.18 m. London, British Museum

259. Alabaster mural relief from the N.W. Palace of Ashurnasirpal II in Nimrud. Height 2.29 m. London, British Museum

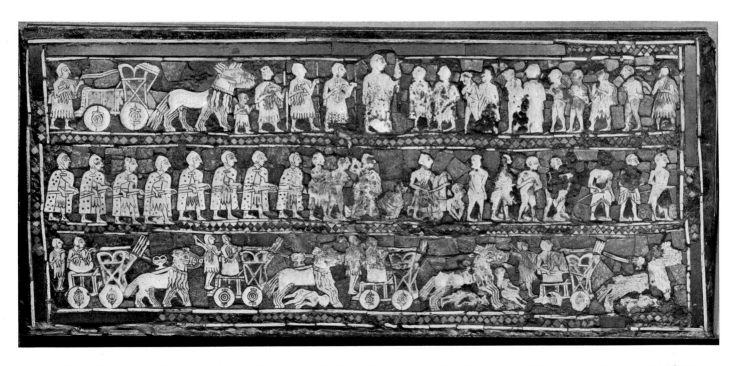

260. Inlaid panel ("Standard") from the Royal Cemetery at Ur, in red limestone, shell and lapis lazuli. Height 20 cm. London, British Museum

261

262

261–263. Alabaster mural reliefs from the N.W. Palace of Ashurnasirpal II in Nimrud. Height *c.* 98 cm. London, British Museum

264

265

264–266. Alabaster mural reliefs from the N.W. Palace of Ashurnasirpal in Nimrud. Height *c.* 95 cm. London, British Museum

267. Alabaster mural reliefs from the N.W. Palace of Ashurnasirpal II in Nimrud. Height *c.* 98 cm. London, British Museum

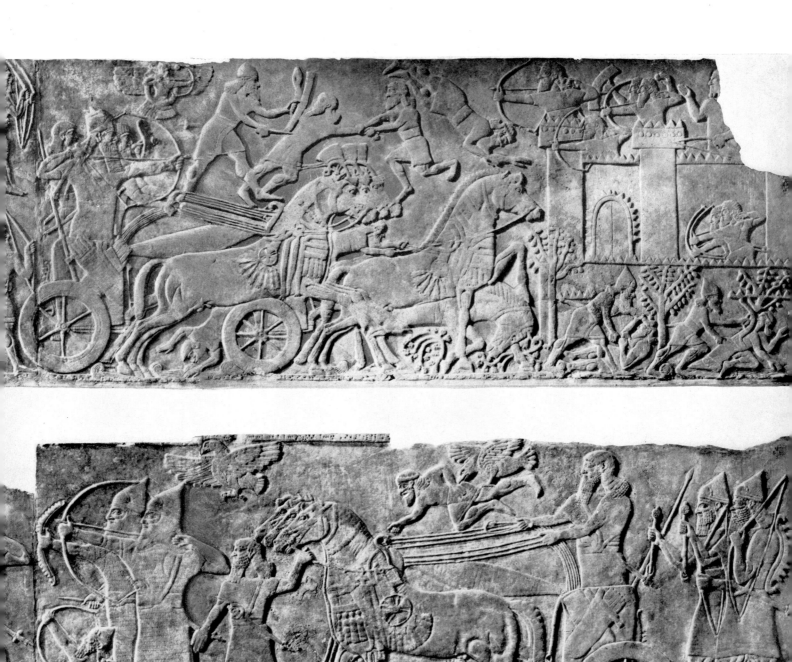

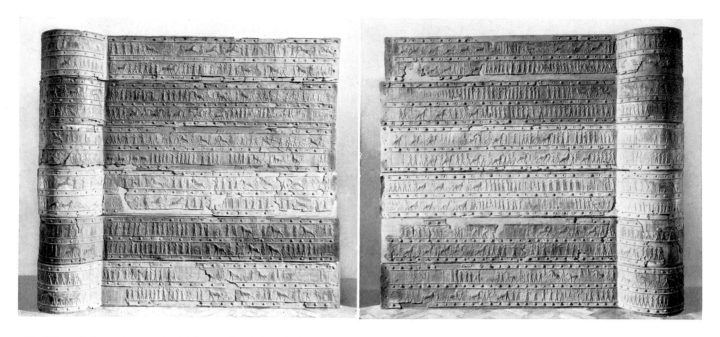

268. Wings of doors decorated with bronze bands in relief, from Balawat. Height 1.62 m. (Reconstruction.) London, British Museum

269. Base of throne of Shalmaneser III in limestone, from 'Fort Shalman eser' in Nimrud. Height of relief 21–29 cm. Baghdad, Iraq Museum

271. Detail of Black Obelisk

270, 271. Black alabaster obelisk of Shalmaneser III ('Black Obelisk'), from Nimrud. Height 2.02 m. London, British Museum

272. Alabaster mural relief from the Central Palace of Tiglathpilesar III in Nimrud. Height 1.32 m. London, British Museum

273. Basalt (?) mural relief from the palace of Sargon II in Khorsabad. Length 1.78 m. London, British Museum

274. Basalt mural relief from the Palace of Sargon II in Khorsabad. Height 1.27 m. Paris, Louvre ▷

275. Alabaster relief from a façade of the throne room at the Palace of Sargon II in Khorsabad. Height 4.70 m. Paris, Louvre

276. Length 3.26 m

277. Length 1.62 m

278. Length 1.48 m

276–278. Alabaster mural reliefs from the S.W. Palace of Sennacheribin Niniveh. London, British Museum

279. Alabaster mural relief from the S.W. Palace of Sennacherib in Niniveh. London, British Museum

280. Height *c.* 22 cm

281. Height *c.* 24 cm

280, 281. Models of sculptures in clay, from Ashur, both in Berlin, Staatliche Museen

282. Stone stele of
Ashurbanipal, from
Babylon (?). Height
36.8 cm. London,
British Museum

283. Detail of mural relief
in alabaster from the
North Palace of
Ashurbanipal in
Niniveh. London,
British Museum

285

285, 286. Details of mural reliefs in alabaster from the North Palace of Ashurbanipal in Niniveh. London, British Museum

◁ 284. Alabaster mural relief from the S.W. Palace of Sennacherib in Niniveh, erected by Ashurbanipal. Height *c.* 2 m. London, British Museum

287. Length c. 1.40 m

287, 288. Alabaster mural reliefs from the North Palace of Ashurbanipal
in Niniveh. Both in London, British Museum

288. Length c. 1.68 m

290. Relief in moulded bricks from the "Processional Way" in Babylon, in glazed terra-cotta. Height 1.05 m. Berlin, Staatliche Museen

291. Relief in moulded bricks from the Ishtar gate in Babylon, in glazed terra-cotta. Height c. 1.10 m. Berlin, Staatliche Museen

◁ 289. Ishtar gate of Nebuchadnezzar II (reconstruction) decorated with moulded glazed bricks, from Babylon. Height 14.30 m. Berlin, Staatliche Museen

292. Detail of the façade of the
    throne room in the palace
    of Nebuchadnezzar II
    (reconstruction) in glazed
    moulded brick, from Babylon.
    Height 12.40 m.
    Berlin, Staatliche Museen

1

2

3

4

5

6

Plate A   Cylinder Seals of the Uruk VI–IV and Jamdat Nasr periods

1a

2

1b

Plate B   Cylinder and Stamp Seals of the Jamdat Nasr period

1

2

3

4

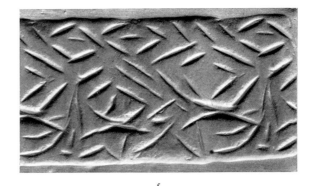

5

6

Plate C   Cylinder Seals of the Jamdat Nasr and the following transitional period

1

3

2

4

Plate D   Cylinder Seals of the Mesilim period and the Imdugud-Sukurru phase

1

2

3

4

Plate E   Cylinder Seals of the Ur I period

1

2

3

4

5

6

7

Plate F   Cylinder Seals of the Akkad period

1

2

3

4

5

6

7

8

9

10

11

Plate G   Cylinder Seals of the Neo-Sumerian and Old-Babylonian periods

1

2

3

4

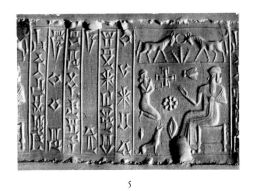

5

6

7

Plate H   Cylinder Seals of the late Old-Babylonian and the Kassite periods

1

2

3

4

5

6

7

8

Plate J   Cylinder Seals of the Old-Assyrian, Hurri-Mitanni and Middle-Assyrian periods

1

2

3

4

5

6

7

Plate K   Cylinder Seals of the Middle-Assyrian period

Plate L   Cylinder Seals of the Uruk VI–IV period (redrawn)

1

2

3

4

Plate M   Cylinder Seals of the Uruk VI–IV period, the Imdugud-Sukurru phase and the Akkad period (redrawn)

1

2

3

4

5

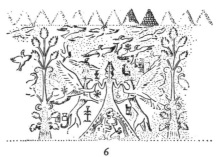

6

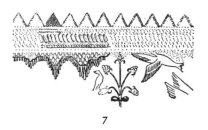

7

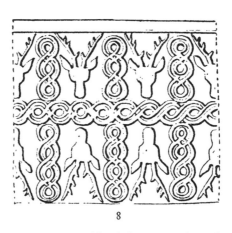

8

Plate N   Cylinder Seals of the Neo-Sumerian, Old Babylonian, Kassite and Hurri-Mitanni periods (redrawn)

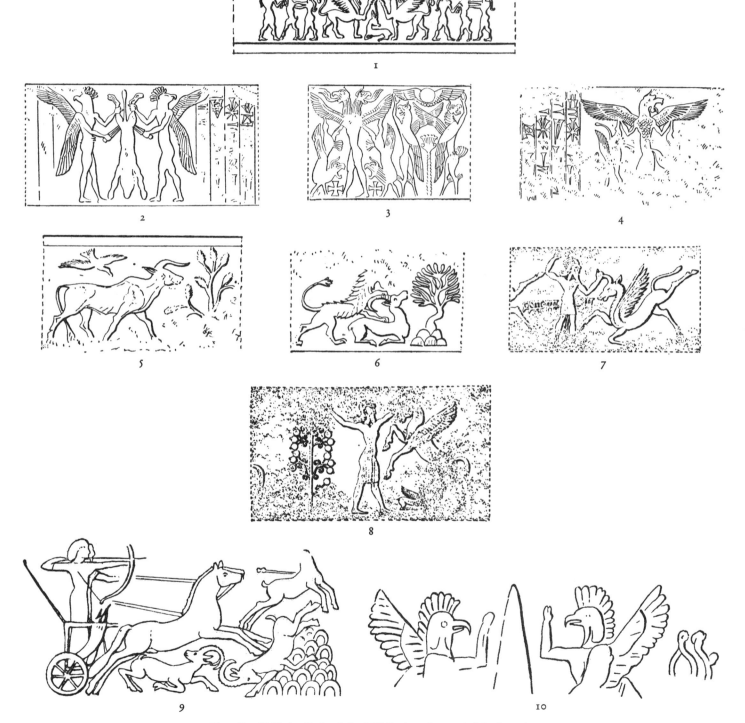

Plate O   Cylinder Seals of the Middle Assyrian period (redrawn)

Abbreviations

AAA = University of Liverpool. Annals of Archaeology and Anthropology. Liverpool

AASOR = Annual of the American Schools of Oriental Research. New Haven, Conn.

AfO = Archiv für Orientforschung

AGF = Wissenschaftliche Abhandlungen der Arbeitsgemeinschaft für Forschung des Landes Nordrhein-Westfalen

AJ = The Antiquaries Journal. London

AMI = Archäologische Mitteilungen aus Iran. Berlin

Amtl. Ber. = Amtliche Berichte. Berliner Museen. Berichte aus den preußischen Kunstsammlungen

AO = Der Alte Orient. Leipzig

Ausgrabungen in Sendschirli = Ausgrabungen in Sendschirli I–V. Berlin 1893–1943. Mitteilungen aus den orientalischen Sammlungen der Berliner Museen XI–XV

BaM = Bagdader Mitt. = Bagdader Mitteilungen. Berlin

BASOR = Bulletin of the American School of Oriental Research in Jerusalem. South Hadley, Mass.

BiOr = Bibliotheca Orientalis. Leiden

BM = British Museum

BMQ = British Museum Quarterly

Contenau, *Ant. Or.* = G. Contenau, *Les Antiquités Orientales Tome I, II.* Musée du Louvre. Paris

Contenau, *Monuments Mésopotamiens* = G. Contenau, *Monuments Mésopotamiens nouvellement acquis ou peu connus.* (Musée du Louvre). Paris 1934

DC = E. de Sarzec/L. Heuzey, *Découvertes en Chaldée.* Paris 1884–1912

Delaporte, *Bibl. Nat.* = L. Delaporte, *Catalogue des cylindres orientaux de la Bibliothèque Nationale.* Paris 1910

Delaporte, *Louvre I, II* = L. Delaporte, Musée du Louvre. *Catalogue des cylindres, cachets et pierres gravées de style oriental.* Tome I, II. Paris

E. Ph. = Encyclopédie photographique de l'Art. Paris

Heinrich, *Fara* = E. Heinrich/W. Andrae, *Fara.* Ergebnisse der Ausgrabungen der Deutschen Orientgesellschaft. Berlin 1931

Heinrich, *Kleinfunde* = E. Heinrich, *Kleinfunde aus den archaischen Tempelschichten in Uruk.* Ausgrabungen der Deutschen Forschungsgemeinschaft in Uruk-Warka. Band 1. Berlin 1936

Hirmer-Strommenger = E. Strommenger/M. Hirmer, *Fünf Jahrtausende Mesopotamien.* München 1962

ILN = The Illustrated London News. London

Iraq = Iraq. London

ITT = Mission française de Chaldée. Inventaire des tablettes de Tello conservées au Musée Impérial Ottoman. Paris

JCS = Journal of Cuneiform Studies. New Haven, Conn.

JEOL = *Ex Oriente Lux.* Jaarbericht van het Vooraziatisch-egyptisch Genootschap. Leiden

JNES = Journal of Near Eastern Studies. Chicago

Luckenbill = D. D. Luckenbill, *Ancient Records of Assyria and Babylonia.* Chicago 1926

MAM = A. Parrot, *Mission archéologique de Mari,* Tome I, II. Paris 1956–59

MAO = G. Contenau, *Manuel d'archéologie orientale.* Tome I–IV. Paris 1927–47

MAOG = Mitteilungen der Altorientalischen Gesellschaft. Leipzig

MDOG = Mitteilungen der Deutschen Orient-Gesellschaft. Berlin

MDP = Délégation en Perse. Mémoires. Paris

MJ = The Museum Journal. Philadelphia

Moortgat, *Bergvölker* = A. Moortgat, *Die bildende Kunst des Alten Orients und die Bergvölker.* Berlin 1932

Moortgat, *Entstehung* = A. Moortgat, *Die Entstehung der sumerischen Hochkultur.* Der Alte Orient 43. Leipzig 1945

Moortgat, *Frühe Bildkunst* = A. Moortgat, *Frühe Bildkunst in Sumer.* MVAeG 40, Heft 3. Leipzig 1935

Moortgat, *VR* = A. Moortgat, *Vorderasiatische Rollsiegel. Ein Beitrag zur Geschichte der Steinschneidekunst.* Berlin 1940

Münchner Jahrbuch = Münchner Jahrbuch der bildenden Kunst. München

MVAeG = Mitteilungen der Vorderasiatisch-Aegyptischen Gesellschaft. Leipzig

OIC = The University of Chicago. Oriental Institute. Communications. Chicago

OIP = The University of Chicago. Oriental Institute. Publications. Chicago

OLZ = Orientalistische Literaturzeitung. Leipzig

Orientalia = Orientalia. Roma

Parrot, *Le temple d'Ishtar* = A. Parrot, *Mission archéologique de Mari;* Tome I, *Le Temple d'Ishtar.* Paris 1956

Pézard-Pottier = M. Pézard/E. Pottier, Musée du Louvre. *Les Antiquités de la Susiane.* Paris 1913

Porada, *Corpus I* = E. Porada, *Corpus of Ancient Near Eastern Seals in North American Collections.* I, *The Collection of the Pierpont Morgan Library.* Washington 1948

Pritchard = J. Pritchard, *The Ancient Near East in Pictures, relating to the Old Testament.* Princeton 1954

RA = Revue d'Assyriologie et d'Archéologie Orientale. Paris

RLA = Reallexikon für Assyriologie und Vorderasiatische Archäologie

RLV = Reallexikon der Vorgeschichte. Berlin

SAK = F. Thureau-Dangin, *Die sumerischen und akkadischen Königsinschriften.* Vorderasiatische Bibliothek Band I. Leipzig 1907

SAOC = The University of Chicago. Oriental Institute Studies in Ancient Oriental Civilizations. Chicago

Schriften M. Frhr. v. Oppenheim-Stiftung = A. Moortgat, *Tell Chuëra in Nordost-Syrien.* Vorläufiger Bericht über die zweite Grabungskampagne 1959. Schriften der Max-Freiherr-von-Oppenheim-Stiftung, Heft 4. Wiesbaden 1960

Starr, *Nuzi* = R. F. S. Starr, *Nuzi. Report on the Excavations at Yorgan Tepa near Kirkuk, Iraq.* Cambridge, Mass. 1939

Sumer = Sumer. Baghdad

Syria = Syria. Paris

Thureau-Dangin, *Arslan-Tash* = F. Thureau-Dangin u. a., *Arslan-Tash. Bibliothèque archéologique et historique,* Tome XVI. Paris 1931

UE = Publications of the Joint Expedition of the British Museum and of the Museum of the University of Pennsylvania to Mesopotamia. Ur Excavations. London

Unger, SAK = E. Unger, *Sumerische und akkadische Kunst.* Breslau 1926

Unger, ABK = E. Unger, *Assyrische und Babylonische Kunst.* Breslau 1927

Ur Excav., see UE

UVB = Vorläufiger Bericht über die von der Notgemeinschaft der Deutschen Wissenschaft in Uruk unternommenen Ausgrabungen. Berlin

VA = Vorderasiatische Abteilung. Museum Ost-Berlin

Vorderasiatische Archäologie, Festschrift Anton Moortgat = *Vorderasiatische Archäologie. Studien und Aufsätze. Anton Moortgat zum 65. Geburtstag gewidmet von Kollegen, Freunden und Schülern.* Berlin 1964

VR, see Moortgat

Woolley, *Alalakh* = L. Woolley, *Alalakh. An Account of the Excavations at Tell Atchana in the Hatay, 1937–1949.* Oxford 1955

WVDOG = Wissenschaftliche Veröffentlichungen der Deutschen Orient-Gesellschaft. Leipzig-Berlin

ZA = Zeitschrift für Assyriologie und Vorderasiatische Archäologie, Leipzig-Berlin. (NF = Neue Folge)

Zervos = C. Zervos, *L'Art de la Mésopotamie.* Basel-Leipzig 1935

Notes

I Sumero-Akkadian Art

1 H. J. Lenzen, ZA NF 15, p. 1 ff., Pls. 1, 2

2 E. Heinrich, ZA NF 15, p. 38 ff.

3 W. Andrae, *Die Urformen des Bauens; E. Heinrich, Schilf und Lehm*

4 UVB 9, p. 28 and Pl. 34 (E. Heinrich)

5 H. J. Lenzen, ZA NF 15, p. 1 ff., Pl. 2

6 E. Heinrich, *Bauwerke in der altsumerischen Bildkunst*, p. 96: cone mosaics, p. 48 ff. the arrangement of niches, including previous interpretations and comments

7 UVB 9, p. 19 ff., UVB 10, p. 21 ff. (E. Heinrich)

8 Seton Lloyd/Fuad Safar, in *Sumer*, Vol. 3, 1947; p. 48 ff.; *Sumer*, Vol. 4, 1948

9 E. Heinrich, *Bauwerke in der altsumerischen Bildkunst*, p. 48 ff.

10 Summarizing: Moortgat, *Entstehung*, p. 74 ff.

11 Seton Lloyd and Fuad Safar, *Tell 'Uqair* = JNES 2, p. 135 ff.

12 M. E. L. Mallowan, *Iraq*, Vol. 9, 1947, Pl. LVII, and also III, IV and I

13 Plan of Eanna: H. J. Lenzen, *Die Entwicklung der Zikkurat*, Pl. 3 (detail), III a–c

14 *Ur Excavations*, Vol. 4, Pl. 20 above and below: *Orientalia* 18 (1949) Pl. VIII

15 J. Jordan, WVDOG 51 Pl. 93 d, e, i: Pl. 94 a–d

16 UVB 5, Pl. 23 a–b

17 WVDOG 51, Pl. 68 below

18 WVDOG 51, Pl. 93 d–e

19 A. Boissier, *Notice sur quelques Monuments assyriens à l'Université de Zürich*, 1912, p. 28 ff.; UVB 16, Pl. 19

20 UVB 16, Pl. 16

21 H. Frankfort, *Art and Architecture*, Pl. 9 B = OIP 60, Pl. 1

22 UVB 16, p. 37 ff., Pls. 17, 18

23 UVB 5, p. 11 ff.; Pls. 12/13

24 W. Nagel, *Das Stempsiegel im frühen Vorderasien* (Dissertation Berlin, 1955, unpublished)

25 Moortgat, *Frühe Bildkunst* = MVAeG 40, 1935, p. 78; summary of material to 1935

26 Moortgat, VR p. 3 ff.; Nos. 1–5

27 H. J. Lenzen, ZA NF 15, 1949, p. 5 ff.

28 UVB 2, Fig. 44

29 UVB 5, Pl. 26 a–d, f

30 Snake-dragon and Imdugud = L. Delaporte, *Louvre*, Vol. 2, Pl. 64, No. 9

31 UVB 2, Fig. 33

32 Moortgat, *Frühe Bildkunst*, Pl. 36, 1

33 UVB 4, Pl. 15 b–d = ZA NF 15, Pl. 3, Fig. 1
   UVB 2, Fig. 34, 35 = ZA NF 15, Pl. 3, Fig. 4

34 Moortgat, *Entstehung*, p. 74 ff.

35 A. Falkenstein, *Archaische Texte aus Uruk*, p. 14

36 Summary in: Moortgat, *Frühe Bildkunst*, p. 47 ff.

37 Spouted ewer with lion: Heinrich, *Kleinfunde*, Pls. 22, 23 a; ZA NF 11, 1939, Pls. I–IV

38 *Amtl. Ber.*, 1930, p. 1. Figs. 1–3

39 Heinrich, *Kleinfunde*, Pl. 38 and 2/3

40 That the alabaster vase belongs to the second half of the Protohistorical Period and not to the first half is confirmed by the site of its discovery, the so-called Building M' of Uruk Level IIIa, where objects from earlier periods have never been found; see Heinrich, *Kleinfunde*, p. 4. Note 1, and H. J. Lenzen, UVB 7, p. 14

41 Moortgat, *Entstehung*, pp. 81–86; id., *Tammuz, Der Unsterblichkeitsglaube in der altorientalischen Bildkunst*, p. 38 ff.; E. Douglas van Buren, *Orientalia*, Vol. 12, 1935, pp. 327–35; more recently, Th. Jacobsen, ZA NF 16, 1957, p. 108 Note

42 On methods of hermeneutics cf. A. Moortgat, *3ème Rencontre Asyriologique* (Leiden 1954) p. 18 ff. For the philological sources: A. Falkenstein, op. cit., p. 41 ff.

43 For the theocratic-state socialist aspects of the Sumerian temple-city cf. A. Falkenstein, *La Cité Temple*, in 'Cahiers d'histoire mondiale', Vol. 1; A. Schneider, *Die sumerische Tempelstadt* in: Plenjes, *Staatswissenschaftliche Beiträge*, Publication no. 4, 1920; Th. Jacobsen, *Early Political Development in Mesopotamia*, ZA NF 16, p. 91 ff.

44 Heinrich, *Kleinfunde*, Pl. 17 c (BM 116 722)

45 Moortgat, VR No. 29, a, b (VA 10537)

46 That the 'man in the net garment' is not only the Royal *Shepherd* of Innin but also her *heroic hunter* has now been very usefully confirmed by M. E. L. Mallowan's publication of the cylinder seal in the British Museum No. 131 440, in: *Bagdader Mitteilungen*, Vol. 3, 1964, p. 65, Pl. 8 a–c

47 UVB 5, Pl. 12 a, b

48 UVB 7, Pl. 24, 2; UVB 9, Pl. 27 a; UVB 11, Pl. 33

49 UVB 11, Pl. 33 a, c

50 Summary: Moortgat, *Frühe Bildkunst*, p. 49 f; Heinrich, *Kleinfunde*, Pl. 9 ff.

51 Heinrich, *Kleinfunde*, Pl. 12 i (recumbent gazelle)

52 VR 10, 29, 30

53 Heinrich, *Kleinfunde*, Pl. 13 a, p. 47

54 Heinrich, *Kleinfunde*, Pl. 13 a, in contrast to all the other animals on Pls. 9–13

55 Heinrich, *Kleinfunde*, Pl. 8 a

56 Heinrich, *Kleinfunde*, Pl. 14 a

57 UVB 7, Pl. 24 b

58 UVB 11, title-page and Pl. 32

59 M. E. L. Mallowan, *Iraq*, Vol. 9, Pl. I

60 M. E. L. Mallowan, *Iraq*, Vol. 9, Pl. II, a–c

61 W. Andrae, *Die archaischen Ischtartempel*, WVDOG 39, Pls. 27 a and 28 c. The original is now in the British Museum; cf. M. E. L. Mallowan, *Early Mesopotamia and Iran*, p. 108, Fig. 119

62 Cf. Note 11

63 Cf. Note 12

64 Heinrich. *Kleinfunde*, Pls. 26 and 27

65 P. Delougaz, *Pottery from the Diyāla Region* = OIP 63, Coloured Plate 6

66 Heinrich, *Kleinfunde*, Pl. 33

67 Heinrich, *Kleinfunde*, Pl. 12 i

68 P. Delougaz, SAOC 7, *Studies in Ancient Oriental Civilization* (Or. Inst. Univ. Chicago); V. Christian, *Altertumskunde des Zweistromlandes*, Vol. 1, p. 171 ff., Pl. 146 ff

69 E. D. van Buren, *Foundation Figurines and Offerings*, pp. 1–10, Pls. I–IV; Mari: A. Parrot, *Le Temple d'Ishtar*, MAM I, p. 51

70 As in the Square Temple in Eshnunna (Tell Asmar): OIP 58, pp. 173/75, Figs. 133/135

71 Temple Oval at Khafaje: OIP 53, Pls. III–VI
    High Temple at Al 'Ubaid: M. E. L. Mallowan, *Iraq*, Vol. 5, p. 1 f.; Eanna at Uruk: H. J. Lenzen, *Entwicklung der Zikkurat*, p. 19, Pl. 5

72 V. Christian, *Altertumskunde des Zweistromlandes*, Pls. 151, 2 (under the Cemetery A on Hill Inghara); E. Mackay, *A Sumerian Palace at Kish, II*, Pl. XX I ff.

73 That the palace at Kish is not an isolated chance occurrence but is a typical Sumerian building of the Mesilim Period has been confirmed recently by the discovery of two ruins in Eridu (Abu Shahrein). Cf. Fuad Safar in *Sumer*, Vol. 6, p. 31 ff., Fig. 3. The alabaster statuette found in the palace at Eridu, op. cit. Pl. III b, suggests that it all should be attributed to the Mesilim Period. Its upper arms lie clear of the chest!

74 UVB 7, p. 41 and City plan Pl. I

75 OIP 58, Pl. 2 a (Sin Temple, Khafaje)

76 OIP 58, Pl. 5 a

77 OIP 58, Pl. 6

78 OIP 58, Pl. 19 A (Earliest Shrine)

79 OIP 58, Pl. 19 B (Archaic Shrine)

80 OIP 58, Pl. 23

81 OIP 58, Pls. 3–6

82 OIP 58, Pls. 26, 27 and Fig. 203 (reconstruction)

83 OIP 58, Fig. 204, p. 289

84 *E. Ph.* 1, p. 175 bottom right.

85 A. Parrot, AfO 12, 1937, 319 ff.; V. E. Crawford, *Bulletin of the Metropolitan Museum of Art*, 1960, p. 245 ff.

86 Cf. Note 39

87 E. g., VR, Figs. 35–64; Moortgat, *Frühe Bildkunst*, p. 52, Vb

88 Examples: OIP 72, Figs. 229, 232, 242, 243, 257, 291, 455 etc.; VR 65, 66, 67

89 *Ur Excavations*, Vol. 3 = L. Legrain, *Archaic Seal Impressions*

90 *Ur Excavations Texts*, Vol. 2 = E. Burrows, *Archaic Texts*: in addition, A. Falkenstein, OLZ 1937, p. 93 ff.

91 Fig. e. g. Legrain, op. cit., nos. 134, 147, 169, 252, 281, 384, 389, 398; simulated writing: op. cit., nos 417, 419, 429, 431/2; UVB 5, Pl. 27 c, *Fara*, Pl. 72 K (VA 6361)

92 A. Moortgat, *Tell Chuēra in Nord-Ost-Syrien* (1958) AGF Vol. 14

93 Zervos, p. 54: *E. Ph.*, p. 176; Moortgat, *Frühe Bildkunst*, Pl. XVI

94 DC, Pl. 5ter, 1

95 OIP 58, Fig. 185, p. 238

96 St. Langdon, *Excavations at Kish*, Vol. I, Pl. XIII, 1, and XLII; E. Mackay, *A Sumerian Palace at Kish*, II, Pl. XXXVI, 1

97 UVB 2, Figs. 24–27

98 Moortgat, *Frühe Bildkunst*, Pl. XVI, 3

99 For a survey of the material cf. Moortgat, *Frühe Bildkunst*, pp. 28–31, as well as OIP 60, Pls. 63, 64, 65, 66, A–C, 67 A–D

100 Moortgat, *Tammuz, Der Unsterblichkeitsglaube in der Altorientalischen Bildkunst*, p. 35 ff.

101 E. Heinrich, *Fara*, Pls. 20 f and 22 a; Moortgat *Frühe Bildkunst*, Pl. XX

102 Cf. Note 191 (Seal no. 51 Bibliothèque Nationale), and cylinder seal from the Cemetery in Ur: *Ur Excavations*, Vol. 2, Pl. 194, 33; 195, 34–39

103 OIP 60, Pl. 63

104 OIC 13, Fig. 44 and *Ur Excavations*, Vol. 2, Pl. 181 below; OIP 60, Pl. 65

105 Moortgat, *Frühe Bildkunst*, Pl. XVIII

106 Heinrich, *Fara*, Pl. 22 a

107 Moortgat, *Frühe Bildkunst*, Pl. XVIII above

108 VR 80, 81

109 VR 77, 78

110 VR 95–97, other examples: OIP 60, p. 18 (Kh. 4, 338)

111 Cf., say, the body of the bull in: O. Weber, *Altorientalische Siegelbilder*, 213, with that in: E. Heinrich, *Fara*, Pl. 20 f.; the lion's mane in the former, Pl. 46 f, with that in the latter, Pl. 22 a; the heroes in the former, Pl. 531, with inlays from Kish: *Excavations at Kish*, Vol. 1, Pl. 36, 3

112 VR 90 and 91

113 VR 91

114 E. Heinrich, *Fara*, Pl. 51, 1

115 OIP 60, Pl. 1 A–D

116 OIP 60, Pl. 61 A

117 OIP 44, Pl. 98–101 A, B and OIP 60, Pl. 95 A, B. Other statuettes: OIP 44, Pl. 102 D–F; OIP 60, Pl. 55

118 VA 3142: cf. OIP 44, Pl. 104. The works from Lagash, DC, Pl. 5, Fig. 2 a and 2 b, are probably somewhat later

119 Cf. Notes 44, 45, 50; Pls. 22, 23

120 OIP 60, Pls. 58–59

121 OIP 60, Pl. 17 A–C

122 OIP 44, Pl. 98 ff.

123 OIP 60, Pl. 33–34

124 OIP 44, and OIP 60

125 OIP 60, Pls. 3, 4, 5

126 OIP 44, Pls. 8, 9, 10; Pl. 46 C–E; Pl. 38 A; OIP 60, Pl. 4 A, B; Pl. 11 B, C; Pl. 87 A, B; Pl. 29, A, B

127 OIP 60, Pls. 89–90; OIP 44, Pls. 23–24

128 One can compare the statuettes of bald-headed men from the Sin Temple in Khafaje: OIP 44, Pls. 36, 37

129 Cf. BaM I, 1960, p. 10 ff; Table 2

130 OIP 44, Pl. 35 A–C

131 OIP 44, Pl. 41 A–D

132 OIP 60, Pls. 82–83; OIP 44, Pl. 5 A and 25 C; OIC 19, Fig. 64; OIP 44, Pls. 4 and 5

133 OIP 44

134 OIP 44

135 BaM I, 1960, 1 ff.

136 OIP 44, Pl. 15 B; 16 AB; 74 AC; 75 A–C; 79 A–C; 84 A; 81 A, B; 83 A–D

137 OIP 44, Pl. 76 A–C; 77 A–C; 77 D–F; OIP 60, Pl. 26 A, B

138 OIP 44, Pl. 76 A–C

139 A. Parrot, *Le Temple d'Ishtar* = MAM I, Pls. 27–30; id., *Mari* (Munich 1953), Pls. 12–15

140 F. Thureau-Dangin had already some years ago (RA 31, 1934, p. 142) declared it was considerably earlier than Ur-Nanshe of Lagash

141 A. Parrot, *Le Temple d'Ishtar*, Pl. 65 (No. 1388), p. 190, Fig. 99

142 *Syria*, Vol. 30, 1953, 209 f; A. Parrot, *Mari* (Munich 1953), Pls. 41–47

143 *Syria*, Vol. 30, 1953, 209 f, Fig. 9

144 OIP 44, Pl. 70 F–H

145 OIP 60, Pl. 32 A–C

146 OIP 60, Pl. 39 B, C

147 OIP 60, Pl. 42 A, B

148 Four views, as in AGF 31, Fig. 12 ff.

149 AGF op. cit., Figs. 16–20

150 AGF op. cit., Fig. 22

151 *Syria*, Vol. 31, 1934, p. 155, Fig. 1 (square type of cella, betylos)

152 OIP 53 (Temple Oval)

153 OIP 44, Pl. 55 A–D

154 OIP 44, Pls. 48–50; on the inscription: OIP 58, p. 295

155 For comparison there is only the very badly preserved figure from Ashur, in WVDOG 39, Pls. 34 c–e, 37 e

156 WVDOG 39, Pl. 32 a–d

157 OIP 60, title-page and Pls. 19–20

158 WVDOG 39, Pl. 30 a–d (VA 8142)

159 An entire series of statuettes from Mari belong to the same phase of development and may therefore be assigned to the second period of transition: *Syria*, Vol. 30, Pl. XXII (Itur-Samagan), ibid., Pl. XXXI, 164, 3; *Syria*, Vol. 31, Pl. XVI, 1; A. Parrot, *Le Temple d'Ishtar*, Pl. XXXI, 164. The statuette of a worshipper with a shaven head and a tufted skirt, found in Level V of the Nintu Temple at Khafaje, must also belong to this group (OIP 60, Pls. 9/10)

160 A. Parrot, *Le Temple d'Ishtar*, Pl. XXX (176); Thureau-Dangin, RA 31, p. 142; J. Gelb, *Old Akkadian Writing and Grammar*, p. 2

161 E. Ph. 1, p. 204 A; UVB 16, Pl. 20

162 G. Contenau, *Monuments Mésopotamiens*, Pl. 1; UVB 16, Pl. 20 a–c

163 *Amtl. Ber.*, 36, 4 p. 73 ff. Also: Th. Jacobsen, *The Sumerian King-List*, p. 183

164 A. Parrot, *Le Temple d'Ishtar*, Pls. XXV/XXXVI (174). Inscription: F. Thureau-Dangin, RA 31, p. 140 f.

165 UE 2, Pl. 150

166 E. Banks, *Bismaya, or the lost city of Adab*, p. 185 ff., Fig. pp. 191–193, Zervos, p. 101; RLV 7, Pls. 131/152; Thureau-Dangin, SAK, p. 152 f, Note 2: probably earlier than Ur-Nanshe

167 A worshipper from Lagash comes from about the same phase: DC, Pl. 6bis, 1 a–c = Zervos, p. 100

168 *Sumer*, Vol. 14, 1958, p. 109 ff.

169 UE 4, Pl. 40

170 The historical last phase of plastic art in the Ur I period can be understood if we examine the statuette of Saud (Salah?) in the Louvre: the inscription describes him as grandson of King Lugal-kisalsi, one of the last kings of Ur before the Akkadian period. In spite of its relatively slender form, the limbs are no longer clear of the bulk of the stone (Contenau, *Monuments Mésopotamiens* Pl. II)

171 E.g., A. Parrot, *Mari*, Fig. 55; *Syria*, Vol. 17, 1936, Pl. 2; E. Ph. I, p. 205 C; OIP 60, Pl. 43, 44 A–B; small head in Munich: *Münchner Jahrbuch*, Vol. 3, p. 60

172 OIP 60, Pl. 24

173 A. Parrot, *Mari*, Figs. 52–53

174 WVDOG 39, Pl. 34 a–b; Pl. 35 a–d

175 This figure has its exact counterpart in the statuettes OIP 44, Pl. 80 and A. Parrot, *Le Temple d'Ishtar*, Pl. XLI (341)

176 BMQ I, Pl. XIX; Zervos, p. 133. For comparison, A. Parrot, *Le Temple d'Ishtar*, Pl. XXXVI (172)

177 A. Parrot, *Le Temple d'Ishtar*, Pl. 39 (304); OIP 44, Pl. 63 C–D; A. Parrot, op. cit. Pl. 40 (178); *Syria*, Vol. 16, Pl. 23, 1; OIP 60, Pl. 94 A, B; E. Ph. Vol. 1, p. 199. The pillar-shaped statuette from Ashur, WVDOG 39, Pl. a–c, is in a special position because of its mantilla-like attire.

178 DC, Pl. 1ter 3 a/b or Zervos, p. 124 f. = L. W. King, *A History of Sumer and Akkad*, p. 40

179 *Sumer*, Vol. 5, p. 131 ff.

180 E. Sollberger, *Sumer*, Vol. 13, p. 62 ff.

181 Cf. the back view especially: OIP 44, Pl. 66

182 *Syria*, Vol 17, Pl. II

183 *Syria*, Vol. 16, Pl. XX, 2 and p. 119, Fig. 9

184 OIP 60, Pl. 8

185 UE 1, Pl. IX, 1 and 2

186 ZA 40, Pls. I/II; Zervos 123

187 The headless seated statue of Dada-ilum from Ur comes from the same phase of development (UE 4, Pl. 41 c); however, it shows already a tendency towards the rounding of all shapes

188 DC, Pl. 6ter, 1 a–b and 47, 2

189 For the development of Style, cf. VR, pp. 13–18

190 E. Heinrich, *Fara*, Pls. 42 b–f; 43 b, i, g, l, m; 44 a, h, l, n; 45 l; cf. VR, p. 13

191 L. Delaporte, *Bibl. Nat.*, No. 51; cf. Note 102

192 DC, Pl. 2bis, Fig. 1, 2

193 UE 2, Pl. 196, 55; VR, p. 14 f.

194 A. de la Fuye, *Documents présargoniques*

195 UE 2, Pls. 207, 214

196 VR 117

197 VR 144

198 Zervos, p. 102

199 The figures of the gods on the incised stone plaques from Nippur (Zervos, pp. 92/93) are scarcely less bulky

200 DC, Pls. 42, 43bis

201 Cf. Notes 210 and 212

202 Scenes from the cycle of the symposium on two fragments from Mari; A. Parrot, MAM I, p. 124, Fig. 69; Sacred Marriage: OIP 44, Pl. 122 A

203 *E. Ph.*, p. 198 = Zervos, p. 150

204 *Amtl. Ber.*, 36, p. 116, Fig. 44 = Zervos, p. 99

205 AJ 6, Pl. 53 = Zervos, p. 85

206 *E. Ph.*, p. 208

207 Summarized in: A. Parrot, *Tello*, p. 90 f. The original publications are also quoted there.

208 DC, Pls. 3–4, 48, 48bis, p. XXXVIII–XLII, F. Thureau-Dangin, SAK, p. 11 ff.

209 *E. Ph.*, 1, p. 193

210 UE I, Al 'Ubaid; cf. Note 201

211 UE 2, *The Royal Cemetery*; A. Moortgat, *Tammuz, Der Unsterblichkeitsglaube in der altorientalischen Bildkunst*, p. 53 f. (which pays special attention to Sumerian beliefs concerning death)

212 UE 1, Al 'Ubaid, Pl. U 32; cf. Note 201

213 UE 2, Pl. 105 (so-called 'Animal Orchestra')

214 UE 2, Pls. 87–89

215 UE 2, Pl. 115

216 W. Hallo, *Early Mesopotamian Royal Titles*

217 The pre-Akkadian level of the Inanna Temple at Nippur must surely also have had the connection between the ante-cella and cella (cf. ILN of 6. 9. 1958, p. 386, Fig. 1); but here it is probably not a case of a cult room divided into two halves

218 AGF, Vol. 24, p. 9 ff., Plan II and III

219 OIC 17, Fig. 20

220 *Iraq* 9, Pl. LX

221 WVDOG 66 = C. Preusser, *Die Paläste in Assur*, p. 6 ff., Pl. 3

222 Op. cit., pp. 10 and 12

223 MDOG 73, p. 2; AfO 15, p. 85

224 MAO 2, p. 666, Fig. 462/3; Unger, SAK, Fig. 33; E. Nassouhi, RA 21, p. 66; Pézard-Pottier, p. 29, No. 1

225 Pézard-Pottier, p. 30, No. 2; Unger, SAK, Fig. 34; Nassouhi, RA 21, p. 72, Figs. 6, 7; Pritchard, Pl. Vol. No. 307. Inscription on fragment with net: MDP 10, p. 7 ff. below

226 E. Unger, RLV 7, 172, Pl. 134 c (Istanbul Mus. No. 5268)

227 *E. Ph.*, 1, p. 225

228 *Syria* 21, p. 14, Pl. VII; *Syria* 20, p. 11 ff., Pl. VII; p. 12, Fig. 8

229 *E. Ph.* 1, p. 203

230 UE 4, Pl. 41 d; The best reproduction: Museum Journal 18, p. 238. Reconstruction of the relief in: J. Pritchard, *Bilder zum Alten Orient*, No. 606; AJ 6, Pl. 54 b; Mededelingen, Vol. 7, Pl. b. Text: UE Text 1 (Text No. 28)

231 UE 4, Pl. 43 below; best reproduction: Zervos, Pls. 210, 211

232 UE 4, Pl. 43 above

233 VA 6980: W. Andrae, WVDOG 39, p. 68, Pls. 38/39

234 DC, Pl. 5bis, 3 a–c; RA 3, p. 113, Pl. IV; Contenau, *Ant. Or.*, Vol. 1, Figs. 12/13

235 *Sumer* 10, 1954, p. 116 ff., Pls. I/II and XIII 1957, p. 222, Figs. 1/2 = Hirmer-Strommenger 118/119

236 A paper by Machteld Mellink, *An Akkadian Illustration of a Campaign in Cilicia*, shows that historical conclusions may also be obtained by purely archaeological means with the use of careful observation and the right methods (*Anatolia*, Vol. 7, 1963, p. 101 ff.). The writer does not attempt to provide an exact date within the Akkadian period. But from the style of the monument it can only belong to the second generation

237 MDP 7, p. 22 f.; *E. Ph.* 1, p. 212

238 For other stelae or fragments of reliefs from thrones cf. P. Amiet in: *La Revue du Louvre et des Musées de France*, 15th Annual Publication 1965, No. 6, pp. 239/244

239 The alabaster statuette from Susa, which was dedicated by an Elamite official Isbum for Manishtusu (MDP 10, p. 1) is a re-used work from the Mesilim Period (E. Strommenger in: ZA NF 19, p. 30 ff., Pl. I, II

240 MDOG 73, p. 2; AfO 15, p. 85

241 *E. Ph.* 1, p. 213 (b); Pézard-Pottier, No. 46; MDP 10, p. 2 and Pl. 2, 1 (Inscription)

242 For the significance of the dress: E. Strommenger in: ZA NF 19, p. 32 and 34

243 W. Andrae, *Das wiedererstandene Assur*, p. 88, Pl. 44 b = MDOG 29, p. 41 ff., Figs. 22/23

244 Pézard-Pottier, No. 47; MAO 2, Fig. 466

245 MDOG 66, p. 27, Fig. 12

246 a) Pézard-Pottier, No. 48; MDP 10, p. 2 and Pl. 2, 2
    b) Pézard-Pottier, No. 49bis; RA 7, p. 103 f.
247 Pézard-Pottier, No. 48
248 *E. Ph.*, 211, B
249 Pézard-Pottier, No. 50, Inscription: MDP 6, p. 2 ff., Pl. 1,
    1; G. A. Barton, *Royal Inscriptions of Sumer and Akkad*,
    p. 142 f.
250 E. Strommenger, in: ZA NF 19, p. 41 f.
251 E. Meyer, *Sumerier und Semiten*, Pl. III; Zervos, Pl. 164;
    Thureau-Dangin, SAK 1, p. 166/7 f.
252 *Iraq*, Vol. 3, p. 104 ff., Pls. V–VII
253 For the attribution to Naram-Sin of the bronze head
    found by Mallowan in Nineveh (*Iraq*, Vol. 3, Pls. 5–7) cf.:
    A. Moortgat, in: A. Scharff – A. Moortgat, *Ägypten und
    Vorderasien im Altertum*, p. 267, and recently: M. Th. Bar-
    relet, in: *Syria*, Vol. 36, p. 20 ff. The fragment of a diorite
    head from Telloh (DC, p. 47 f., Pl. 21, 1) comes from an
    exact counterpart to the bronze head from Nineveh
254 MDP 1, Pl. 10; MDP 2, Pl. 11; *E. Ph.* 1, Pls. 214/215;
    E. Meyer, *Sumerier und Semiten*, Pl. IV; Zervos, Pl. 165 f.;
    Inscriptions: MDP 2, p. 53 and MDP 3, p. 40
255 E. Strommenger, in: *Bagdader Mitteilungen*, Vol. 2;
    p. 83 ff. Recent photographs of the whole relief and of its
    details have now made it possible to identify a Late Su-
    merian cap and stylization of the beard, which would be
    more suitable on a ruler of the Third Dynasty of Ur, such
    as Shulgi, than on Naram-Sin. Until now no Akkadian
    male face with a rectangular beard has been known. And the
    alabaster head with inlaid eyes from Bismaya (E. J. Banks,
    Bismaya, p. 25 b = OIP 60, Pls. 68–69), which also has a
    variety of Late Sumerian cap, has a truly Semitic pointed
    beard. The stylization of the beard on the figure of
    Darband-i-Gawr resembles in all its details the beard of
    Ur-Nammu on his great stele from Ur (photograph of
    detail)
256 R. M. Boehmer, *Die Entwicklung der Glyptik während der
    Akkad-Zeit*, Untersuchungen zur Assyriologie und vorder-
    asiatischen Archäologie, Vol. 4
257 OIP 72, Pl. 65, No. 701
258 Cf. R. M. Boehmer, op. cit., p. XVIII (Introduction),
    where this early Sargonic glyptic is called 'Akkadian Ia'.
259 UE 2, Pl. 212, No. 307
260 UE 2, Pl. 212, No. 309 = UE 3, Pl. 31, No. 537
261 R. M. Boehmer, op. cit., Fig. 326 f.
262 Cf. the list of dated seals of E. Unger, under 'Glyptik' in:
    RLV, Vol. 4, 2, p. 370
263 L. Delaporte, Louvre I, Pl. 9 (T. 106) = H. Frankfort,
    Cylinder Seals, p. 99, Fig. 31
264 VR, Pl. B 1 = H. Frankfort, *Cylinder Seals*, Pl. 17 c
265 E. g., VR 188 and UE 10, Pl. 15, Fig. 186
266 L. Delaporte, *Louvre I*, (T. 107), Pl. 9, No. 11 a and b; DC,
    Pl. 32bis, Fig. 6; p. 282, Fig. B
267 L. Speleers, *Catalogue des Intailles des Mus. du Cinquan-
    tenaire*, Vol. 1, p. 222, No. 452 = H. Frankfort, *Cylinder
    Seals*, Pl. 24 a; further, op. cit., Fig. 36

268 VR 234, 235
269 The identification of the hero with the six curls of hair (docu-
    mented in Ancient Near Eastern art from the Protohisto-
    rical Period and shown fighting lions to protect the herds)
    as Gilgamesh, is one of the deep-rooted misinterpretations
    of our branch of learning. Although it has been refuted as
    baseless for decades, it is always reappearing in literature,
    especially in philological literature (cf. recently, the VIIe
    Rencontre Assyriologique Internationale Paris 1958)
270 For Sumero-Akkadian mythology, cf. recently: S. N.
    Kramer, *Mythologies of the ancient World*, p. 95 ff.
271 VR p. 23 ff.; H. Frankfort, *Cylinder Seals*, p. 62 ff.
272 G. A. Eisen, *Ancient Oriental Seals*, Collection Moore
    (OIP 47), No. 37 = Excav. at Kish, Vol. 4, Pl. 34, 3
273 Seal of the scribe Adda, BM 89 115 = O. Weber, *Altorien-
    talische Siegelbilder*, Fig. 375 = H. Frankfort, *Cylinder
    Seals*, Pl. 19 a
274 A. Scharff / A. Moortgat, *Geschichte Ägyptens und Vorder-
    asiens im Altertum*, p. 272 ff.
275 WVDOG 39, p. 95 ff.
276 Cf. Note 92
277 OIP 72, p. 33, Pl. 64, No. 689–691
278 Cf. *Syria*, Vol. 19, Pl. IV and VI, 4, p. 16 f.; Pl. VII 2.
    Recently: A. Parrot, MAM 2, *Le Palais, Documents et
    Monuments*, p. 14 ff., Pl. XII
279 E. D. van Buren, *Foundation Figurines and Offerings*,
    Fig. 10 ff.; *E. Ph.*, I, p. 242, A and B
280 MDP 6, Pl. 2
281 E. D. van Buren, op. cit., Fig. 16
282 UE, Vol. 5 = C. L. Woolley, *The Ziggurat and its Sur-
    roundings*, Pl. 68 and 86
283 Ground-plan: UE, Vol. 5, Pl. 68; View of the ruins, op.
    cit., Pl. 40 ff.; Reconstruction: op. cit., Pl. 48 ff.
284 H. J. Lenzen, *Die Entwicklung der Zikkurat*, Pls. 9–11,
    27 a and p. 20 ff.
285 For the Kukunnum cf.: R. Ghirsman, *Troisième Campagne
    de fouilles à Tschoga-Zanbil près Suse*, 'Arts Asiatiques',
    Vol. I, 1954, pp. 91–93 (Inscriptions of Untash-Huban)
286 Plan: AJ, Vol. 4, Pl. XLIV
287 AJ, Vol. 10, Pl. XXXVII a
288 Seton Lloyd, *The Gimilsin Temple* = OIP 43, Pl. 1
289 Seton Lloyd, *The Gimilsin Temple* = OIP 43, Pl. 1
290 AJ 6, 1926, p. 382, Pl. 57
291 Ashur: cf. Note 220; Tell Brak: cf. Note 221
292 With Woolley's Notes on these tombs cf. the still provision-
    al AJ 11, p. 347 ff., Pl. 45
293 A. Moortgat, *Tammuz, Der Unsterblichkeitsglaube in der
    altorientalischen Bildkunst*, p. 53 ff.
294 A. Parrot, MAM 2, *Le Palais, Architecture*, p. 255 ff.
295 Summary of all the Gudea statues with bibliography in
    A. Parrot, *Tello*, p. 160 ff., Pls. XIII–XVIII
296 DC, Pls. 11 and 13, 2 = Zervos, p. 181 = *E. Ph.* 1, p. 232/
    33; DC, Pl. 15, 5 and 20; DC, Pls. 10 and 13, 1 = Zervos,
    p. 184 = *E. Ph.* 1, p. 230; DC, Pls. 14/15 = Zervos, p. 183;
    DC, Pls. 16/19 = Zervos, p. 182 = *E. Ph.* 1, pp. 234/36

297 M. Lambert – J. R. Tournay, *La Statue de Gudea,* in RA 45, 1951, p. 90 ff.; DC, Pl. 16 ff.; SAK, p. 73; *E. Ph.* 1, p. 234 ff.

298 Cf. back view of the 'architecte au plan' = DC, Pl. 16

299 *E. Ph.,* p. 237

300 F. Thureau-Dangin, in: *Monuments Piot.* 28, Pl. 8

301 DC, Pls. 7/8 = Zervos, p. 177

302 DC, Pl. 12, 2; Zervos, p. 179; E. Meyer, *Sumerier und Semiten,* Pl. 6 (VA 2910); and D. Opitz, in: AfO 7, p. 127 ff.

303 SAK, p. 67 ff.

304 M. Lambert – J. R. Tournay, op. cit., in: RA 45, p. 60 ff.

305 *E. Ph.* pp. 228/29; SAK, p. 86 f.

306 E. Sollberger, in: JCS 10, 1956, p. 11 ff.

307 B. Meissner, *Die babylonische Literatur,* Vol. 1; Zervos, p. 222

308 RA 27, 1930, p. 162 f., Pls. I/II

309 F. Thureau-Dangin, in: *Monuments Piot.* 27, 1928, p. 104 ff.; Zervos, p. 218 ff.

310 DC, Pl. 21bis 3; AJ 6, Pl. 51c; DC, Pl. 21, 4 (Iraq Museum, U. 6306)

311 *Syria,* Vol. 17, p. 24 f., Pl. VII, Fig. 13; Vol. 19, Pl. IV; MAM 2, *Le Palais, Documents et Monuments,* p. 2 ff., Pl. I ff.

312 AJ 6 (U. 6306; IM 1173), Pl. LI, c

313 DC, Pl. 21bis, 3

314 DC, Pl. 21, 4

315 A. Parrot, *Syria,* Vol. 19, Pl. VII, 1; MAM 2, *Le Palais Documents et Monuments,* p. 16 ff., Pls. IX–XI

316 WVDOG 55, Pl. 21 a–d, or Pl. 22 a–d

317 E. Unger, *Sumerisch-Akkadische Kunst,* Fig. 52

318 E. Nassouhi, AfO 3, p. 109; F. Thureau-Dangin, in: RA 34, p. 73; G. Dossin, in: *Syria,* Vol. 21, p. 164 f.

319 WVDOG 55, Pl. 21 d

320 Pézard-Pottier, No. 55, SB 57

321 OIP 43, p. 185

322 Contenau, *Ant. Or.,* Vol. 1, Figs. 26, 31 = Zervos, pp. 206/207 = *E. Ph.* 1, p. 244 A. The best statue in the round of a woman from this period may well be the statue of Enannatuma, daughter of Ishme-Dagan of Isin (AJ 6, Pl. 52), but the reconstruction (L. Legrain, MJ 185, 223, Fig. 224 ff.) usually printed in all the histories of art creates a false impression

323 UE Texts I, No. 103, p. 23, Pl. XVIII, and as well: OLZ 1931, p. 115 ff. and *Iraq,* Vol. 13, p. 38 f.; AfO 17, pp. 25 and 46; before restoration: AJ 6, Pl. LIIa, after restoration: MJ 18, p. 224 ff. = Zervos, 114

324 DC, Pl. 26bis. 1; 2

325 H. de Genouillac, *Fouilles de Tello,* Pl. 84, 1

326 DC, Pl. 25, 5 (Ningirsu with the goddess Baba on his knees)

327 DC, Pl. 25, 4

328 DC, Pl. 44, 2 a, b, c; Zervos, pp. 200/201

329 E. D. van Buren, *The God with streams*

330 Zervos, p. 214 f.; DC, Pl. 24, 3 and 4

331 H. Lenzen, *Die Entwicklung der Zikkurat,* Pl. 9, Q; G. Cros, *Nouvelles fouilles de Tello,* p. 283

332 AJ III, p. 319 ff.; VI, p. 371 ff.; Pl. XLVI, b

333 G. Cros, *Nouvelles fouilles de Tello,* Pl. X, 1

334 A. Parrot, *Tello,* p. 181, Fig. 37

335 E. Meyer, *Sumerier und Semiten,* Pl. VII

336 Delaporte, *Louvre I* (T. 108), Pl. X

337 E. Meyer, op. cit., p. 55, Pl. VIII, right and left

338 RA 30, pp. 111–115; AJ 5, p. 397 ff., Pls. 46–48; MJ 16, p. 50 ff. and 5 ff.

339 UE Texts I, No. 44

340 MJ 16, p. 52

341 *E. Ph.,* p. 227

342 RA 30, Pl. I above

343 *E. Ph.,* p. 230 B

344 RA 30, Pl. II below or Heuzey, *Origines Orientales,* Pl. II

345 MJ 16, pp. 48/49 or Zervos p. 204

346 AfO 19, p. 1 ff.

347 E. Strommenger, *Das Felsrelief von Darband-i-Gawr,* in: *Bagdader Mitteilungen,* Vol. 2, p. 83, Pl. 15 ff. A comparison of the head-dress and beard of the victorious king at Darband-i-Gawr with those of Naram-Sin on his two reliefs and on the bronze head from Nineveh (cf. Notes 251, 252, 254, 255) shows that the rock relief should not be assigned to Naram-Sin

348 Porada, *Corpus I,* Pl. XLIII, 274

349 R. M. Boehmer, *Die Entwicklung der Glyptik während der Akkad-Zeit*

350 E. D. van Buren, ZA 50, p. 92 ff.

351 Delaporte, *Louvre I,* Pl. 8 (T. 66, T. 73/74)

352 OIP 43, Fig. 100 A, B. There is no reason to query the dating of this seal in the period of Ibbi-Sin, as W. Nagel does in: AfO 18, p. 100, Note 24, and especially not now that a relief of Shu-Sin with the same motif has been confirmed in a text

353 A. Parrot, *Sumer,* p. 275

354 A. Parrot, MAM 2, *Le Palais, Peintures murales*

355 A. Parrot, MAM 2, *Le Palais, Peintures murales*

356 A. Parrot, MAM 2, *Le Palais, Documents et Monuments.* Cf. this with the various statues of Ishtup-ilum, Puzur-Ishtar, Laasgan and Idi-ilum, as well as with what is said below on the 'Statue Cabane' and the goddess with the aryballos vase

357 A. Moortgat, *Die Wandgemälde im Palast zu Mari und ihre historische Einordnung,* in: *Bagdader Mitteilungen,* Vol. 3, 1964 (= Festschrift, E. Heinrich), p. 68 ff.

358 A. Parrot, op. cit., p. 53 ff., Pls. A and VII–XIV

359 A. Parrot, op. cit., *Peintures murales,* Pls. X/XI

360 A. Parrot, op. cit., Pls. IX/XI

361 A. Parrot, op. cit., *Documents et Monuments,* p. 189 ff.

362 A. Parrot, op. cit., Pls. 41/42

363 W. Eilers, Die *Gesetzesstelle Chammurabis* = AO 31, Nos. 3/4, p. 5, Note 4

364 A. Parrot, op. cit., *Peintures murales,* p. 16 ff.

365 A. Parrot, op. cit., Fig. 18 = A. Parrot, *Sumer,* Fig. 345

366 A. Parrot, op. cit., Pl. B, a = A. Parrot, *Sumer,* Fig. 344

367 This could only be an enthroned god, as we may infer from the scene, similar in its content and composition, on a fine Syrian cylinder seal in the Morgan Collection (Porada, *Corpus I,* No. 910, or also in: H. Frankfort, *Cylinder Seals,* Pl. 42 ff.). I am grateful to U. Moortgat-Correns for this suggestion

368 U. Moortgat-Correns, *Westsemitisches in der Bildkunst Mesopotamiens,* in: AfO 16, p. 287 ff. Cf. with this stele under *Altbabylonische Kunst,* Note 26

369 J. Læssøe, *The Shemshara Tablets* (1959)

370 One cannot separate this second group of wall paintings from countless other fragments which A. Parrot has summarized in MAM 2, *Le Palais, Peintures murales,* p. 1 ff., Fig. 6 ff. The style of their drawing and painting are identical in technique and style with that of the second group, though they contribute a great number of new pictorial motifs. These fragments all originate from Court 31 and Room 34, the centre of the so-called royal residence within the palace. Therefore this part of the palace probably dates from the period of Iasmah-Adad

371 A. Parrot, op. cit. p. 70 ff., Pls. XVI–XXI, B, b; E, Fig. 57

372 A. Parrot, op. cit., Pl. E

373 L. Legrain, MJ, Vol. 18, p. 96

374 G. Cros, Nouvelles Fouilles de Tello, p. 285, Pl. IX, 2, 3

375 Cf. Akkadian impressions on clay tablets from Telloh, cf. R. M. Boehmer, *Die Entwicklung der Glyptik während der Akkad-Zeit,* Pls. LXII and LXIII

376 Cf. A. Moortgat, *Die Wandgemälde des Palastes zu Mari und ihre historische Einordnung,* in: Festschrift E. Heinrich = *Bagdader Mitteilungen,* Vol. 3, 1965, p. 68 ff. (cf. also Note 357)

II Old Babylonian Art

1 A. v. Haller, *Die Heiligtümer in Assur* = WVDOG 67, p. 17, Fig. 2

2 A. Parrot, *Syria,* Vol. 41, p. 6, Fig. 1

3 OIC 20, p. 74 ff., Fig. 60, OIP 72, inclusive plan Pl. 96

4 *Sumer,* Vol. 2, No. 2 (after p. 30); *Sumer,* Vol. 3, pp. 22, 24

5 Seton Lloyd, *The Gimilsin Temple and the Palace of the Rulers,* OIP 43, p. 97 ff., Fig. 87 f.

6 Seton Williams, *Palestine Temples,* Iraq, Vol. 11, p. 77 ff.

7 Dagan Temple in Ugarit, Temple at Level I in Alalakh

8 L. Woolley, *Alalakh. An Account of the Excavations at Tell Atchana,* Fig. 35

9 A. Parrot, MAM 2, *Le Palais, Architecture*

10 A. Parrot, MAM 2, *Le Palais, Documents et Monuments,* p. 11 ff., Pls. VII–VIII

11 Seton Lloyd, OIP 43, p. 27 ff., Pl. I

12 VR, Section *Glyptik der Altbabylonischen Zeit,* p. 31 ff.

13 Cf. Note II 18

14 E. Unger, in: RLV (see under Glyptik), Vol. 4, p. 365 ff.; VR, p. 30 ff.; Summary of the seal impressions on documents of the Old Babylonian Period from Sumu-abum to Samsu-ditana. – W. Nagel, in: AfO 18, p. 319 f.

15 J. Kupper, *L'iconographie du Dieu Amurru*

16 Both the wife of Singashid, Salurtum, the daughter of Sumulailu, and the wife of Rim-Sin, Beltani, have left us a seal with this theme on it: Atlantis No. 7, 1961, p. 390; *Bagdader Mitteilungen,* Vol. 2, 1963, p. 6 and Pl. 7, 1 (Seal impression on jug stopper); VR 322

17 I. e. VR 467–470

18 MAM 2, *Le Palais, Documents et Monuments,* p. 189 ff., Pls. 41/42

19 MAM 2, op. cit., p. 169 ff., Pl. 48; Fig. 104

20 MAM 2, Le Palais, *Peintures murales,* p. 8 ff.

21 A. Parrot, MAM 2, op. cit., Fig. 7

22 A. Parrot, MAM 2, op. cit., Fig. 23

23 A. Parrot, MAM 2, op. cit., Fig. 35

24 A. Parrot, MAM 2, op. cit., p. 6 ff., Fig. 4 ff. and Pl. III

25 A. Moortgat, in: BiOr 9 (1952), p. 92 ff.

26 *E. Ph.* 257

27 OIP 60, Pl. 75 A, No. 336; p. 21

28 OIP 43, p. 116 ff.

29 H. R. Hall, *Babylonian and Assyrian Sculpture in the British Museum,* Pl. IX above, left

30 H. Schmökel, *Hammurabi von Babylon,* p. 104

31 *E. Ph.* 259; MDP 4, p. 11 ff.; Pl. 3 ff.

32 W. Eilers, *Der Codex Hammurabi,* AO 31, Issue 3/4, p. 5, Note 4

33 *E. Ph.* 247

34 H. Schäfer, *Von Ägyptischer Kunst,* 4th edition, Wiesbaden, 1964, with epilogue by E. Brunner-Traut (Die Aspektive)

35 Cf. Note 16

36 *E. Ph.* p. 247

37 R. Opificius, *Das altbabylonische Terrakottarelief,* Untersuchungen zur Assyriologie und Vorderasiatischen Archäologie, Vol. 2

38 Op. cit., No. 488, Pl. 13

39 Also the well-known Burney terra-cotta relief – with the scene of a nude winged goddess, with bird claws instead of feet, standing upright on a recumbent lion between two owls, with the whole group shown on a mountain – can be dated in the Hammurabi period because of its almost exaggeratedly high relief. It is a work of high quality and, owing to the scarcity of works of art from the Hammurabi period, it is regarded as one of our best examples of this period's art (AfO 11, p. 350, Fig. 1).

40 R. Opificius, op. cit., no. 208, p. 73

41 D. Opitz, in: AfO, p. 350 ff., Fig. 1

42 E. Strommenger, *Bagdader Mitteilungen,* Vol. 11, p. 73, Pl. 21

43 F. Thureau-Dangin, RA 31, 1934, p. 144; *Mélanges Syriens* (R. Dussaud, 1939, p. 158

44 J. Pritchard, *The Ancient Near East in Pictures,* p. 175, No. 517

45 WVDOG 61, Pl. 242; cf. also: 1) R. M. Boehmer, *Die Ent-wicklung der Glyptik während der Akkad-Zeit*, Nos. 392, 393, 430; 2) MAM 2, *Le Palais, Peintures murales*, Pl. XVII; XX, 1; E; Fig. 60; 3) UVB 1, Pl. 15; 4) WVDOG 53, Pl. 1; 5) WVDOG 66, Pl. 25 a, b

46 *Syria*, Vol. 18, p. 78 Pls. XIII–XIV

47 OIP 60, Pls. 77, 78 or 79 and 80

48 Op. cit., p. 21

49 W. Nagel, in: AfO 18, p. 323, Fig. 1

50 Cf. in the glyptic: for instance VR 523

51 MAM 1, *Le Temple d'Ishtar*, p. 111, Pl. XLV

52 G. Contenau, *Ant. Or.* 14/15 = E. Ph., pp. 216/217

53 R. Dussaud in: *Monuments Piot.* 33, p. 1 ff.; *E. Ph.* 1, p. 261 B

54 R. Dussaud in: *Monuments Piot.* 33, p. 1 ff.; *E. Ph.* 1, p. 261 C

55 Pézard-Pottier, No. 58; E. Ph. 1, p. 262

56 Pézard-Pottier, op. cit., Nos. 54, 55, 56, 57, 63

57 MAO, Vol. 4, p. 2125, Fig. 1174, where for the first time the significance of this head is pointed out = E. Ph., p. 257 A/B

58 Cf. the summary in VR, Section *Altbabylon. Zeit, Aus-gang*, p. 44 ff.

59 VR, 497 ff.

60 F. Böhl, in: JEOL 8, p. 725 ff., Pl. XXXV

61 W. Andrae, in: *Amtl. Ber.* Jahrg. 58, 34 f. and Fig. 4

62 MAM 2, *Le Palais, Documents et Monuments*, Pl. XVI ff., p. 33 ff.

63 Op. cit., p. 36, Fig. 30 (1129); Pl. XVII

III Middle Babylonian (Kassite) Art

1 F. Delitzsch, *Die Sprache der Kossäer*; K. Balkan, *Kassitenstudien*

2 UVB 1, p. 53

3 UVB 1, Pl. 10

4 UVB 1, Pls. 15–17

5 Moortgat, *Bergvölker*, Pl. 96

6 UE, Vol. 5, p. 49; UE, Vol. 8, pp. 3, 64

7 Remains in the Baghdad Museum, reference in Hirmer-Strommenger, p. 90

8 *Iraq*, Suppl. 1944/45, pp. 11–13

9 *Eurasia Septentrionalis Antiqua*, Vol. 10, 1936, pp. 115–117

10 RA 35, 1938, p. 179 ff., pp. 227, 426, 427 = 11 and 12

11 AJ 5, p. 387, Fig. 6; UE, Vol. 8, Pl. 47 ff.

12 JEOL 9, p. 184 ff.

13 *Iraq*, Suppl. 1945, Pl. I

14 *Iraq*, 8, Pl. XXII

15 *Iraq*, Suppl. 1945, Pl. II

16 *Iraq*, 8, Pl. IX

17 *Iraq*, Suppl. 1945, Pl. XVI

18 *Iraq*, 8, Fig. 2

19 *Iraq*, op. cit., Pl. XVII

20 *Iraq*, 8, Pl. XV, Fig. 9 = Hirmer-Strommenger; Ph. XXXII

21 *Iraq*, 8, Pl. XIV = Hirmer-Strommenger, Pl. 171

22 *Iraq*, 8, Pls. XI–XIV

23 G. Contenau, MAO Vol. II, p. 898, Fig. 621

24 F. Steinmetzer, *Über den Grundbesitz in Babylonien zur Kassitenzeit*, in: AO Vol. 19, Issue I

25 A. Parrot, AfO 12, p. 319; V. E. Crawford, *Bulletin of the Metropolitan Museum of Art*, 1960, p. 245 ff., Fig. 5 a–d

26 Berl. Diss., Ursula Seidl, 1965 (unpublished)

27 L. W. King, *Babylonian Boundary Stones*, Pl. I, p. 3

28 MDP I, p. 167 ff.; Pézard-Pottier, p. 47 ff.

29 MDP I, p. 168, Fig. 379

30 MDP I, Pl. XVI = E. Ph., 265

31 E. Ph., 264

32 L. W. King, op. cit., Pl. XXIII

33 MDP 4, Pls. 16, 17

34 MDP 7, Pl. XXVIII = E. Ph., pp. 266/67

35 Th. Beran, *Die Babylonische Glyptik d. Kassitenzeit*, in: AfO 18, p. 255 ff.

36 Th. Beran, op. cit., Fig. 1 = Porada, *Corpus* I, No. 577, Seal of an official of Burraburiash

37 Th. Beran, op. cit., Figs. 5–8

38 Th. Beran, op. cit., Figs. 9–12

IV Assyrian Art

1 T. Özgüc, in: *Ausgrabungen in Kültepe*. (Türk Tarih Ku-rumu Yayinlarindan, No. 12, 1953, p. 226 ff.)

2 VR 505, 506, 507, 508, 513, 516

3 A. Goetze, *Kulturgeschichte des Alten Orients*, Vol. 3; *Kleinasien*. 2, Edn. 1956, Fig. 12

4 C. Preusser – W. Andrae, *Die Paläste und Häuser in Assur*, WVDOG 66

5 W. Andrae, *Das wiedererstandene Assur*, p. 88, Pl. 44 a–d

6 H. de Genouillac, in: RA 7, p. 151 ff., Pls. V, VI; *E. Ph.*, p. 257 C; A. Goetze in: RA 46, p. 155 ff.

7 U. Moortgat-Correns, *Westsemitisches in der Bildkunst Mesopotamiens*, in: AfO 16, p. 287 ff.

8 RA 46, p. 155 ff.

9 OIP 43, p. 215, Fig. 100

10 W. Andrae, *Das wiedererstandene Assur*, Fig. 44; WVDOG 67, p. 84 ff.

11 Reconstruction: W. Andrae, op. cit., p. 98 ff., Fig. 45

12 R. F. S. Starr, *Nuzi*, (Temple A) p. 87 ff., Pl. 13; C. L. Woolley, *Tell Atchana-Alalakh* (Palace of Niqmepa), p. 115, Fig. 45

13 C. L. Woolley, *Tell Atchana-Alalakh*, Fig. 45 (Palace of Niqmepa); H. Frankfort, *The Origins of the Bit Hilani*, Iraq, Vol. 14, p. 120 ff.

14 C. Preusser, WVDOG 66, Pl. 4

15 R. F. S. Starr, *Nuzi*, Pl. 13

16 R. F. S. Starr, *Nuzi, Report on the Excavations at Yorgan Tepe*, 1937/39

17 M. E. L. Mallowan, *Iraq, 8 & 9; 25 Years of Mesopotamian Discovery*, p. 12 ff.

18 C. L. Woolley, *Alalakh, An Account of the Excavations at Tell Atchana*, Oxford 1955

19 OIP 79, *Soundings at Tell Fakhariya*; AGF Issue 62 (1955): Vol. 7 (1956)

20 AGF, Vol. 14 (1958)

21 E. Porada, *Seal Impressions of Nuzi* (= AASOR 24)

22 Th. Beran, *Die assyr. Glyptik des 14. Jahrh. und ihre Stellung im vorderasiat. Bereich*, Diss. Berlin 1954 = ZA NF 18 (1957), p. 141 ff.

23 VR 95, Pl. D 3

24 R. F. S. Starr. *Nuzi*, Pls. 128/129 = A. Moortgat, *Altvorderasiat. Malerei*, Pl. 15

25 AJ 19, Pl. XII = C. L. Woolley, Alalakh, Pl. XLV

26 R. F. S. Starr, *Nuzi*, Pl. 112 A

27 Kumarbi myth and Kronos myth: for the literary references, see *Wörterbuch der Mythologie I*, p. 185

28 Tell Chuera; AGF Vol. 24, p. 20, Fig. 15; also cf. A. Moortgat, *Bergvölker*, p. 28 ff.

29 B. Hrouda, *Die bemalte Keramik des 2. Jahrtausends*

30 Hirmer-Strommenger, Pl. 177

31 S. Smith, *The statue of Idrimi*

32 Cf. also: H. Otten, *Hethitische Totenrituale* (1958)

33 Cf. Tell Chuera: AGF Vol. 24, p. 35 ff.

34 It is possible that the statuettes of the Mesilim Period from Tell Chuera were not just figures of worshippers, but were also ancestor cult images, which had originally stood in the wall niches of the small temple *in antis* of Level 4. (A. Moortgat, Tell Chuera in Nordost-Syrien. Report on the fifth expedition 1964, publications of the M. von Oppenheim Foundation, Issue 6)

35 *E. Ph.*, 105

36 WVDOG 58: W. Andrae, *Die jüngeren Ischtar-Tempel*, Pl. 34

37 H. Bossert, *Altanatolien*, Nos. 577–580 = C. L. Woolley, *Alalakh*, Pl. 49

38 R. D. Barnett, *The Nimrud Ivories*, p. 198, Fig. 82 = ILN of the 29. 7. 1950, p. 182, Fig. 14

39 Cf. finally: O. W. Muscarella, *Lion bowls from Hasanlu*, in: *Archaeology 18*, No. I, p. 41 f.

40 WVDOG 53, W. Andrae, *Das Kultrelief aus dem Brunnen des Assurtempels zu Assur*, Pl. 1 ff.

41 Th. Beran, *Assyrische Glyptik des 14. Jahrhunderts*: ZA NF 18, 1957, p. 141 ff.

42 Th. Beran, op. cit., Fig. 1 = VR 53, Pl. C 2

43 Th. Beran, op. cit., Fig. 2, 17, 18

44 Th. Beran, op. cit., Nos. 33 and 38

45 VR 586

46 A. Haller, *Die Gräber und Grüfte von Assur* = WVDOG 65, Tomb 45 (Ass. 14630)

47 F. W. von Bissing, in: ZA 46, 1940, p. 149 ff.

48 Drawing of reconstruction by U. Moortgat-Correns

49 ZA 47, 1942, p. 49, Fig. 36

50 R. F. S. Starr, *Nuzi*, Vol. 2, p. 421, Pl. 101, I, 1–4. For an interpretation of all the details of this figure, its half-masculine and half-feminine features as well as its general resemblance to the particulars given in a Hittite description of the goddess Shaushga of Hurrian origin, cf. the recent contribution by Machteld Mellink, *A Hittite Figurine from Nuzi*, in: *Vorderasiatische Archäologie, Festschrift A. Moortgat*, p. 155 ff., Pl. 20, 1–4

51 As in: W. Andrae, WVDOG 65, p. 123 ff.

52 WVDOG 65, Pl. 30 a, b; p. 135, Fig. 163 a/b

53 WVDOG 65, Fig. 161

54 W. Andrae, *Die Festungswerke von Assur* = WVDOG 23, Pl. 84, p. 69 ff.; B. Hrouda, *Keramik des 2. Jahrtausends*, Pls. 2, 3; E. Herzfeld, AMI 8, 3, Pl. 9, Figs. 108 and 152 (reconstructer)

55 B. Meissner – D. Opitz, *Die Reliefs im Nordpalast des Assurbanipli in Nineve*, Pl. XVII

56 *Amtl. Ber.*, 59, p.14 ff. = WVDOG 66, Pls. 25/26; p. 30; W. Andrae, *Das wiedererstandene Assur*, Pl. 54

57 U. Moortgat-Correns, *Beiträge zur mittelassyrischen Glyptik*, in: *Vorderasiatische Archäologie, Festschrift A. Moortgat*, p. 170, Fig. 4

58 ZA 47, p. 52 ff.

59 Only a brief exploration of the Level of Shalmaneser I was carried out (*Iraq*, Vol. 18, p. 19 ff.)

60 E. Ebeling / B. Meissner / E. Weidner, *Die Inschriften der altassyrischen Könige* (1926)

61 C. Preusser, *Die Paläste in Assur* (= WVDOG 66)

62 WVDOG 66, Pl. 4

63 C. Preusser, op. cit., p. 18

64 W. Andrae, *Das wiedererstandene Assur*, pp. 115 and 123

65 W. Andrae, *Das wiedererstandene Assur*, p. 92, Fig. 42

66 W. Andrae, *Die jüngeren Ischtar-Tempel in Assur* (= WVDOG 58)

67 W. Andrae, *Das wiedererstandene Assur*, Fig. 47

68 W. Andrae, *Das wiedererstandene Assur*, Fig. 48

69 C. Preusser, WVDOG 66, p. 13, Pl. 12 d; 13 a

70 W. Andrae, *Farbige Keramik aus Assur*, Pls. 1–4

71 Op. cit., Pl. 2

72 Op. cit., Pl. 5 a–c

73 WVDOG 23, Pl. 84 (1958, 1972 and 6868)

74 Cf. with this U. Moortgat-Correns, *Beiträge zur mittelassyrischen Glyptik* in: *Vorderasiatische Archäologie, Festschrift A. Moortgat*, p. 172, Fig. 6

75 A. Moortgat, *Assyrische Glyptik des 13. Jahrhunderts*, in ZA 47, p. 50 ff.

76 e. g. E. Porada, *Corpus I*, 601 = ZA 47, Fig. 29 = BM 89557, in: D. J. Wiseman, *Götter und Menschen im Rollsiegel Westasiens*, No. 61

77 Cf. the enlarged drawing of the so-called sherd in U. Moortgat-Correns, op. cit., Fig. 6

78 Sherd from the pottery room; WVDOG 23, Pl. 84 = Herzfeld, AMI 8, Pl. X, Fig. 114

79 ZA 47, p. 76, Fig. 52 = Southesk Collection, Pl. VII, Qc 11; O. Weber, *Altorientalische Siegelbilder*, 513

80 W. Andrae, *Das wiedererstandene Assur*, Pl. 49 b = *Amtl. Ber.* 59, p. 39 f.; D. Opitz, AfO 13, p. 219 ff.

81 For the group of the symbol pedestal; W. Andrae, *Die jüngeren Ischtar-Tempel* (WVDOG 58), p. 57 ff., Pl. 29 ff.

82 Op. cit., Pl. 30

83 Op. cit., Pl. 30

84 OIP 79, p. 73, Pl. No. 16; ZA 47, NF 13, p. 54, Fig. 4 = BM 89862; Southesk Collection II Qc 35, Pl. 8 = ZA, p. 63 ff., Fig. 25; E. Porada, *Corpus I*, 601

85 Cf. Note 60

86 *Wörterbuch der Mythologie I*, p. 40 f.; 279 ff.

87 *E. Ph.* 2, 31

88 H. R. Hall, *La sculpture Babylonienne et Assyrienne au British Museum*, (= Ars Asiatica 11) Pl. XI

89 E. F. Weidner, AfO 10, p. 1 ff.; D. Opitz, op. cit., p. 48 ff.; A. Moortgat, ZANF 14, 23 ff.; Th. Beran, ZA NF 18, p. 141 ff.

90 Chariot hunt of Ninurta-Tukul-Ashur and seal of Rimani with winged demons: D. Opitz, in: AfO X, p. 49, Figs. 1–4; p. 50, Figs. 5–8

91 Luckenbill, Vol. 1, p. 91 ff.

92 C. F. Lehmann-Haupt, *Materialien zur älteren Geschichte Babyloniens und Assyriens*, p. 16 ff.; Figs. 6, 7 a–b

93 ZA 48, p. 43, Fig. 46

94 Inscription: Luckenbill, Vol. 1, p. 118 ff.; Relief: E. A. W. Budge – L. W. King, *The Annals of the Kings of Assyria*, p. 108 ff.; Unger, ABK, Fig. 32; Moortgat, *Bergvölker*, Pl. 26; Parrot, *Assur*, 40 C; its attribution to Ashurbelkala: E. F. Weidner, AfO 6, p. 75 ff.

95 Recently: Hirmer-Strommenger, Pl. 188 below

96 E. Unger, MAOG 6, Issue 1–2, p. 1 ff.; Pls. I–XVII

97 Seen best in the re-drawing of it in: E. Unger, op. cit., Pl. XVII

98 Cf. E. Unger, op. cit., Pls. II, VIII, XIII etc.

99 Cf. R. D. Barnett, *Assyrische Palastreliefs*, Pl. 24, 25

100 R. D. Barnett, op. cit., Pl. 28

101 R. D. Barnett, op. cit., Pl. 14

102 E. Unger, MAOG 6, illustrated friezes A 2, B 5, D 7, D 1

103 Cf. the marble disk (= lid of jar) with battle scene, cf. Note 80

104 R. J. Tournay/Soubhi-Saouaf, *Annales archéologiques de Syrie*, Vol. 2, 1952, pp. 169–190; H. Schmökel, *Ur, Assur und Babylon*, Pl. 83, p. 283; H. G. Güterbock, in: JNES 16, 1957, p. 123

105 M. E. L. Mallowan, *The Excavations at Nimrud*, 1951, in: *Iraq*, Vol. 14, p. 7 ff.; D. J. Wiseman, *A New Stela of Ashurnasirapli*, in: *Iraq*, Vol. 14, p. 24 ff., Pl. II ff. Note the remarkable parallel between the banquet of Ashurnasirpal II, after the completion of the North-West Palace, with the people of Kalakh and all the surrounding peoples, and the meal which lasted seven days provided by Solomon for the people of Israel after the building of the Temple (I Kings, VIII, 65)

106 H. A. Layard, *Nineveh and its remains*, Plan II

107 *Iraq*, Vol. 20, Pl. 13

108 F. Thureau-Dangin *inter alios*, *Arslan Tash*, p. 16 ff.; R. D. Barnett, *The Nimrud Ivories*, p. 2 f; G. Loud, in: RA 23, p. 153

109 R. D. Barnett, op. cit., p. 3, Note 8; M. E. L. Mallowan, in: Iraq, Vol. 15, p. 30 ff., Fig. 3

110 R. D. Barnett, op. cit., p. 3

111 F. Thureau-Dangin *inter alios*, *Arslan Tash*, p. 41 ff.

112 F. Thureau-Dangin, *Arslan Tash*, p. 47 ff.

113 R. Koldewey, *Ausgrabungen in Sendschirli*, Vol. 2, 1898, Pl. XXII

114 H. Weidhaas, *Der bit hilani*, in: ZA NF 11, p. 108 ff.

115 Example from the latest excavations: Lamassu in the N. W. Palace: M. E. L. Mallowan, *Twenty-five years of Mesopotamian Discovery*, 1956, Pl. I

116 Layard had already found several Lamassu figures in the area of the N. W. Palace: E. A. Budge, *Assyrian Sculptures in The British Museum, Reign of Ashur-Nasir-pal*, Pls. IV–VI

117 If W. Andrae is correct in his observations (*Das wiedererstandene Assur*, p. 135 top), Tiglathpileser I was the earliest Assyrian king to have portal sculpture erected in Ashur. For some of the fragments referred to by Andrae see now too: C. Preusser, *Die Paläste in Assur*, WVDOG 66, Pl. 23; with p. 26 f (cf. H. Schmökel, *Ur, Babylon Assur*, Pl. 80)

118 W. Andrae, *Farbige Keramik aus Assur*, p. 12 ff., Pls. 7–9

119 AAA 18, Pl. 31

120 W. Andrae, op. cit., Pl. 8

121 AAA 18, Pl. 31

122 *Die Stelenreihen von Assur*, WVDOG 24, p. 6 ff., Fig. 3

123 J. B. Stearns, *Reliefs from the Palace of Ashur-nasirpal II*, AfO Supplement 15, p. 72 (restoration of Room B)

124 E. A. Budge, *Assyrian Sculpture in the B. M.*, Pl. XI

125 Moortgat, *Entstehung*, p. 83 ff.; id., *Tammuz, Der Unsterblichkeitsglaube in der altorientalischen Bildkunst*, p. 27 ff.; p. 134 ff.; id., *Geschichte Vorderasiens bis zum Hellenismus*, p. 220 ff.

126 For the development and history of this whole pictorial theme in the art of the Ancient Near East cf. A. Moortgat, *Tammuz Der Unsterblichkeitsglaube in der altorientalischen Bildkunst*, Chapter II, A; IV B

127 H. A. Layard, *Nineveh and its remains*, p. 384 ff.; J. B. Stearns, AfO Supplement 15 (1961)

128 Cf. A. Moortgat, *Geschichte Vorderasiens bis zum Hellenismus*, in: A. Scharff u. A. Moortgat, *Ägypten und Vorderasien im Altertum*, p. 429 ff.

129 Examples of polychrome in Late Assyrian wall relief: H. A. Layard, *Monuments of Nineveh* II, p. 306; cf. also P. E. Botta / E. Flandin, *Monuments de Ninive*, Vol. I, Pls. 43, 53

130 A. Moortgat, *Die Bildgliederung des jungassyrischen Wandreliefs*, in: *Jahrbuch der Preussischen Kunstsammlungen*, 51 1930, p. 141 ff.

131 L. Curtius, *Antike Kunst* I (1913), p. 270 ff.

132 A. Moortgat, *Die Bildgliederung des jungassyrischen Wandreliefs*, cf. Note 130

133 *Ur, Excav.*, Vol. 2, *The Royal Cemetery*, Pls. 90–93, p. 61 ff. The best figure in: Hirmer-Strommenger, Pl. 72, below

134 British Museum, Nimrud Gallery, Nos. 5 b–6 b, the lower halves, of which the upper halves together form the storming of a citadel surrounded by water (op. cit., nos. 5 a–6 a)

135 British Museum, Nimrud Gallery, Nos. 3 a–4 a and nos. 3 b–4 b

136 British Museum, Nimrud Gallery, nos. 7 a–10 a

137 W. Andrae, *Das wiedererstandene Assur*, p. 140 ff.

138 B. M. 118885; recently in: Hirmer-Strommenger, Pl. 208

139 Fort Shalmaneser: ILN of 24. XI. and 1. XII. 1962; most recent plan: *Iraq*, Vol. 25, 1963, Pl. II; description and significance of the building, see: D. Oates, in: *Iraq*, Vol. 25, p. 6 ff.

140 L. W. King, *The Bronze Reliefs from the Gates of Shalmaneser*, 1915: H. Rassam, *Ashur and the Land of Nimrud*, p. 201 ff.; most recent publication on the 'Ekalmasharti', in: M. E. L. Mallowan, *Nimrud and its Remains*, Ch. XVI–XVII, Pl. VIII

141 R. D. Barnett, *Assyrische Palastreliefs*, p. 13, Note 29

142 R. D. Barnett, op. cit., Pls. 138/139

143 ILN of 1. XII. 1962; D. Oates, in: *Iraq*, Vol. 25, 1962, p. 6 ff., Pl. II

144 D. Oates, in: *Iraq*, Vol. 25, p. 7 ff. (State Apartments)

145 ILN of 1. XII. 1962, p. 880 ff.; D. Oates, in: *Iraq*, Vol. 25, p. 10 ff., Pls. III–VII; P. Hulin, *The Inscriptions on the carved Throne-Base of Shalmaneser III*, in: *Iraq*, Vol. 25, p. 48 ff.

146 D. Oates, in: *Iraq*, Vol. 25, p. 20, Pl. VII C

147 ILN of 1. XII. 1962, pp. 880/881; *Iraq*, Vol. 25, pp. 16–19, Pls. IV–VII

148 C. J. Gadd, *The Stones of Assyria*, p. 147 f.; cf. Note 138

149 F. Thureau-Dangin, M. Dunand *inter alios*, *Til Barsip*, Paris, 1936

150 A. Parrot, *Assur* (Die Mesopotamische Kunst vom XII. vorchristlichen Jahrhundert bis zum Tode Alexanders des Großen) 1961, Coloured Plate 109 ff.

151 *Til Barsip*, op cit., p. 25 ff.

152 *Til Barsip*, op. cit., Ch. IIA, *Le palais assyrien*, p. 8 ff., Plan B

153 *Til Barsip*, op. cit., p. 42 ff.

154 Explained in: *Syria*, Vol. 11, p. 123

155 A. Parrot, *Assur*, p. 100 ff.

156 F. Thureau-Dangin, *Til Barsip*, op. cit., p. 141 ff.

157 *Til Barsip*, op. cit., Pl. LII = A. Parrot, *Assur*, Fig. 113

158 *Til Barsip*, op. cit., Pl. XLIX = A. Parrot, *Assur*, Fig. 112

159 *Til Barsip*, op. cit., p. 72 ff.

160 *Til Barsip*, op. cit., p. 73

161 *Til Barsip*, Pl. XLIX = A. Parrot, *Assur*, Figs. 112, 117 and 344

162 R. D. Barnett / M. Falkner, *The Sculptures of Assur-nasirapli II, Tiglath-Pileser III, Esar-haddon from the Central and South-West Palace at Nimrud*, p. 1 ff. I (The Central Palace)

163 ZA NF 11, p. 108 ff.

164 E. Unger, *Die Reliefs Tiglathpilesers III, aus Arslan Tasch*, Publications des Musées d'Antiquités de Stamboul, VII; F. Thureau-Dangin, A. Barrois, G. Dossin et M. Dunand, *Arslan Tash*, p. 77 ff., Pl. VII ff.

165 E. Unger, Die Reliefs Tiglathpilesers III aus Nimrud = Publikationen der Kaiserlich Osmanischen Museen, Vol. 5; R. D. Barnett / M. Falkner, op. cit.

166 Barnett / Falkner, op. cit., p. 35

167 See the general comparison between the two groups in: R. D. Barnett / M. Falkner, op. cit., p. 34

168 S. Smith. *Assyrian Sculptures in the British Museum, from Shalmaneser III to Sennacherib*, Pl. VIII

169 R. D. Barnett / M. Falkner, op. cit., p. 35, Pls. IX, X

170 S. Smith, op. cit., Pl. XI, above and below

171 P. E. Botta / E. Flandin, Monuments de Nineve, 1867/70; G. Loud, H. Frankfort and Th. Jacobsen, Khorsabad I = OIP 38, 1936, G. Loud and Ch. B. Altmann, Khorsabad II = OIP 40, 1938

172 Cf. 38, p. 66 ff., Figs. 79/80

173 OIP 38, p. 66 ff., Figs. 79/80

174 OIP 40, Pl. 76

175 OIP 40, Khorsabad II, Pl. 75 (Rooms 17–19)

176 P. E. Botta / E. Flandin, *Monuments de Nineve*, Vol. 2, Pl. 107/114; OIP 38, p. 71 ff.

177 OIP 38, p. 28 ff., Fig. 28 f.

178 K. F. Müller, in WVAeG 41, p. 59 ff.

179 Cf. the reconstruction of the gates to the Throne Room VII with Lamassus and 'Gilgamesh': OIP 38, Fig. 45; cf. also Notes 125, 126

180 P. E. Botta / E. Flandin, op. cit., Vol. 2, Pl. 7 and separate plates

181 P. E. Botta / E. Flandin, op. cit., Vol. 2, Pl. 118

182 E. g., P. E. Botta / E. Flandin, op. cit., Vol. 1, Pl. 55 ff., 70 ff., etc.

183 OIP 38, Figs. 51–55

184 P. E. Botta / E. Flandin, op. cit., Vol. 2, Pls. 107–1014 = OIP 38, p. 71 ff., Room 7, Figs. 83–89

185 S. Smith, *Assyrian Sculpture in the British Museum from Shalmaneser III to Sennacherib*, p. 14, Pl. XXXI (Cf. this to the passage in: E. Ph. 318)

186 Cf. H. Schäfer, *Von ägyptischer Kunst*, p. 86 ff.

187 Cf. von Soden, *Der Nahe Osten im Altertum*, in: *Propyläen Weltgeschichte*, p. 112 ff.

188 D. J. Wiseman, *The Vassal-Treaties of Esarhaddon*, in: *Iraq*, Vol. 20, p. 1 ff., Pl. III ff.

189 See U. Moortgat-Correns, *Dissertation über Südwest-Palast auf Kujundschik*, Berlin 1945 (unpublished)

190 A. Paterson, *Assyrian Sculptures, Palace of Sin-acherib*, (Den Haag 1912), Pl. 75; U. Moortgat-Correns, op. cit., Plan 3; Palace plan from: A. H. Layard, *Monuments of Nineveh*, Vol. 2, Pl. 71

191 Literature in: U. Moortgat-Correns, op. cit., Cf. recently:

B. Hrouda, *Der assyrische Palastbau nach zeitgenössischen Darstellungen*, in: Bonner Jahrbuch, 164, pp. 15–26

192 Cf. the side-building on the Throne Room of Palace F (Rooms 16–18); OIP 40, Pl. 75; D. Oates, *The Excavations at Nimrud*, 1961, in: *Iraq*, Vol. 24, p. 1 ff., Pl. 1 (Royal Apartments)

193 The new palace, which Ashurbanipal, after he had begun by using the South-West palace of his grandfather, built in place of the Riduti Palace on the northern tip of Kuyunjik: this so-called North Palace is in too fragmentary a condition to be used when forming any conclusions on architecture.
(B. Meissner – D. Opitz, *Studien zum Bit-Hilani im Nordpalast des Assurbanipli zu Ninive*. (Abh. der Preuss. Akad. der Wissenschaften, Berlin 1940) with plan after Loftus-Boutcher on Pl. 1)

194 Cf. B. Hrouda, *Die Kulturgeschichte des assyrischen Flachbildes*, p. 61; Note 60

195 S. Smith, *Assyrian Sculptures in the British Museum from Shalmaneser III to Sennacherib*, Pls. 66–69

196 C. J. Gadd, *The Stones of Assyria*, p. 176 and 216, Pl. 22. Original slabs partly in the Vorderasiatischen Museum in East Berlin. Cf. Dissertation U. Moortgat-Correns, op. cit., (Dating of the ramp from the Palace to the Ishtar Temple in relation to the South-West Palace and individual rooms)

197 Cf. with this: L. Curtius, *Die antike Kunst, Vol. 1, Ägypten und Vorderasien*, Berlin 1913, p. 276 ff.

198 S. Smith, op. cit., Pls. 42, 43, 47, 49, 56, 58, 59

199 A. Paterson, *Assyrian Sculptures, Palace of Sinnacherib*, Pls. 68–77

200 S. Smith, op. cit., Pls. 53/54 inter alia

201 F. Thureau-Dangin, *Til Barsip*, op. cit., Fig. 16; A. Parrot, *Assur*, Pl. 336/40

202 W. Andrae, *Das wiedererstandene Assur*, Pl. 74 a, p. 159

203 W. Andrae, op. cit., Pl. 74 b

204 B. Hrouda, *Die Kulturgeschichte des assyrischen Flachbildes* (= Saarbrücker Beiträge zur Altertumskunde, Vol. 2, Bonn 1965), p. 115 ff., Pl. 8 ff.

205 New illustration of the stele: *The Guide to the Babylonian and Assyrian Antiquities*, 1922, Pl. XXVIII, from a British Museum photograph

206 M. Streck, Assurbanipal (= VAB 7) 2. Part, p. 261

207 B. Meissner / D. Opitz, *Studien zum Bit-hilani*, Pls. X–XI

208 E. Ph. 226 A, B

209 W. von Soden, *Der Nahe Osten im Altertum*, in: *Propyläen-Weltgeschichte*, p. 114 ff.

210 B. Meissner / D. Opitz, *Studien zum Bit-hilani*, p. 4 ff.

211 B. Hrouda, op. cit., p. 117 ff.

212 R. D. Barnett, *Assyrische Palastreliefs*, Pl. 60 ff.

V Neo-Babylonian Epilogue

1 F. Wetzel / F. H. Weissbach, *Das Hauptheiligtum des Marduk in Babylon, Esagila u. Etemenanki* (= WVDOG 59); R. Koldewey / F. Wetzel, *Die Königsburgen von Babylon*. I: *Die Südburg* (WVDOG 54), II: Die Hauptburg (WVDOG 55)

2 For Herodotus and the city wall of Babylon: F. Wetzel, in: ZA NF 14, 1944, p. 45 ff.

3 R. Koldewey, *Das Ischtar-Tor in Babylon* (WVDOG 32)

4 R. Koldewey, *Die Tempel von Babylon und Borsippa* (WVDOG 15)

5 WVDOG 15, Pl. III

6 WVDOG 15, Pls. VI/VII

7 Cf. the neo-Babylonian ground-plan of the cella with the ground-plan of the cella in the *gigparku* of the Third Dynasty of Ur (AJ 6, Pl. XLII)

8 F. Wetzel, *Das Hauptheiligtum des Marduk in Babylon*, WVDOG 50, Pl. 2. Also the reconstructed model from: F. Wetzel, *Assur und Babylon*, 1949

9 Cf. the plan of the whole Nanna Shrine at Ur (UE 2, Pl. 1) and Eanna during the Third Dynasty in Uruk (UVB 16, Pl. 38)

10 R. Koldewey / F. Wetzel, *Die Königsburgen von Babylon*. I: Die Südburg, WVDOG 54, Pl. II

11 A. Moortgat, *Nebukadnezars Südburg*, in MDOG 69, p. 1 ff.

12 A. Moortgat, op. cit., Fig. 2

13 R. Koldewey, *Das Ischtar-Tor in Babylon* (= WVDOG 32), Pl. 10 ff.

14 Moortgat, *Frühe Bildkunst*, p. 63 ff., Pl. 9; 33

15 R. Koldewey, *Das wiedererstehende Babylon*, 1925, p. 28 ff. (for the technique and style of the enamelled ornamental bricks, cf. in the same work Figs. 16–21)

16 Recently reliefs of moulded bricks have also been substantiated as early as the period of Sid-iddinam of Larsa (UE 8, pp. 3 and 91)

Sources of Illustrations

Plates

Deutsches Archäologisches Institut, Baghdad (Jürgen Fehrmann)
10, 11, 37, 38, 42, 48, 51, 57, 58, 63, 86, 87, 88, 89, 105, 154, 178, 224, 225, 269

Dr. Boehmer, Berlin 64

Institut für Vorderasiatische Altertumskunde, Free University, Berlin 15, 16, 17, 18, 26, 44, 53, 77, 82, 83, 85, 98, 115, 132, 139, 140, 142, 144, 147, 148, 149, 150, 151, 152, 168, 169, 171, 172, 173, 174, 189, 190, 194, 195, 198, 199, 201, 213, 223, 226, 227, 228, 236, 243, 244, 245, 246, 247, 289

Gebr. Mann Verlag, Berlin 240

Staatliche Museen zu Berlin, Berlin 2, 3, 4, 5, 22, 23, 25, 45, 46, 143, 181, 182, 191, 192, 193, 238, 239, 241, 242, 280, 281, 291, 292

Bildarchiv DuMont Schauberg, Cologne 19

Ny Carlsberg Glyptotek, Copenhagen 107

British Museum, London 29, 116, 133, 237, 251, 268, 273, 276, 277, 278, 279, 283

Hirmer Verlag, Munich 1, 13, 14, 20, 21, 24, 49, 52, 61, 68, 69, 78, 79, 80, 84, 94, 96, 101, 102, 103, 106, 109, 114, 119, 120, 121, 125, 134, 136, 137, 138, 155, 161, 162, 163, 166, 170, 175, 176, 177, 179, 180, 183, 200, 203, 206, 208, 209, 214, 215, 218, 221, 222, 234, 235, 257, 258, 259, 260, 261, 262, 263, 264, 265, 266, 267, 270, 271, 272, 275, 282, 284, 285, 286, 287, 290

Hanns Reich Verlag, Munich 66, 90, 91, 92, 95

The Metropolitan Museum of Art, New York 31, 32, 33, 34, 35

The Pierpont Morgan Library, New York 159

Professor Dr. H. Schmökel, Northeim 254, 255

Ashmolean Museum, Oxford 39, 40, 41

Musée du Louvre (Musées Nationaux), Paris 6, 7, 35, 47, 97, 99, 100, 104, 108, 113, 118, 126, 127, 128, 146, 158, 160, 164, 165, 185, 186, 204, 205, 229, 230, 231, 233, 248, 249, 274

University Museum, Philadelphia, Pa. 130, 131

Archäologisches Institut der Universität, Zürich 8, 9, 10

The following photographs have been supplied by the author 27, 28, 30, 43, 50, 54, 55, 56, 59, 60, 62, 65, 67, 70, 71, 72, 73, 74, 75, 76, 81, 91, 93, 110, 111, 112, 117, 122, 123, 124, 129, 135, 141, 145, 153, 156, 157, 167, 184, 187, 188, 196, 197, 202, 207, 210, 211, 212, 216, 217, 219, 232, 250, 252, 253, 256, 288

Impressions of Seals

Pl. A   1   Moortgat, *Frühe Bildkunst*, Pl. XXXVI, 2
2   Moortgat, VR 1
3   Moortgat, VR 2
4   BaM 3 (1964), Pl. 8 b
5   Heinrich, *Kleinfunde*, Pl. 17 b
6   Moortgat, *Frühe Bildkunst*, Pl. XXVI, 3

Pl. B   1 a, b   Moortgat, VR 29 a, b
2   Moortgat, *Frühe Bildkunst*, Pl. XXVI, 2

Pl. C   1   Moortgat, VR 41
2   Moortgat, VR 53
3   Moortgat, VR 48
4   Moortgat, VR 65
5   Moortgat, VR 66
6   Moortgat, VR 67

Pl. D   1   Moortgat, VR 99
2   Moortgat, *Frühe Bildkunst*, Pl. XXII, 3
3   Moortgat, VR 95
4   Delaporte, *Louvre II*, Pl. 68, 4

Pl. E   1   Frankfort, *Cylinder Seals*, Pl. XII, c
2   UE II, Pl. 193, 18
3   Moortgat, VR 117
4   Moortgat, VR 144

Pl. F   1   Moortgat, VR, Pl. B 1
2   Moortgat, VR 188
3   UE X, 186
4   OIP 47, No. 37
5   Frankfort, *Cylinder Seals*, Pl. XIX, a
6   Moortgat, VR 234
7   R. M. Boehmer, *Die Entwicklung der Glyptik während der Akkad-Zeit* (Berlin 1965), Fig. 721

Pl. G   1   Porada, *Corpus I*, 274
2   Moortgat, VR 253
3   Moortgat, VR 252
4   Moortgat, VR 254
5   J. Pritchard, *The Ancient Near East in Pictures, relating to the Old Testament* (Princeton. N. J., 1954), No. 699
6   Moortgat, VR 410
7   Moortgat, VR 322
8   OIP 72, No. 770

**Map of
Ancient Mesopotamia**

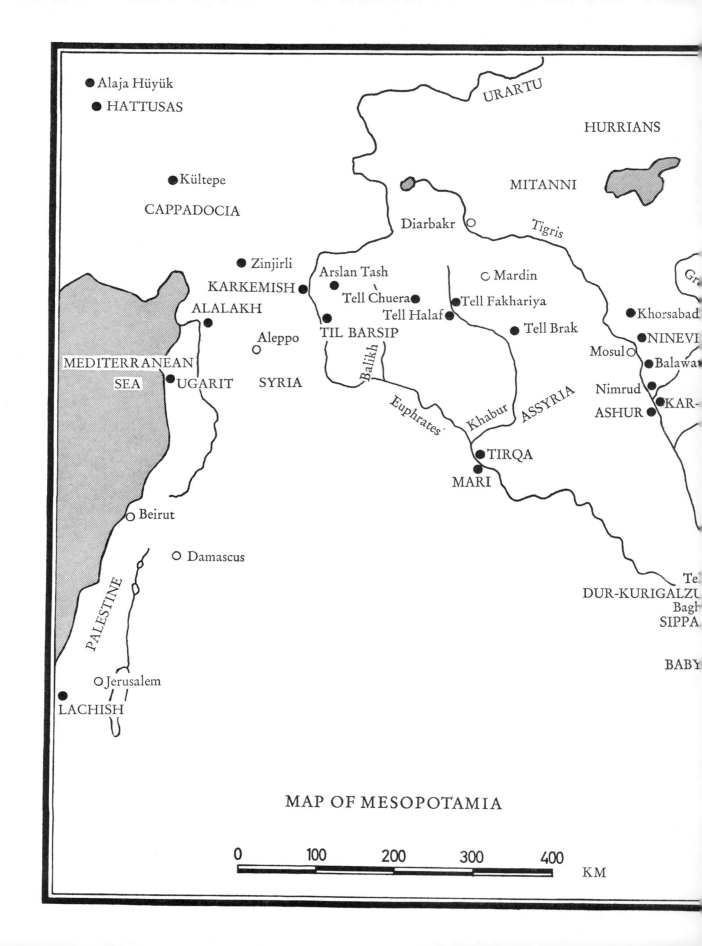

MAP OF MESOPOTAMIA

0   100   200   300   400
                                    KM

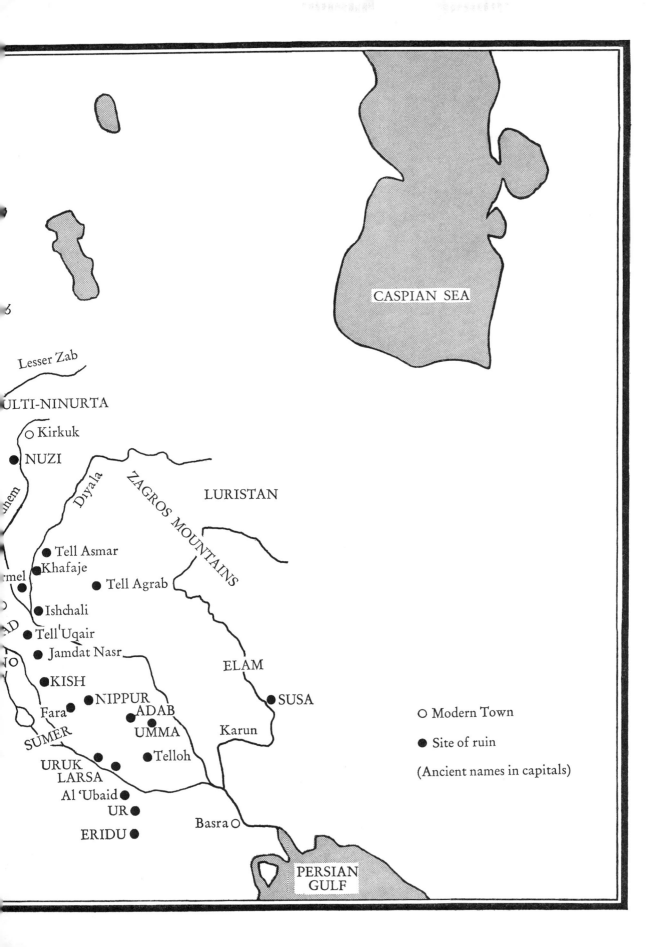

CASPIAN SEA

Lesser Zab

ULTI-NINURTA

○ Kirkuk

● NUZI

Diyala

LURISTAN

ZAGROS MOUNTAINS

● Tell Asmar

●Khafaje

mel

● Tell Agrab

● Ishchali

● Tell Uqair

● Jamdat Nasr

ELAM

● KISH

● NIPPUR

● SUSA

Fara ● ● ADAB

UMMA

Karun

● Telloh

SUMER

URUK

● LARSA

Al 'Ubaid ●

UR ●

Basra ○

ERIDU ●

○ Modern Town

● Site of ruin

(Ancient names in capitals)

PERSIAN GULF

Index

DATE DUE